MARKETING ON THE INTERNET

Sixth Edition

Seven Steps to Building the
Internet Into Your Business

Jan Zimmerman

MAXIMUM PRESS
605 Silverthorn Road
Gulf Breeze, FL 32561
(850) 934-0819
www.maxpress.com

Publisher: Jim Hoskins

Manager of Finance/Administration: Joyce Reedy

Production Manager: ReNae Grant

Cover Designer: Lauren Smith Designs

Compositor: PageCrafters Inc.

Copyeditor: Ellen Falk, Scott Falk

Proofreader: Jacquie Wallace

Indexer: Susan Olason

Printer: Malloy, Inc.

Library of Congress Cataloging-in-Publication Data

Zimmerman, Jan.

   Marketing on the Internet / Jan Zimmerman. — 6th ed.

     p. cm.

   Includes index.

   ISBN 1-885068-80-8

   1. Internet advertising. 2. Internet marketing. 3. Internet.

I. Title.

HF6146.I58Z56 2002

658.8'4—dc21

2002005820

For my mother with love and admiration,
as she celebrates 80 years of common sense
and uncommon strength

Acknowledgments

This book would not have happened without months of extraordinary assistance from Alex Knox, whose Web research talents are without peer. Not only did he handle all the fact checking and updating for this edition, he also produced the tables and graphs and managed somehow to find Web sites that were good examples of X, Y, or Z. I don't know how this book could happen without him. I also enjoyed the assistance of Aries Light and Tenley Zumwalt. Ms. Light spent hours on the phone locating appropriate companies and conducting interviews for model sites, while Ms. Zumwalt produced all the screen shots (complete with Photoshop processing!) and organized the art and clearance process. She worked far beyond the call of duty to clear copyrights and meet deadlines. I am enormously grateful to them all for their skills, their commitment, and their patience. There is no thank-you big enough.

I want to thank my clients, from whom I learn every day about innovative ways to market on the Internet. They provide me with a reason to search the Web perpetually for new discoveries, and their challenges certainly keep me from getting bored. My thanks also to the vendors and organizations that answered endless questions and gave copyright permission. The companies appearing as model sites were especially generous with their time and information.

With the Internet changing so rapidly, I can only hope that all my errors and omissions will be overtaken by a new reality before they are noticed.

Disclaimer

The purchase of computer software or hardware is an important and costly business decision. Although the author and publisher of this book have made reasonable efforts to ensure the accuracy and timeliness of the information contained herein, the author and publisher assume no liability with respect to loss or damage caused or alleged to be caused by reliance on any information contained herein and disclaim any and all warranties, expressed or implied, as to the accuracy or reliability of said information.

This book is not intended to replace the manufacturer's product documentation or personnel in determining the specifications and capabilities of the products mentioned in this book. The manufacturer's product documentation should always be consulted, because the specifications and capabilities of computer hardware and software products are subject to frequent modification. The reader is solely responsible for the choice of computer hardware and software. All configurations and applications of computer hardware and software should be reviewed with manufacturers' representatives prior to choosing or using any computer hardware and software.

Trademarks

The words contained in this text that are believed to be trademarked or service-marked, or otherwise to hold proprietary rights, have been designated as such by use of initial capitalization. No attempt has been made to designate as trademarked or service-marked any personal computer words or terms in which proprietary rights might exist. Inclusion, exclusion, or definition of a word or term is not intended to affect, or to express judgment upon, the validity of legal status of any proprietary right that may be claimed for a specific word or term.

Foreword

The Internet, like all disruptive technologies before it—electricity, the telephone and manned flight—has emerged from a state of zany euphoria to a more business-like reality. But like those world-altering inventions before it, the reality—that e-business is just business—does not limit the vast potential and opportunities the Internet presents.

No longer obscured by the dazzle of get-rich quick schemes built on unsustainable business models, the Internet is seen today very clearly for what it is, for what it's always been—a tool that enables innovation and integration.

The benefit of that innovation is in how we redefine our lives, run our schools or manage our businesses. How we do that is through integration. As an integrating medium, the Internet makes possible the unification of information and processes that heretofore have been splintered across companies and institutions in the rush to decentralize over the last few decades.

The Internet transforms every process and transaction that matters most to schools, institutions and businesses—transactions with students, citizens and customers. Transactions with business suppliers, partners, employees, shareholders, and even inanimate objects, such as cars, vending machines and pacemakers. Businesses of all sizes are moving rapidly to link their processes and transactions to the Web for cost efficiencies and competitive advantage. In many ways, the marketing aspects covered in this book—e-commerce and the formation of electronic relationships with customers—represents the first wave of millions of digitized transactions sweeping across an enterprise. From order intake on the front end to procurement, inventory control and billing on the back end.

Driving the Net's explosive growth is a competitive access provider market, sophisticated new server, software and storage technology, as well as a growing movement toward open standards and technologies such as Linux and Java. What's more, within the next year, 700 million personal computers will be accessing the World Wide Web, but they'll be dwarfed by other kinds of networked access devices: personal digital assistants, Net-enabled cell phones and game consoles. A billion wireless appliances will connect to the Net in the next several years. Following these new end user devices will be a trillion or more connected "things"—things not conceived as "computers" but which will be able to do specified levels of transaction computing as well as data storage. You're probably sitting on such a "thing" at this very moment, or maybe you're surrounded on all four sides by these "things."

The unbounded potential of the Internet promises a world in which millions of enterprises connected to billions of people by trillions of devices will make computing as pervasive and unobtrusive as electricity. Meanwhile, as the Internet moves toward its adolescence, open-ended questions ranging from security and privacy issues to potentially restrictive regulations that could alter or slow down this organic, user-driven medium remain unanswered. As with all new innovations, these issues will work themselves through in time.

And ultimately, it will be the end-user—not the technology—who will mine the Net's limitless opportunities to address the challenges we face as businessmen and women, as parents and as citizens. Ultimately, it won't be about the technology at all. It will be about what we choose to do with it through participation, creativity and responsible action and interaction.

Hoon Meng Ong,
Vice President, Global Small & Medium Business Marketing,
IBM Corporation

Table of Contents

Chapter 4:
Step 4: Create and Distribute Info-Tools

103

Chapter 5:
Step 5a: Plan Your Web Site   137

Chapter 6:
Step 5b: Design an Effective Web Site   179

Chapter 7:
Step 5c: Build an Effective Storefront   219

Chapter 10:
Step 7b: Market Your Internet
Presence Online and Offline   308

Chapter 11:
Step 7c: Market Your Internet
Presence with Search Engines   328

Chapter 12:
Step 7d: Market Your Internet
Presence with Online Advertising   349

Chapter 13:
Model Web Sites   376

Chapter 14:
The Future Is Yours   395

About This Book

Whether your business is small, large, or merely a glimmer of a dot-com dream, *Marketing on the Internet* is *the* book to read for all aspects of doing business online. It covers every step from integrating Web efforts into your overall business plan to building a Web site that works for you. Whether you are already on the Web or are trying to make the online decision, the sixth edition of *Marketing on the Internet* will provide you with invaluable advice, worksheets, and resources to ensure success.

This edition has been updated to keep business owners, CEOs, and marketing managers current on the status of online sales and marketing. With new material that places the Web in the context of basic principles of marketing, this edition should be helpful to business school faculty and students. It has already proved useful as a resource for Web developers, graphic designers, and Web-promotion companies looking for new ideas to assist their clients. It's an unbeatable one-stop reference book on all aspects of Internet marketing, from how to select vendors to how to accept payment online. The book is organized to work equally well whether read straight through or consulted on specific points of research.

The popular first edition, published in 1995, sold over 10,000 copies in the first two months and went on to become the publisher's best-selling title. The sixth edition has been expanded to include the needs of an increasingly sophisticated audience of Web businesses, many of which are launching their second-, third-, or even tenth-generation Web sites. It has been rearranged to function effectively in a classroom environment as well. This new volume includes:

- The latest statistics to give you a solid base of information on Internet demographics, user buying habits, and business transactions

- Many new Web sites to stimulate your imagination and serve as models for Web development

- Lessons in looking at sites to understand their effectiveness from design, content, navigation, and marketing perspectives

- Tips for Tired Sites to rejuvenate sites that aren't producing

- A brand-new section about marketing basics, including Maslow's hierarchy of needs

- New information about financial objectives, including computing return on investment, breakeven point, and conversion rates for a Web site

- More information on photography, marketing communications, and human factors for Web design

- A complete chapter on building an effective online storefront, from catalogs to shopping carts, and from merchandising to handling secure transactions

- Expanded chapters on Web promotion on-site, online, through search engines, and with paid advertising

- Ten new model sites that illustrate the principles of online marketing

- The latest trends to prepare you for the fast-changing world of electronic commerce.

Here is what's inside:

- Chapter 1 reviews the congruence of marketing principles online and offline, as well as providing an overview of Web activities and techniques for evaluating Web sites.

- Chapter 2 outlines basic marketing theory and the seven steps for online marketing success.

- Chapter 3 initiates the process with the first three steps: observing the Web; knowing your business, including your infrastructure and back office needs; and writing an online business plan with financial objectives.

- Chapter 4 describes low-cost Internet tools to initiate Internet marketing, such as signature files, press releases, newsgroups, e-mail marketing, and online services.

- Chapter 5 details the steps for planning a Web site, from estimating costs and establishing a budget to selecting various Web service providers, understanding the design process, and registering a domain name.

- Chapter 6 explores the principles of effective Web design, including marketing communications concepts, writing for the Web, rich media, hints for a successful site, and popular lists of free resources.

- Chapter 7 is dedicated to constructing an effective storefront, from an analysis of store-building options to merchandising and accepting payment.

- Chapter 8 explains the importance of maintaining and updating a Web site, and monitoring the traffic it receives.

- Chapter 9 tells how to use the site itself for promotion through such techniques as chat rooms, message boards, and calls to action.

- Chapter 10 looks at Web promotion with online and offline resources, including Word-of-Web campaigns, inbound links, and site launches.

- Chapter 11 focuses specifically on search engine techniques, including tips to optimize pages for better search engine rankings.

- Chapter 12 considers trends in Web advertising, explaining different types of online ads, ad rates, search engine advertising, and online classifieds.

- Chapter 13 analyzes ten model Web sites that successfully apply specific online marketing techniques.

- Chapter 14 discusses global e-commerce, privacy, security, legal considerations, and long-range trends in technology, government, taxation, and trade. It reiterates the importance of integrating online marketing with other business operations.

Your "Members Only" Web Site

The online business world changes almost daily. That's why a companion Web site is associated with this book. On this site you will find Internet resources, expanded information, and a living table of contents that allows you to link to all the URLs in the book. However, you have to be a member of the Marketing on the Internet Club to gain access to this site.

When you purchased this book, you automatically became a member. (In fact, that's the only way to join.) To access the companion Web site, go to the Maximum Press Web site located at *http://www.maxpress.com* and follow the links to the Marketing on the Internet companion Web site area. To enter the Web site, you will be prompted for a user ID and a password. Type in the following:

- For User ID: *mktint6e*

- For Password: *friends*

You will then be granted full access to the "Members Only" area. Once you arrive, bookmark the page in your browser and you will never have to enter the user ID and password again. Visit the site often and enjoy the Internet resources and information with our compliments— and thanks for buying the book. We ask that you not share the user ID and password for this site with anyone else.

If you would like to suggest topics or Web sites for the next edition, or if you have questions about this edition, you can e-mail the author from the companion Web site.

Introduction

Outer space may be "the final frontier" for "Star Trek," but cyberspace is the latest frontier for marketing. Since its expansion as a visual medium in 1993, the Internet has opened a whole new dimension for promoting, marketing, buying, and selling both products and services.

Multinational companies such as Ford and J.P. Morgan, traditional retailers like Wal-Mart and J.C. Penney, and millions of specialty businesses have expanded onto the Web, along with Prince Andrew, the rock star Prince, travel agencies, breweries, movie studios, Girl Scout cookies, and pizzerias. Commercial companies now operate about 28 million active Web sites—up from only 414,000 commercial sites five years ago.

The Internet audience has grown apace. By August 2001, the Internet had reached more than 500 million users in 320 countries and territories. This growth far outruns that of any other telecommunications technology in history. It took less than five years to get the first 50 million people online; it took radio 38 years, television 13 years, and cable 10 years to reach audiences of equal size!

The Internet has unleashed creativity, business opportunities, and phenomenal growth in software, hardware, and services to support its expansion. One recent study showed that the contribution of the Internet to the U.S. economy, including infrastructure and advertising, exceeded $700 billion by the end of 2001. That statistic helps explain many trends in our economy: the deeply intertwined telecommunications and computer industries, the merger and acquisition of top Internet companies, and the battle for control between content providers and access channels.

Businesses selling everything from socks to socket wrenches see the information superhighway as a route to profits. What's most often ignored, however, is that most of those socks and socket wrenches, soups and space station parts, are sold to another business, not to the end user. U.S. business-to-business (B2B) online sales, projected at $721 billion in 2003, will far outdistance business-to-consumer (B2C) sales of only $100 billion.

You needn't think of the Web as only a venue for selling. Although some find it a great way to generate revenue, many more businesses use it to:

- Increase brand or product awareness

- Enhance corporate image

- Provide information or display samples of goods or services

- Generate lists of prospects

- Build relationships with customers

- Improve customer service

- Gather information about customer needs and preferences for future product development

- Better understand customer demographics

- Test consumer response to discounts or special offers

- Find business partners, dealers, franchisees, or vendors

- Recruit talent, members, employees, or subscribers

- Save money by lowering the cost of customer communication and support, reducing the cost of order fulfillment, shortening the time frame for acquiring inventory, reducing stock on hand, and simplifying distribution channels.

Several themes echo throughout this book. First, you need a good business plan before investing marketing dollars online. There is no point in establishing an e-commerce Web site if you don't have the back office infrastructure and the financial resources to support it. A good business plan confirms that you've covered all these bases and forces you to set clear goals and objectives.

Further, with competition on the Web driving down profit margins, it's critical to make sure that the cost of new-customer acquisition will not exceed the money you can make. Many now-failed dot-coms (and their investors) were shocked to realize that the more sales they made, the more money they lost. The Web may continually spawn new technology, but the basics of business are old. "Breakeven" and "Return on Investment" can be found in any Business 101 course from 1950, but they apply to Web sites in the new millennium. In the words of a French proverb, "The more things change, the more they stay the same."

Second, you must commit to constant research and continual site updates. You need to remain alert to new technologies and online techniques that are appropriate to your business, adding relevant interactive features that increase time online and build customer loyalty. It's become a truism to describe Internet time in dog years, with one year online now representing the business changes that used to occur over a seven-year period. At that speed of change, just being online is not enough to succeed online.

Third, Internet marketing is just another part of your overall marketing effort. Many businesses built a Web site only to discover that the visitors did not come. Without actively marketing their sites online and offline, too many companies have found that only their Web developers made any money from their investment. The Web has spawned its own forms of advertising, but traditional methods of getting out the word should not be ignored.

Finally, staying customer-focused is just as important online as it is offline. Remnants of Web companies litter the cyberscape. They were unable to manage their inventory, ship product, answer e-mail, or fulfill customer requests in a timely fashion. Ultimately, the companies that succeed online make it easy to do business from start to finish. That means making it easy to contact the company; making the Web site clear and easy to navigate; and making sure the site just plain works!

This book will help you decide whether the Internet and the Web can make your business more successful and more profitable. If the answer is yes, it will help you implement your electronic vision. Use this book as a reference, dipping into chapters as needed for "how-to" directions and online resources. Review it with your own marketing needs in mind and your own marketing staff involved. By all means read this book with one eye on the screen and the other on your business plan, one hand on a mouse and the other on your financial statement. But read it also with an open mind, with an active imagination, and with passion for your business in your heart.

1

How to Succeed in Online Business by Really Trying

The lifetime of the Internet is a brief 33 years, yet it has profoundly changed how we search for knowledge in an age when knowledge is power. The **World Wide Web** (also known as **W3, WWW,** or the **Web**)— that graphical, easily accessible portion of the Internet—has energized its growth over the past decade. It has also, and rather unexpectedly, had a profound effect on the way business is conducted.

In this chapter we'll look at how the Internet, especially the Web, is redefining marketing communications, altering distribution channels and sales models, modifying consumer behavior, and mediating the relationship not only between businesses and individual consumers, but on the business-to-business level as well.

In spite of the dot-com debacle, Internet revenues of all types, including infrastructure and advertising, exceeded $700 billion by the end of 2001. As seen in Figure 1.1 online retail sales (called **B2C** for business-to-consumer) for all market segments in the United States reached almost $50 billion in 2001 and are projected to reach over $100 billion by the end of 2003. U.S. business-to-business (**B2B**) online commerce dwarfs these numbers, ballooning from $306 billion in 2001, to estimates of over $720 billion in 2003. If you do the arithmetic, you'll see that B2B e-commerce in the U.S. accounts for nearly 90 per-

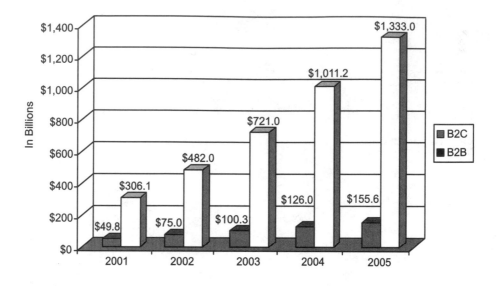

Figure 1.1. U.S. e-commerce 2001-2005, B2B vs. B2C, Source: North America E-Commerce: B2C and B2B Executive Summary, *http://www.eMarketer.com.* Courtesy eMarketer, Inc.

cent of online dollars. On a global scale, B2C is expected to reach $550 billion by 2005 and B2B e-commerce is estimated at more than $2.7 trillion by 2004.

Should part of these revenues be yours? Should you invest your time, energy, money, and other resources to market and/or sell over the Internet? Or should you expend those scarce resources on offline marketing techniques that you know will work? The decision isn't an easy one.

To help you, this chapter provides some context for doing business online. We'll cover a little history, offer some statistics about market potential, and provide you with basic tools for analyzing Web sites. Armed with this information and the review of your business, marketing strategy, and customers in Chapters 2 and 3, you can determine whether selling or marketing online is for you. Specifically, we'll discuss

- How marketing and selling online are the same as or different from offline marketing and sales

- The technology and history of the Internet and World Wide Web

- The range of activities users undertake online

- Opportunities in both the business-to-consumer (B2C) and business-to-business (B2B) online worlds

- How to analyze a site for concept, content, navigation, decoration, and marketing effectiveness

The Entrepreneur's Eye View

To early Internet entrepreneurs, the Web looked like a perfect business opportunity: all up-side, no risk. Indeed, some of the first companies online did well: Competition was limited, even though the audience was small, and they enjoyed the novelty of being first. As Web sites proliferated, venture capitalists entered the arena under the assumption that the Internet would generate as much cash as a winning slot machine. Soon, however, it became apparent that selling online had its own challenges.

Not only were many more companies competing for attention, but getting new customers and fulfilling their orders proved to be an expensive challenge. For instance, it was only after 6 years of money-losing operations that *Amazon.com*, the largest online retailer, reported a profit in the fourth quarter of 2001. The dot-com shakeout of the late '90s found too many dollars chasing too many sites with untested products, premises, and business models. Many of the disappearing dot-coms had spent so much money to acquire customers that they advertised themselves into financial oblivion.

At the same time, large catalog companies like REI, with deep pockets and the back-office experience to handle fulfillment, went online, driving smaller, underfunded sites out of business. Some large brick-and-mortar retailers, such as Toys R Us, discovered that doing business online was not the "slam dunk" they anticipated. Well-publicized holiday shipping problems, lack of inventory control, and inadequate server capacity to handle site traffic led many large sites into the swamp.

While the demise of hundreds of venture-funded dot-coms attracted press attention, hundreds of thousands of other small businesses discovered Web profitability by following basic business principles. What did these successful online businesses realize that so many others forgot? Viewing the Web not as an end, but as a means to improve customer service and build customer loyalty, these businesses saw value in using the Web for more than just online sales. They used the Web to advertise, provide company background, offer product and service information, and generate leads. They recognized that the Web was better used for target marketing than for broad audience, mass marketing. They also understood, in some cases intuitively, that there are more similarities between online and offline marketing than there are differences.

What's the Same about Web Marketing

Whether you sell only online as an **e-tailer,** or whether you are creating a Web site to supplement your offline business activities, the essentials of business are the same:

- It is profit, not gross revenues, that counts. You can't make money by increasing sales if you lose $1 every time you ship a product.

- It's easier to sell a second product to an existing customer than to acquire a new customer.

- If you're going to open an online store, you need to give it at least the level of care and feeding that you would a brick-and-mortar storefront.

- Customer satisfaction is the driving principle behind all successful businesses, whether they are online or offline.

Basic sales techniques also apply online, whether your approach is soft-sell or hard-sell.

WIIFM

What's In It For Me? That question must be answered, implicitly or explicitly, every time a customer walks into a store or visits a Web site for the first time. Customers must understand immediately what you have to offer that might meet their needs, solve their problems, or provide entertainment or information. If visitors don't understand what's on your site for them within a few seconds of arriving at your home page, they will click away before giving you a chance to explain. Every successful online business knows that. Test it as you surf the Web. You'll see.

You

Successful businesses, online and offline, understand that what the customer wants to buy is much more important than what the business needs to sell. In marketing language, successful businesses focus on the benefits of the product or service, not on its features. To accomplish this, they couch online text or sales text in second person ("You'll love this because...") instead of first person ("We have 16 bells and 8 whistles."). Whether good companies are looking at ease of use of their Web site or the layout of their store, they are more concerned with the customer's experience than with their own skill.

Free

"Free" is the "open sesame" of sales—no word opens a pocketbook faster. It's human nature to want to "get a deal" or, better yet, to get something for nothing. Whether it's a special discount, free information, or a free 30-day warranty, be sure to offer your customers something of value on your Web site.

AIDA

Savvy Web marketers apply the four-step process of direct mail marketing to the Internet. The acronym **AIDA** sums it up:

- *Attention.* In any marketing approach, you must first get your prospect's attention. Use good graphics, attention-grabbing headlines, and a benefits-based lead to draw viewers to your site.

- *Interest.* You need to pique their interest to pull people to internal pages of your site. Whether by telling viewers where to find information or entertainment, or stimulating them with the sense that a good value is waiting at the next click, you can use additional pages of your site to intrigue your viewers.

- *Desire*. Let the viewer's desire increase by moving through your site to locate the answers needed for a buying decision. Building desire to obtain a particular service or product is tricky. Good copy and graphics help, and you can take advantage of the interactivity of the Web. For instance, look at the interactive materials calculator seen in Figure 1.2 at *http://www.todayshomeowner.com/ calculators/index.html*.

- *Action*. A **call to action**, an explicit step that directs people to take a step toward a purchase, is critical. On the Web, it's easy to have a viewer take concrete actions. With most other forms of advertising, you have to wait until viewers have switched to

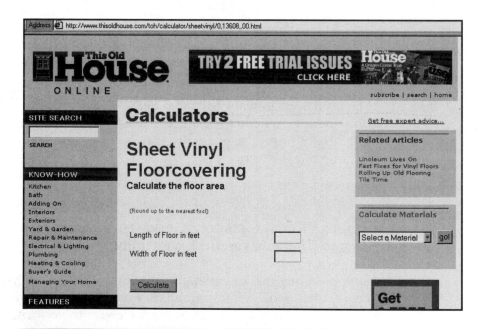

Figure 1.2. Interactive materials calculator, *http://www.todayshomeowner.com/ calculators/index.html*. Courtesy of This Old House Ventures, Inc. Copyright © 2002 This Old House Ventures, Inc. All rights reserved.

another activity after hearing or seeing an ad. On the Web, they are already at their computers, mouse at hand, just two clicks away from a purchase.

Get on the Winning Side

Surveys by Verizon SuperPages, IDC, and eMarketer all show small businesses increasing their use of the Web as a tool for customer relations, marketing, advertising, and communications. As of October 2001, almost three-quarters of all small businesses had Internet access, which they used for e-mail and research, and more than 30 percent had a Web site (see Figure 1.3). However only 11 percent of small businesses sold directly online and they averaged only a few sales per month. For those businesses that did sell online, on-site sales as a percent of total sales grew 23 percent between 2000 and 2001.

Two-thirds of small businesses with sites in the Verizon study said their Web site is important to their business, and about 57 percent reported that the site provided at least a 100 percent **return on investment (ROI)**, whatever its purpose. More than half responded that they expected the amount of business generated from their site to increase. With some strategic planning, well-planned work, and modest funds, you can create or upgrade your Web site and online marketing efforts to produce these results for your business.

TIPS FOR TIRED SITES

AIDA to your aid. Do your site statistics show that visitors leave within a few seconds instead of delving deeper into your site? Do they visit only once? If you're not converting browsers to buyers, take a good look at your site. What does your home page do to attract attention? Is there a tempting headline that makes a promise you can keep? Are you directing people to something of value on the next page to increase their interest? To build desire for your product or service on internal pages, do you talk about the benefits for the shopper? Do you have a specific call to action, such as a "Buy Now" link? Is the purchasing opportunity available within two clicks?

Estimated 7.56 million small businesses in 2001

(In thousands)	1998	1999	2000	2001	% of all businesses
Online	3,863	4,290	5,010	5,594	74.0%
Have Home Page	1,169	1,565	2,092	2,344	31.0%
Conduct e-Commerce	400	540	725	Est. 809	10.7%

Figure 1.3. U.S. small business Internet use, *http://cyberatlas.internet.com/ markets/smallbiz/article/0,,10098_860861,00.html.* © 2002 INT Media Group, Inc. All rights reserved.

A Brief History of the Internet and the Web

To better understand the marketing opportunity the Web offers, it will help to have a little history. The Internet is the worldwide interconnection of many different computer networks that allow their users to share information, programs, and equipment, and to communicate with one another. By hooking together **servers**, the large computers that manage individual networks, the Internet allows more than 500 million people around the world to access information stored on hundreds of thousands of computers. The Internet transmits messages between servers much the way the telephone system does, using satellites, microwaves, and dedicated cables such as Ethernet lines, fiber optic cables, cable television, or even the simple phone lines in your home.

Originally, computer networks on the Internet could exchange only text messages. Now the Web portion of the Internet allows users to exchange graphics, still photos, animation, voice, and even full-motion video.

The Web is the fastest-growing, most user-friendly, and most commercially popular segment of the Internet. Any computer on the Internet equipped with a **browser** (software designed to look at Internet resources) and small pieces of specialized software called **plug-ins** can access different kinds of text, images, and sound. A **page** (part of a site) on the Web can be connected to another page with related information using a **link**, even if the computer hosting the other page is halfway around the earth, orbiting in the space shuttle, or sitting on Mars. How did all this come to be?

A Government Heritage

The Internet owes its existence to the Pentagon and the Cold War. To solve the problem of a centralized computer system vulnerable to a single well-placed bomb, scientists at the Rand Corporation developed the concept of a **centerless network** in 1964. They envisioned thousands of computers connected with communication redundancy, much the way the human brain is wired, so that the loss of a few "neurons" or connecting cables would not result in a total loss of function.

In 1969, two **nodes** (computers connected to a network) were linked for the first time on the ARPAnet, the precursor to today's Internet. (ARPAnet was named after the Defense Department's Advanced Research Projects Agency, which sponsored its development.)

As the ARPAnet grew, researchers at UCLA, MIT, Stanford Research International, Bolt Baranek & Newman, and the British National Physical Laboratory defined a way to bundle information into structures called **packets**, which were labeled with the **network address** of the recipient's computer. Like a message in a bottle, a packet of information is cast adrift in the sea of computers on the network. Each computer forwards the packet closer to the address on the bottle. Once the packet reaches its destination, the packet structure (i.e., the bottle) dissolves, leaving the message intact. All computer networks now use this packet scheme to package and deliver messages reliably. The **protocol** that moves these packets of information along Internet pathways is called **TCP/IP** or **Transmission Control Protocol/Internet Protocol**.

When the ARPAnet was decommissioned in 1989, NSFnet supplanted it as the main high-speed transmission line, or **backbone**, with support from the National Science Foundation. Perhaps because its original government funding mandated public ownership of the enabling technology, or perhaps because of an open-development process through public **Requests for Comments (RFCs)**, the Internet grew of its own accord to meet the needs of its users. The Internet is now self-sustained by a network of interested parties, both public and private.

Without a doubt, the rapid spread of sophisticated desktop computers in the 1980s and 1990s enabled the Internet to take off. ARPAnet was founded in the days of large mainframes located at universities and major corporations; NSFnet was originally funded to connect five supercomputer centers. Without personal computers there never would have been so many computers to connect!

The 1993 release of Mosaic, the first browser capable of reading graphical information, provided the mechanism for user-friendly access and gave birth to the Web. Suddenly, Internet usage parameters that had been doubling each year began doubling in three months.

Curious? For more information on the history of the Internet, try *http://info.isoc.org/internet/history* or *http://www.pbs.org/internet/timeline*.

Spectacular Growth

By any criterion—number of computers connected, domain names, active Web sites, Web pages, or people connected—the growth of the Internet has been spectacular. In its first 15 years, the Internet barely topped 1,000 **hosts** (computer systems connected to the Internet). In its second 15 years, it exploded like a supernova. As seen in Figure 1.4, by January 2002 the Internet comprised over 147 million hosts. These hosts serve more than 500 million users worldwide in 320 countries and territories around the world.

As of January 2002 the total number of **domain names** (Web site names) registered worldwide topped 44 million (not all are active). Within the past year, the number of new names versus resold names has dropped dramatically. Now almost 70 percent of names being registered are names

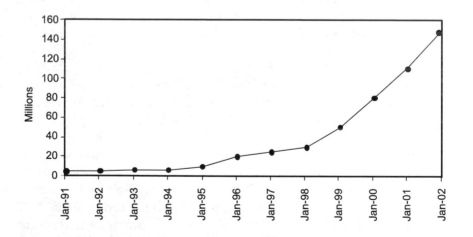

Figure 1.4. Internet domain survey host count, *http://www.isc.org/ds/hosts.html*. Partially based on data from the Internet Software Consortium (*http://www.isc.org*). Courtesy Internet Software Consortium.

whose original registration has expired. (We'll discuss domain registration in Chapter 5.) Figure 1.5 shows the growth of domain-name registration in graphic terms. About 8 percent of registered names become active sites, with 4,400 new sites posted each day. By the end of 2002, the number of pages on the Web is expected to exceed 6 billion, more than the world's population!

The number of Web sites in the commercial (*.com*) and network domains far outpaces that of educational institutions (*.edu*), the military, and the government, which represent a negligible fraction of names. Partly due to the lack of available names in the *.com* domain, the number of names has grown lately in other top-level domains like *.net* and *.org*, in newly-created domains like *.biz*, and in countries outside the United States. Commercial domains represented over 30 percent of all registered domains in January 2002.

Internet access, particularly since the development of the World Wide Web, has grown faster than any other communications technology in history. Consider this: It took 38 years for 30 percent of U.S. households to have a telephone; 17 years to have a television; 13 years to

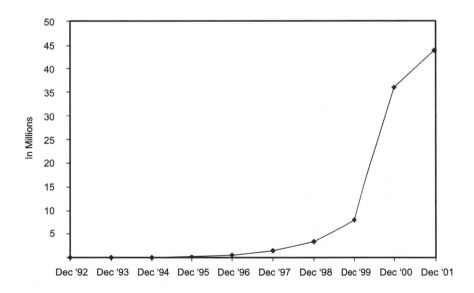

Figure 1.5. Growth in registered domain names, *http://www.networksolutions. com*. Network Solutions domain name registration data is used with permission of Network Solutions, Inc. Copyright Network Solutions, Inc.

have a computer. The World Wide Web took less than 7 years to reach the same 30 percent! This is one of the truly remarkable stories of technological innovation.

For online marketing purposes, the implications of all these numbers are staggering. For current statistical information, check out:

- *http://www.forrester.com*

- *http://www.eMarketer.com*

- *http://www.isc.org/ds/WWW-200201/index.html*

- *http://www.internetstats.com*

- *http://www.netcraft.com*

- *http://www.nua.ie*

- *http://www.cyberatlas.internet.com/markets*

What's Happening in Cyberspace?

How your customers obtain Internet access and the kinds of information they are able to receive affects your ability to reach your desired audience. It matters that in the year 2001 the installed base of computers was already over 182 million in the United States and 625 million worldwide. It matters that more than 51 percent of U.S. homes (54 million households) had at least one computer in 2000, up from 42 percent in 1998. Of those households, more than 80 percent are online, a significant increase from fewer than 50 percent of households with computers going online in 1997. In Chapter 3, we'll take a deeper look at these numbers for market segmentation, since computer ownership and Internet access are not equitably spread across all segments of the population.

Prices on computers have fallen low enough that multiple computer/Web-access homes are becoming commonplace, with PCs sometimes connected to each other with a phone-based, mini-networking card, or a switcher, router, or hub. In other cases, the second unit will be an

Internet appliance, or hand-held wireless device. Personal digital assistants like the Palm Pilot, cell phones with special built-in Internet browsers, WebTV, or **Web appliances**—which integrate home organization with Web access and e-mail—have gained minor market share as alternate forms of Internet access.

Figure 1.6 shows that users connect to the Internet at faster and faster speeds. Although home users still overwhelmingly use dial-up connections (83.7 million) from their **Internet Service Providers (ISPs)**, 13 percent (17.7 million) enjoyed high-speed (sometimes called **broadband**) access through cable modems, **digital subscriber lines (DSLs)**, or other dedicated lines. With high-speed capability reaching a potential 75 percent of U.S. households by the end of 2001, the number of high-speed subscribers will increase, especially if providers bring down the initial and monthly cost. A higher percentage of business users than home users have high-speed Internet access.

For those 63.4 percent of all users who dial into the Web at 56 Kbps, *actual* modem connection speed averages 38 percent slower than modem or ISP capability. As a result, home users continue to be easily frustrated by graphics-intensive, feature-laden sites. Faster access also affects how people interact with the Web, as seen in Figure 1.7. Broadband access increases dramatically the number of Web visits (sessions) users make, the time they spend online, and the number of pages they view (130 percent more). It also affects what types of sites they are

Connection Speed	July 2000 (000)	% of Total 2000	July 2001 (000)	% of Total 2001
High Speed*	8,003	9.2%	17,703	17.5%
56K Modem	49,666	57.0%	64,290	63.4%
28.8/33.6K Modem	24,205	27.8%	15,523	15.3%
14.4K Modem	5,304	6.0%	3,907	3.8%
Total	*87,178*	*100.0%*	*101,423*	*100.0%*

*High-speed access includes ISDN, LAN, cable modems and DSL.
Source: Nielsen//NetRatings

Figure 1.6.   Internet use by connection speed, *http://cyberatlas.internet.com/ markets/broadband/article/0,,10099_870841,00.html#table2.* © 2002 INT Media Group, Inc. All rights reserved.

	Before Broadband January 2001	After Broadband July 2001	Percent Change
Page Views (000)	2.4 billion	5.5 billion	130%
Pages per Person	757	1,170	55%
Sessions	22.03	27.5	25%
Time Spent Online per Person (hr:min:sec)	12:21:50	15:14:00	23%

Figure 1.7. How broadband changes Internet use, *http://cyberatlas.internet.com/markets/broadband/article/0,,10099_870841,00.html#table2.* © 2002 INT Media Group, Inc. All rights reserved.

likely to view: Broadband users are more likely to download music, listen to music, watch video, or conduct personal banking and stock-related activities. With download speed a significant design issue, you may need to adjust your Web site based on whether your target audience is more likely to log on from home or work, and what their access speed is likely to be.

It even matters to you which hardware platforms, browsers, and browser versions viewers use, since Web sites don't look equally good in all environments. The most popular browsers, Netscape's Navigator (now less than 10 percent market share) and Microsoft's Internet Explorer (about 90 percent market share) have long since supplanted Mosaic. These browsers allow access to e-mail, newsgroups, and mailing lists, as well as the Web, as long as an ISP handles them. Alternative browsers like Opera (*http://www.opera.com*) have such a small market share that you don't currently need to test for compatibility.

What's going on that has more than 58 million Americans logging on every day, many of them multiple times? In 2001 users spent about 83 minutes per session (down from 90 minutes in 2000), reducing the time they spent watching television, shopping in stores, or reading newspapers to go online, as seen in Figure 1.8. A March 2002 survey by the Pew Internet & American Life Project (*http://www.pewinternet.org/reports/pdfs/PIP_Getting_Serious_Online.pdf*) found that the Web has now become more necessity than novelty. More people use the Web to work from home than previously, and more of them use it for utilitarian purposes, such as conducting a transaction, or seeking specific information, particularly from health-care or government sites. (See Figure 1.9.)

Has the Internet increased, decreased, or had no change on the amount of time you spend...	Increased	Decreased	No Change
Watching television	3%	25%	72%
Shopping in stores	4%	18%	78%
Working at home	14%	5%	81%
Reading newspapers	5%	14%	81%
Working at the office	10%	6%	84%
Spending time with family	6%	6%	88%
Spending time with friends	8%	2%	90%
Commuting in traffic	1%	6%	92%
Attending social events	5%	2%	93%

Figure 1.8. The Internet and time use. Source: Pew Internet & American Life Project. March 2001 Survey; asked of Internet users, n=862 for March 2001; margin of error is ±4%. From "Getting Serious Online," March 3, 2002 pg. 19, *http://www.pewinternet.org/reports/pdfs/PIP_Getting_Serious_online.pdf.* Downloaded April 05, 2002, 2:36 pm.

Top 15 Daily Internet Activities	% of those with Internet Access
Go online	58%
Send e-mail	54%
Get news	26%
Surf the Web for fun	20%
Look for info. on a hobby	20%
Do any type of research for work	20%
Seek political news/info.	17%
Check the weather	17%
Internet search to answer specific question	14%
Send an instant message	14%
Research a product or service before buying it	14%
Get financial information	13%
Check sports scores	10%
Look for information about movies, books, other leisure activities	9%
Research for school or training	8%

Figure 1.9. Top 15 daily Internet activities, *http://www.pewinternet.org/reports/chart.asp?img=Internet_Activities.jpg.* Source: Pew Internet & American Life Project. These data come from different months of the Pew tracking survey. Please consult the Pew Internet & American Life Project Web site (*http://www.pewinternet.org/reports*) for exact dates and methodology information. March 2000-December 2001. Downloaded April 09, 2002, 5:06 pm.

E-Mail and Instant Messaging

Electronic mail (**e-mail**), one of the original uses of the Internet, remains the most essential activity, with over half of all users saying it is their most common use. With e-mail, one person sends a message to the computer mailbox of another. E-mail also allows someone to broadcast a message to many people simultaneously. Most e-mail programs permit users to attach a computer file containing any type of information, from spreadsheets to software programs. With over 505 million e-mail boxes expected worldwide by the end of 2002, users will flood the Internet with 10 billion personal messages a day. By 2005, the number of mailboxes is expected to reach 1.2 billion, with 36 billion daily messages, or about 30 per person. This does not count the potential 200 billion commercial messages to be sent per day by 2004, a large percentage of which will be unwanted and unread.

Instant messaging (**IM**), personal online chatting conducted by simultaneously exchanging e-mail messages, has exploded as a form of communication, especially among younger users. Jupiter Media reports that between 2000 and 2001, the number of IM users rose 34 percent to 13.4 million users at work and 28 percent to 53.8 million users at home. Three providers offer mutually incompatible IM services: AOL, Microsoft Network (MSN), and Yahoo!

Mailing Lists

An Internet **mailing list** stores the names and associated e-mail addresses of users with a common interest in a particular topic. Once an **opt-in** mailing list is started, Internet users can add their names and e-mail addresses to the list (called **subscribing**). These public lists generally fall into the genre of "several-subscribers-to-many-subscribers." About 21 percent of e-mail users subscribe to one or more-mailing lists, whose subscriber base ranges from a few dozen to tens of thousands.

Over 48,000 public mailing lists cover every subject imaginable. Scientists use-mailing lists for peer discussion of theories and experiments. Philosophers use them. Priests use them. Techies and Dead Heads use them. Even marketers use them. On the Internet all kinds of people use-mailing lists to stay informed of important events, exchanging data on everything from the flight path of killer bees to changes in concert schedules.

Newsgroups

Mailing lists are accessed via e-mail, but **newsgroups,** a worldwide system of over 21,000 discussion groups on a portion of the Internet called USEnet, require full Internet accounts and newsgroup reader software provided by an ISP. Newsgroups function like-mailing lists in some ways, but they offer several different methods of sending messages. A user can **post** a message for everyone in the group, or respond to someone else's comments on a particular topic. In the latter case, only those who read the original comments see the response.

A few of the more popular newsgroups have as many as 300,000 users at a particular time. More commonly, subscribers range from 200 to 10,000. Whether a newsgroup will be a valuable marketing tool for you depends on your business and your target market. We'll discuss this more in Chapter 4.

The World Wide Web

The World Wide Web consists of those servers on the Internet programmed to handle specific information requests from browser software. To locate any resource on the Internet that is part of the Web, you enter an address into your browser in a standard format called a **URL** (**Uniform Resource Locator**). Typical Web addresses look like this: *http:// www.watermelonweb.com.* The acronym **http** (**HyperText Transport Protocol**) indicates a special method of moving **HyperText** files, which contain links to other Web pages, across the Internet. The **www** after the double slash (*//*) means that the information is located on a dedicated Web server. Browsers allow users to **bookmark** any sites (by saving the URL address) they want to recall in the future.

By the Numbers: Business on the Internet

About 53 percent of U.S. Web users—over 50 million people—report having purchased something online at least once, up from 47 percent in 2001, 40 percent in 1999, 26 percent in 1998 and 15 percent in 1996. (See Figure 1.10.) Some of these buyers are "regulars": Even if they don't actually buy on the Web, over 90 percent of online consumers

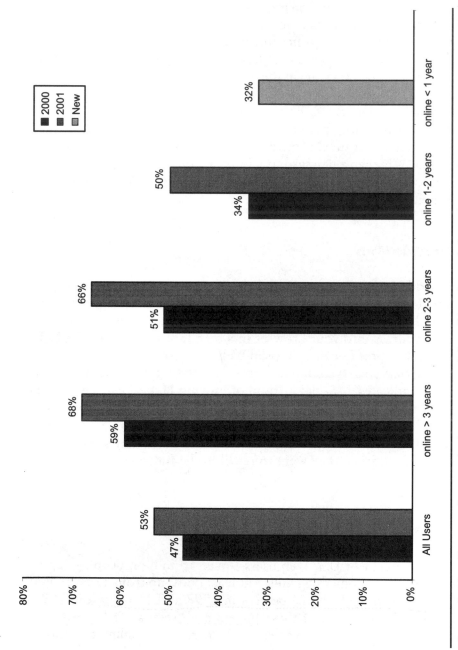

Figure 1.10. Percent of users who have ever used the Web to buy products. Source: Pew Internet & American Life Project. "Getting Serious Online," March 3, 2002, pg. 22. *http://www.pewinternet.org/reports/pdfs/ PIP_Getting_Serious_Online.pdf.* Downloaded March 28, 2002, 12:00 pm.

obtain product information or research future purchases, especially for cars, books, and computers. Figure 1.11 compares the millions of consumers (by number of users) who research (the shoppers) to those who purchase by category (the buyers). These numbers are a persuasive argument for going online to display your products even if you choose not to sell there.

Who's Selling What to Whom

The nature of online selling—what sells, what doesn't—has changed as the Internet has evolved, and as the characteristics of the online population have changed.

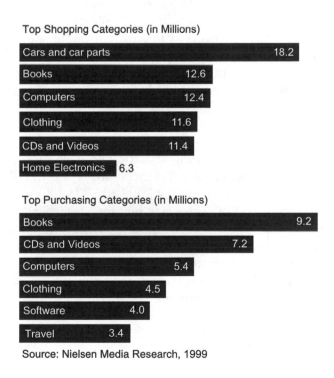

Top Shopping Categories (in Millions)

Category	
Cars and car parts	18.2
Books	12.6
Computers	12.4
Clothing	11.6
CDs and Videos	11.4
Home Electronics	6.3

Top Purchasing Categories (in Millions)

Category	
Books	9.2
CDs and Videos	7.2
Computers	5.4
Clothing	4.5
Software	4.0
Travel	3.4

Source: Nielsen Media Research, 1999

Figure 1.11. Comparison of online shoppers vs. buyers, *http://www.emarketer. com/images/062899naecom.gif*. Courtesy eMarketer, Inc.

B2C

Some products sell better on the Web than others. Brokerage houses and sites selling computer hardware and software, travel, and collectibles (often found on auction sites) are among the most lucrative. Music/ video, books, tickets, and flowers all do well on the Web; their dollar volume is lower because the price of the products is relatively low.

Travel is another growth story. Total online commerce related to travel and leisure is expected to reach $64 billion in 2006, up from $18 billion in 2000, with visitors attracted by such sites as CentralAmerica.com (*http://www.centralamerica.com/cr/parks/index.htm*). Close to 58 percent of online consumers have used the Web to research travel destinations and prices, and about one-half of those will book online. Travel is now the biggest retail category on the Web, with online revenues greater than those of cars, clothes, and books combined.

The number of real estate sites has also grown, from huge sites like *http://www.realtor.com* to individual residential brokers' sites. It is difficult to quantify the dollar value of real estate sold because sales are initiated online but closed offline. The latest surge of Web sites among small businesses has been in the service sector: financial, real estate, and insurance, with a growth rate of 160 percent in sites from 1999 to 2001.

B2B

Perhaps the most interesting statistic about commerce on the Web is that most of it is business-to-business, not retail. U.S. B2B numbers are staggering, with projections for 2003 of $721 billion, more than seven times that of U.S. B2C sales (see Figure 1.1 earlier). Of course, a B2B sale is generally for a larger amount than a retail transaction. These forecasts are also fueled by the increasing use of industry-wide, online buying sites for corporate giants in the automotive, airline, and computer industries. Small businesses are expected to generate about 13 percent of total online commerce in 2002.

How People Find Sites

It's important to understand how people find the Web sites they visit, because this will affect your Web promotion strategy. Already newspapers and TV shows review Web sites and announce Web happenings, from scheduled chats with stars, athletes, and political personalities to live Webcasts of entertainment events. News programs, movies, and all forms of advertising now include URLs in their promotional matter—just watch an evening of television or tabulate the print ads with URLs in your favorite magazine.

A survey posted in June 2000 on Business Week Online *(http:// www.businessweek.com)* ranked users' common strategies for finding new Web sites in the following order. The four most common were

- Search engines, 45.8%

- Word-of-mouth, 20.3%

- Random surfing, 19.9%

- Magazines, 4.4%

If you sell B2C online, potential customers may locate you through price-and-feature comparison sites like *http://www.mysimon.com* or *http:// www.DealPilot.com.* Bid sites like *http://www.priceline.com* allow consumers to set a target price to try to obtain the best bargain on their desired products. Other consumer-oriented sites like *http://www. accompany.com* aggregate buyers to leverage group purchasing power for better prices.

Other sites offer shopping-specific search engines devoted exclusively to retail sales, like *http://eshop.msn.com* (Figure 1.12) or *http:// ivillage.catalogcity.com.* After the user enters a desired product, the engine returns information about locations and prices.

Mass vs. Target Marketing

A perennial advertising debate rages over Web promotion: Is the Web 90 percent brand imaging? Or is it 90 percent niche marketing? Should you aim for mass markets, maximizing your total exposure and the total number of viewers who see your name? Or should you aim at narrow demographic prospects who are more likely to turn into customers? Let's look at ad costs and results.

Advertisers use the term **CPM** to represent the cost per thousand possible viewers or listeners (M is the Roman numeral for 1,000). Generally,

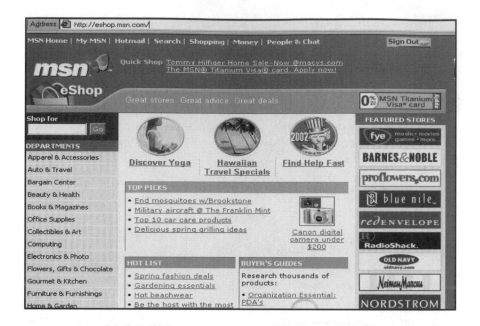

Figure 1.12. Shopping search engine, *http://eshop.msn.com.* ©1996-2002 Microsoft Corporation and/or its suppliers, One Microsoft Way, Redmond, Washington, 98052-6399 U.S.A. All rights reserved.

the higher the CPM, the smaller but more targeted the audience in terms of geography or demographics. The table in Figure 1.13 compares typical CPMs for various media. The key, as always, is whether the viewers you reach are the right targets for the product or service you sell.

Even though its CPM may be low, the actual costs or minimum rates for an ad may not be. A 30-second Super Bowl 2002 ad, with a CPM of $15, sold for slightly less than $2 million to reach 130 million viewers.

By comparison, the average CPM for a Web banner ad by the end of 2001 was $13-$20, down for the fifth year in a row, partly due to the loss of advertising dollars as a result of the dot-com shakeout, and partly due to excess online advertising space. Actual costs range from a few hundred dollars per year to tens of thousands of dollars per week. You'll need to balance your budget against your desired audience size and demographics.

Based on these numbers, unless you are a major corporation already managing brand imaging in national newspapers, network TV,

Forms of Media	Typical Range CPM
Web Site	$10-$70 average $13-$20
National Newspaper	$18-$40
Prime Time Network TV	$9-$40 average $12-$20
Superbowl	$15
Outdoors	$1.50-$2
Consumer Magazine	$35

Figure 1.13.   CPM by media.

radio and glossy magazines, you will be better off with a tightly-targeted, guerrilla marketing approach. The cost of exposure-driven marketing is likely to empty all but the deepest pockets. Spend your precious dollars where they will reach the most likely buyers. We'll talk more about advertising in Chapter 12.

To stay abreast of Internet statistics, watch sites such as:

- *http://www.openmarket.com/intindex.cfm*

- *http://www.internetindicators.com*

- *http://www.internetstats.com*

- *http://www.emarketer.com/estats*

There's More to a Site Than Meets the Eye

Before we leave this preparatory chapter, we need to review what makes a Web site work. As with art, you can move beyond the perspective of "I don't know anything about it, but I know what I like." By learning to evaluate Web design and functionality, you can intelligently discuss other Web sites and improve your own. The better you can articulate what makes a particular Web site effective, the better you can communicate with your designer, colleagues, customers, and even your boss. We'll talk more in Chapter 6 about how to incorporate the five elements below into your Web site itself:

A good website [handwritten annotation]

- Concept

- Content

- Navigation

- Decoration

- Marketing Effectiveness

Start a collection now of sites that you like or dislike. Bookmark these sites whenever you're surfing the Web, and print out pages to save in a Web planning notebook. For a start, look at Inc. Magazine's award-winning sites at *http://www.inc.com/home*. This collection will be of invaluable assistance to your Web developer later.

Concept

A Web site is an exercise in marketing communications, just like the development of logos, advertisements, or brochures. The first impression a site creates is the most important; it is formed by the elements of graphic design—colors, layout, and images—well before a viewer reads anything more than the headline at the top of the home page. The concept, the visual metaphor or unifying theme that underlies a Web site design, "sells the sizzle, not the steak." It enables you to decode the audiences and purposes the site is intended to serve. Ask yourself what message the audience of a site is expected to take away. Only in the context of its goals and audience can you evaluate how effective a site is and whether the most appropriate means of communication have been used.

As you surf Web sites, you'll quickly realize that the good ones maintain the same visual concept throughout. This consistency not only reinforces the chosen message and image of the company, it also makes it easier for viewers to navigate the site. The concept may be a concrete metaphor, like that of eWatch (*http://www.eWatch.com*) shown in Figure 1.14, or strictly pictorial, as with Valley K Greenhouses (*http://www.valleyk.com*) shown in Figure 1.15.

The concept for a Web site can be folksy or formal, avant-garde or retro, academic or playful, sophisticated or slapstick, droll or determined. It only matters that it's consistent throughout the site and con-

Figure 1.14. Concept as a concrete metaphor, *http://www.ewatch.com.* Courtesy PR Newswire.

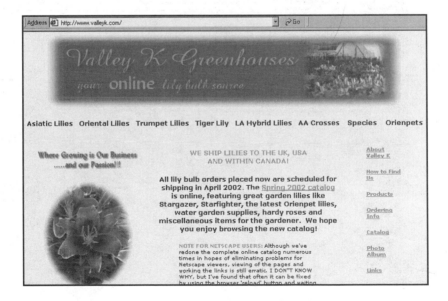

Figure 1.15. Pictorial metaphor, *http://www.valleyk.com.* Courtesy Valley K Greenhouses.

gruent with the purpose and audience for the site. If the concept of the site contradicts the message it intended to convey or turns off the audience it is trying to reach, it will not achieve its marketing goals no matter how beautifully it is executed.

Content

To fulfill the purpose of a site, **content**—the words, pictures, and multimedia on the screen—must be relevant, stated clearly, and communicated quickly. How quickly does the headline grab you? Does the content stay focused on the purpose of the site? Can you tell whether someone wrote for the Web as a unique medium, or tried to save money by adapting older content? Hint: Old copy may be too wordy, too long, or too passive for the inherently interactive Web. (We'll discuss writing for the Web in Chapter 6.) Like everything else on the Web, creating good content, like that in Figure 1.16 (*http://www.visionpaper.com*), is an art.

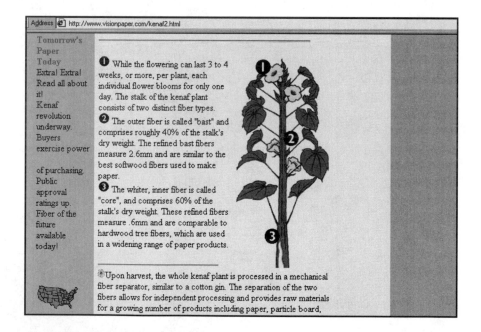

Figure 1.16.   Site with good content, *http://www.visionpaper.com*. Courtesy www.Visionpaper.com.

Don't feel that you have to overwhelm visitors with every single bit of information ever created about your company. In fact, a site that stays tightly focused on your marketing mission will be more satisfactory to both the viewer and your bottom line.

Navigation

How well can the viewer get around a site? Is it obvious? Intuitive? Does it leave a trail of "pixel crumbs" so viewers know where they've been in case they want to go back? Does the site provide clues to what users will find at future destinations? Are they led gently along a garden path to the next panorama or left to wander through a maze?

Site designers can facilitate navigation in many ways that we'll explore in Chapter 6. For now, just ask yourself whether a site:

- offers a clear, complete home page that is always accessible with a link from other pages

- lets users know with a menu on the home page how the content is organized, much like the table of contents in a book or magazine, whether that menu is linear or spatial, as in *www.aromanaturals.com*, seen in Figure 1.17

- keeps the main menu available on every page

- restrains the number of main on-screen options to no more than 6 to 10

- allows viewers to reach any place on the site within two or three clicks

- guides users with consistent visual cues such as buttons, layout, and prompts, as done at *http://www.bc.com*, shown in Figure 1.18

Decoration

The unique style of a site—what most people think of as Web design—is actually the servant of concept, content, and navigation. **Decoration**

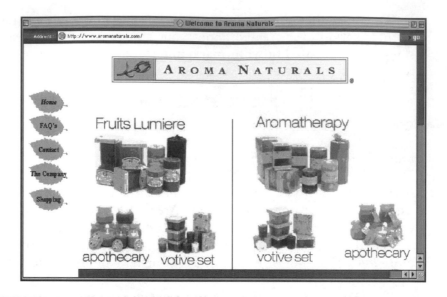

Figure 1.17.   Site with a clear spatial menu. *http://www.aromanaturals.com.* Copyright Thomas M. Dionisio.

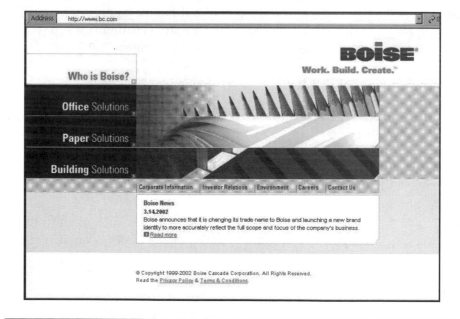

Figure 1.18.   Site with consistent visual cues, *http://www.bc.com.* Copyright Boise Cascade Corporation. All rights reserved.

refers to the graphic and multimedia elements that are as unique to a site as your logo is to your company name.

Designers are fond of a saying by the architect Mies van der Rohe, "God is in the details." Does a company's image sparkle through the decorative details on its site? Take a look at the two screenshots in Figures 1.19 (*http://www.freelancefarm.com*), and 1.20 (*http://www.finecoffee.com*). Would you be likely to confuse the corporate identity of any of these sites, each of which has its own unique Web decoration and concept?

Marketing Effectiveness

Marketing effectiveness is a summary assessment of how well a site conveys a central message, addresses the needs of its target audiences, and moves the audience to take action. It takes into account the appropriate use of features for promoting a site within its own pages, which we'll address in Chapter 9. You can use Figure 1.21 as a rating sheet to evaluate your own or others' sites.

Figure 1.19. Unique style, *http://www.freelancefarm.com*. Courtesy Freelancefarm.

First, evaluate your site's content, concept, navigation, decoration, and marketing effectiveness yourself. Try to be honest and imagine yourself as someone visiting the site for the first time. Then ask several customers, employees, and viewers at a cyber-café to evaluate your site using the form on page 31. By all means, give them a promotional item with your URL, a credit for additional time at the cyber-café, or something else of value in thanks. Or ask online visitors to evaluate your site online in exchange for a coupon or discount on their next purchase. Compare their answers to yours. Mark the areas that need improvement for discussion with your Web developer for your next site upgrade.

The Bottom Line

The array of data in this chapter should convince you of several things: The Internet is here to stay, usage is growing, and the rate of change in the business world will only increase. Using online market research to en-

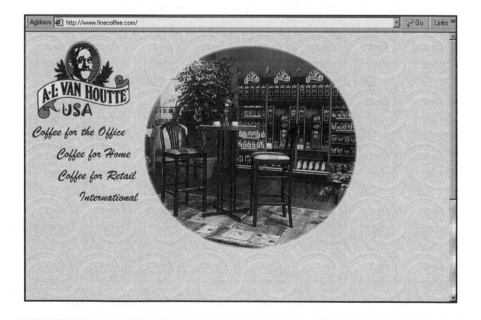

Figure 1.20. Unique style, *http://www.finecoffee.com*. Courtesy Jim Hood, Fruba, Inc. dba College Hill Coffee Shop.

Based on the imagery and the content, who is the audience for this site and what purposes does the site serve? Rank each item below from 1-5 with 5 being best. Subtotal each category, then total the site overall.

CONCEPT
How well is a coherent visual metaphor carried through the site? 1 2 3 4 5
How well is that metaphor carried through on each screen? 1 2 3 4 5
How well does the metaphor fit the company image? 1 2 3 4 5
How well does the metaphor suit the purpose of the site? 1 2 3 4 5
How well does the metaphor suit the target audience? 1 2 3 4 5
Concept Subtotal_____

CONTENT
How appropriate is the text-intensiveness of the site? 1 2 3 4 5
How well does the site answer any questions you may have? 1 2 3 4 5
If you have unanswered questions, how easy is it to ask questions
  via e-mail and/or phone? How prompt is the response? 1 2 3 4 5
How well does the content suit the purpose of the site? 1 2 3 4 5
How well does the content suit the target audience? 1 2 3 4 5
Content Subtotal_____

NAVIGATION
How consistent is the navigation? 1 2 3 4 5
How obvious, simple, or intuitive is the navigation? 1 2 3 4 5
How easy is the access to the menu, site index, and
  home on each screen? 1 2 3 4 5
How accessible are navigation tools (screen visibility/position)? 1 2 3 4 5
How effectively are internal links used to move through the site? 1 2 3 4 5
How well arranged is the content (e.g. number of clicks needed)? 1 2 3 4 5
Navigation Subtotal_____

DECORATION
How attractive is the decoration? 1 2 3 4 5
How well does the decoration support the concept? 1 2 3 4 5
How well does the decoration support the content? 1 2 3 4 5
How well does the decoration support the navigation? 1 2 3 4 5
How well does the decoration suit the purpose of the site? 1 2 3 4 5
How well does the decoration suit the target audience? 1 2 3 4 5
Decoration Subtotal_____

MARKETING EFFECTIVENESS
How well does the site convey its central value message? 1 2 3 4 5
How well does it meet the buying needs of its target audience? 1 2 3 4 5
How effectively does it use calls to action? 1 2 3 4 5
How well does the site promote itself within its own pages? 1 2 3 4 5
Marketing Subtotal_____
Site Total_____

Figure 1.21. Web site evaluation form. © 2001-2002 Watermelon Mountain Web Marketing.

hance your efforts may seem daunting, but it can help you achieve your business goals. And contrary to expectations, it is possible to analyze any Web site, including yours, for its effectiveness in achieving its goals.

The most complex problems you'll face are not technology-based, but business-based: finding your target market, turning prospects into customers, and keeping those customers as repeat buyers of your product or service. The Internet and the Web are just other methods for solving those problems. You'll learn more about implementing your Internet marketing options and integrating your Web plans with offline business activities in the next two chapters.

2

The ABCs of Business Are the XYZs of Internet Marketing

The Internet is at once an advertising medium, a form of sales literature, a distribution channel, a sales channel, a supplier chain, a method of customer service, and a source of operational cost savings. You should avoid the temptation to go online simply because everyone else is, but you also want to evaluate the potential benefits of the Web in the broadest possible way. To do that, you must have a clear understanding of your business goals.

Be creative and free-thinking in terms of what makes sense for your business. Molly's Manicures, with a clientele drawn from a single high-rise office building, might take advantage of the Web as follows: Clients could schedule appointments online, saving Molly time on the telephone. A client could request a specialty nail polish so it will be in stock for her appointment, leading to greater customer satisfaction. The site could accept orders for glue-on nails with rhinestone studs and Molly could deliver in the building or by mail. By developing alliances with other shops in the same skyscraper, Molly may be able to extend her delivery service (and thus her revenues and profits) to include everything from dry cleaning or breakfast muffins to neck massages or birthday gifts that her busy clients don't have time to buy.

Of course, that kind of ambition means that you must think not only about a Web site, but about all the implications a site will have for your business, from personnel to inventory to strategic partnerships. Then you can decide whether you want to join the 31 percent of all small businesses that already have a Web site. By the end of this chapter you will be familiar with

- The importance of good business practices to online success

- The purposes and theories of marketing

- Abraham Maslow's hierarchy of needs

- The seven steps to Internet success

Is the Internet Right for Your Business?

What kinds of businesses work on the Web? All kinds: genealogy search services (*http://www.geneologysearch.com*), career and placement (*http://careerlab.com/letters/default.htm*), private investigators (*http://www.via-investigators.com*), reference support (*http://www.surfchina.com*), coupon services (*http://www.hotcoupons.com*), crafts (*http://www.origamido.com*), gifts (*http://www.gifts.com*). If you're thinking of starting a computer-based, virtual company but are not sure what you want to do, try browsing through such lists as Work-at-Home Ideas on the news group *biz.general*. (See Chapter 4 for more information on news groups.)

As we saw in Chapter 1, some products sell better online than others. Consider:

- Products that appeal to tech-savvy users or that relate to computer use

- Collectibles and specialty items that are otherwise hard to find

- Products that sell on an **"informed purchase"** basis (i.e., that require research)

- Products than can be sold less expensively online than offline

You Can Do Much More Than Sell Online

Selling electronically instead of through a print catalog is usually the first thought that comes to mind with the Web, but you can do much more. In fact, only a minority of businesses actually conduct transactions online. Far more of them use the Web to accomplish other marketing goals, such as:

- Increasing brand or product awareness

- Enhancing corporate image

- Achieving market leadership

- Providing information and/or displaying samples of goods or services

- Generating a list of prospective customers (**lead generation**)

- Qualifying leads

- Building loyal relationships with customers

- Improving customer service

- Gathering information about customer needs and preferences to guide future product development

- Improving knowledge of customer demographics

- Testing consumer response to discounts or other special offers

- Finding strategic business partners, dealers, franchisees, or suppliers

- Recruiting employees, members, subscribers, or investors

- Saving money through automation, streamlined distribution channels, reduced cost of order fulfillment, or smaller inventories.

How many of these goals do you want your Web site to accomplish? The goals you select determine which methods you will use
and how you will define success. As seen in the survey of fast-growth
companies in Figure 2.1, large companies view their sites as multi-

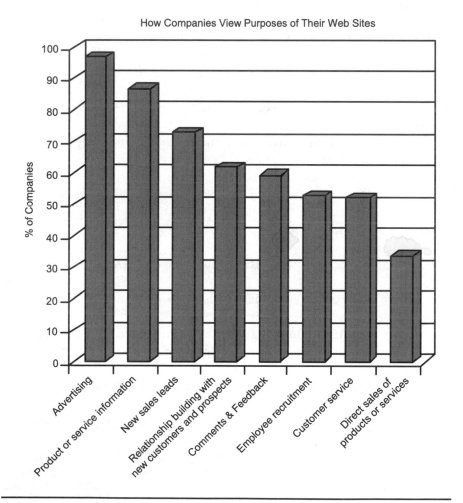

Figure 2.1. Purposes of corporate Web sites, *http://www.barometersurveys.com/ pr/tb980910.html.* Courtesy Pricewaterhouse Coopers' "Trendsetter Barometer."

purpose in nature. This is equally true for small businesses. Thirty-six percent of small companies with Web sites use them for advertising and providing information; only 11 percent established their sites to sell online. According to the Small Business Internet survey conducted for Verizon Wireless in 2001, more than half the businesses with Web sites are interested in adding functionality in the coming year to meet other goals, ranging from online lead generation to scheduling applications.

Essential Questions for Web Value

If you're still uncertain whether the Web is right for your company, ask yourself these questions:

1. Is your business local in nature? That's not necessarily a deterrent; local sites now draw Web audiences for information and customer support.

2. Does your business depend on face-to-face contact with customers? Can you rethink it to add new services like The Shoe Guy.com (*http://www.shoeguy.com*), shown in Figure 2.2?

3. Could you benefit from a national or global reach?

4. Do you have an unusual product or service that's difficult for customers to find?

5. Can you ship your product by mail or courier service? Will you ship yourself, or will your product be drop-shipped by manufacturers or distributors? Can you provide some aspect of your service online?

6. Are your customers able and willing to use the Internet to obtain support or information?

Here's the ultimate question: Will an investment in Internet marketing pay off by increasing the value of your company? Will it contribute to your bottom line? If the answer to that question is still no, then satisfy your Web cravings as a buyer, not a seller.

Figure 2.2. Unusual service site, *http://www.shoeguy.com*. Courtesy Shoeguy.com.

Essential Questions for Readiness

Once you are convinced that the Web has potential value for your company, you need to consider your overall business readiness. Your answers to these questions will contribute to your business plan, as you'll discover in the next chapter.

1. Do you have an existing business, or is this a new venture? A new venture requires much more planning, from suppliers to financing, than expanding an existing business to cyberspace.

2. Will this be an online-only business, or an online addition to an offline business, sometimes called a **"bricks-and-clicks"** or **"clicks-and-mortar"** operation? Integrated businesses have specific concerns from stocking to pricing, from cannibalizing storefronts outlet to support the Web, to maintaining good relationships within alternative distribution chains.

3. Do you currently have an Internet connection and e-mail at your business? What speed connection do you have?

4. What kind of budget do you have for creating a Web site? For marketing it? For updating it? Will the money come from diverting funds currently budgeted for other forms of sales, marketing, or advertising, or will this be a new investment?

5. What about personnel? Can you identify someone to spearhead the Web effort, learn about online marketing, and remain committed to staying up-to-date on the field? Do you have someone in house to write copy for the Web site and take photos, or will you need outside support? What about someone to handle e-mail inquiries and phone calls? Communication demands will increase once your Web site is up.

6. If you are planning to sell online, do you personally buy goods or services online? If you don't buy products/services online like the ones you plan to sell, why would someone else? As one essential piece of research, buy a product from at least three of your online competitors: one large company, one medium-size company, and one small company. How easy is it to use their sites? Do you receive an e-mail confirmation? What happens if you have a question or you want to return your purchase? This is no different from playing "mystery shopper" at one of your competitor's storefronts, where you would check out the window display, merchandise quality, and variety, pricing, service, and return policies.

7. If you are selling products, do you have a system already in place to process and fulfill orders, or will you need to develop one that meets online buyers' expectations?

8. How will you handle customer service issues such as order status, returns, offline payment requests, warranties, technical support, and alternate shipping arrangements?

9. Do you already have a merchant card account? Will you qualify for one, or will you need to explore online payment alternatives, as described in Chapter 7?

The Importance of Good Business Practices

Stories of easy dollars flowing in Internet commerce may leave you fantasizing about the cyberwealth of Bill Gates, or at least of Midas. The media may glorify Web winners, but business online is not all a bed of virtual roses.

For instance, if you can't fulfill customer orders promptly, you may easily go through cyber-crisis, as too many businesses found out with the $7-billion crush of online orders during the 1999 Christmas season. Amazon.com, Barnes & Noble, and Toys R Us all had well-publicized problems that year processing orders online, managing inventory and delivering in time for the holiday. But they learned. By 2001 the percentage of shoppers satisfied with their online holiday shopping experiences grew to 72 percent, up from 55 percent in 2000. The number of dissatisfied buyers dropped to 27 percent from 42 percent in the same time period. How did they do it? The E-tailing Group's survey for the Direct Marketing Association (DMA), seen in Figure 2.3, indicates the improvements online retailers made in site quality between 2000 and

	2000	2001
Shoppers who were satisfied with all their online holiday shopping experiences	55%	73%
Shoppers who were unsatisfied with some aspect of their online holiday shopping experiences	42%	26%
Average number of clicks to checkout	8.76	5.36
Real-time inventory status	42%	54%
Sites offering gift searches	14%	46%
Link to privacy policies from home page	90%	90%
Shipping confirmations by e-mail	54%	80%
Online shipping status	76%	79%
Toll-free numbers	98%	99%
Requires membership	86%	54%
List customer service hours	72%	74%

Figure 2.3. Online retailer site improvements 2000 vs. 2001. Available on *www.e-tailing.com/research/mystery_summary.html*. Also courtesy Retail Forward, Inc. Source: DMA and e-tailing group, 2002 "Mystery Shopping" Report.

2001. These changes will now become the baseline performance expected of other sellers.

One note of caution. A study by Jupiter Media Metrix, summarized in Figure 2.4, shows a poor level of response to customer service e-mails, especially from 40 percent of online-only retailers who took 3 days or more to respond, if they responded at all.

Like prompt response time, online security is critical. If purchasing data and credit card information gathered online is not kept private and secure, customers will lose confidence about shopping in cyberspace, just as they would if their credit card numbers were stolen after charging dinner at a local restaurant. The implications are clear: If you plan to sell online, you need to focus on service to attract and keep customers. There's nothing new about that.

If you are selling, consider in advance how you will fulfill increased orders promptly. In addition to personnel issues, do you have access to the needed inventory or the space to store it? Can you arrange just-in-time contracts or drop-shipping with your suppliers? Can you process orders more efficiently? Can you meet price pressure on the Web? Will you be able to renegotiate pricing with your suppliers? Cut costs elsewhere? Do your forecasts show that you can increase volume to counteract a smaller profit margin?

As you experiment online, don't stop marketing your products and services in ways that sell. If you succeed online, you may decide to shift your marketing mix or open an all-online division, but wait for proof. In the meantime, keep doing what works. As you'll see throughout this book, a well-conceived Internet marketing strategy will complement your traditional marketing efforts and vice versa.

Time Frame	Brick-and-Mortar	Online-Only	Both
Within 6 hours	28%	33%	30%
6-24 hours	22%	13%	18%
1-3 Days	22%	13%	18%
Longer than 3 days or no response at all	28%	40%	33%

Figure 2.4. Response time for retailers responding to online customer service e-mail inquiries, *http://cyberatlas.internet.com/markets/retailing/article/0,,6061_948461,00.html.* © 2002 INT Media Group, Inc. All rights reserved.

Marketing Basics

Studying successful people in the late 1960s, humanistic psychologist Abraham Maslow created a "hierarchy of needs," often called **Maslow's Triangle**. Under this theory, everyone seeks love, happiness, and personal growth, but has to satisfy certain needs before they can achieve their maximum potential for creativity, wisdom, and altruism. According to Maslow, when one need is satisfied (and only then), the next one pops up. Let's look at Maslow's Triangle in greater detail.

Why People Buy: Maslow's Hierarchy of Needs

When applied to marketing, Maslow's theory is often cited to establish motivation for purchasing certain products or seeking certain types of information, with the variation that a person may seek different products or information to meet different needs at the same time. Maslow defined five needs, illustrated in Figure 2.5. The two levels at the bottom of the triangle are basic needs; the three at the top are considered growth needs.

1. **Physiological Needs.** Biological needs for oxygen, food, water, sleep, sex, health, and shelter must be satisfied first because they are essential for survival. At this level, people seek basic "coping information" and purchase the essentials for living: homes or rental apartments, clothing, groceries, dental and medical care.

2. **Safety Needs.** Though most widely experienced by children, adults seek security in times of emergency (earthquakes, floods, terrorist attacks), social disorganization (rioting or a crime wave), or as a result of personal trauma (rape, domestic violence, assault). A predictable, fair, and generally routine world offers a sense of stability. To satisfy safety needs, people seek "helping information," such as a hotline number for battered women, fire evacuation plans, or emergency supplies. They purchase items like home fire extinguishers, earthquake kits, car alarms, or GPS systems.

3. **Social Needs.** To escape a sense of loneliness and alienation, people need to give and receive love and affection. We crave a

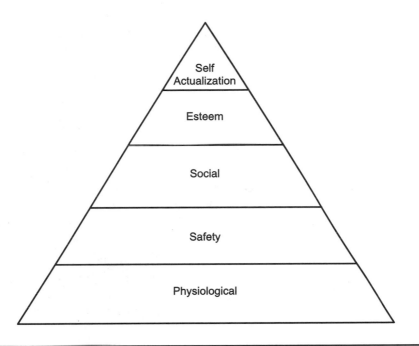

Figure 2.5. Maslow's hierarchy of needs.

sense of caring and belonging. Readers searching for "enlightening information" about their relationships with others may buy self-help books or read popular magazines on such topics as how to improve their marriages, get more friends, be more popular, or meet their mates. For activities, they seek hobbies, clubs, family gatherings, civic activities, and church groups. They buy hobby products, marriage counseling services, memberships, and items they believe will make them more attractive to others. To meet these needs, people may join online affinity groups.

4. **Esteem Needs.** To feel satisfied, self-confident and valuable, people need both a high level of self-respect and respect from others. Without self-esteem, which incorporates feelings of competence, achievement, and mastery, people may feel weak, inferior, helpless, or worthless. Respect from others may take the form of simple courtesy, fair treatment in the public arena, ac-

ceptance by a group, recognition for achievements, reputation, or tangible appreciation for effort. It is here that status and prestige come into play, exemplified by purchases like sports cars or motorcycles, jewelry, monogrammed leather goods, and expensive watches. People seek "empowering information" on personal growth and personal development, such as overcoming shyness, dressing for success, or achieving recognition at work.

5. **Self-Actualization Needs.** Maslow believed that very few people actually achieve self-fulfillment, the sense of having found one's "calling." To reach this peak, people move through "understanding and knowledge" (the need to satisfy curiosity, discover things, solve problems, seek meaning, and meet intellectual challenges) to "aesthetics" (the presence of beauty in their surroundings). In Maslow's theory, self-actualization is an ongoing process, in which individuals are involved in something outside themselves. As he put it, "a musician must make music, an artist must paint, and a poet must write." People in this category may search for "edifying" moral and spiritual information through religion, education, music and art. They may purchase classes, concert tickets, and art.

Information is one of the most valuable resources of the Internet. If you match the information you provide on your site with the category of Maslow's Triangle into which your product or service falls, you will enhance your ability to appeal successfully to your target audience. It goes without saying that a successful sales pitch shows how your product can meet those needs.

TIPS FOR TIRED SITES

If your Web site is attracting viewers, but not converting them into buyers, try to apply Maslow's theory. Which category of needs does your product or service fulfill? What kind of information are people looking for at that level? Do you provide it? Does your sales copy reflect those needs, or is it oriented toward something different? Trying to sell a home-alarm system on status (other perhaps than a personal bodyguard or bullet-proof limousine!) is not likely to be as successful as selling it on peace of mind, stressing constant police monitoring and fast response time to panic-button calls.

Why People Buy Online

In our time-deprived society, customers shop online for convenience, not price, as you can see in Figure 2.6 from a Department of Commerce survey conducted in 1998 (*http://www.ecommerce.gov/emerging.htm*). Consequently, poor performance that interferes with convenience is a sure way to lose a customer. Sites that make their products hard to find, forcing people to go through page after page on the Web, are just as discouraging as stores with similar products scattered across several departments on different floors.

Conversion Rates: Browser to Buyer

Not every visitor who walks past a store window or links to a Web site becomes a buyer. Whether in real-space or cyberspace, it takes effort to convert a browser into a buyer. Like the funnel in Figure 2.7, the marketing process narrows during this progression. Using the AIDA acronym for direct marketing that we discussed in the last chapter, you can move people from one stage to another.

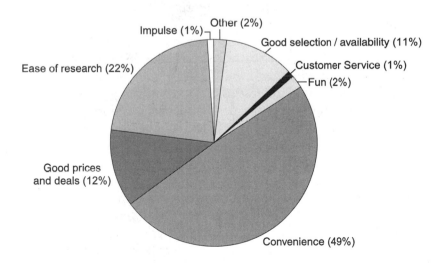

Figure 2.6.   Best thing about online shopping, *http://home.doc.gov/ Electronic_Commerce/Publications_and_Reports*

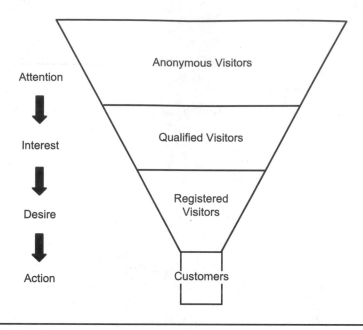

Figure 2.7.   Conversion rate in direct marketing terms.

The first step is to attract attention. A storefront may do this with a window display, a sandwich board, signage, or advertising. A Web site must do this with ads, a home page, or splash (introductory marketing) pages. When someone walks through the door, makes a phone call, or clicks on another page of the Web site, they become a browser.

You must build interest to convert visitors to browsers. A storefront does this through attractive merchandising, positioning new products near the entrance perhaps, or sometimes arranging the store so customers view "impulse" items on their way to what they came for. Compare a grocery store, where merchandising techniques are fairly obvious, to your Web site. What can you do to get people to your online catalog? An on-site search engine to find the products they're looking for? Perhaps the results show several variations of the product at different prices levels or styles. Once they've reached the catalog level, you have a shopper.

Interactivity is one of the most intriguing ways to build browsers' interest. You can move your viewer toward a "buy" decision by having them take specific actions. Consider the interactive materials calculator at Arranger on the Better Homes and Gardens site (*http://www.bhg.com/*

bhg/file.jhtml?item=/dswmedia/index&temp=yes) or Nike's sneaker design program (*http://www.nikeid/nike.com/nikeid_home.jsp*) seen in Figure 2.8. Nike lets users customize their sneakers from upper to sole and add their own signature.

Many Web shoppers arrive with a desire for a specific product. Here the standards of offline selling become a factor:

- Product and product mix

- Positioning

- Price

- Presentation

Your product or service must offer benefits to buyers and meet their needs. It's pretty hard to sell a poor-quality product that the market doesn't

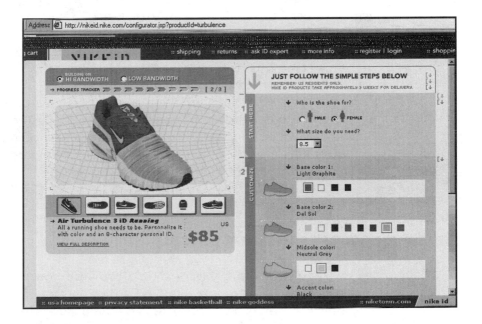

Figure 2.8.   Interactive online tool, *http://nikeid.nike.com/nikeid_home.jsp*. Courtesy Nike, Inc.

want. Positioning refers to your product compared to your competitors' offerings. What unique value do you add that would make someone purchase from you instead of someone else? Your product must be priced competitively. There is far more price pressure online than off, since it's easy to compare prices on the Web. Finally, it must be presented well. Here's where online sales copy and imagery become critical.

The last step, converting shoppers to buyers, is the most difficult. It's never easy to get people to part with their money! You not only need to ask for the sale, but you must make it easy to buy. All along the way, you must remove any reason to say "no" to a purchase, ensuring that people feel secure giving credit card numbers online, that they can return unwanted products, that shipping will be prompt. Given that more than 60 percent of buyers abandon their shopping carts in cyber-aisles before completing their purchase, this last step can be a tough one!

What can you expect as a conversion rate? For the first step, from visitors to browsers, you'll do well do get 1.5 to 2 percent, a standard response rate for direct marketing. That means only 2 percent of viewers who get to your home page may continue on to the next page. As you move down the funnel, the conversion rate between steps increases to as much as 40 percent since you're already working with an interested audience. While every business is different and a great deal depends on your ability to draw a highly targeted, pre-qualified audience to your site, it may take 250 visits or more to generate one sale. You can see why site designers say "two clicks to purchase."

It's also obvious why so much attention goes to retaining customers! As anyone in business knows, it's much easier—and cheaper—to sell a second item to an existing buyer than to acquire a new customer. Repeat customers start near the base of the funnel, where your conversion rate is closer to 25 percent than to 2 percent.

The Seven Steps to Internet Success

The above review of marketing basics should convince you that the "more things have changed, the more they have stayed the same." Translating these familiar business principles from an offline marketing environment to the Web, however, may take some work. The seven-step process below will help you make that transition:

1. Observe the Web.

2. Know your business.

3. Write an online business plan.

4. Create and distribute info-tools.

5. Plan and create an effective Web site.

6. Maintain and montior your site.

7. Market your Internet presence.

After a brief introduction to these steps, we'll discuss them in detail in the chapters to follow.

Step 1: Observe the Web

It's time for research that won't ever go to waste. One of the easiest ways to get a feel for the way information, advertising, and sales move across the Web is to check out an online service. Use a free Web service like *www.juno.com*, a portal site like *www.msn.com*, or one of those ubiquitous free offers from America Online (*www.aol.com*). Evaluate how companies advertise on the site and how they place their ads. Do they catch users with a special offer when they first sign on? Does a display ad pop up on the viewing screen? What types of ads appear on a news page? On a search page? Can you figure out whom these advertisers are trying to reach?

Look at their shopping malls, like the one in Figure 2.9. What would you have to do to showcase your product? Visit a company that sells products or services like yours. What do they offer online—their full range of products, or a subset? What promises do they make to customers? How do they handle customer support? E-mail an inquiry to see how long it takes to receive a response.

Now go to an online forum or message board in your area of interest, whether it is computer hardware, politics, or travel. (On AOL, select a community and click on Message Boards.) Sign up for several and read

Figure 2.9. AOL shopping mall, *http://webcenter.shop.aol.com/office/index.adp*. AOL screenshot. © 2002 America Online, Inc. Used with permission.

some of the postings. Are people advertising on the boards? Sign onto a business chat room or a room with people who would be part of your target audience, even if you don't write anything. Are rumors flying? Do participants "bash" companies? Do they exchange useful information?

If you haven't already done so, purchase something from a small-, medium-, and large-sized competitor to follow the process all the way through to payment, shipment, and product quality. If your competitors aren't on one of these sites, find them through one of the major search engines, like *www.yahoo.com*, *www.google.com*, or *www. metacrawler.com*

Sites You Love/Sites You Love to Hate

As mentioned in Chapter 1, tracking good sites and bad ones will help your own site design or redesign efforts. In addition to bookmarking them in folders, you may want to print out examples to keep in a notebook. Note the aspect of the site that you find appealing or appalling: concept, content, navigation, decoration, marketing effectiveness. If you're an online retailer, add to that the quality of the site's catalog, shopping cart and checkout stand, shipping, customer service, and/or product mix. Your site review should include not only those you commonly visit, but those visited by your customers, posted by your competitors, and sought out by your vendors, distributors, manufacturers, or others that you deal with.

Customers

If you are already in business, ask your customers whether they are online, at what speed, what they use the Internet for, and what they have bought online. Ask for the names of other sites they visit, and check those out. These sites may give you ideas for features your customers will appreciate, the types of graphics they enjoy, and potential ad placement. You can conduct a brief postcard survey using your mailing list, or ask customers who come into the store. If you already have a Web site, post a survey on your site, along with an opportunity to provide feedback on your current design. Whichever way you solicit opinion, give people something in exchange for their time: a coupon, an instant discount, or a promotional item.

Competitors

It's fairly obvious what your competitors will offer:

- Pricing research (Are some of your competitors selling items at different prices online and off?)

- A performance baseline for viewer expectations in terms of site features, design, and ease of use

- What kind of traffic they are receiving, should your competitors be naive enough to post their "hit" or visitor rate

- Great ideas you can borrow (You can't duplicate a copyrighted design, but you can identify specific features or ideas that you want to implement.)

Vendors and Others

Why bother to understand what your vendors are doing? For one thing, some of your vendors may be selling to others who have discovered that they can use their Web sites to save money by increasing purchasing efficiency. Many companies create a password-protected portion of their site on which they post "requests for quotes," allow suppliers to offer bids, monitor inventory, or issue resupply requests automatically. If other firms are able to reduce costs, they can beat you on price and still maintain their profit margins. You owe it to yourself to see if that's true. By all means, ask other business owners whether they are online and check out their sites. Most noncompeting businesses will share their experiences, perhaps including the cost of development and whether they have seen a return on their investment.

Step 2: Know Your Business

With online research animating your brain, evaluate your current business situation. Now that you understand where your customers congregate on the Internet, the best way to reach them, and how to support the sale, what changes must you make in your business operations? How will your Web site fit with your existing business and marketing plans? Can you afford a Web site? Can you afford not to have a Web site?

Marketing on the Internet may be faster and cheaper in absolute dollars than traditional methods of advertising, but it is not always as cost-

TIPS FOR TIRED SITES

If you have received complaints from customers (even if it's just one or two) about payment problems, shipping costs or delays, or product quality, review your own internal operations. Compare what you're doing or charging to what your competitors are doing and offering online. If they have established a performance baseline beyond yours, you will lose sales and market share. The Web makes it very simple to compare service and quality, as well as prices. You can use one of the price comparison sites that also rates sites for performance, like *www.bizrate.com*, to find a well-regarded competitor. Price what it would cost to upgrade your site or revise your policies. Can you afford *not* to make changes?

effective. Will online marketing fit your operations as well as it does those of Red Hen Turf, a company that allows viewers to place advance orders online for turf pick-up or delivery (*http:// www.redhenturf.com*). You can test promotion costs offline versus online by trying a similar promotion using both methods. You may find that not enough of your customers use the Internet or that your true clientele is local, not national. It is tempting to avoid dealing with printers, mailing houses, bulk mail regulations, and the post office, but coping with an arrogant Web host, bugs in Web page programming, and slow Internet access can be just as aggravating.

If you can't make the numbers work for your own site, consider online auctions as a simple and inexpensive alternative. The Web's unique ability to link a critical mass of buyers and sellers in real time establishes market-driven prices on a dynamic basis. Auctions are also an excellent way to test pricing on a new product or to liquidate discontinued stock.

To see if becoming an "auction-preneur" is for you, head for the pioneering auction site eBay, Inc. at *http://www.ebay.com*. eBay has long been one of the most profitable sites on the Web, posting its highest quarterly revenue ever in the fourth quarter of 2001. With more than 6 million items listed at any time, eBay is the most popular shopping site on the Web measured by total user minutes. The site, shown in Figure 2.10, counts more than 42 million registered users, millions of which are small businesses.

Step 3: Write an Online Business Plan

Goals, objectives, and methods are the currency of a business plan, offline as well as online. As we'll discuss in greater detail in Chapter 3, your online plan should establish the goals for your site first, and define quantifiable objectives to measure your progress toward each goal. Try to be as specific as you can. It's also important to be realistic about the time frame for going online and what it's going to cost. As with almost any new project, it makes sense to start in a small way and then expand your efforts as you learn what works. For example, you may decide to establish an online presence for six months before selling online.

If you are going to sell online, you may want to select only a portion of your product line to start. If possible, pick products with a successful and reliable sales history through direct marketing, thus removing one of the variables in your online experiment. Once you are certain that

Figure 2.10. eBay auction site, *http://www.ebay.com*. Courtesy eBay, Inc.

everything works smoothly, from online order taking through order fulfillment and payment, you can expand to hundreds of products or put your entire catalog on line.

By the same token, if you want to expand your corporate presence, think what aspect of your company is best portrayed through the Web. With multimedia capabilities, it's possible to showcase everything from musical talent to video histories. Consider the geographic area in which you want to provide your service. Now that you can sell nationally, maybe you should create an auxiliary product, such as an audio CD for customers located too far away to hire your jazz trio to play at their next Christmas party.

If you don't receive at least minimal interest on your Web site after six months, whether measured in terms of unique visitors to your Web site or online sales, you may need to rethink your approach. Perhaps people have not found your site and you need to expand your online and offline promotion efforts. Perhaps your Web design isn't appealing to the audience you've drawn. If you're getting hits but not making sales online, perhaps your retail prices are too high for this electronic location. Alternately, perhaps others too easily match your product or you haven't asked for the sale effectively. Like any other business plan, your online plan will need to tested, revised, and updated as the real world overtakes your plans.

Step 4: Create and Distribute Info-Tools

To succeed online, you will need to restructure existing promotional material or create new materials to meet Internet users' insatiable demand for information. In many cases, the marketing value of a site comes from perceiving your company as a source of useful information, completely independent of any point-of-sale activity.

In addition, you will need to publicize your site to ensure that large numbers of Web surfers continually learn about you. Some of the most cost-effective methods involve only e-mail. As you'll see in Chapter 4, **info-tools** can be short messages, reports, newsletters, press releases, or prepared e-mail responses.

Whether you have a new way of making peanut butter or sell an old-fashioned item like paper clips, tell people about your product with an interesting, informative angle. Describe how to make the world's longest paper-clip chain, or list 1,001 things that can be made from recycled peanut shells. Find a way to make your business sound fresh to the world, or at least new to the Internet universe. Graphic versions of text-based info-tools can later be placed on your Web site.

One company that successfully uses information as an online tool is Wine.com (*http://www.wine.com*), which provides help for everyone from wine neophytes to connoisseurs.

Step 5: Plan and Create an Effective Web Site

How do you develop a site that will work well for you? Do you do it yourself or get help? In most cases, unless you have preexisting technical sophistication or can utilize a prepackaged template, you're better off contracting with a Web developer to create your site and a Web hosting service to maintain it. Often, one company will offer both services, with Web developers reselling hosting services, and hosting services offering either template-based or custom development as part of a value-added package.

To manage more than a simple home page in-house, you may need a local area network, server hardware and software, a high-speed connection to the Internet, and access to technical support, including a Web programmer, a graphic artist, and an **MIS** (**management information system**) specialist to oversee the project. Even when you out-source Web development and hosting, there will be more than enough for you to do!

Anything truly valuable takes time or money to develop—generally both. As a guideline, a small, static brochure site may cost anywhere from $500 to $2,500. For a less expensive option, consider a template-based site offered as part of a hosting package. A "typical Web site"— a *custom* design with eight to twelve pages of customer-supplied text, several forms, and one or two special features might run from $3,500 to $5,500. Custom-designed retail and B2B sites, with online transaction capability and a database-driven catalog, often start around $10,000. Again template-based storefronts can be found at e-commerce hosts for less money. There is no limit at the high-end. High-end prices in May 2001 ranged from $65,000 for a small site to $125,000 for a medium-sized site and $250,000 for a large site! We'll talk more about site budgets in Chapter 5.

Web hosting itself runs anywhere from $5 to $100 per month plus setup fees for a small-to-medium site. Of course, there are additional costs of maintaining, monitoring, and promoting a site and handling additional customer demands. Because of these variations, it makes sense to establish your budget first and then figure out what you can afford for those prices, rather than to work the Web problem the other way around.

Step 6: Maintain and Monitor Your Site

You can't determine whether you have met the goals of your plan unless you build in measurement methods. In Chapter 8 you'll learn about specific services that are available through your Web host or other companies to measure precisely how well your Web site is working. If computers are good at anything, they are good at counting, so a great deal of information is available to analyze the performance of your site.

Everyone talks about **hits** (total number of times any file on a site is accessed), but that number is essentially meaningless. It's far more valuable to know how many unique visitors reached your site and how many pages they viewed. You might also want to track how long people stay on your site, the path they follow through it, and whether they return. You will certainly want to know how they reached you (**referral links**) and which specific pages interested them.

If you are selling online, be sure you are able to track the source, amount, and item number of each sale. This enables you to compute your cost of sales more accurately and to compare the value of selling online with the value of selling through other methods, such as traditional mail catalogs.

Sites that accept advertising should be able to track both the number of visitors who see each ad and those who actually link to your site from the ad. All major services and **portals** (large Web sites used as a launching pad for other sites) offer sophisticated demographic analysis of their users. A list of some portals is found in Figure 2.11.

Automated statistical tools like those described above should be included with Web hosting fees or shopping cart packages. For e-mail and mailing list results, you have to maintain your own records, or purchase relatively expensive e-mail tracking software.

Step 7: Market Your Internet Presence

No matter how successful a Web site you create, you must attract people to it. It does no good to have the best site on the Web if no one knows how or why to find you. One of the most important parts of successful

> http://www.about.com
> http://www.amazon.com
> http://www.aol.com
> http://www.cnet.com
> http://www.google.com
> http://www.msn.com
> http://www.terralycos.com
> http://www.vivendiuniversal.com

Figure 2.11. Major portals on the Internet.

marketing on the Internet is achieving exposure amid overwhelming amounts of information. The Web is such a busy intersection on the Information Superhighway that you have to tell potential visitors which way to turn. To succeed, you'll need to develop a marketing plan that includes on-site marketing, online marketing such as search engines and inbound links, and offline marketing.

To get the maximum effect from your online marketing, all your offline advertising in print, TV, or radio should mention your Web address. Be sure to place your e-mail and Web addresses on your letterhead, mailers, flyers, business cards, and promotional items as well. These offline additions to your Web presence let the world know you are an electronic player.

Web addresses now appear in all kinds of advertising. You might expect Mitsubishi to advertise its URL in Newsweek, but did you realize that more than 75 percent of the ads in America's top 50 magazines, including women's publications, now use URLs or e-mail to drive traffic to the Web? Just look at the statistics in Figure 2.12.

As you get more sophisticated, you can coordinate Web site activities with traditional advertising and promotional activities, such as an event, special sale, contest, customer feedback line, or PR campaign.

PC World	100%
Business Week	93%
Forbes	93%
National Geographic	88%
Car and Driver	77%
Martha Stewart Living	74%
Seventeen	69%
Parents	68%
Prevention	64%
Star	55%
The National Enquirer	55%

Figure 2.12. Percent of ads using URLs in major magazines, *http://www.npd.com/corp/content/news/releases/press_000508.htm.* Courtesy The NPD Group, Inc.

A More Level Marketing Field?

Any business can appear significant and powerful online. By following the design concepts discussed later in the book, you can have a Web site as effective as Epicurious's at *http://www.epicurious.com*, shown in Figure 2.13. The look and feel of your site can have all the flash of the big guys—for a price.

You can market online at all levels: very cheap, the equivalent of a photocopied handbill (black ink on colored stock); moderately inexpensive, like a used car commercial on cable TV; moderately expensive, the Web equivalent of a four-color, glossy brochure with lots of photos; and the all-out extravaganza, the electronic equivalent of a one-minute spot broadcast in prime time on the three major networks. The amount you spend will depend on your available budget, the nature of your company and its products or services, the kind of audience you are trying to reach, and the extent to which you need to use interactive multimedia on your site.

Figure 2.13.   Sample large site, *http://eat.epicurious.com*. Courtesy Epicurious Food. Copyright 1999-2002 Conde Net, Inc. All rights reserved.

How many people will use your site? One of the most popular sites in Internet history, NASA's Pathfinder photographs from the 1997 mission to Mars (*http://mpf.www.jpl.nasa.gov*), received more than 100 million hits from all its mirror sites combined in just one day, and 500 million during the month of July 1997. Even a moderate-size but well-publicized site like Kids Crosswords (*http://www.kidscrosswords.com*) received over 2.7 million hits in October 2001.

Realistically, few sites attract these numbers. The Internet viewing population for most businesses is closer to the number of viewers that an infomercial receives on late-night television. Even if your Internet marketing is solely designed to provide corporate presence, set a goal for the number of viewers you want to attract.

Customer Service Is the Name of the Game

As you've learned in this chapter, the Internet doesn't free you from doing what every business must do to get and keep customers: Provide good service. Whatever you promise—quick shipment, high quality, cheap price, individual attention—do it. Promises can be explicit (free monogramming) or implicit (e-mail us). Don't risk customer goodwill by falling down on the job. Think not about how Internet marketing differs from what you are already doing, but about how your successful business practices can be incorporated online.

Now it's time to turn your plan into reality. Take this opportunity to create folders on your hard drive to bookmark sites for various service providers, model sites, and potential advertising or link sites. You might also want to start a large three-ring binder to track your Web planning efforts. Make ten dividers for:

1. Online Marketing Plan (goals, objectives, target market, methods)

2. Development Schedule and Tasking

3. Budget (initial and maintenance)

4. Info-Tools

5. ISP and Hosting Selection

6. Web Developer/Subcontractor Selection

7. Site Content & Acquisition

8. Site Statistics & Maintenance

9. Site Feedback & Bug Reports

10. Web Site Promotion & Advertising

We'll look at the first three steps toward Internet success in greater detail in the next chapter: observing the Web, knowing your business, and writing an online business plan.

3

Build the Foundation with Steps 1–3

In this chapter we'll look in greater detail at the first three steps to Web success: Observing the Web, Knowing Your Business, and Writing an Online Business Plan. Like any brick-and-mortar business, your online business will benefit from basic market research and business planning. You may be surprised to find that the same tools you use for assessing risk and establishing performance criteria for an offline business also apply to a Web-based enterprise.

Under the category of Observing the Web, we'll go beyond the site visits and shopping experiments discussed in the prior chapter. Here we'll look at the demographics of the overall Web audience and discuss how you can use the Web as a resource to estimate the size and nature of your potential market. You'll learn how to characterize your target audience and assess how many Internet users share your desired demographics. Depending on your business, your online and offline audiences may differ.

You don't want to guess when it comes to deciding whether your Web site is likely to produce a significant return on investment (ROI). You can use traditional financial analysis techniques, such as calculating a break-even point, to determine whether your Web site will be worthwhile. Establishing quantifiable and measurable objectives will help you compare the performance of your site against expectations. With this perspective, Web expenditures become an investment, rather than a straight expense. That realization alone can reduce stress!

Finally, we'll consider the benefits of preparing an online business plan. Writing a plan forces you to think about business processes, costs, and other issues that you might overlook. Writing a plan ensures that you will have the essential tools for bottom-line success: a budget, a development timeline, and financial projections.

By the end of this chapter, you'll understand:

- how to use online market research to analyze your target market

- the value of setting quantifiable objectives for your site, including the break-even point

- the basic elements of an online business plan

Step 1: Observe the Web—Know Your Audience

Understanding the profile of your target audience is critical. Whether your audience is individual consumers or other businesses, if they don't use the Internet, does it make sense for your business to be there? This isn't an automatic no, but it should make you consider the size of your investment. Could Web marketing be important to other target audiences, such as suppliers, potential employees, or possible business partners? Could e-mail marketing without a Web site be effective?

It's also important to understand whether your target audience is more likely to use the Internet at work (more likely to go online during business hours with high-speed access) or at home (more likely to surf evenings or weekends on slower connections). Currently, more than half of American adults access the Internet from home, 28 percent access it from work, and 19 percent use other locations, like libraries or cyber-cafés.

Try to find out what else your customers do online. E-mail? Newsgroups? Subscribe to mailing lists? Use AOL, MSN, or free Internet services? The more information you have, the better you can target your site design and marketing activities to meet your target audience's needs and expectations.

Researching your customers has another benefit. When you figure out how many users with your desired profile are floating around in cyberspace, you can better gauge the size of your potential target market. Let's take a look at overall Web statistics and where you might find audiences who share a particular demographic feature, such as age, gender, or race. Because it's the World Wide Web, not the U.S.-wide Web, we'll also look at international users and language preference.

Online Demographics

One word of caution: No Internet demographic study is ever 100 percent reliable because the Web changes so rapidly. Watch the fine print on any statistics you use; one study might measure all Internet users over the age of six, another measures only users over age 16, or includes Canada as well as the United States. Income brackets and even ethnic categories may be defined differently.

What do we think we know about Web users? The current estimate of 500 million users worldwide represents only 6 percent of the planet's inhabitants, but this is expected to double to 1 billion users by 2005. By November 2001 over 127 million Internet users over the age of 18 in the United States had accessed the Web from work, home, or other locations. This represented 64 percent of all U.S. adults, up 1 percent and 6 million users from the previous year. This percentage is much higher than the percentage worldwide, reflecting uneven access to Internet services and a global digital divide.

Trends lines in Internet use also tell us that the rate of growth in the number of Internet users in the United States is slowing down and may soon peak. Since about one-third of the people in the United States who could use the Internet choose not to, future growth in the number of users will come from elsewhere around the world. Reports show that the number of households subscribing to Internet services declined slightly in 2001. This may indicate that the total number of household connections—roughly 42 percent of all U.S. households—has topped out, or that some families felt the effects of the economic downturn and canceled their ISP contracts.

These reports also found that U.S. subscribers to more expensive, high-speed Internet services increased, while subscribers to free services and Internet TV took a dive. Online services like AOL experienced their slowest rate of growth.

Don't confuse the number of users online with the time spent online. For most of 2001, average weekly time online continued to rise, with home surfers reporting 3 hours 11 minutes per week and office users spending 6 hours 7 minutes.

The Implications for Web Marketing. You may find yourself thinking globally sooner than you expected. Broadband access ups the ante for Web design, with users both more willing to spend time online, and seeking more sophisticated sites that previously took too long to download.

Income and Education

Internet use is not evenly distributed by age, income, or ethnicity. Although the online community has started to mirror the overall population more closely, we're not there yet. Consider the results of the Harris Interactive 2001 Survey shown in Figure 3.1, which compared Web users with the general U.S. adult population.

The online community is still skewed toward the more affluent and the better educated, although the past year saw increases in Internet use from women, minorities and those in modest-income ($30,000–$50,000) households, especially those with children at home. Increased online activities include sending e-mail, getting news, browsing for fun, pursuing hobbies, and buying products.

Only 19 percent of those online have household incomes of $25,000 or less, but they comprise 25 percent of the total U.S. population. By comparison, 45 percent of those online have household incomes over $50,000, but they represent only 32 percent of the population. Since education level generally correlates closely to income, it's not surprising to see that 62 percent of Internet users have at least some college, while that group represents only 48 percent of the overall population.

The Implications for Web Marketing. The nature and dollar value of purchases change with the amount of disposable income, as well as with an individual's stage in the life cycle. Changes in the composition of Web users affect advertising, product sales, and information-based sites.

Age Distribution

Figure 3.1 also shows the distribution of the U.S. online population by age. Young adults are still overrepresented in the online population,

Profile of U.S. Online Population

	Online Adults	All Adults
Age		
18 to 29	28%	22%
30 to 39	23%	22%
40 to 49	23%	20%
50 to 64	18%	18%
65+	7%	16%
Gender		
Men	49%	48%
Women	51%	52%
Race/Ethnicity		
White	76%	76%
Black	10%	12%
Hispanic	10%	10%
Other	2%	2%
Education		
High school or less	38%	52%
Some College	30%	26%
College grad/post grad	32%	22%
Household Income		
$25,000 or less	19%	25%
$25,001 to $50,000	23%	29%
$50,001 and over	45%	32%

Figure 3.1. Demographics of Internet users, Source: Harris Interactive, *http://www.harrisinteractive.com/harris_poll/index.asp?PID=266*. Courtesy Harris Interactive.[SM]

while those over 65 are still underrepresented. You can count on one thing: The participation of every age group is increasing. Some numbers may surprise you.

The number of users age 50 and over is growing quickly. For sites devoted to seniors, you might want to target:

- Elder Web: *http://www.elderweb.com* (information resources)

- Elderhostel: *http://www.elderhostel.org* (educational programs)

- Gold Violin: *http://www.goldviolin.com* (sells items for seeing, hearing, and moving better, gifts for older people)

- Senior Net: *http://www.seniornet.com* (computer training site)

- Senior Sites: *http://www.seniorsites.com* (nonprofit services)

- Senior.com: *http://www.senior.com* (information resources)

The Implications for Web Marketing. While their percentage is small, seniors who are online are dedicated users of e-mail, and use the Web to gather information to manage their lives, whether for healthcare, financial planning, or travel.

If there are seniors online, there are kids and teens galore! The number of 5- to 17-year-olds online—now 65 million—has more than doubled since 2000. This group spends a mind-boggling $60 billion in disposable income each year. Boys and girls seek out different Web sites, with boys looking for novelty and entertainment (e.g., online games), while girls like to fulfill goals (e.g., applying to college) and prefer to feel part of a community, making extensive use of instant messaging to communicate with their friends. While teenagers are often unimpressed by generic teen sites, a number of companies try to design sites that address specific interests, particularly those of preteen girls:

- *http://www.Cosmogirl.com*

- *http://www.Blink182.com*

- *http://www.dELiAs.com*

- *http://www.gurlmail.com*

- *http://www.seventeen.com*

- *http://www.smartgirl.com*

- *http://www.spacegirl.org*

Older teens and college students spend hours online on music-downloading sites, such as Audiogalaxy (*http://www.audiogalaxy.com*).

The Implications for Web Marketing. Site design for the teen population differs distinctly from site design for older audiences. Frequent updates are critical to stay on top of trends, if not to create them, and products must rotate often.

Gender Distribution

Most significantly, the adult gender gap has closed: By June 2001, 52 percent of Internet users were female, up from 38 percent in 1996 and from 5 percent only eight years ago. Men may still go online 11 percent more often than women, and spend 16 percent more time online, but when it comes to spending money, women have become the driving force. Some 58 percent of online orders for Christmas 2001 were placed by women, up from only 39 percent in 1998.

Women are more utilitarian than men, returning to sites that save them time and money, rather than surfing many different sites. Women seek health and religious information or research jobs online, while men prefer news, sports, and financial information. Women are responsible for the growth in sales in such categories as Home & Garden, or Toys & Games, compared to the more traditional, male-driven categories of Electronic Gadgets and Computer Hardware. Undoubtedly, these statistics were in the minds of those who created three of the major Web sites aimed at women:

- *http://www.ivillage.com*

- *http://www.oxygen.com*

- *http://www.women.com*

iVillage, which went public in March 1999, counts NBC among its investors. Oxygen Media—the umbrella name for several sites (BeFearless, Oprah, Thriveonline, ka-Ching) with a direct tie-in to a cable channel of the same name—has funding from AOL, Disney/ABC TV, and Oprah Winfrey's media machine. Hearst Corporation (Redbook and Cosmopolitan magazines) backs Women.com.

These sites are not slouches, but like other sites dependent on ad revenue, they joined dot-coms in the Spring 2000 stock downturn. Some smaller, less-expensive, women-oriented sites are surviving well:

- *http://www.womenswire.com*

- *http://www.chickclick.com* (a Web ring that includes the "grrls" sites that follow)

- *http://www.webgrrls.com*

- *http://www.cybergrrl.com*

- *http://www.feminista.com*

- *http://www.hissyfit.com*

- *http://www.femina.cybergrrl.com* (a search engine for women)

The Implications for Web Marketing.   The increasing number of women shopping online signifies one of the most important trends for Internet marketing. Women traditionally control household budgets. They are responsible for 70 percent of all retail sales and 80 percent of sales of personal and household goods.

Racial Distribution

The Internet still does not look like the world when it comes to race. As seen in Figure 3.2, the "World White Web," as one AP writer called it, remains a serious problem.

As the statistics in Figure 3.1 show, the situation in the United States has improved since the release of the 1999 report from the U.S. Department of Commerce, "Falling Through the Net: Defining the Digital Divide." As a result of that report, which showed that racial disparity in computer ownership and Internet access was not just a matter of income, the federal government adopted several initiatives to make low-cost Internet access available in rural, low-income, and minority communities.

The effort seems to have paid off, with the percentage of individual African-American and Hispanic users now roughly proportional to their share of the general population. About 44 percent of African-American households and 42 percent of Hispanic households are now online. Compare this to 70 percent of Asian-American households and 58 per-

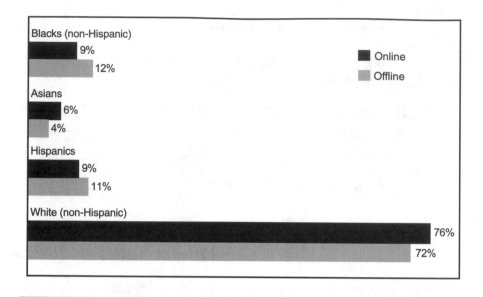

Figure 3.2. Distribution of ethnic groups within online population vs. overall population (2000) *http://www.emarketer.com/analysis/edemographics/052900_race.html*. Data from U.S. Census Bureau, 2000. Courtesy eMarketer, Inc.

cent of white households. Taken together, these numbers imply that minority users may be accessing the Web from work, libraries, or other sources, rather than having Internet access at home.

To reach an African-American audience, you might want to search out such sites as:

- African American Internetwork (*http://www.africanamerican.com*), the first publicly traded African-American content site

- Africana (*http://www.africana.com*)

- AfroNet (*http://www.afronet.com*)

- Black Entertainment Television (*http://www.BET.com*), which has funding from Microsoft, three major media companies, and two major black organizations. It offers content similar to its companion cable channel, with black celebrities, health, food, and finances, and sells products like books and music by black artists.

- Black Planet (*http://www.blackplanet.com*)

- Black Voices (*http://www.blackvoices.com*)

- NetNoir (*http://www.netnoir.com*)

If one segment of your target audience is U.S. Hispanics, you might want to focus online marketing efforts on Prodigy (*http://myhome. prodigy.net/espanol*), which offers a Spanish-language Internet access service ($9.95–$21.95 per month) or AOL Mexico at *www.aol.com.mx*. Both hope to bridge the language barrier that has restrained the number of Hispanics online. (Only 3 percent of Web sites are in Spanish; 68 percent are in English.)

Like African-American sites, many Hispanic-oriented portals and sites are struggling to stay alive:

- Advancing Women: *http://www.advancingwomen.com/hispbiz.html*

- Hispanic Business: *http://www.hispanicbusiness.com*

- Hispano: *http://www.hispano.com* (professional job market)

- Latin World: *http://www.latinworld.com* (Hispanic search engine, including kids' sites)

- Que Pasa: *http://www.quepasa.com* (portal)

- Saludos Hispanos: *http://www.saludos.com* (employment service)

- Star Media: *http://www.starmedia.com* (worldwide Spanish and Portuguese site)

- U.S. Hispanic Chamber: *http://www.ushcc.com*

Although Asian Americans participate actively online, they have fewer ethnic portals, but you might consider *http://www.moshix2.com*, *http://www.japan.asiaco.com*, or *http://www.dragonfield.com*. Native Americans lag farthest behind in Internet use, particularly those rural tribes with limited telephone access. Many Native American sites focus on selling traditional arts and crafts or explaining their culture to outsiders, such as *http://www.nativeweb.org* or *http://www.500nations.com*. Even as the digital divide is softening among individual users, it remains a significant factor among minority-owned businesses, which are less likely to have Web sites than their Caucasian counterparts.

The Implications for Web Marketing.   Identifying an ethnic group online is valuable if you have a product or service targeted to one of these audiences, but it might be more difficult than you expect. Like sites in other categories, some of the ethnically oriented sites don't draw enough traffic to sustain themselves. Be sure to check traffic statistics on these and any other sites you explore.

Global Use

Remember, it is the *World* Wide Web. U.S. Web dominance has begun to decline as other countries install infrastructure and reduce obstacles to Internet access. Experts estimate that by 2003, about 65 percent of Web users (up from 57 percent in 2001) will be from outside the United States. After the United States, China, the UK, Germany, and Japan currently have the greatest number of online users, as seen in Figure 3.3. The U.S. share of B2C and B2B global e-commerce will drop from 70 percent in 2002 to 55 percent by 2006, as Asian-Pacific and European nations become more active. Details can be seen in Figure 3.4.

The next area of growth for online commerce is likely to be Europe, where Internet access is expanding quickly. The Euro has simplified electronic currency exchange and the European Union has removed barriers to online commerce. European e-commerce is estimated to jump from $195 billion in 2001 to $1.53 trillion by 2004. European B2C spending focuses on travel, computers and electronics, groceries, books, apparel, music, and other categories. By comparison, Latin American online spending is projected to grow from $6.8 billion in 2001 to $81.8 billion by 2004, with an emphasis on personal computers, travel, groceries, and books.

Don't make the mistake of treating Europe as a marketing monolith. The Scandinavian countries are fully and enthusiastically wired, with Britain, Switzerland, the Netherlands, and Germany close behind. France, which since 1981 has had Minitel, its own non-Web online service, has only recently reached the 10-percent mark in Internet use. Southern and Eastern European countries lag behind Western Europe.

Country	Total Population	Online Population
United States	278.0 million	149 million
China	1.3 billion	33.7 million
United Kingdom	59.6 million	33.0 million
Germany	83.0 million	26.0 million
Japan	126.8 million	22.0 million
South Korea	47.9 million	16.7 million
Canada	31.6 million	14.2 million
France	60.0 million	11.0 million
Italy	57.7 million	11.0 million
Russia	145 million	7.5 million
Spain	40.0 million	7.0 million
The Netherlands	16.0 million	6.8 million
Taiwan	22.3 million	6.4 million
Brazil	174.5 million	6.1 million
Australia	19.4 million	5.0 million
India	1.0 billion	5.0 million

Figure 3.3. Global online populations, *http://cyberatlas.internet.com/big_ picture/geographics/article/0,,5911_151151,00.html.* © 2002 INT Media Group, Inc. All rights reserved.

Asian countries are recovering from the economic downturn in the late 1990s, but significant Internet presence outside Japan is several years away. Still, Asia-Pacific use is expected to rival Europe by 2005. Internet use and electronic commerce in Latin America is just starting to pick up, but is also growing quickly. Once again, there is great variation among nations, with Brazil, Mexico, and Argentina having the largest online populations and greatest volume of online retail sales in that order.

The developing world is still on the far shore of the digital divide, although the G-8 summit in July 2000 pledged to create a "dot force" to expand Internet access and reduce its cost in developing nations.

The Implications for Web Marketing. There will be lots of opportunity to sell to the worldwide market. If you have a product that can ship internationally, or that can be marketed through agents or distributors in other countries, start planning now to become globally competitive in the future. Among those countries with your target audience, focus

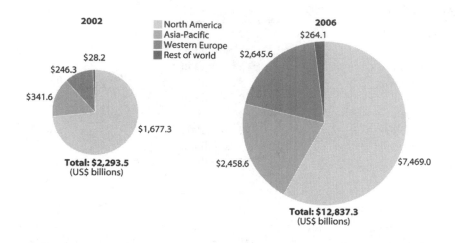

Figure 3.4.   Worldwide e-commerce growth. Source: Forrester Research Report, 12/26/01, "Global Online Trade Will Climb to 18% of Sales." ©2002 Forrester Research Inc.

first on the ones with the most developed infrastructure and largest online populations.

Language

Let's consider what the world market looks like from a language perspective. The percent of Internet users who speak English as their preferred language is dropping quickly. As recently as 2000, English-speakers had a slight majority online, but by 2002, only 40 percent of those with Internet access spoke English; 34 percent spoke a non-English European language; and the remaining 26 percent spoke an Asian or other language, as seen in Figure 3.5. The distribution of languages appears in Figure 3.6.

Although many people in Europe and Asia speak English as a second language, they prefer to access the Web in their native language. Try to translate several key pages of your Web site into any target languages, and promote language-specific gateways to your site in each country. Companies like Global Reach (*http://www.glreach.com*) assert that this may raise the number of non-native English speakers visiting your site from 15 percent to 50 percent or more.

	Internet access (in M)	% of world's online pop.	Internet access 2003 (est. in M)	Total pop. in 2003 (est. in M)
English	228	40.2%	270	567
Non-English	339	59.8%	510	5,633
Total World	567	100.0%	780	6,200
European Languages (non-English)	192.3	33.9%	259.3	1,218
Asian Languages	146.2	26.1%	254	487

Figure 3.5. Percent of world population with Internet access by major language groups, *http://glreach.com/globstats.* Courtesy Global Reach.

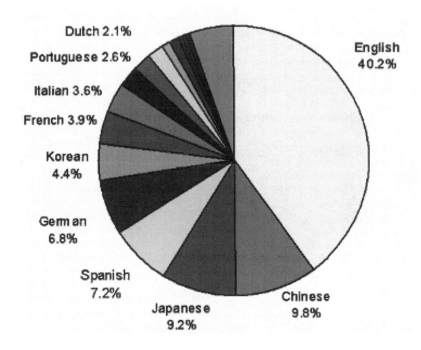

Figure 3.6. Online language populations, *http://www.glreach.com/globstats.* Courtesy Global Reach.

The Implications for Web Marketing. How are you going to sell to non-English markets? As former German chancellor Willy Brandt put it, "If I'm selling to you, I speak your language. If I'm buying, *dann müssen Sie Deutsch sprechen*" [then you must speak German]. You may find that you need to budget for translation services, international marketing support, and/or domain registration in other countries.

Online Market-Research Sources

The information above may seem overwhelming, but it represents only a small fraction of what you can discover through online market research. You might find such intriguing nuggets of information as the average amount spent per online shopper during Christmas 2001 ($392), or that 43 percent of all Internet surfers use the Web to window-shop, but go to the mall to close the deal.

You can use the Web itself as a source of data on everything from demographics to what sites are the best sellers. Take a look at sites like the ones below to get a sense of where to look for various types of information.

- *http://www.clickz.com/tools_resources*

- *http://www.commerce.net/research/stats/stats.html*

- *http://cyberatlas.internet.com/big_picture/stats_toolbox/article*

- *http://cyberatlas.internet.com/big_picture/traffic_patterns*

- *http://www.internetstats.com*

- *http://www.domainstats.com*

- *http://www.glreach.com/globstats*

- *http://www.internetindicators.com*

- *http://www.internet.com*

- *http://www.isc.org/ds*

- *http://www.marketingsherpa.com*

- *http://www.nua.ie/surveys*

- *http://www.pm.netratings.com/nnpm/owa/print_home_page_new*

For information on store performance and top-selling sites, see:

- *http://www.bizrate.com/ratings_guide/guide.xpml?de_id=335*
  (seen in Figure 3.7)

- *http://www.consumerreports.org/main/home.jsp* (paid site)

- *http://www.economy.com/store* (industry research)

- *http://www.emarketer.com* (paid reports by market segment)

Figure 3.7. Customer ratings of online stores, *http://www.bizrate.com/ratings_guide/guide.xpml?de_id=335*. Courtesy Bizrate.com.

You can question other marketing experts by subscribing to online discussion groups like Internet Marketing at *www.iMarketing.com* or the Online-Advertising Group at *www.o-a.com*. For information on specific Web sites, install the Alexa toolbar (*http://download.alexa.com/alexa6/quicktour.html?p=&u=*) on your browser. It offers contact information, traffic statistics, and related categories for any site you visit. Google's toolbar (*http://toolbar.google.com*) is more limited, but it will give you the Google ranking of each page.

Step 2: Know Your Business

If you are already in business, use the development or re-launch of your Web site to evaluate critically all aspects of your business operations. Understanding the problems you already face is essential before deciding whether the Web will help overcome them or merely magnify them. The Internet is not a panacea for other business difficulties, nor is it a get-rich-quick scheme. For that, stick to late-night infomercials. Profit margins are under enormous pressure on the Web. In the crowded and competitive cyber-marketplace, small businesses are particularly vulnerable as larger, more traditional companies get online with the financial resources to produce sophisticated Web sites and to advertise heavily for online customers.

Do you already have a program for advertising or other marketing? If not, you have lots of company: A recent survey found that 91 percent of small businesses rely solely on word of mouth and referrals for customers. But to compete with millions of other online businesses, you will need to let people know about your site. You'll have to become a smart guerrilla marketer, savvy when it comes to selecting cyber-niches. If you do start advertising online, will be you able to handle additional business? Would you need to expand a manufacturing facility or contract with a fulfillment house?

Site Goals

As a precursor to writing an online plan, you need to think seriously about what you want your site to achieve as part of your overall business needs and reality. Is your business new? Is it online only? Will you need to integrate online and offline operations? Defining your goals and objectives will guide everyone on your development team, from the programmer to the copywriter and the photographer. It may help to think about your site in terms of four stages of the Web site life cycle.

Web Site Life Cycle

While some sites flow through the four stages of development in sequence, many sit contentedly into only one category for their lifetime. Where do your goals place you on the art shown in Figure 3.8?

- **Informative:** a static site that presents passive material or advertising about a company or product; the Web equivalent of a brochure

- **Interactive:** a site that engages viewers to take action online, such as searching a catalog, taking a survey, playing a game, or checking the status of a shipment

- **Transactive:** a site that sells product or services and accepts payment online

- **Transformative:** a site that affects basic business processes, such as accepting bids from vendors or providing technical support to existing clients

Site Objectives

To ensure success, you need to decide what will constitute achievement of your goals, at least in broad terms. Whenever possible, quantify at least one specific, measurable objective for each goal—for example, $25,000 in sales over the first year, 600 visitors a day learning about your business on the Web, speeding order fulfillment by two days, obtaining six new bookings as a wedding photographer, or hiring three new employees. Use a Web planning form like the one in Figure 3.9 to organize this. Different goals may also have different target audiences, so also be sure to identify the people you need to reach. Thinking through

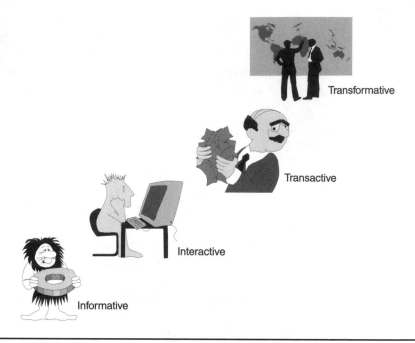

Figure 3.8.   Stages of Web development.

specific objectives reduces the risk of establishing a Web site, and will help you determine a realistic budget. The point of a Web site is not to increase your expenses; it's to increase your business!

Whatever objectives you define, if you're not making progress toward achieving them within six months of launch, you may need to analyze the situation and rethink your approach.

Let's look at some examples of objectives to get a better sense of this element of the Web planning process.

Financial Objectives

If you have an e-commerce site, you will undoubtedly have specific sales objectives, including total dollar value per day/week/month, sales volume (number of sales), average dollar sale, number of repeat sales, and sales per product or product line. Knowing what you want to measure is critical, because you'll need to confirm that the shopping cart and

WEB PLANNING FORM FOR _____ (URL)
(can do for entire site, a section of site, or individual pages)

Prepared by:_____   Date:_____

Page Name:_____

Goal 1:
Target Audience 1:

Traffic Objective	_____		within _____	(timeframe)
Conversion Objective	_____%		within _____	(timeframe)
Break-even Objective	_____		within _____	(timeframe)
ROI Objective	_____		within _____	(timeframe)
Sales Objective 1	$_____		within _____	(timeframe)
Other Objective	_____		within _____	(timeframe)

Goal 2:
Target Audience 2:

Traffic Objective	_____		within _____	(timeframe)
Conversion Objective	_____%		within _____	(timeframe)
Break-even Objective	_____		within _____	(timeframe)
ROI Objective	_____		within _____	(timeframe
Sales Objective 1	$_____		within _____	(timeframe)
Other Objective	_____		within _____	(timeframe)

Figure 3.9. Web planning form. ©2002 Watermelon Mountain Web Marketing.

checkstand you use will support your reporting needs. If you plan to track sales back to specific customers who arrive from specific ads, there are implications for site development, such as the need for **cookies,** small files placed on users' machines to identify the users and track their path through the site.

Even if you're not selling online, you may have indirect monetary objectives. You may want to see if the Web can help you increase your market share, or generate leads that turn into offline sales or attendance at an event. Perhaps you want to increase the number of gift certificates sold, free trial offers accepted, or coupons redeemed for purchase. Whatever your financial objective, keep your eye on the bottom line. Remember, it's profit, not gross revenue, that defines success.

Traffic Objectives

Do you want to increase the total traffic arriving at your site? Or, if you're seeing a lot of meaningless traffic instead of prospects, you might actually want to reduce the number of visitors, going for a smaller number of better-screened visitors, or at least sorting out the "looky-loos" quickly. Perhaps you want to keep people on your site longer, increase the number of page views per visitor, or increase the number of people who sign up for your e-mail newsletter. If you intend to generate income by selling advertising online, then site traffic is your ultimate measuring stick—what you sell is your audience.

As you'll see in Chapter 8, statistics from your existing site can provide the baseline. Be sure that the statistical package you use lets you analyze traffic the way you want. Statistics are so important that you may need to switch Web hosts to get the package you want, or invest in a statistical package of your own. Once again, your objectives will affect dozens of other decisions.

Conversion Rate Objectives

In the last chapter, we spoke about the conversion rate: the ratio between browsers who arrive at your site to buyers who take a desired action at the conclusion of their experience on your site. If your site traffic leaves in less than a minute, or drops off before completing the desired action, then you may want to establish a specific conversion rate, even between pages, as an objective. For instance, you may want to set a 2-percent rate for visitors who arrive at the home page to click on your catalog or other secondary page, and a 25-percent rate for those who open a shopping cart to actually buy. As you monitor the results, you would keep tweaking the site to achieve those objectives, looking at such things as navigation, copy, and the quality of the offer being made to attract users further into the site. Establishing conversion objectives is especially critical for an e-commerce site.

ROI & Break-even Objectives

Whatever your goal, you will feel better about your investment in a Web site if you establish objectives that let you know whether it has paid off. If you have an information-only brochure site, you may want to see whether site expenses are offset by cost-savings in advertising or printing. If you have opted for an interactive site without online sales, you might want to compare the costs of customer acquisition or lead generation online to similar costs offline. A typical retail storefront spends $20 to $30 for new customer acquisition. Are you spending more or less than that on the Web? (Many dot-coms failed in the 2001 bust because they were spending as much as $60 to $75 to acquire each new customer.)

If you have a transformational site (using your site to change the way you do business), consider **ROI** (return on investment) objectives that compare the cost of providing customer support online, the cost of processing a transaction through your accounting system, the cost of processing an order, or the cost of maintaining inventory.

Sites that sell online can benefit from the most traditional analysis of all: computing the **break-even point** for your Web site. By definition, break-even is the point at which revenues equal total costs; units sold above this point contribute to profit. Here's how to calculate a simple estimate of the break-even point (number of sales needed) for a single product:

1. Subtract what you pay to manufacture or acquire the goods (known as the **cost of goods**) from your selling price. This gives you the **gross margin** on your product.

2. Divide your total **fixed costs** (overhead costs like rent, utilities, Web hosting, and developer fees) by the gross margin to determine the number of units you need to sell. That's your break-even point!

Computing break-even for an entire store is more complicated, since each product may have a different gross margin. In that case, estimate the *average* selling price and the *average* gross margin. If you have these numbers from your existing brick-and-mortar or mail order business, use those. If not, do some research online or contact your local Small Business Development Center (see Figure 3.10) for assistance with this calculation.

For greater accuracy, compute break-even using the concept of **contribution margin**, instead of gross margin. To establish your contribution margin, subtract both the cost of goods and the cost of sales from your selling price. The difference is the contribution margin. Then divide total fixed costs by the contribution margin.

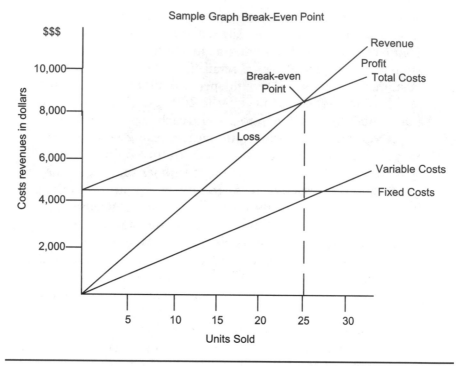

Figure 3.10. Calculating break-even points. U.S. Small Business Administration.

The cost of sales are variable costs that depend on the number of units sold or the number of visitors to your site. For an online store, cost of sales might include:

- shipping and handling

- merchant card fees (percent of transaction)

- variable charges for Web hosting based on traffic

- customer support

The graph in Figure 3.10 illustrates how this works. If you create a spreadsheet for break-even analysis, you'll easily be able to review "what if" scenarios, considering best case and worst case cost analyses. You may be surprised at the number of sales you need to break-even. How does it compare to break-even offline? Is it reasonable given the conversion rate that you established as an objective above? Can you absorb the costs until the break-even point is reached?

If not, stop to catch your breath! Will you be able to get financing to see you through? Can you revise your pricing, cost of goods or cost of sale, product mix, or business model to make the numbers work? Keep revising your Web plans until you have a realistic chance of reaching break-even without losing your shirt!

Hidden Costs of Readiness

One of the most common errors in estimating the cost of a Web site is ignoring expenses that may be necessary to support the online effort. As part of knowing your business, survey your internal resources. This is critical if you expect to host your own site, sell online, offer customer support, or receive a large number of new e-mail messages. You may need to invest in new computer equipment, install additional phone lines, upgrade to a high-speed Internet connection, or train staff on new software. Some items come with a substantial price tag, so you'll want to be sure they are included in the budget for your site.

TIPS FOR TIRED SITES

Has your Web site become a sink for dollars without a payoff? Take time to do or redo the numbers. Is your impression wrong? Perhaps the site is paying for itself in cost-savings that you didn't realize. Were your prior expectations for traffic, conversion rates, or averages sales price unrealistic? If you bring those into line, what would it cost to modify your site to achieve your new objectives? If you can't make the numbers work, it may be time to unplug the Web site, or cutback to a small brochure site. Put your marketing dollars to work for you in conventional venues that you know will help your business grow. Sometimes life on the Web just isn't fair.

Telecommunication Needs

As a top priority, maximize the speed at which you access the Web. Try to get the fastest method that your local telecommunications infrastructure will support. At the very minimum, you should have a 56K dial-up modem via **POTS** (Plain Old Telephone Service). **Broadband** or high-speed access has exploded in past two years, especially via **DSL** (**digital subscriber line**) and cable modem. Other broadband options come from the telephone world, such as ISDN and T1/T3 leased lines, while wireless and satellite access are still in the early stages of adoption. The table in Figure 3.11 compares the different methods of online access, with sample rates, setup fees, purposes, and benefits. The rates for these options, which vary around the country, may run anywhere from tens to several thousand dollars per month, depending on your needs and usage.

Cable companies, which compete with phone companies' DSL lines, seem to be winning the battle for high-speed market share in residences, home offices, and small businesses. Cable is both more widely available and more widely subscribed to than DSL. In August 2001 a Salomon Smith Barney report predicted that by 2005 cable modems will have 59 percent of the market for high-speed access compared to only 34 percent for DSL. Broadband access over T1/T3 lines is more common for large companies.

DSL

Because DSL lets users carry both data and voice on the same phone line, it is especially attractive to residential users with only one line into their homes. Unfortunately, only one computer can be used on a phone line. **ADSL** (Asymmetric DSL) lines upload more slowly than they download. DSL lines, and sometimes even adequate copper phone lines, may not be available in rural counties or in all urban neighborhoods. Even large metropolitan areas may not have enough lines available or the lines may be too old to be reliable. For more information on DSL and other telephone line-based options, check out these sites:

- *http://www.PacBell.com/Products/business/fastrak/networking/ISDN*

- *http://www.dslreports.com*

Type of Access	Bandwidth	Typical User	Monthly Rates	Installation/ Equipment	Positives (+) / Negatives (-)
POTS(Plain Old Telephone Service)	Up to 56K	Home	Free- $21.95+ ISP charges	phone installation; 56K modem $30-$100	+ some free Internet services available, affordable, easy set up - slow, no guarantee of speed, uploads slower than download
ISDN	64 Kbps to 128K	Small-medium business, multiple users	$20-$40 fixed hours + $1.50 each addr'l hour	line installation; ISDN modem $200	+ guaranteed speed, can talk and browse simultaneously - can't support a server; availability limited to within 3.6 miles of central office
DSL	256 Kbps, up to 6–8 Mbps	Residential or small business	$50 for 256 Kbps, $80-$100 for 8 Mbps and up	$100-$500 may not include required ($200) DSL modem; often resold by ISPs	+ always on, works well with LAN/server, very fast, voice and data using same phone line - increased security risk and complexity; availability limited to locations close to central office
Burstable T1 Lines	1.5 Mbps	Large Business	$200-$1500	$1,000 installation, plus additional support equipment like routers to deliver service to different users	+ T1 excellent Internet connection - cost, limited availability

Figure 3.11. Telecommunication rates and Internet access. *(continued on next page)*

Type of Access	Bandwidth	Typical User	Monthly Rates	Installation/ Equipment	Positives (+) / Negatives (-)
Full T1	1.5 Mbps	Large business	$1000-$1500	$1000-$1500 for installation plus additional support and equipment	+ T1 excellent Internet connection - cost, limited availability
Full T3	44.7 Mbps	Large business	call phone company fractional installations available	$2000 or waived depending on contract	+ T3 needed for full-motion, full-screen video - cost, limited availability
Cable Modem	1.5-3.0 Mbps download;	Residence or small business	$40-$100	$80-$250 for cable modem plus cost of installation	+ always on, good value - shared service can cause slowdowns, limited availability, no choice of ISPs
Satellite	400 Kbps		$70 and up	$300-$700 for dish, box, and PC card; $200 installation	+ very fast, great for remote locations, always on, speed constant, 2-way broad band at slower rates - expensive, requires outside dish that may be affected by weather, broadband inbound, but require 56K modem outbound for e-mail and attachments

Figure 3.11. Telecommunication rates and Internet access. *(continued from previous page)*

- *http://www.specialty.com/hiband*

Cable Modem

Cable companies have become very cost competitive with DSL. They have the added advantage of allowing multiple computers to share the same online connection. Small home or office networks can reduce their online fees by using cable modem services, which often will include basic cable TV in the service bundle. Cable companies and providers like AOL remain engaged in a battle over whether consumers must use a cable company's bundled Internet service, or whether they enjoy open access to other ISPs. For more information on cable modems and other options, try the following Web sites:

- *http://www.multichannel.com/bband.shtml*

- *http://www.cnet.com*

- *http://cyberatlas.internet.com/big_picture/hardware/hardware_index.html*

ISDN

ISDN (Integrated Services Digital Network) has been available for a long time as a dial-up service in metropolitan areas. ISDN, which requires a separate line and an ISDN modem (I-modem) costing several hundred dollars, remains primarily a small business option.

T1/T3 Leased Lines

T1/T3 leased lines require rewiring an office building, which can be logistically and financially difficult. T1 lines, roughly equivalent to 6 ISDN lines, are often used to connect networks to the Internet, but it takes a T3 line to carry full-motion, full-screen video. Additional equipment is needed to divide the resources among different servers. If you host your own site and expect increased traffic, you'll need to confirm that you have the telecommunications capacity to handle more simultaneous users without slowing down. You may need to upgrade to a dedicated fractional T1 or T3 line.

Wireless Broadband & Satellite

Generally, satellite-based Internet service, such as that from DirecPC *(http://www.DirecPC.com)*, offers great download speed (400 Kbps), but constrains uploads to a 56 Kbps phone modem. Newer technology allows uploads without a telephone line, which may resolve the problem of Internet access for rural areas, albeit at a high cost. For those who already have a satellite dish, the monthly cost of adding an ISP service may be competitive, but combined monthly service charges may really add up. For instance, DISH Network adds monthly fees for WebTV to its own monthly programming charges *(http://www.dishnetwork.com)*.

Narrowband wireless access is used predominantly for handheld Personal Digital Assistants (**PDAs**). Web access on PDAs is generally limited to special text-only sites created in a different programming language than that used for regular Web sites.

Hardware and Software In-House

Take this opportunity to survey the hardware, operating systems, applications software and browsers you currently use. Will any of your operating systems or application software constrain the development environment for your Web site? If so, that may affect your selection of a Web host and developer. Will you need more equipment or space if you bring on additional employees to handle demand generated by the site? Will you need to purchase a digital camera to take product shots? Photo processing software like PhotoShop to enhance the images? Database software to accept automatic downloads of registration information? Mail-order management software?

If your company is on a network, discuss your Web project with your system administrator to see if additional equipment will be needed. You may require more routers or other network upgrades, for instance, if many more people will be online at the same time.

Hosting your own site is recommended only if computer technology is already one of the core competencies of your organization. If you intend to host your own site, it's critical to select the correct **server**, a computer with the software and telecommunications capacity to act as a host. The complexity and size of your site and the amount of traffic you anticipate will affect your decision. At a minimum, expect to pay $4,000 to $6,000 for an in-house system, plus staff time for programming and maintenance.

The operating system you use will affect other decisions downstream, including selection of Web development and server software, whose costs range from free to thousands of dollars. Your choice of other application packages, such as security, catalog, or multimedia software, will also be affected. Consult with your systems engineer or IT manager on all these issues before proceeding.

The general guideline for buying hardware definitely holds with purchases related to the Internet. Invest in computers with the fastest processor and most memory that you can afford. Any VGA monitor will do, although larger screens make it easier to see Web images without scrolling.

Step 3: Write an Online Business Plan

Once you've analyzed your current business situation, established goals and set quantifiable objectives for your site, it's time to put together a written **online business plan** for how to achieve them. If you don't already have a plan for your business, write at least a short draft before you go online. If your plan is sitting on a shelf, dust it off and update it for your Web venture. If you plan to start a new enterprise that exists only on the Web or intend to seek investors for your dot-com start-up, it's absolutely critical to have a detailed business plan.

For help with business plans, check out a Small Business Development Center (SBDC), generally located at a local community college. For the one nearest you, call the Small Business Administration (SBA) Answer Desk at 1-800-827-5722 or check out the SBA Web site (*http://www.sbaonline.sba.gov*) for this and other information useful for small businesses. Definitions of various online business models may be found at *http://www.digitalenterprise.org/models/models.html*.

Obviously, the business plan for a Web-based purveyor of "cookie bouquets" will differ from the plan for a minority executive search firm.

Look at their Web sites in Figures 3.12 and 3.13 to see how those businesses take advantage of the Internet's potential.

Many businesses write a plan only when they go to a bank to borrow money, but wise business owners write one annually as an internal gyroscope. They use the plan to set milestones for the coming year, to introduce a new product, or before entering another geographic (or virtual) territory.

Use the Internet itself to help write and implement your business plan. For instance, through online research you might find new suppliers who can give you a better price, just-in-time delivery, or higher-quality goods. You can check whether the Web has fostered new competition. With manufacturers, wholesalers, and retailers all selling on the Web, distribution channels—and price points—are shifting rapidly. You may need to adjust sales projections according to what you learn from your online research.

You can use the Web to conduct a cyber-focus group to explore the opinions of your customers with a moderated online chat session. You

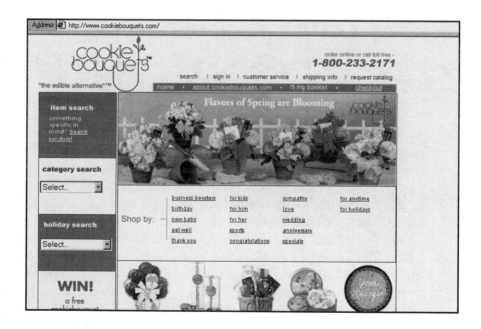

Figure 3.12. Sample small business Web site, *http://www.cookiebouquets.com.* Courtesy Cookie Bouquets.

Figure 3.13. Sample small business Web site, *http://www.minorityexecsearch.com.* Courtesy Minority Executive Search, Inc.

can do this yourself or use one of several companies that specialize in recruiting participants and moderating such sessions: e-Focus Groups (*http://www.e-focusgroups.com/online.html*), Insights Online (*http://www.insightsonline.com/olg.htm*), or (*http://www.surveysite.com/newsite/docs/onlinefocus.htm*).

For additional small business assistance, try these Web sites:

- *http://www.SmallBizPlanet.com*

- *http://www.onvia.com*

- *http://www.wilsonweb.com*

- *http://www.smallbiztechnology.com*

- *http://www.inc.com/home*

Elements of a Business Plan

Whether you're writing a complete business plan for a new enterprise, or a plan confined only to your online presence, a business plan generally includes the following sections:

1. A Brief Executive Summary

2. Mission/type of business or Web site (e.g., manufacturing, wholesale, retail, catalog, service) and goals

3. Description of product or service

4. Competition (online and offline)

5. Marketing

   a. Target market (customer description or demographics)

   b. Why there's a market for your product or service and market size in customers and dollars

   c. Your objectives for market penetration and revenue

   d. Marketing strategy and methods, including positioning vis-à-vis the competition and your competitive edge

   e. Promotion and advertising strategy (online and offline)

6. Sales plan

   a. Pricing

   b. Distribution channels, including any issues raised by selling online

   c. Sales methods (e.g., sales force, agents, reps, telemarketing, Web)

   d. Order-fulfillment process

7. Operations

    a. Facilities (e.g., location, size, equipment) including status of space, access, hours

    b. Manufacturing methods (if applicable)

    c. Raw materials or inventory needed and suppliers

    d. Customer service and support

    e. Staff, including numbers and types of employees and hiring plans

    f. Development timeline

8. Management and financial

    a. Resumes of key management and time available, including board members or other advisers if applicable

    b. Any legal, licensing, zoning, code requirements, insurance issues, etc.

    c. Sources of funding and how funds will be spent

    d. Financial statements (current, if any)

    e. Projected revenues and expenses (one to five years) with break-even analysis and detailed Web budget

In Chapter 5, we'll talk more about the Development Timeline (7f) and Web budget (8e). In the meantime, if you stick to the basics below as you write and implement your plan, you'll be able to analyze most of the challenges you'll face and consider ways to overcome them.

- Plan your work; work your plan.

- View the Web as a means to your business ends, not as an end in itself.

- Understand how an online presence will affect your overall business operations, paying particular attention to the integration of offline and online activities, and to the essential contribution of back-office operations to online success.

Integrate Bricks-and-Clicks

If you have (or plan to have) both an offline business and an e-commerce site, you face particular challenges. In this situation, you might want to think of your Web site as another storefront. Ask yourself the same questions you would ask about locating a new building and about integrating operations across multiple locations.

It's Still One Business

Plan ahead to keep your business operations in sync. No matter how many retail outlets you have, your customers, vendors, and service providers think of you as one business. Your accounting software, inventory software, and contact databases need to be compatible with each other and the Web. You would no more use different sets of SKU (product) numbers in your Tallahassee and Tampa stores than you would between your Walla Walla store and your Web site.

With a well-thought strategy, your Web site and storefront will complement each other, instead of competing. Think of all the different ways that customers might interact between the Web and reality. They might:

- Research a product online, but buy it in the store

- Research an item in person, but order it using an in-store kiosk connected to the Web (as the outfitter REI provides in its stores) to reduce waiting time at the checkout desk or to arrange quickly for shipping to someone else

- Buy a gift certificate in the store and give it to someone who shops online, or vice versa

- Call the storefront to ask questions about the Web site

- Use the Web site to determine closest store locations, hours, sales, and inventory

- Use an online coupon designed for use in the store, or vice versa

- Buy an item online, but bring it to the store for return

- Order an item online, but pick it up in person

The combinations are endless, but you need to think through the options you want to implement. Software for **Customer Relationship Management (CRM)** can smooth out some potential glitches, allowing both online telephone support personnel and sales associates in the store to view a single, shared customer record.

Don't Eat Your Young

Manufacturers or distributors who plan to sell online face another potentially treacherous problem: cannibalizing their distribution **channels**. A channel is the path a product takes from manufacturer to consumer. A product might be sold directly from a factory outlet, sold through a wholesaler, or pass through both a distributor and retailer until it reaches the end user. If you divert retail sales to your Web site, you may not only see no net gain in sales, but risk alienating existing distributors or retailers. To overcome potential channel conflicts, consider using some of the following strategies:

- Talk to your retailers and distributors about your online plans; don't surprise them.

- Don't undercut them on price.

- Sell only some of your inventory online, leaving retailers and distributors exclusivity on certain product lines.

- Allow your retailers to return unsold merchandise and use the Web site for liquidation.

- Make yours a B2B site to streamline order-taking and fulfillment with your distributors and leave the B2C world to them.

- Offer retailers/distributors free advertising on your Web site.

- Redirect customers to retailers' Web sites or store locations for actual purchases.

Plan for Back-Office Operations

A pretty Web face is simply not enough: Customers expect cyber-service levels to match the level of service in the real world. There's a high price to pay for failure: In its 1999 study, BizRate.com found that online shoppers who experienced trouble were 73 percent less likely to buy from that Internet merchant again. Figure 3.14 shows the high correlation between customer satisfaction and repeat purchases. E-commerce companies have taken heed, with shoppers reporting improvements in 2001 from prior years.

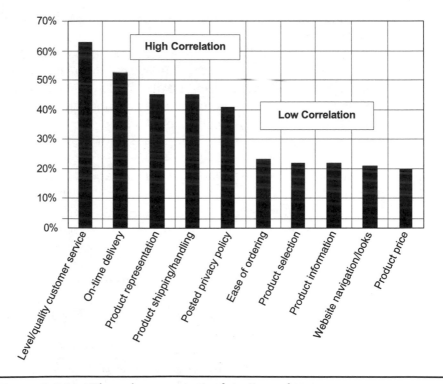

Figure 3.14. Why e-shoppers return, *http://www.bizrate.com.*
Source: BizRate.com, Consumer Online Report, First Quarter 1999.

With new performance benchmarks well established, your job as an online merchant has become more difficult. Your order-fulfillment process must satisfy customer expectations on everything from order taking and responding to e-mail to warehousing and shipping. It may require that you establish:

- Drop-shipping from a supplier and/or participation in a "fulfillment net" to automate drop-shipping from multiple vendors and track orders

- Accurate online inventory information so customers don't order out-of-stock items

- Adequate server capacity to handle maximum traffic loads without crashing or slowing down the site

- Order tracking, either online or by well-trained customer support representatives

- A method for handling returns. Bricks-and-clicks businesses with a physical storefront have an advantage over pure "e-tailers," since customers can more easily return a product and pick out a replacement

- A transportation network for immediate home delivery, such as done by Peapod.com (*http://www.peapod.com*), an online grocery seller with delivery

- Large warehouses with bar-code scanners and inventory management systems that package and ship items quickly and accurately (whether run by your company or outsourced)

- Online shipping and tracking services via one or more common carriers

Shipping

Shipping can be easily integrated into a Web site. If your Web host doesn't offer a shipping module with your online storefront (see Chapter 7), ask about incorporating applications from Federal Express, the U.S.

Postal Service, or UPS. Generally, a shipper is happy to provide free software and technical support to guarantee that it will get your business. When the customer selects a delivery date and method, the data is transmitted to the shipper, who generates a bill of lading, schedules a pickup, and forwards the information to you, all automatically. Some shipping software allows customers to track their orders from your Web site or the shipper's and provides e-mail notification before and after delivery. For more information, check out these sites:

- *http://webapi.fedex.com*

- *http://www.ec.ups.com/ecommerce/solutions/index.html*

- *http://164.109.64.160/front2.asp* (U.S. Postal Service)

Be cautious about offering free shipping; some 37 percent of online retailers cite shipping costs as a major headache. If your profit margins aren't high enough to support free shipping, incorporate the cost into the product price. Or offer customers the option of ordering online, but picking up the item at your storefront to save shipping charges. So many companies have lost money on shipping and handling that more and more are using drop-shipping from their suppliers or joining fulfillment nets, a new service that automates and tracks drop shipments from multiple suppliers to one customer.

Warehousing

Preexisting distribution networks geared to moving large truckloads of items from warehouses to retailers just don't cut it! Web e-tailers can take advantage of knowledge that offline catalog companies figured out long ago. For instance the Keystone Internet Services unit of Hanover Direct, Inc. *(http://www.keystonefulfillment.com),* provides fulfillment service to KBkids.com. Dirt Devil outsources shipment of its vacuum cleaner accessories to Fulfillment Plus *(http://www.ffplus.com).* Other fulfillment companies include Rush Order, Inc. *(http://www.rushorder.com),* and Young America *(http://www.young-america.com).*

It may cost more per order to outsource, but it's worth it if you don't have the capital or expertise to manage the process yourself. When selecting a fulfillment house, check references from their other clients and make sure that:

- Their management software, whether database, inventory, or accounting, will be technically compatible and easy to integrate.

- The fulfillment house has experience packaging your type of product.

- The company has large clients who provide a good revenue base and will help ensure that the fulfillment company is stable.

- The company offers high-quality customer service.

- The warehouse is close to a shipping hub and the company maintains good relationships with shippers.

While it may not be easy to build a Web site, building a good online business is even more of a challenge.

TIPS FOR TIRED SITES

You can't fix back-office problems until you know what they are. Try ordering something from your own Web site as a mystery shopper. Did you find any problems? How easy was it to create your order? If you have a form that visitors must fill out instead of an automated shopping cart, you may be losing a large percentage of probable sales. It's time to upgrade! Were you able to determine shipping and handling costs early in the process? Did you receive email confirmation? Did you have an express shipping option? How long did it take to receive your order? Could you track your shipment? Send a product question by email to see how long it takes your staff to respond. Call your 800-number or customer-service phone line to see how your staff responds to messages that are left during off-hours.

To meet customer demand for convenience, you should offer a variety of payment options, including online credit cards and printing out an order form to fax back. Any form with payment information should reside on a secure server. E-mail orders with credit card numbers are not secure and should not be used. If you have an older site that doesn't accept credit cards online, it's time to re-think that process (see Chapter 7). New offerings make it easy, even if you don't have a merchant card account.

Moving Forward

In this chapter, we've covered the first three steps for Web success: observing the Web, knowing your business, and writing an online business plan. You should have Web planning sheets that lay out goals, measurable objectives, and target audiences for your site, and perhaps computations of your break-even point and other criteria to assess your return on investment. Your Web notebook should by now include an online business plan, with a few blanks for budget and schedule, which we'll address in Chapter 5. First, let's take a look in the next chapter at inexpensive methods of Internet marketing besides your Web site. Like any good marketer, you'll want to have a lot of different arrows in your online quiver.

4

Step 4: Create and Distribute Info-Tools

In this chapter we'll discuss Step 4 for Internet success: creating and distributing info-tools. Although Web sites receive the most commercial attention, there are many other ways to take advantage of the Internet for marketing by distributing messages via e-mail, **listservers**, **newsgroups**, or chat rooms. You can participate in message boards and libraries on the old, text-intensive portion of the Internet, or conduct instant messaging and real-time conferences on other Web sites.

Info-tools and real-time communication alternatives offer an opportunity to generate interest and attention, while establishing credibility. You give away information while you tie in related products or services. Handled properly, the information you spread around the Internet will produce new customers or leads.

These low-cost, easy-to-implement strategies are enough for some small businesses. Other firms test their audiences with these less-risky alternatives before inaugurating a full-scale online effort, or use them to amplify their Web presence. The largest companies integrate them into a full-spectrum program of Internet activities to build an online "buzz" about their business as part of their **site launch** and to maintain customer relationships.

To provide concrete examples, we'll look over the shoulder of a fictional business, The Perfect Kernel Popcorn Company. The Perfect Kernel, a maker of organically grown gourmet popcorn, has annual sales of $2.5 million and employs 25 people. Marketing Manager Jane Ogilvie has been assigned the task of developing and executing an on-line marketing plan for The Perfect Kernel's new line of flavored popcorn. By the end of this chapter, you'll know how to:

- Create info-tools, from signature files to FAQ files

- Distribute these tools via e-mail, listservers, and newsgroups

- Understand how to manage an effective e-mail marketing campaign

- Take advantage of message boards, chats, conferences and software libraries available on major online services

Creating Info-Tools

Before you wade into the whitecapped marketing waters of cyberspace, you should create six info-tools related to your product or service:

1. Signature files

2. Blurbs

3. Reports and white papers

4. Newsletters and e-zines

5. Press releases

6. Lists of frequently asked questions (FAQs)

These simple tools, which can be kept in the Info-Tools section of your notebook and on your hard drive, will be valuable regardless of the distribution method you select. You can create them with your word processor as simple text files, without any special formatting. Later, you can convert these into HTML format for a fancier presentation, or modify them for inclusion on your Web site.

Signature Files

The electronic equivalent of your business card, a three- to six-line, text-only **signature file** should be appended to the end of every e-mail message, blurb, report, or other posting. Not only does it include all critical information about how to reach you, it also incorporates a brief marketing phrase that positions your business (**tag line**). Like your business card, your signature file is distributed far, wide, and often. This little self-promotional file is not considered advertising, so you can use it everywhere you go on the Internet.

Be sure to include all feasible ways to contact you. If you have a toll-free number, show it. If you want users to visit your Web site, provide the URL. If you can be reached by carrier pigeon, give directions a bird can follow. The make-believe signature file that Jane Ogilvie creates for The Perfect Kernel is shown in Figure 4.1. She may change the e-mail address line to direct responses to appropriate individuals or to track the source of the inquiry. Or she may change the call to action ("Discover our latest flavors...") according to the target audience or the purpose of the message.

Most e-mail programs have a simple procedure for creating a signature file. (Check "Help" to find instructions.) Once you have created a

Jane Ogilvie
The Perfect Kernel
Specializing in Naturally Grown Popcorn
1234 Main Street, Waterloo, Iowa 50701
T: 800-555-POPS F: 319-555-6666 E: Ogilvie@theperfectkernel.com
After The Perfect Kernel has a Website, she'll add:
Discover our latest flavors at *http://www.theperfectkernel.com*

(If The Perfect Kernel has a separate listserver address, she'll show that, too.)

Figure 4.1. Signature file for The Perfect Kernel.

signature file, it can be attached automatically to every message you send. On older versions of some e-mail programs, you may need to create a text file and paste it into messages manually.

Blurbs

Blurbs are short, pre-packaged messages about your business, products, services, or a related topic that can be sent quickly in response to inquiries. The text can be lifted from an existing news release, newsletter, or brochure, or created from scratch. Be sure to tell readers how to contact you to place orders or get more information, including your e-mail address and Web site.

Your blurb may eventually enjoy wide distribution online—a kind of electronic word of mouth—so check it for spelling and typographical errors, and edit it for readability. Follow basic principles for "revving" your copy with energy:

- Use the first person (I, we) or second (you), not the third.

- Use positive phrasing, such as "buy now" instead of "don't hesitate to buy."

- Use short, commonly used words.

- Use active verbs; try to avoid forms of the verb *to be*.

- Use numbers and details, such as "ultramarine, mint green, and mango," instead of "many colors."

- Spark your text with vivid, emotive words (e.g., munchies, sun-dried, guilt, money).

- View your blurb both on screen and in print to ensure there are no problems.

Jane at The Perfect Kernel created the blurb in Figure 4.2 for use in electronic marketing. She will append her signature file, coding the address line to track the source of resulting inquiries.

Gourmet popcorn, a low-fat alternative to other munchies, is great for your entire family. With only 5% of calories from fat and almost no cholesterol, popcorn is a healthy way to snack without guilt. Our "savory" flavors—cheddar, sun-dried tomato and green chili—tease the taste buds with grown-up flavor. The Perfect Kernel's Gourmet Popcorn places good health and good taste at the top of our priorities.

For a free sample of The Perfect Kernel's organically-grown flavored popcorn, just hit REPLY. Type ONLY your name and address in the message field. (Follow with signature file)

Figure 4.2. Sample blurb for The Perfect Kernel.

Reports and White Papers

Reports or **white papers**, which are longer than blurbs, are information-intensive files for the interested reader. They help establish your credibility as a resource or expert, but they don't contain much more marketing content than a signature file. You will upload these report files to strategically placed areas on the Internet that attract your target audience. On occasion, you may use them as attachments to e-mail requests for information.

These reports should not be particularly time critical, or you will have to update them continually. They might be short feature stories that could appear in a trade journal, or product fact sheets that are appropriate in a few newsgroups. You could create such items as a trivia-question game about your industry, questionnaires with a free gift for completion, or industry-related crossword puzzles. Or you could write an informative background article on your subject. Be creative, but soft-pedal marketing appeals in these reports. Since they may appear in places that restrict advertising, keep the content factor high. People can always go to your Web site, or contact you by phone or e-mail for more information.

For The Perfect Kernel, Jane creates several reports. One deals with cultivation of corn by Native Americans; another describes different corn species used for popcorn, animal feed, and corn on the cob. A third covers how popcorn is made, and yet another talks about the wide variety of flavored popcorns now available. As always, Jane appends her signature file.

Newsletters and E-Zines

Like their print counterparts, electronic newsletters may appear either regularly or irregularly, but change their content. Organizations from Symantec (*http://smallbiz.symantec.com*) to the U.S. Social Security Administration (*http://www.ssa.gov/enews*) use targeted electronic newsletters to communicate with specific audiences. Don't oversell your product or service in a newsletter, but let readers know what you have available while providing them with useful information. As before, include your signature file. Figure 4.3 shows excerpts of an online newsletter distributed by E-Mazing, (*http://www.emazing.com*), which e-mails newsletters on any topic viewers pick, from window treatments to chicken salad recipes to baseball trivia.

E-zines, longer online publications that generally are found on a Web site, contain several stories or articles from multiple authors. They are a much more ambitious publication effort, but can also be effective marketing tools.

Press Releases

One of the most-used forms of self-promotion, the press release is as effective online as off. Update old press releases for electronic placement. Create new ones as you go along, covering everything from product announcements to news about changes in your Web site and notices of promotions or awards. You'll post these releases, along with reports, in appropriate areas of the Internet, as well as in an archive file on your Web site. Be sure to include your signature file, designating the appropriate contact person for your organization. (Figure 4.4 displays one of Jane Ogilvie's fictional press releases.) See Chapter 10 for more information on conducting an online PR campaign.

FAQs

Files of answers to **frequently asked questions (FAQs)** can be extremely useful with Internet newsgroups and some-mailing lists. Create several of these files in question-and-answer format. FAQ files usually contain little about your company except "Provided by" and your signature file. Users that provide valuable information about your industry or innovative ways

E-mail Newsletter

Small Business Tip of the Day
Monday April 1, 2002

Save Money On Your Mortgage NOW!!

New home loan, refinancing, home equity loan, debt consolidation, home improvement, FHA/VA loan available. Get a free mortgage quote. Click here for more details.

Develop A Disaster Chain-Of-Command For Your Business

In many small businesses, the owner has a critical role that is difficult for the business to replace. If you find that to be true in your business, you need a contingency plan in the event you are incapacitated.

Pick an individual who can function for you in your absence on behalf of the business. Through a limited power of attorney, you can give this individual as much or as little control as you'd like. If there's not a logical candidate for this role within your business, pick someone outside who could function appropriately.

Don't let your absence close down your business. A properly drawn legal document can insure that your wishes are honored when you can't see to it yourself.

- Rick Fields

FIVE Sony CDs of your choice!

EMAZING.com is giving away cool Sony stuff every day! You could win Today's Prize! Click here to enter.

ARCHIVES   MAIL TO A FRIEND

Figure 4.3. E-mail newsletter, *http://www.emazing.com*. Emazing.com is a service of Emazing, Inc. Copyright 2002. All rights reserved.

to use your product. Also create several product-specific FAQs to be used in locations other than newsgroups or to respond to e-mail.

FAQ files for newsgroups must conform to a specific format. To obtain this information, read the FAQs for the newsgroup you want to join. Files that smack of blatant advertising or promotion generally are not acceptable. Once FAQ files are posted, you can update them whenever you want. (Later in this chapter, you'll learn more about newsgroups.)

FOR IMMEDIATE RELEASE
CONTACT: JANE OGILVIE
DATE: MARCH 23, 2000
ogilvie@theperfectkernel.com

Lip-smacking, finger licking, caramel apple popcorn. Fragrant memories of amusement parks, dunking for apples, and Thanksgiving pies burst from freshly-popped kernels of The Perfect Kernel's latest popcorn flavor.

Caramel Crunch joins The Perfect Kernel's product line-up on Monday, March 29, 2002. It initiates a "Sweet String" of flavors to come. The Perfect Kernel's current "Savories" line includes white cheddar, sun-dried tomato, and green chili.

Katherine Gadsden, president of The Perfect Kernel, says, "This new line will satisfy the sweet tooth of baby boomers, without adding fat, cholesterol, or high calorie count. Our studies show this population worries more about salt than sugar."

The Perfect Kernel's Popcorn (www.theperfectkernel.com) is the premier supplier of gourmet popcorn to upscale movie theaters, restaurants, gift shops, and specialty food distributors.

For more information, call Marketing Manager Jane Ogilvie at 800-555-POPS, or go to our Web site at *http://www.theperfectkernel.com.*

Figure 4.4.   Sample press release for The Perfect Kernel.

TIPS FOR TIRED SITES

Do you make creative use of e-mail to drive traffic to and from your Web site? Can users e-mail their questions easily from every page of your site? When you collect e-mail addresses, do you ask people for permission to send information in the future, or are you wasting your time (and theirs) with a passive "guestbook"? Do you include sample reports, newsletters, or FAQs on your Web site to indicate their value? Sometimes you may deliberately choose to leave information off your Web site to pre-qualify a lead. By e-mailing for a price quote or calling about a free analysis, prospective customers indicate their interest and offer your sales staff an opportunity to move the sales process forward in person.

Newsgroups

Newsgroups are virtual communities of people who choose to discuss a shared interest on the Internet. Called USEnet, this older portion of the Internet hosts more than 100,000 discussions with millions of people participating worldwide. A given newsgroup that reaches even 0.01 percent of the Internet population is extraordinary—that's over 50,000 pre-qualified prospects interested in something related to your business. Over the 20 year history of USEnet, more than 700 million USEnet messages have been archived, creating a fascinating history of the Internet. Even now, about 1 **gigabyte** (billion bytes) of new information is circulated daily through this Internet function.

To find a list of newsgroups, point your browser to one of the following sites, where you can search newsgroups by keyword:

- *http://www.cyberfiber.com*

- *http://www.groups.google.com*

- *http://www.newsville.com/news/groups*

- *http://tile.net/news*

Major newsgroup categories are shown in Figure 4.5. Each of these categories is divided hierarchically into minor groups and then into more

BIZ	Business	SCI	Science topics
COMP	Computer-related topics	SOC	Social issues
MISC	Miscellaneous topics	TALK	Like Talk Radio—anything goes
NEWS	Current events	ALT	Other topics not covered above
REC	Recreation-related topics		

Figure 4.5. Major newsgroup categories.

detailed subgroups. Groups are named by continually appending words to the right of the prior word, separated by a period. The longer the name, the more focused the group. Jane Ogilvie might find newsgroups related to The Perfect Kernel at *rec.food.recipes* or *alt.college.food*. In most cases, you don't even need to subscribe; just click to read the messages that interest you.

For instance, point your browser to a listing of newsgroups and browse for likely ones, such as those shown in Figure 4.6. Select the desired subgroup(s) and read their FAQs. With most systems, you just click an icon to post your message. You can find out which of the biz newsgroups allow advertising, press releases, or product announcements by looking at their FAQs at *http://www.bizynet.com/faq-news.htm*. The Internet changes so rapidly that you should search for relevant newsgroups at least every six months. You can buy special software, such as News Rover (*http://www. newsrover.com*), to search newsgroups for you.

In a newsgroup you can post a message of your own or respond to a message someone else has submitted. The former is better because everyone in the group will receive your message. An answer to a message

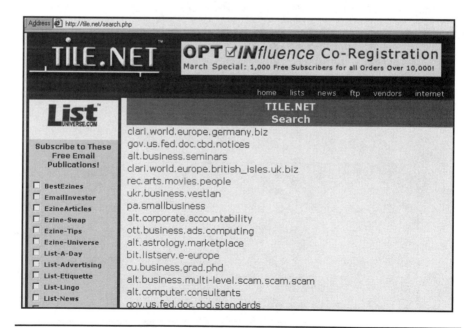

Figure 4.6. Sample listing of business newsgroups, *http://tile.net/search.php*. Courtesy List-Universe.com.

on a prior topic, called a **thread**, is sent only to those who have read the prior message. Although some newsgroups boast large numbers of participants, any one message may be seen by only a small percentage of them. Thus, the best strategy for newsgroups is to post consistently and frequently to an active thread.

The information you distribute online, called a **posting**, can be as short as one or two sentences or as long as a multimedia presentation. If you post a message that is nothing more than an ad on an inappropriate newsgroup, you will be considered a **spammer** and may be asked to leave the group. Generally, your postings will be effective as long as they contain real information of value to readers.

Some newsgroups are moderated by people who review messages for relevance before posting. Many readers prefer moderated groups because they tend to have higher-quality, less-repetitious content. As always, play observer initially. Stay in the background (**lurk**) for several weeks, reading messages without sending any of your own.

Once you find a few appropriate newsgroups, post messages asking for names of related groups. Follow those leads until you think you have located the majority of newsgroups appropriate to your business. Don't forget that asking questions enables you to leave your signature file, which builds recognition for your business.

To manage your newsgroup participation, create a series of folders and mailboxes using e-mail programs such as Eudora Pro (*http://www.eudora.com*) or Outlook Express (*http://www.microsoft.co/office/outlook/default.htm*). They enable you to place newsgroup postings or incoming mailing list subscriptions into appropriate folders, and allow you to **scan** (view subject lines without opening a message) them quickly each day.

Some people advocate using fake names in signature files and "From" lines of newsgroups to avoid receiving junk mail, but you may regret it from a business perspective. As Chris Gunn of BIZynet puts it, "That's like trying to do business with an unlisted phone number." Instead, direct newsgroup postings to an alternate e-mail address.

Net Courtesy

When you participate in the non-Web portion of the Internet, especially newsgroups, you're invading areas of cyberspace that people guard avidly against commercialization. If you don't honor the rules, you may get **flamed** (sent derogatory messages), receive spam, or be ousted by your ISP. Here are a few basic rules:

- If you use newsgroups or public mailing lists, be subtle.

- Never post blatant advertising in newsgroups. Use the third-party technique of a satisfied customer talking about your products or services in a positive way. You can also answer a question asked by someone else in the group.

- Keep your contributions full of real information.

- CAPITAL LETTERS are considered rude.

- Distribute information through e-mail only to those who have expressed an interest in receiving it.

- If you run your own newsgroup, always let people remove their names easily (unsubscribe).

E-mail Marketing

E-mail marketing has several components: One is simply handling e-mail correspondence promptly and professionally, essential to creating a good first impression for your company. Another is using e-mail to distribute the portfolio of info-tools you have just created. The third is crafting a special e-mail campaign designed to achieve sales or marketing objectives. With 10 billion e-mail messages per day sent in 2000, a number that is expected to rise to 35 billion per day by 2005, you can't afford to ignore this communication channel. E-mail reaches almost everyone on the Internet, even those with free e-mail accounts from Juno, Hotmail, Yahoo, or other Web sites.

Responding to E-mail

Set up an organized method of folders and files to categorize your saved e-mail correspondence, or use the tools in your e-mail program to organize your mail. To simplify your e-mail tasks and reduce the time it takes you to respond to inquiries, create a standard greeting that you can personalize quickly as a preface. This can be as simple as

> *Dear* _____,
>
> *Thank you for your interest in* _____. *You will find the answer to your question in the report that follows. Please let me know if I can be of further assistance.*

Then select or create a series of text files for the most common replies, or use any of your info-tools—FAQ files, reports, or blurbs—as prepackaged answers to speed response time. While you want to reduce the amount of time you spend responding to e-mail, you also want to get your reply opened. Be sure to use an intriguing subject line. Incorporate a **call to action** within your e-mail replies or info-tools. For example, invite readers to join your mailing list, respond with another e-mail, or visit your Web site (always include your URL with a hypertext link). And as always, end with your signature file, using a customized tag line or reply address if appropriate.

For an example, look at Figure 4.7, which provides excerpts from a marketing e-mail sent by AOL in response to a request for information. Large companies frequently take advantage of this low-cost method of communicating with their customers.

Try to keep your e-mail responses short and always check spelling and grammar. If possible, avoid attachments because many people either can't or won't open them due to a legitimate fear of viruses. Most of all, do not send unsolicited e-mail (**spam**) of any type. Spam generates ill will that no business can afford. The safest bet is to mail only to people who have requested information directly from you, have a preestablished business relationship, or who have subscribed to a mailing list.

Managing e-mail can become daunting when the number of messages reaches 300,000 a month, as it does for Dell. The task has become so complex that firms like MessageMedia (*http://www.messagemedia.com*) have grabbed this opportunity to manage e-mail for large companies. Right Now Technologies (*http://www.rightnow.com*) and Kana (*http://www.kana.com*) are among the other companies that offer expensive software to sort inquiries, generate automated responses, and tie the results into sophisticated e-commerce analyses.

Subj: AOL Advertising

Thank you for your interest in America Online (AOL). I have outlined some of AOL's advertising opportunities below. You have several options, however I recommend you look at the "search term" area of NetFind as one of the most cost effective forms of advertising on AOL. Please review the information and feel free to call or e-mail me with any questions.

You can find more advertising information online at AOL keyword MediaSpace , or on the web at *http://media.aol.com* (also fax on demand 800-832-8220). AOL offers special packages for any investment to help you harness the power of this medium. AOL can either drive traffic to your existing web site with banners located in highly targeted content areas or give you opportunities for content sponsorship.

Please feel free to contact me soon, if possible, as our most popular Search Terms are selling out rapidly. I have a number of success stories about businesses like yours who have used AOL very profitably. Please call me and tell me about your business so that I can help craft an online strategy with you. Thank you for your interest in advertising with AOL.

Best Regards,

Exxxx Tyyyyyyyy

AOL Interactive Marketing

415-XXX-XXXX, ETyyyyyyyy@aol.com

Figure 4.7. Responsive e-mailed blurb from AOL. "America Online," and "AOL" are registered trademarks of America Online, Inc. ©1997–2002 America Online, Inc. All rights reserved. Used with permission.

Mailbots

There is another option for responding to a high volume of e-mail. Newer e-mail programs and ISPs can help you respond automatically to routine messages using a program called a **mailbot** (a cross between mail and robot) or **autoresponder.** As seen in Figure 4.8, a mailbot automatically sends an appropriate message to anyone who sends an e-mail. Mailbots are often used to confirm receipt of an order placed at a Web site, or to acknowledge a support inquiry.

Hello. (This is an automated response. There is no need to reply.)

Your message regarding:
[NMT Web Help #514] /TBD/stats
has been received and assigned a request number of 514.
We will respond to this problem as quickly as possible.

In order to help us track the progress of this request, we ask that you include
the string [NMT Web Help #514] in the subject line of any further mail about
this particular request.

For example:
Subject: [NMT Web Help #514] /TBD/stats

You may do this simply by replying to this email.

Figure 4.8. Service mailbot from New Mexico TechNet, *http://www.technet. nm.org.* Courtesy New Mexico Technet.

The easiest way to set up a mailbot is to designate a separate e-mail address under your master account or create an alternate one. When a mailbot is active, you can't receive regular e-mail messages, so put only the alternate address into an auto-reply status, sometimes called **vacation mode.** (Vacation mode is usually used to tell senders you are away and direct them elsewhere for immediate assistance.) Or you can specify that messages with certain words in the subject line receive a particular reply.

Instead of a vacation message, write a blurb about a product or service. If you want to get more specific, create different mailbots at different addresses or with different subject lines, each used for a different reply. Jane Ogilvie's fictional mailbot is shown in Figure 4.9. You can see why this powerful and inexpensive Internet tool may be worth your time.

Many new versions of e-mail programs like Netscape Communicator, Eudora, and Outlook Express let you set up automated replies easily with their own "rule" functions. In a large company, you may need to ask your network administrator how to handle this. Software like VarPro (*http://www.varpro.com*) lets you manage multiple autoresponder

> Your free sample of The Perfect Kernel's Flavored Popcorn is on the way! For a full list of products, check out our Web site, The Perfect Kernel (*http://www.theperfect kernel.com*). You may place your order online or by fax. In a hurry? Call 800-555-POPS. Thank you for your interest in The Perfect Kernel's Popcorn.
>
> (Follow with signature file).

Figure 4.9. Sample mailbot for The Perfect Kernel.

messages. To establish mailbots from your Web site, ask your developer or Web host for assistance. Some may charge a modest setup and/or a monthly fee and offer their users 25–30K of free storage space for each incoming message. You can usually find information about vacation mode or mailbots in your e-mail program's help section, or in the FAQ file from your ISP or Web host.

Listservers for Info-Tool Distribution

Once you've invested time creating info-tools, it's worth distributing them more broadly than individual responses to e-mail queries. A **listbot** or **listserver** program automatically processes a series of requests for information. Unlike an ordinary mailbot, a listserver can be **concatenated**. That is, prospects and customers who mail to it can be asked to do something that will result in another message being e-mailed without further intervention. A listserver acts like an automated sales clerk or fax-back service, responding to requests for more information by sending the appropriate document. You can save enormous time and costs by having dozens (or hundreds) of different files sent automatically to different audience segments.

Listservers are often used when viewers register on a Web site to receive e-mails in the future. The approach where people must actively **opt-in** to receive information is considered more ethical than requiring users to "opt-out." And, of course, always provide directions in each message about how users can **unsubscribe** (remove their names) from the list. Many Web sites let users specify what type of e-mail they want: Special offers only? Industry information? New product releases or upgrades? Monthly newsletter? This approach not only helps viewers control their e-mail, but increases the positive response to your mailings.

Because these recipients have requested information, you can offer marketing materials with as hard or soft a sell as you find appropriate. A soft-sell newsletter, e-zine, or info-tool with links to further information is a great way to utilize a listserver, but so are product spec sheets, catalogs, new-product announcements, trade-show invitations, or hard-edged discount offers. As usual, include your signature file and your URL.

Choosing who maintains your listserver depends on convenience and price. If you don't have a database of e-mail addresses, or aren't collecting them on your Web site, you can distribute info-tools through opt-in public mailing lists or rented lists of e-mail addresses. If you already have addresses, check with your ISP or Web host about setting up a listserver, or use a Web mailing service that offers everything from e-mail templates to list management and reporting.

Existing Public Mailing Lists

Once you've decided what your mailing will be about—swimwear, space aliens, wok cooking, Elvis Presley, hood ornaments for Mustangs—whatever is related to your product or service—you can search for public e-mail lists on that topic. These opt-in lists consist of people who have actively subscribed by sending their e-mail addresses to a listserver. There are over 53,000 public mailing lists (out of more than 200,000 total lists) on the Internet, packed with millions of pre-qualified prospects.

As seen on TopicA (*http://www.topica.com*) in Figure 4.10, you can search for appropriate lists by keyword. There are additional lists of lists at:

- *http://paml.net*

- *http://tile.net/lists*

- *http://www.lsoft.com/lists/listref.html*

From most of these sites, you can subscribe to a list or **upload** desired text to the listserver. Once you have subscribed, you will receive an updated list of the most recent messages. From then on, you will get a copy via e-mail of anything posted by any other subscriber and you can post an e-mail message that will be distributed to everyone else.

As an exercise, subscribe to the iMarketing list, which deals with Internet marketing. Send an e-mail to *imarketing-subscribe@topica.com*. In the subject line and body of the message, type *subscribe imarketing*. That's it!

Figure 4.10. Mailing list (newsletter) search, *http://www.topica.com.* ©2002 Topica, Inc.

Before you start posting to a list, always study incoming messages to understand the nature of the list and acceptable communications. A few lists, such as the Internet Advertising Discussion List at *http://www.o-a.com/index.html* with its 10,000 names, allow specific sponsors and promotions (e.g., a discount for readers who buy from your site). Others strongly resist such messages.

Although you can usually find the e-mail addresses of others who are on the list, never, never, send them unsolicited, private e-mail, although you can offer to let them contact you for additional information. You can certainly scan that information to confirm that you are participating in a list with an appropriate target audience for your company. Whether you use a public mailing list, your own list of names, or rent a list, be sure you subscribe to the list yourself!

Back at The Perfect Kernel, Jane Ogilvie decides that she'll start with a public mailing list, but that developing her own list of e-mail addresses needs to become a priority.

Rent-a-Reader

If you can't find a public mailing list, and don't have enough names on your own list, you can always rent e-mail addresses from opt-in list brokers. Because these lists are relatively new, they are not always "clean" leads. Most of them, like PostMasterDirect.com (*http://www.postmaster direct.com*) or Colonize (*http://www.colonize.com*, seen in Figure 4.11), send your e-mail for you, without actually providing you the addresses. If you rent a list, encourage recipients to link to your own mailing list subscription form so you capture these names for yourself. Rented names may not be as well qualified as names on a list you build yourself; although they are supposed to have opted-in, recipients may think that what you're sending fits in their junk-mail category. Hundreds of places rent lists. In addition to the above, try:

- NetCreations: *http://www.netcreations.com*

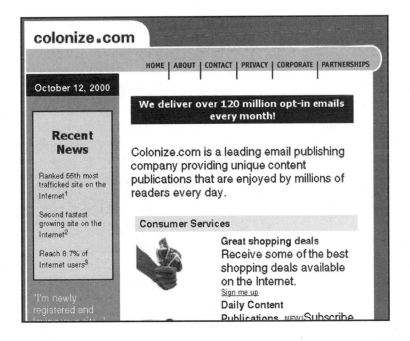

Figure 4.11. An opt-in e-mail company, *http://www.colonize.com*. Courtesy Colonize.com, Inc.

- The Direct E-mail List Source: *http://www.copywriter.com/lists*

- Best Mailing: *http://www.bestmailing.com*

Or go to one of the search engines for a list. For example, look at *http://dir.yahoo.com/Business_and_Economy/Business_to_Business /Marketing_and_Advertising/Direct_Marketing/Direct_Email.*

Create Your Own Mailing Lists

As any sales or marketing person knows, names and addresses are worth their weight in gold. Make a commitment to develop a solid database of customers, leads, and qualified prospects over the long-term. Where will you find all those names? Adding a subscription link to your Web site and signature file is a no-brainer. But names and e-mail addresses may come from many sources besides the opt-in form on your Web site. For instance, you can collect e-mail addresses:

- during customer service or tech-support calls

- at trade shows or association meetings, and from business cards

- from e-mail you receive

- from written guestbooks at parties, seminars, speeches, or other events you host

- from records kept by sales & marketing, customer service, and accounting staff

The Direct Marketing Association considers it acceptable to send an initial e-mail to people with whom you already have a minimal business relationship. This initial e-mail should ask permission to continue sending messages, with either a link to subscribe or a simple way to unsubscribe (**opt-out**).

Distributing Your Information

If you've collected your own list of e-mail addresses, you need to find a service to actually manage the distribution. You can use a free distribution service like TopicA (*http://www.topica.com*), as long as you are willing to post sponsorship notices or advertisers. Yahoo offers something similar at *http://groups.yahoo.com*. If you don't want someone else's messages to appear, look at for-fee offerings or at a mailing list management company like-mail-List.com (*http://www.mail-list.com*). Alternately, you can ask your ISP provider for prices, which may range from nothing to $100 for setup and/or a monthly fee of $5 to $30 depending on the size and nature of your list. Some ISPs and listserver services offer an annual rate or charge a transaction fee instead of a monthly fee. For instance, Bcentral.com offers a listbot at *http://www.bcentral.com/products/lb/default.asp*. Their monthly plan runs $29.95 for 1,000 e-mails, while their "value" program charges $299 for an annual plan with up to 10,000 e-mails a month.

The service may ask you to select from options like those that follow to establish the appropriate listserver for your needs:

- **Auto:** The listserver performs all subscription requests without your prior approval.

- **Open:** Users can add or drop themselves, but not someone else, without prior approval.

- **Closed:** You, as owner, approve all subscriptions. This is often used for a paid subscription list.

- **Private:** Only people who are on the list can see who else is on the list.

- **Fully moderated:** You approve any incoming message before it can be-mailed to the list. Potential participants view moderated lists as an indication of stronger content.

- **Externally moderated:** You approve only messages from outside the-mailing list.

- **Maximum message length:** You must approve any e-mail larger than the preset length you've established.

It may take several days to set up your mailing list. As the list owner, you will receive e-mail notification of all "subscribe" and "unsubscribe" requests. Like bulk mail at the post office, e-mail to lists is usually given a lower priority than regular e-mail and will take longer to be sent from a server over the Internet. Most list software allows you to send an automatic "probe" message to confirm the e-mail addresses of subscribers and remove any faulty addresses. Above all, subscribe to your own list!

Post to a List of Lists

Once your mailing list is running, place announcements around the Internet giving the listserver address, which will be something like *info-newsletter@theperfectkernel.com*. Be sure to add it to several "Lists of Mailing Lists." Your mailing list address will be copied to hundreds of nodes where major network users reside, enabling you to build a larger list. Some services ask you to send an e-mail message with your announcement to the-mail master. Others have you fill out a questionnaire, such as the one at Tile.Net, *http://tile.net/lists/signup.php*.

You should soon receive dozens of messages telling you that someone has joined or dropped off your list. Neither requires any action on your part. To find out how your list is doing at any given time, simply send the message "Who" to your own list. The e-mail addresses of all subscribers should bounce back to you. Unless you have restricted access, any subscriber on your list can do the same thing.

You will need to nurture your list. Set up a regular schedule to monitor the traffic. This is a good time to create a chronological **info-log**, like the one in Figure 4.12. Note each scheduled task, and log when tools are created, when they are posted, and the volume of response each one generates.

If responses to your mailing list start to lag, keep the postings hot and encourage others to do the same. Invite important and interesting people to subscribe, or take several aliases and stir up discussion yourself.

This is your list, so you can end each of your messages with a call to action. Invite recipients to ask for your sales literature through private e-mail, to visit your Web site, or to request ordering information. Of course, include your signature file.

Secrets of Effective E-mail Marketing

An offline direct-mail campaign requires that you design and print a flyer or other material, purchase or rent multiple direct-mailing lists,

Scheduled Task	Description	By	Date Created	Date Posted	Location & Notes (e.g. # responses)
Signature File	J. Ogilvie;	jo	11/14/01	11/14/01	
Blurb #1	New flavor announcement	jo	12/1/01	12/1/01	
Report #1	Corn species	jo	12/5/01	12/10/01	
Press Release	Corporate backgrounder	jo	1/12/02	1/12/02	
FAQ	Making good popcorn	jo	1/15/02	1/15/02	
Newsletter	January issue	jo	1/20/02	1/23/02	
Subscribe RITIM-L	mailing list on imarketing	jo	1/26/02	1/26/02	
Ck newsgroup	alt.college.food	jo	1/28/02	1/29/02	
FAQ	franchising	jo	2/13/02	2/15/02	
Ck. newsgroup	rec.food.recipe	jo	2/18/02	2/18/02	
New mailing list	healthy snack food eaters	jo	2/26/02	2/26/02	
Announce list	at mail-list.com	jo	2/27/02	2/27/02	
Post Report #1	to mailing list	jo	2/28/02	2/28/02	
Create mailbot	for auto-response to list	jo	3/4/02	3/402	

Figure 4.12.   Chronological info-log.

and mail it out. You may have to buy or rent many mailing lists to have a significant number of "real" prospects for your products and services. Old-fashioned direct mail can cost anywhere from several dollars to several hundred dollars per lead. For much less—perhaps fractions of a penny per message—you can e-mail your announcement or newsletter to tens of thousands.

Are e-mail campaigns worth the effort? Absolutely! Research shows that direct e-mail can produce a response rate at least as good as the 1- to 2-percent response of regular direct mail. Some studies show results 20 times as cost effective as print, leading to a higher return on investment.

According to DoubleClick, in 2001 more than 37 percent of shoppers purchased immediately after clicking through from a permission-based (opt-in) e-mail. That's up from 20 percent in 2000.

The immediacy of direct e-mail makes it great for impatient business owners. The "Click Here" call to action generally leads to a response within 48 hours of e-mail delivery. Furthermore, it's easy to segment your list to tailor your message to the audience most likely to respond. Asking readers on the sign-up page what type of messages (sometimes called opt-in interest categories) they want to receive is likely to produce a better response rate and ultimately, increased revenues.

Creating and mailing electronic newsletters has become far simpler than it used to be. Many Web-based services like Constant Contact (*http://www.constantcontact.com/home.jsp*) provide pre-formatted HTML templates, e-mail testing, mailing list uploads, automatic tracking, and reports on click-through results. Similar programs may be found at:

- *http://www.exacttarget.com*

- *http://www.mailermailer.com*

- *http://www.postmastergeneral.com*

- *http://www.bcentral.com/products/lb/default.asp*

Ready, Set, Mail

As with any advertising compaign, success will derive 40 percent from the right audience (the list); 40 percent from the right offer (the content), and 20 percent from the right creative (the style of your mailing). An e-mail campaign benefits from standard direct mail techniques that you would use offline:

- Research your target audience. Know what matters to them and what other newsletters they read.

- Subscribe to competing newsletters and to others with similar topics.

- Be sure your name is on the list of recipients.

- Use pre-publicity to build anticipation and encourage recipients to open the-mail. In any case, publicize the newsletter.

- Even a short-term product campaign should have a minimum of three repeat mailings.

- For an effective branding program, stick to a schedule.

Of course, there are a few cyber-only requirements:

- Test your mailing first with a few recipients on all the major e-mail services, and ascertain which recipients can handle text only and which ones can handle HTML.

- The subject line must grab readers' attention strongly enough to open the message.

- Be prepared to handle unsubscribe requests, complaints, flaming, questions, and sales. Make sure you have staff who can promptly answer each e-mail you receive.

HTML vs. Text E-mail

The debate over text versus HTML e-mail has generated megabytes of online discussion. Text e-mail files are very small, accepted by all e-mail programs, easy to create, and flexible.

By comparison, HTML newsletters offer better presentation (see Figure 4.13). They are easier to read, with stylish graphics and formatting that maintain the look and feel of your Web site. Unlike text e-mails, which must be tracked by hand, it's possible to track automatically when HTML files have been opened and monitor click-throughs by link. On the downside, HTML newsletters are slower to download, take longer to create, and may crash old browser and e-mail applications.

There are some ways to overcome these difficulties. If you're planning a mailing in the thousands or more, work with a firm that specializes in e-mail. They can send out a **sniffer**, a test e-mail that determines which addresses on your list accept text and which accept HTML. While it's cheaper to do your own list, there's no easy way to know which

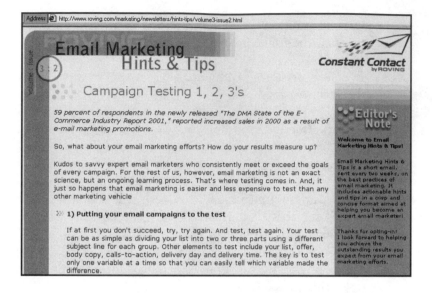

Figure 4.13. Sample HTML newsletter sent by e-mail, *http://www.roving.com/ marketing/newsletters/hints-tips/volume3_issue2.html*. Courtesy Roving Software, Inc. creator of Constant Contact.®

recipients are which. Furthermore, your ISP or Web host may limit the quantity of names on your list or block the-mailing as spam.

By creating at least two versions of your newsletter, one in text and one in HTML, you can avoid crash-and-burn aggravation on HTML files. Some companies also produce a separate version for AOL. If you don't use an e-mail service, create your own templates and use them consistently to reduce the time and cost of creating newsletters.

In the end, it's a business decision. Does the information you want to convey justify using graphics? Will HTML produce a higher response rate? Is that enough to justify increased production costs or the use of a Web-based e-mail service provider?

Enticing E-mail

Not surprisingly, many of the same principles of good print direct mail pieces also apply to online newsletters. Utilize the principles of AIDA, described in Chapter 1: Attention, Interest, Desire, Action. A powerful appeal in the Subject line of the e-mail message attracts attention and increases the likelihood that the e-mail will be opened. Keep it short and include a benefit. Good content—something that is more than one long sales pitch—builds interest. A clean layout, with plenty of white space, will help. Detailing benefits helps create desire. The calls to action are simple and effective, usually links to your Web site.

From a content perspective, keep the copy interesting, informative, and vibrant. Obviously the material you use will be driven by the nature of your business and audience, what interests them, and the goal of the publication. Consider commenting on industry issues or providing case studies, testimonials, or success stories. For hobby sites, a "how to" story works well. For many products, hints or tips on how to get the best out of a purchase will build interest. Some readers may respond to features like sweepstakes or contests; others may find them offensive.

Keep the newsletter to less than three pages. Use color and layout to make the newsletter easy to read. Here are some other design tips to consider:

- For branding purposes, try to keep the newsletter consistent with your Web site design.

- Limit the file size to 25K, which means go easy on the graphics, especially photos, unless they are really essential.

- Avoid tables.

- When linking to pages of your Web site, be sure to include the actual URL, not just "click here." Use links from a Table of Contents at the top of the newsletter so readers can immediately reach their area of interest.

- Include only a brief summary of a story in a newsletter, perhaps no more than two paragraphs. Link to a more complete article on your Web site.

- Follow the Web writing principles discussed in Chapter 6 and absolutely, positively proof your work.

- Include a privacy statement and remind readers why they are receiving the newsletter (e.g., where they signed up for it).

- Let readers know that back issues are archived on the Web site (use a link). On that page of the site, include a call to action to send the page to a friend.

- Provide obvious links for actions to forward the newsletter to a colleague, subscribe, unsubscribe, change preferences, provide feedback, or print a text version.

You'll find an excellent product guide for e-mail marketing at Netpreneur (*http://www.netpreneur.org/connect/am/email_mktg/#1*). For additional information about e-mail marketing, check out:

- *http://www.everythinge-mail.net*

- *http://www.wilsonweb.com/cat/cat.cfm?page=1&subcat=me_Email-Gen*

- *http://www.ezine-tips.com*

- *http://www.clickz.com/em_mkt/em_mkt*

- *http://www.optinnews.com*

- *http://www.digitrends.net/marketing/13640.html*

Reaping What You've Sown

You can use the power of e-mail to follow up on hundreds of leads by responding with another, already-created info-tool. When you see from a message that someone is ready to become a customer, you may want to individualize the response or close the sale offline.

This process works for The Perfect Kernel. A few days after announcing her own list, Jane watches it begin to grow. When she reaches 100 members, she posts some of her previously created info-tools and starts to participate actively. Over time, her list increases to more than

3,000 people and the volume of retail sales goes up by 10 percent due to electronic orders.

You now have several distribution channels for your info-tools: standard e-mail for manual responses, mailbots for automated responses, public e-mailing lists, and your own list on an automated listserver. Whenever you change or add to your info-tools, be sure to post them to the various lists and newsgroups you've joined. Now let's turn to online services as yet another way to establish an electronic presence on the Internet.

Marketing on Online Services

More than 50 million people currently subscribe to an online service that provides e-mail, Internet access, and content. By far the largest is America Online (AOL), with 33 million subscribers. It far outdistances its closest competitor, the Microsoft Network (MSN), which has over 7 million paid subscribers and 6.3 percent of the market. The free service at United Online (Juno and Netzero) has 6.1 million users, while Prodigy and CompuServe are down to 3.5 million and 1.8 million respectively.

These services offer a self-contained online universe, complete with shopping, news, and communications services like chat rooms. Subscribers who are timid about the Web or who have slow modems may use only an online service. Since the majority of subscribers to these vendors are families at home, online services may represent a significant market for you depending on your product or business.

If you choose to market directly to online service customers, be aware that membership changes rapidly and that demographics can be difficult to nail down. Web portals have to some extent replaced these services as destination points and gateways. Online services are price-competitive with ISPs, averaging $20 to $25 per month for unlimited user access.

Depending on your business, you may want to subscribe to all or none of these services. At the very least, try each of their free-trial offers to see whether your target audience uses the service. As with everything else on the Internet, the best way to learn about an online service's customers and culture is to observe quietly in the background. Of course, you will drop any online service whose marketing results after several months do not cover at least the monthly expense of that service.

Online Communities of Interest

Communities on online services cover everything from aquariums to zoology, from politics to pop stars. Since they combine real-time chats, conferences, and/or instant messaging with close equivalents of newsgroups (message boards) and mailing lists (on-demand libraries), communities offer the potential for multi-format, repeat communication with potential customers. Such repeat visibility helps visitors remember your name and company.

Search the available communities for the ones most likely to attract users who fit your profile of a good prospect. For instance, on AOL you might select the Workplace community (seen in Figure 4.14); on MSN, the Business category. If you sell a product or service that would be of interest to those in another area, choose that community. Prodigy strongly discourages advertising and promotion, but you might try the Small Business/Home Forum, as long as you are subtle. Otherwise, your

Figure 4.14. Workplace community on AOL. AOL screenshot ©2002 America Online, Inc. Used with permission.

Prodigy marketing will be restricted to purchased advertising. Remember, the purpose of all this is to create easy pathways to the largest possible number of potential customers.

Each community has a system operator, or **Sysop**, who is responsible for managing its activities and publicizing it on the online service. Each time you move to a new community, study it until you understand its style and the quirks of its Sysop. If you are an expert on a subject, you can use these communities to become better known, to establish credibility, and by extension to promote your company.

You'll usually find three or four elements to a community:

- **Message boards,** sometimes called **bulletin boards,** operate like newsgroups, with people posting comments or queries on a topic and others responding at different times. Message boards can be thought of as a no-host radio call-in program, limited only by the topic. Many individual sites, not just the online services, include message boards.

- **Chats, Instant Messaging, Conferences,** or **Forums** for real-time communication—These may or may not be scheduled and may or may not be moderated. In the case of scheduled and moderated conferences or forums, the session may include a guest expert. Again, many individual sites now offer similar features in an effort to build their own loyal communities of interest.

- **Personal Web Pages**—Instead of posting text-based material, most of these online communities now offer the opportunity for everyone to create a small, template-based home page.

- **Libraries** are "on-demand" application programs uploaded by others, including both free and **shareware** (low-cost) programs. At any time, you can get a report of how many people have downloaded your program from the library. If your program is fun or useful, expect hundreds of downloads per month.

Visit communities on the online services by going to one of the following:

- *http://communities.msn.com/home*

- *http://www.aol.com/community/directory.html*

- *http://geocities.yahoo.com/home* (a community of free Web pages)

- *http://www.communities.prodigy.net*

At The Perfect Kernel, Jane decides to start by joining AOL, then adding MSN and other online services. First, she creates a template-based home page for The Perfect Kernel at *http://hometown.aol.com/ hmtwn123/index.htm*, using some of her previously created reports as content. Then she asks her programmer to create a screensaver and wallpaper of popcorn popping with the company name appearing in the kernels. She uploads this to the screensaver section in Fun & Games portion of software libraries. With these tasks accomplished, she'll be ready to announce their availability and her AOL home page to relevant AOL online communities.

More about Message Boards

Once you contribute a program or home page, announce it in the message board and in chat rooms for that community and on any other appropriate (meaning on-topic) board. Always include your signature file so that members will be exposed to your company name and know how to reach you.

Then start reading postings regularly, respond to questions if you know the answer, and comment on the messages posted by others. If people ask for information about your products, forward a blurb and tell them where to find other info-tools you have uploaded. If their request appears in the message section, post your blurb there. If the request comes from private e-mail, send your blurb to the individual's e-mail address only. Be sure to track all these actions, as well as the number of responses from each source, in your info-log.

Jane selects two channels for The Perfect Kernel—"Careers & Work (Workplace)" and the "Food & Recipe" section of "House & Home." She sends a notice about the screensaver to several of the "Food & Recipe" message boards and begins to respond to queries. As her e-mail inbox fills with requests for information from AOL subscribers, Jane responds with a blurb. Jane cycles the questions she gets into more info-tools, blurbs, and reports, which she adds to her online marketing arsenal.

Jane finds several other areas indirectly related to her marketing needs. The franchising message board draws participants looking for business opportunities. As it happens, The Perfect Kernel offers franchises to qualified people who want to distribute its popcorn or open a storefront of their own. While she can't advertise on that message board, she is able to identify some potential franchisees. As a result of her online activity, Jane sells six franchises around the country over the next few months—excellent results from these early online marketing steps.

Chats, Instant Messaging, Conferences, and Forums

Conferences on CompuServe or Forums on AOL allow you to showcase your own and your company's experience. You can always participate in conferences arranged by others, which at least permits you to leave your signature file. It's better, however, to host a conference in your area of expertise. The Sysop of the particular forum or board arranges conferences. Sysops may be hard to reach, and it may be difficult to schedule a conference on a particularly busy forum.

As the moderator of a conference, you may make a presentation, perhaps with files delivered before hand to conference attendees. Participants could number from several dozen to several thousand. During the conference, any attendee can type in a comment that other participants can then respond to.

Make sure all attendees know how to reach you afterward, since you can't market your services directly during the conference. Conference participants are a self-selected list of likely prospects. You're on your own, though, to follow up on leads from people who contact you later. For The Perfect Kernel, Jane arranges with the Sysop to lead a chat on unusual ways to use popcorn in cooking.

What's Next?

In this chapter, you've seen how to use info-tools as an independent marketing effort, and as a way to drive traffic. As you have seen, some of these info-tools are the online equivalent of offline direct-marketing techniques, from business cards (signature files) to direct mail (e-mail campaigns). Other tools are unique to the Internet: chat rooms, conferences, software upload centers, and others. All these techniques help get

TIPS FOR TIRED SITES

Trying to draw a specific audience to your Web site from among the likely subscribers to AOL, MSN, or another online service without paying high advertising rates? Create a free home page that is designed specifically for that target market on that service. Put a link on the mini-home page to your "real" Web site. Don't forget to announce your page in message boards, chat rooms, and elsewhere on the online service, using your signature block whenever possible. You can do this on as many services as you like, including Geocities, which is free.

your name out to the audience you are trying to reach, build credibility, and set you apart from your competition.

Many of the real-time communication techniques described in the online service section also take place on the Web through portals like Yahoo and iVillage. Be sure to search for existing chats, online seminars, and message boards on topics relevant to your business. In Chapter 9, we'll look at how to use online communication techniques—chat rooms, instant messaging, message boards, and online conferences—to build a community of interest on your own site. Using these methods to build site loyalty and bring visitors back for return visits will eventually pay off in new customers and increased sales.

The business planning and non-Web preliminaries are over! It's time to tackle your Web site. We're still not at the pretty picture stage, but it's getting close. In the next chapter we'll look at the essential steps for planning site development, including budgets, timelines, issuing a request for quote, selecting service providers, and picking a domain name.

5

Step 5a: Plan Your Web Site

As you've realized by now, the Internet is a sinfully rich marketing and sales tool. To truly take advantage of the Internet, you must develop a Web site that meets your business goals while ensuring customer satisfaction. In this chapter we'll explore planning a Web site, from estimating costs and selecting service providers to choosing a domain name. These issues, along with the design and storefront considerations discussed in the next two chapters, will enable you to complete the fifth step of Internet success: building an effective Web site.

Since you will most likely contract with other companies for Web design and hosting, we will consider how to select companies that best meet your needs. Most of all, we will focus on the importance of planning and research before you start spending money. In this chapter you'll learn about:

- Preplanning your site, including staff, budget and timeline

- Hiring service providers: ISP, Web host, designer and/or programmer

- Issuing a Request for Quote (RFQ) or Request for Proposal (RFP)

- The design process

- Registering a domain name

Preplanning Pays Off

Your online business plan was strategic; now it's time for tactics. First, review your Web planning form, which tied together your goals, objectives and audience in Figure 3.9, and your online business plan. You can use these tools to explain the project when talking to service providers, to recruit Web team participants, to forge consensus, or to justify the project to higher-ups. Add one more planning document to your stack, the Web implementation worksheet seen in Figure 5.1.

Web Site _____ Date _____

Web Producer/Coordinator _____ Contact_____

Webmaster/Developer   _____ Contact_____

Web Content Editor   _____ Contact_____

Other Staff (Name/Title)   _____ Contact_____

Goal/Target Audience   _____

Summary Description:

Schedule

Developer Conference   _____   Navigation to test   _____

Comps   _____   Content ready to install   _____

Standards Book   _____   Site testing starts   _____

Templates   _____   Site Launch   _____

Budget   **Objectives**

Outside Development   _____   Viewers/month   _____

Special Elements   Sales #/month   _____

 (e.g. Animation)   _____   Average $/sales   _____

Marketing   _____   Revenue/month   _____

In-House Labor   _____   ROI   _____

Figure 5.1. Web implementation worksheet. ©2002 Watermelon Mountain Web Marketing.

Start the document with a short summary statement for your site. Do you remember cereal-box contests, where you had to complete the phrase "I like fruity SugarOhs because..." in 25 words or less? Writing the summary statement for your Web site is much like that. If you can't say what you want your site to accomplish and how you will do it in less than one paragraph, you haven't fully thought it through.

As you go through various planning steps, complete the sections about staffing, budget, and timeline. This worksheet and all the cost estimates belong in your Web notebook with your other planning documents.

Set Up a Team

Developing a Web site can be daunting. Leonardo da Vinci was probably the only person who could have done it all himself—from stunning graphic design to elegant code, from mastering the aesthetic vocabulary of six different media to computing bandwidth requirements. Ordinary mortals need to designate a team and team leader (is that you?) to select and meet with various Web providers. The team will also evaluate and test designs, provide content, suggest site structure, schedule material for updates, and coordinate with other business operations. "Team" notwithstanding, you still need a senior person with decision-making authority who has the final say and who signs off on everything.

Besides those involved with information systems, the team should include representatives from any department that will provide content and/or is expected to interact with users. This may mean representatives from corporate communications, human resources, customer service, or marketing. If you plan to generate revenue from your site, include product/service managers and staff from sales, order processing, shipping, accounting, and catalog development.

Launching and publicizing your site when it is ready may be an in-house marketing responsibility, or it may be handled by your Web designer, Web host, PR firm, or advertising agency. In any case, you'll want a marketing person to oversee the activities conducted by these contractors and ensure that Web promotion is coordinated with overall business marketing.

There are no fixed roles for participants in a Web project, but there are responsibilities that must be covered. Nor are there rules saying what must be done in-house and what should be done by an outside provider. Even the distribution of labor among outside providers is in flux. Both hosting services and developers, for example, may offer to do such initial promotion tasks as submitting to search engines. Some developers do graphic design; others do not.

A Web site is not a one-time project. Like Tennyson's river, it goes on forever. In your staffing plans, be sure to identify who will be responsible downstream for:

- Managing the site

- Ensuring that users receive technical and customer support

- Updating the site

- Responding to communications from users via phone and e-mail

- Monitoring and analyzing site traffic and providing feedback.

Consider preexisting workloads before tasking members of your team. What you think will be a one-time, 20-hour task completed within a month may easily turn into a task that takes 20 hours per week indefinitely. You may need a minimum of three people with different skill sets:

1. **Web development coordinator/producer:** As the primary contact for all the various vendors and in-house personnel, this person assumes overall responsibility for acquiring and delivering any content needed for the main pages of the site, deciding which upgrades and features to add, monitoring performance, and following through when decisions are made.

2. **Web editor:** Someone must be responsible for creating the initial content (or at least providing raw material to a copywriter) and making content changes on an ongoing basis. If you have an online store, the editor or another person must be responsible for merchandising, product copy and photography, and decisions about pricing, sales events, and special promotions.

3. **Webmaster:** This person, who is often supplied by your Web development company, is responsible for fixing technical problems with the Web site. If the site is down, if a link needs to be changed,

if there are performance problems, or if users e-mail a complaint about site operations, the Webmaster is the person who will respond.

In a really small business, the first two hats may be worn by the owner, who already has a complete millinery wardrobe! Larger companies may create a larger Web unit within their organization.

Plan for Updates

Fresh content keeps your site interesting to repeat visitors. Updating your site daily, weekly, or monthly is an important consideration. You'll need to decide who will be responsible for providing new content, as well as who will actually make the changes. If your site has many pages that change frequently, it will become expensive to pay your developer for changes by the hour. Tell your developer which pages you want to be able to change on your own; you may even want the ability to add and remove pages yourself. You can request an administrative form accessible from ordinary word processors or browsers for changing text and uploading new graphics.

If you want to be able to update many pages, it may be cost-effective to buy a tool like Page Publisher content-updating software (*http://www.interactivetools.com/products/pagepublisher/*) that lets many non-technical staff share content-updating responsibilities and upload changes to the site without learning HTML. New site-updating services, such as Suite Source (*http://www.suitesource.com*), let you update standard pages without developer assistance for a per-page, monthly fee.

Establish User Hardware/Software Needs for Your Site

You rarely have a guarantee about your users' computer skills, equipment, software, or navigational savvy on the Web, but this is helpful for site development. If you are upgrading an existing site, you may have statistics showing the platforms, browsers, and browser versions that your visitors currently use. If not, plan a quick survey or at least ascertain whether your audience is more likely to access your site during the day from work, or during the evening from home. Plan to have in-house whatever hardware and software you expect most of your customers to have. Although the majority of testing is the responsibility of your Web developer, you should duplicate a typical viewer's experience before signing off and accepting the work.

Remember that the more multimedia you put on your site, the more sophisticated the user software and hardware required, and the more likely some viewers will be shut out.

Budget

A budget allows you to manage expenses for the Web site. It lets you compare estimated costs for online advertising, sales, and customer support. It ensures that you have thought through potentially hidden expenses and forces you to set priorities in terms of features and time. As we discussed in previous chapters, thinking about money makes you ask whether the investment of time and dollars for a Web site will produce the desired results, or whether there are better ways to expend limited financial and personnel resources.

Costs for Web development range from free (see "Freebies and Features" in Chapter 6) to tens of thousands of dollars. As you can surmise by looking at some of the sites in this book, there is no upper limit. A Fortune 500 company may spend anywhere from $500,000 to more than $5 million to create a transaction-intensive, electronic commerce site!

Why the range? Prices for Web development vary by size and complexity of the site, geographic region (vendors on the coasts are more expensive), and the size and reputation of the design house you select. Some businesses have found that Web developers outside the country are less expensive than those in the United States.

Costs for full-service Web development have dropped in the last year, with the collapse of the dot-com culture and more Web development companies chasing fewer customers. As the chart in Figure 5.2 indicates, the range of Web site budgets leaves room for businesses of any size. For context, consider a recent BtoBonline survey *(http://www.btobonline.com/webPriceIndex)*, which showed *median* development costs in 2001 as:

- $65,000 for a small, high-end brochureware site, with an Intranet database, a little Flash animation, and some updating tools

Budget	Total Sample	Type of site Media/Portals/ Info/Publishers	Exclusively Online Sales
None	4%	7%	4%
$1 to 100	2%	3%	1%
$100 to 500	9%	10%	6%
$501 to 1,000	10%	5%	11%
$1,001 to 5,000	34%	20%	31%
$5,001 to 10,000	13%	11%	7%
$10,001 to 99,999	22%	28%	27%
$100,000 to 999,999	8%	15%	9%
over $1Million	1%	2%	3%
Average	$36,579	$77,788	$67,858

Figure 5.2.   Budget range for Web site investment, *http://cyberatlas.internet. com/big_picture/hardware/article/0,1323,5921_234331,00.html.* Reprinted with permission. ©2002 INT Media Group, Inc. All rights reserved.

- $125,000 for a medium-size site, with secure e-commerce capabilities, searchable document database, threaded message board, and user registration

- Up to $250,000 for a large e-commerce marketplace portal redesign with real-time news feeds, advanced e-commerce features for buyers and sellers, and links to wireless devices

These budgets include development and hosting only, not the additional costs of internal labor, maintenance, infrastructure, or site promotion. Good thing that **median** means half the quotes are for less than these prices—a lot less!

Before you panic, most small businesses can put up a modest, custom site with a little basic marketing for $750 to $2,500 plus internal labor. You can create even less expensive Web pages using low-cost, off-the-shelf templates from a Web host or provider. (For example, see *http://www.clientready.com* or *http://www.tripod.lycos.com.*) You'll find an infinite number of pricing packages and methods. Some companies offer introductory packages in the $60 to $800 range for a 3- to 5-page, template-based brochure site, as long as you host with them for a year.

In Chapter 7, we'll discuss many economical e-commerce store-builder sites as well.

Don't make the mistake of using a "free" Web site that doesn't let you assign your own domain name: You can't market the site and search engines won't index it. If you must use such a site, take advantage of services like *http://www.mydomain.com* to redirect users from your registered URL to your free site. A well-organized, simple site that offers value and is well promoted will make sales or draw people to your business initially. If you save your profits, you'll soon have enough in the piggy bank to expand your site.

Other developers price by the page ($60 to $200 for roughly an 8.5" × 11" page), with add-on fees for custom design and multimedia. Still others charge only by the hour, though you can set a limit on the number of hours, prioritizing what will be eliminated if you run out of money. Hourly rates vary by task complexity. Basic HTML programming is at the low end of the scale ($50–$80/hour), with Java, Perl, cgi, database programming, and strategic planning at the high end ($90–$150/hour). Generally, it doesn't pay to custom code back office elements or functions like catalogs. Use standard software when possible to reduce costs.

The budget worksheet in Figure 5.3 provides some rough budgets for startup and annual maintenance costs for mini, small, and medium sites. Except for the mini site, which is done by modifying a template offered by a Web hosting service, the table assumes contracting with a Web designer to build and maintain the site. The mini, small, and medium sites use a Web hosting service, while the large site is self-hosted. Both the mini and small sites are text and graphics only. The medium site adds multimedia in the form of Flash animation, while the large-site budget includes some streaming media.

In this model, all except the static mini site do some form of online sales. The small site starts selling online, adding a small, free catalog and shopping cart from its Web host, and using an online service like PayPal for credit card payments. The medium site adds real-time payment processing and a merchant card account. Note the oft-ignored

---

RULE OF THUMB

Estimate an average of $100 per page for site development.

Item	Mini Site Setup/Annual	Small Site Setup/Annual	Medium Site Setup/Annual	Your Site Setup/Annual
Hardware	$700 optional 1x	$1,500 optional 1x	$3,000 optional 1x	
Software	$200	$1,200	$2,000-$5,000	
Register Domain	$70/$35	$70/$35	$140/$70 (2 names)	
ISP	$300	$300	$480	
Web Host	$25/$240	$50/$360	$100/$1,200	
Web Design 1 yr updates	free template 5-8 pages	$1,800 for 20 Pages	$5,000 for 50 Pages	
Telecomm	$0/$480 @ $40/month POTS 56K	$60/$600 @ $50/mo cable modem	$60/$600 DSL @ $50/mo	
Multimedia and extras	None	cgi-script $25	audio/animation $1,500	
Shopping Support	None	from Web Host –$120 for secure server @ $10/mo	$150/$1,200 for real-time gateway	
Statistics	From Web Host	From Web Host	$700 buy stat software	
Minimum Set-up Costs without Hardware	$115	$780	$3,150	
Development and Annual Outside Cost	$1,055	$3,440	$10,050	
Annual Marketing @ 40% Site Cost	$468	$1,688	$5,280	
First Year Site Cost without Labor	$1,638	$5,908	$18,480	
Estimated # Visitors	10,000	60,000	200,000	
Estimated CPM	$164	$98.46	$92.40	
In House Labor	$4,000	$12,000	$40,000	
Total Cost with Labor	$5,638	$17,908	$58,480	
Estimated Sales (#/$)	500 sales @ $25 = $12,500	3,000 sales @ $40 = $120,000	10,000 sales @ $60 = $600,000	
Cost per Sale	$11.27	$5.97	$5.85	
ROI	2.22	6.70	10.26	

Figure 5.3. Web site budget worksheet. © 2002 Watermelon Mountain Web Marketing.

Tips for Tired Sites

Did you spend a small fortune on a Web site that is not receiving much traffic? As a quick check, divide your marketing costs by unique viewers in thousands to estimate your CPM (cost per thousand visitors). How does this CPM compare to the CPM for your other advertising, whether by newspaper, direct mail, or TV? How does the cost of customer acquisition (those who actually purchase) compare to the cost of acquiring customers for your brick-and-mortar store? How do these numbers jibe with the ROI you computed in Chapter 3? If there are discrepancies, review your Web promotional budget to bring expectations and expenses into line.

---

line item for in-house labor to service the site, from providing content updates to communicating with the Webmaster and customers.

Given that vendors' bids for developing and maintaining the same Web site may be separated by several orders of magnitude, start with an internal estimate of how much you are willing to spend. After your first round of bids, finalize a budget—and stick to it. If you don't establish a limit, Web expenditures can quickly balloon out of control.

One of the most difficult numbers to estimate is the cost of marketing. How much should you spend to acquire visitors to your site? Some now-defunct, venture-funded dot-coms spent anywhere from 70 percent to 125 percent of their revenues on marketing, including branding, customer acquisition, and loyalty-building! We'll talk more about this in Chapters 9 through 12, but for now expect to spend about 20 percent to 40 percent of your *total* business budget for all forms of marketing if you're a Web-only business. You may get away with as little as 5 percent in additional marketing costs if you shift some of your marketing budget from an existing brick-and-mortar business to Web-site promotion. Another way to think about it is to allocate half-again of what you're budgeting for Web site development to your promotional effort.

Use the categories and numbers in Figure 5.3 as a guide to create your own spreadsheet. Fill out your cost estimates as you proceed through the development process. Be careful: A 1999 Gartner Group study found that most companies budgeted only 50 percent to 75 percent of what their site eventually cost. The most often underestimated factor was labor, which accounts for 79 percent of total site expenses, followed by hosting fees and servers.

RULE OF THUMB

Most sites will cost twice as much as initially budgeted and take twice as long as initially planned.

Timeline

You must establish the initial timeline just as you do the budget. If you don't set a deadline and a schedule for achieving it, your Web project may never be done! Obviously, a timeline will vary with your situation and with the complexity of your site. For instance, you may require an introductory site in conjunction with a scheduled event or product launch. One criterion for selecting Web designers will be their availability to work to your timetable, but be realistic: Good sites take time. Even the simplest sites usually need at least a week of planning, although putting them up may take only a day. Many sites take months. If you have a deadline, try to give everyone enough lead time to do a good job.

As you can see in Figure 5.4, you should expect to spend about half the time available for your project in the planning and design phase. The remaining half will be split almost equally between development and testing. These ratios, which are typical for both media production and programming, may seem excessive on the front end. They aren't. The time you spend planning will save you dollars in the end.

You don't have to launch all the pages on your site at once. It's better to get a site up and begin to establish your online presence than to wait until everything is perfect. Continue to build, test, and publicize pages over time. Sequencing development not only spreads out the costs, it also enables you to see how well a specific page works. If you're not sure how to accomplish this, prioritize the goals and target audiences in

RULE OF THUMB

Allow half your timeline for planning, one-quarter for programming, and one-quarter for testing and debugging.

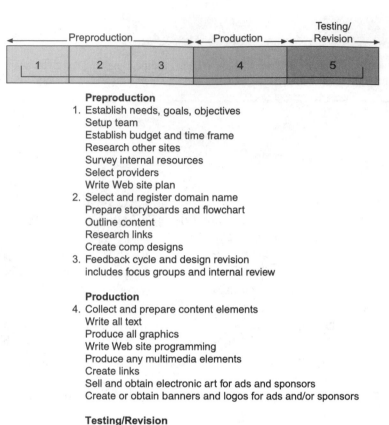

Preproduction
1. Establish needs, goals, objectives
   Setup team
   Establish budget and time frame
   Research other sites
   Survey internal resources
   Select providers
   Write Web site plan
2. Select and register domain name
   Prepare storyboards and flowchart
   Outline content
   Research links
   Create comp designs
3. Feedback cycle and design revision
   includes focus groups and internal review

Production
4. Collect and prepare content elements
   Write all text
   Produce all graphics
   Write Web site programming
   Produce any multimedia elements
   Create links
   Sell and obtain electronic art for ads and sponsors
   Create or obtain banners and logos for ads and/or sponsors

Testing/Revision
5. Test programming, including syntax and links
   Test user interface/acceptability (internal)
   Review content for accuracy
   Test trial site with limited number of users (external)
   Launch

Figure 5.4. Development timeline.

your business plan. You may want to delay all multimedia until the basic site is up.

You should also create a schedule for additions, monitoring, and updates. As you'll learn in Chapters 9 and 10, changes on a site offer opportunities for promotion. By spreading out development and updates, you'll generate multiple promotional announcements, drawing new or repeat viewers each time.

TIPS FOR TIRED SITES

Has your initial traffic fallen off? Depending on the purpose of your site and the nature of your business, some element of your site should change at least once a month to keep it fresh and interesting to viewers. New content might be a press release, a product announcement, a special offer, or simply different graphics. Unless your business is completely static, your Web site shouldn't be. There is a fine line between adding new information to draw repeat visitors and making changes for the sake of change. If your site successfully serves repeat customers, leave key functions well enough alone.

Selecting Service Providers

The first decision is whether to handle your site in-house or to hire others. With the right resources and skilled personnel on staff, it is certainly possible for a large company to become its own ISP, host its own site, and handle all design and promotion internally. Many do. Large companies staff a Web unit with 4 to 12 people, including content, programming, and marketing specialists; others create an entire online division as an independent profit center to market and sell products on the Web.

Small high-tech companies may have the in-house skills to create, maintain, and host a modest site, and contract out only for ISP, marketing, and graphic design support. A one-person, Web-based, home business with modest needs might start with a site-building template from their host.

DIY?

Many companies, in an effort to save money, hire an owner's teenaged relative or send an administrative assistant to a class in Web design. Occasionally, the results are great, but most do-it-yourself Web sites resemble newsletters produced in the early days of desktop publishing. Be very cautious about hiring inexperienced friends or relatives to do your site. If your site looks amateurish, it may never contribute to your business success. Any savings you find are likely to be false.

Realistically, most small companies just don't have people with Web development skills in-house, and their staff is often stretched thin. Their best options are to use a one-stop template-based host, to hire a Webmaster, or to outsource the development.

There is no one right solution. In business you usually have to spend money to make money. That probably means going with a pro, either in-house or outside. The more complex your site in terms of transactions, multimedia, or size, the more you need professional help. If you are serious about the Web, it is worth an investment to make the site easy to use, graphically appealing, and effective for marketing and sales. Otherwise, your Web expense may never return cost savings or increased revenue.

Selecting an Internet Service Provider (ISP)

Chances are you long ago selected one of the more than 6,000 ISPs in the United States to connect your business or home office to the Internet. (Point to *http://thelist.internet.com* for a directory sorted by country, state, and area code.) How else could you have done all this research? You may also have established accounts with one or more of the online services that you want to keep for marketing reasons, such as AOL for $23 per month.

Criteria for ISP selection are a subset of those used to select a Web hosting service. To obtain Internet access for your company, you probably looked at such factors as:

- Rates for connect time; unlimited service is best for a business.

- Free local access numbers and cost-free, dial-in access when out of town. Most ISPs support Internet mail access at the very least. Many regional or local ISPs charge for access when you use a toll-free number; this can add up if you travel a great deal. Otherwise travelers have to find a cyber-cafe with Internet access by the hour.

RULE OF THUMB

You can have it good; you can have it fast; you can have it cheap. Pick any two.

- Reliability and speed of access to the Internet and to your office. POTS (Plain Old Telephone Service) at 56K may be a limiting factor. Not all ISPs can bring in leased lines, T1, or DSL service, so be sure they offer the access speed you need. Other limitations include the number of customers (the average ISP has several thousand) and the connection speed between the ISP and the Internet backbone.

- The availability of basic services, such as e-mail, newsgroups and FTP.

- The number of e-mail boxes provided under one account.

- The quality of technical support.

- Supplying and supporting the latest browser versions.

- Security and backup procedures, including redundant servers.

- A free trial period or month-to-month contract option, so you can assess your satisfaction before signing a long-term contract.

- Compatibility with existing and planned hardware and telecommunications capabilities.

- Whether they also offer Web hosting.

Unhappy with your ISP? Join the crowd: Some 47 percent of customers have complained about the quality of their Internet connections. More than 75 percent report that their connection is frequently or often interrupted. Other complaints leading people to switch ISPs are a need for faster data rates and lower prices. In a 2001 survey, the average level of ISP satisfaction, scored on a scale of 1 to 4, was only 2.62, with ISDN ranked at 2.76, cable at 2.73, wireless at 2.71, DSL at 2.69, and dial-up at 2.58.

ISPs are entering an era of commodity pricing similar to that of long distance. Competition from "free" ISP services, which are advertiser-supported, has declined as their subscriber lists have fallen. Most ISPs now offer unlimited 56K dial-up Internet access for $15 or less per month for basic service, including one e-mail account and 3 to 5 MB of free

Web space. However, they vary widely in the availability of free local access numbers, the number of calls they can handle at any one time, the nature of their own connection to the Internet, and the space for personal home pages. Of course, DSL, cable, and other connections cost more, as discussed in Chapter 3.

For serious Internet use, look for an ISP that can provide multiple e-mail addresses, mailing list programs (listservers), mailbots, newsgroup access, and FTP (**file transfer protocol**). The provider must give you a **SLIP/PPP** account (Serial Line Internet Protocol/Point-to-Point Protocol—the Internet protocols that support Web and FTP servers). If an ISP can't provide all or most of these functions, keep shopping. Some, but not all, ISPs also host Web sites.

Some ISPs have a start-up fee; others offer a discount for year-long contracts; some charge extra for services like-mailbots and listservers. Compare costs for start-up, first year, and subsequent years of service, as well as connection track record, business history, and customer rating. The lowest-priced service may not be the best bargain; sometimes you get what you pay for.

For references, check with existing customers or review customer rankings of ISPs in your area at *http://www.cnet.com/internet/0-3761.html*, or look at the ISP buyer's guide at *http://www.thelist.com*. Figure 5.5 provides an ISP selection checklist. Based on your online marketing plan, decide on the services you will need, customize the checklist in Figure 5.5, and request bids from several providers based on the same set of services.

Selecting a Web Host

Not all ISPs host Web sites, and not all Web hosts are ISPs. Depending on your choices, you may end up with two different providers or you may find some, such as AplusNet *(http://www.aplus.net/services/services.html)* or Earthlink *(http://www.earthlink.net/business)*, that offer an integrated business package encompassing both. In this virtual world, a Web host with a server thousands of miles away may host your site, but a local ISP with a free access number may be used for e-mail and Internet searching. If your ISP and Web host are different companies, decide whether you want the Web host to forward mail received at your site address to another e-mail name (called an **alias**). Although there are some 10,000 hosting companies world-wide, a few large companies account for the majority of hosting services.

ISP Name _____   Date _____

Item	Y/N	Description	Cost
General			
Length of time in business?			
Staff qualifications/turnover?			
Client references? (get 3)			
System			
Local access numbers?			
Access numbers nationally?			
800-number access? Surcharge?			
Web e-mail option?			
Type of Internet connection?			
What connection speeds does the ISP cater to/handle?			
How much traffic at once?			
Security, e.g. firewalls?			
What % of time was server available during past 3 months?			
Server/connection redundancy?			
Back-up policy?			
Pricing			
What is the pricing structure?			
Monthly Flat Rate?			
Hourly?			
Add-on and over-quota rates?			
Long-term discounts?			
On/off connection fees?			
Technical Services			
Software pre-configured for use on your end?			
Will they support reconfiguration of your existing set-up, if needed?			
Can they support mailing lists? Newsgroups? Mailbots?			
What level/hours is technical support provided?			
What are the charges for technical support? Set-up? Troubleshooting?			
Other			
Free personal Web space? Size?			
How many free mailboxes with account? Cost for additional?			

Figure 5.5.   ISP selection checklist. ©1997-2002 Watermelon Mountain Web Marketing.

You will need to communicate directly to your site, perhaps via FTP, for uploading new content files, downloading transaction records, or checking statistics. Your Web host should provide you with directions for doing this. Some of the statistical analyses discussed in Chapter 8 should come with your hosting contract at no additional charge. Hosting services may not support all Web development packages equally. If a certain site development package is critical, perhaps due to an existing **legacy site**, that must become a selection criterion.

Depending on your needs, there will be additional technical questions, such as

- The bandwidth available, which determines the number of visitors your site can handle at once. Approximately 1,500 Kbps bandwidth (a T1 line) will handle 50K hits per month, assuming traffic is spread evenly. However, traffic spikes may occur at certain times of day, with special offers or events or with other forms of site promotion.

- What operating system and Web development packages the host uses/supports. Of the two most commonly used operating systems, UNIX is generally used for large sites that expect high traffic volume, while Microsoft NT is acceptable for smaller sites. Other server operating systems are sometimes used, so check compatibility.

- The connection between the host server and the Internet backbone, especially if you need high speed and wide bandwidth for multimedia.

- Whether you need a server solely for use by your company (**dedicated server**) instead of a **shared server** used by many other companies. Dedicated servers are faster and more flexible; shared servers are less expensive and generally used for smaller sites.

- Whether the Web host has redundant equipment in case a server goes down.

- The Web host's provisions for backups, data security, and tech support.

- What statistics will be available to analyze traffic to your site.

- Which database, catalog, shopping cart, and checkstand packages are supported, and what provisions exist for secure credit card processing.

- Whether the site supports **CGI** (Common Gateway Interface) programs that allow non-Web information to be turned into a Web document on the fly. You'll need cgi forms for on-site event registration, newsletter sign-ups, electronic orders, or surveys.

- What other services are offered, such as Web design, Web mall operation, site promotion, or audited statistics for advertising traffic.

Most companies have an initial setup fee plus monthly charges, and add fees for special services. Most offer discounts for long-term contracts. Identify several Web hosts that can provide the services you need, then compare prices on a spreadsheet. Web hosting fees, which vary widely, may be based on:

- The amount of space needed on the server. Estimate 10 Kb per page of Web text; graphics or multimedia will take more space.

- The amount of traffic you estimate per month.

- The frequency and size of data transfers.

- The number of domain names supported.

- Support for specialized programs, such as streaming video, database software, or particular e-mail or security programs.

- Support for specialized electronic commerce services, including access to a secure server. Some Web hosts specialize in transaction-intensive sites, with prices based on catalog size.

- Additional statistical analysis.

As with ISP selection, analyze start-up costs, first-year total costs, and subsequent-year costs independently. A small business should be able to find a solution for between $5 and $250 per month, depending on the size and complexity of its site. Cost, however, should be only one factor in your decision. Pay particular attention to business history, performance history, technical support, and customer service. There are already many sad stories of Web hosts and developers going out of business leaving their customers stranded. Almost all Web hosts provide a list of customers on their own site. For references, e-mail the Webmasters of several sites similar in scope to yours.

You can check the monthly ratings of the Top 25 Web Hosts and find other information at such sites as:

- *http://www.webhostingratings.com/hostdir.html* (reviews 900 hosts)

- *http://www.hostindex.com*

- *http://www.hostcompare.com/checklist.htm*

- *http://www.tophosts.com*

The checklist in Figure 5.6 summarizes selection criteria for a Web host. Before you start the process, check off the items you need and estimate quantitative entries, such as the number of expected hits per month (average and maximum) and the total space needed in megabytes. You may need assistance from your Web developer to fill in some of these blanks.

Selecting a Designer and/or Programmer

Web development has become the latest career fad for computer whiz kids, hackers, and underemployed artists, but a business site requires a great deal more skill and sophistication than a personal home page. Not all Web designers are created equal. Highly skilled programming houses don't always have graphics and marketing communications knowhow. Wonderful graphics artists and ad agencies don't always understand the Web implications of their designs in terms of download speed or navigation.

Not all developers have the knowledge to build effective order-taking mechanisms; not all are familiar with specific feature code; not all have business experience. Different developers may use specific development environments and e-commerce packages, so you must find a

Web Host Name _____   Date _____

Item	Y/N	Details	Cost
General			
Length of time in business?			
Staff qualifications/turnover?			
System			
Type of connection to the Internet?			
What connection speeds?			
How much traffic can they handle at a time?			
What provisions do they have for security, e.g. firewalls?			
Server/connection redundancy?			
Back-up policy?			
Dedicated or shared servers?			
Pricing			
What is the pricing structure?			
Monthly flat rate? For space in MB? Hits in K?			
Add-on and over-quota rates for space or hits?			
Long-term discounts?			
On/off connection fees?			
Technical Services			
UNIX, NT, or other?			
What level/hours is technical support provided?			
What are the charges for technical support? Setup? Trouble shooting?			
How easy will it be to make changes to the Web site?			
Frequency and fees for updating?			
What kind of statistical reports are available? How often?			
Web Development Support			
What Web development packages do they support?			
What kinds of streaming media/multimedia can they support?			
Do they support graphics libraries?			
Do they support interactive pages? CGI? or Perl?			
Which database programs do they support?			
Transaction Support			
What catalog, shopping cart, and/or checkstand software?			
Secure server (SSL minimum) Digital ID? Encryption?			
Which real-time transaction gateways? (e.g. Cybercash)			

Figure 5.6. Web host selection checklist. © 2000-2002 Watermelon Mountain Web Marketing.

developer and host to match the software you want to use. You are more likely to find providers with excellent technical and/or graphic skills than those with a marketing background. *You* must add the marketing insight to the process.

If you can't find all the skills you want in one person or company, consider using a graphic designer to create the overall look-and-feel, and a separate programmer to create the Web site. If you go this route, insist that the parties communicate closely. If artists are not familiar with the exigencies of the Web, their designs may take forever to download or be hard to navigate. They may deliver art that appears completely different on a low-resolution monitor with the limited color palette of the Web, or one that is difficult for programmers to execute. Similarly, Web engineers may not understand the importance of a particular graphic element and give it short shrift.

Be sure that the designer/developer team you hire has

- References and a portfolio of existing sites

- A reasonable business history

- The skills and experience to do the job you need, including specific expertise in e-commerce if needed

- The time and staff to produce the work according to your timeline

- The flexibility to work within your budget

- The willingness to contract for site updates on a regular basis

- Experience with standard business and programming practices, from business contracts to commenting code

An ISP, Web host, or advertising agency may offer Web development services, or you can check for Web developers in your city's creative directory or with an Internet professional association. On sites you like (go back to the list of sites you love in your notebook), look for the developer's name at the bottom of the home page or on the "About Us" page. You can always ask for a referral from a business whose site you want to emulate. Finally you can search for design companies online at such sites as:

- SiteMine.com Developer Directory: *http://www.sitemine.com/ developer.asp*

- Web Designer Directory: *http://www.aaadesignlist.com*

- Digital Spinner's Web Developer Directory: *http://digitalspinner .com/directory*

Always, always, always look at a developer's work online; almost all have a portfolio of links on their own site. (If they don't, ask yourself, "Why not?") Call or e-mail several of their clients to check references. (E-mail addressed to Webmaster often forwards to the developer, so contact the clients' marketing or communications department directly.) While a Web host may be located anywhere, a local Web developer may be more convenient for face-to-face meetings. If you can't find the skills you need locally, look for companies adept at combining audio teleconferencing with online posting to work with clients long distance. Development costs may be lower if you select someone away from either coast. Only you can weigh the factor of convenience versus cost.

If you're satisfied with a basic site, you can short-circuit the design process by signing up with a Web host such as Wyenet (see Figure 5.7,

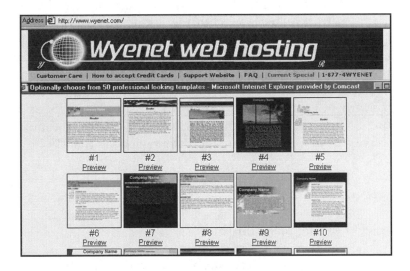

Figure 5.7. Web site templates, *http://www.wyenet.com*. Courtesy Wyenet Services, LLC, www.wyenet.com. 1-877-4WYENET.

http://www.wyenet.com), which offers Web site templates. For a low-cost, high-quality compromise, identify a local graphic artist with the skills to customize a template. An experienced eye can quickly select colors, typefaces, and buttons that add a sophisticated veneer to an otherwise pedestrian design. (See the Freebies section at the end of Chapter 6 for other template sources.) Your needs, as well the developer's rates, skills, and availability, will determine the best provider for you.

Selecting a Web developer is a multistep process. First, assemble a list of 8 to 12 potential providers based on referrals, sites you've collected, and/or directories. After looking at their on-site portfolios, select no more than 6 whose work you like. Then use the questionnaire in Figure 5.8 modified according to your Web plan, to prequalify potential Web designers by phone or e-mail. At this point, you can narrow your list to 3 or so that you will ask for a bid.

Requests for Quote or Proposal

A Request for Quote (RFQ) and a Request for Proposal (RFP) are similar. However, bidders will generally respond to an RFQ only with pricing and contractual details, like payment schedules and deliverables. If you want bidders to generate a design as part of their bid, or to provide a detailed work plan, label your request an RFP.

To solicit more bids than just a few from companies you have prequalified, you can e-mail your RFP to a number of Web developers; notify business associations, local ISP, or Internet organization sites; or post it on your own purchasing pages. Many large corporations and government agencies are required to do such postings as a matter of purchasing policy or law respectively. Of course, the more bids you receive, the more work you will have reviewing them!

Elements of an RFQ/RFP

An RFQ or RFP may consist of:

- A cover letter requesting a bid, the due date for a response, and the way the response should be delivered

- Your 25-word summary statement about the site, its goals, objectives, and target audience

Web Developer Questionnaire

1. How long have you been in business? How long have you been designing Web sites?

2. If not already available, please provide the URLs and client references for at least three sites you have designed, preferably ones similar to ours. Describe what services you performed for each of these sites.

3. Which Web services do you offer?

   a. Graphic design and page layout?

   b. Copywriting?

   c. Basic HTML programming?

   d. cgi scripting?

   e. Java/Shockwave (for animations)?

   f. Database programming?

   g. Other (e.g. Perl)?

4. Do you design banner ads?

5. What is your policy on site updates?

6. Do you perform site testing? If so, on which browsers, which versions, which platforms?

7. Will you do site verification, e.g. code, dead links, spelling, etc.? How often?

8. Do you offer any promotional services?

9. Do you work with a team or alone? If a team, who would be our contact point? Who are the other members of the team?

10. What is your process for working with clients? e.g. comps? review stages? testing?

11. Our development schedule is: _____. What is your availability?

12. Do you price by job, page, or hour? What are your basic rates and/or rates for each service you offer?

    If applicable, add:

13. We are thinking of adding multimedia (specify type) in the future. What relevant multimedia production experience do you have? (Get URL and reference)

14. We are thinking of adding a special feature (e.g. chat line, forum) in the future. Have you done this before? (Get URL and reference)

15. This will be a transaction site, with X (number of) products that are paid for by (Y) payment processes. We expect Z (number of) purchases per week. What access to and experience with storebuilding, checkstand and payment software modules do you have? Are you tied to development and/or support of particular products?

16. Do you understand that this will be a work for hire and copyright will belong to us?

Figure 5.8. Web developer questionnaire. ©1997-2002 Watermelon Mountain Web Marketing.

- A list of desired features (e.g., a message board, chat room, flash animation, or searchable database)

- A draft site index (to be discussed in Chapter 6), including the estimated number of pages and the number of items in an online catalog

- A list of any other Web development services needed (e.g., do you want illustrations from the graphic artist delivered as PhotoShop layers? Do you need photos scanned? Copy written? Administrative pages? Ongoing maintenance?)

- An expected price range, or at least an upper limit

- The timeline for development, including target launch date

- Any other conditions or additional services (e.g., do you want the developer to include costs for hosting and/or Web marketing, for backing up the site quarterly on CD-ROM, or for exporting data from an online form into your contact management database software?)

- How and when proposals will be assessed

The more detailed your RFQ/RFP, the more accurate the bids you will receive. The fictional RFP shown in Figure 5.9 will give you an idea. Unless you use a standard RFP for your site, it may be impossible to compare prices and services from different developers. With answers and bids in hand, you should have the information to make a selection.

Evaluation Criteria

Before you issue your RFP or RFQ, decide which factors really matter to you. Price is usually not the only thing to consider. You might want to assign a maximum point value to each factor to indicate how much it will count toward your decision. It's a good idea to share the evaluation criteria with your prospective bidders as part of the RFP/RFQ. Here are a few ideas with arbitrary weighting to consider:

- Responsiveness to the RFP (20 points)

SuperSillyStuff, Inc., which manufactures and sells a variety of novelty clothing lines, invites you to bid on Web site development and hosting for a new e-commerce site at *www.sillysox.com*. (The domain name is already registered.) The new site will sell a line of novelty sox for women and children. This site will have:

- 5 pages of HTML text created as administrative pages for user updating without tech support

- flash animation on the home page (code supplied)

- 3 interactive children's games (code supplied)

- a cgi-form for newsletter registration

- a 100-item catalog, with text, photos, prices, and inventory up-datable without tech support

- a secure server for transactions, including screening out children too young to purchase

- a complete set of traffic and sales statistics

The online store should use a pre-packaged store-builder, including catalog, shopping cart and checkstand with real-time credit card processing. Graphic design elements will be provided by our designer as JPEGs, subject to modification for the Web. We will supply digital photos, text and metatags. Another contractor will handle all Web promotion including search engine submission. SuperSillyStuff, Inc. will own the copyright and other intellectual property rights to the site and to any code produced as a work for hire. The complete RFP includes a detailed scope of work, a site index, a background questionnaire, the criteria for selection, lists of our other Web sites, and a list of competing sites. Please let us know by 5/24/02 if you intend to bid.

Schedule

Bids due electronically	6/03/02	Developer selection	6/13/02
Initial developer conference	6/17/02	Comps due	6/30/02
Initial site ready for testing	8/01/02	Site Launch	8/22/02

Figure 5.9. Fictional RFQ.

- Practicality of the approach for your situation (20 points)

- Experience of the bidder on similar sites (20 points)

- Capability for handling future work (10 points)

- References (10 points)

- Cost (20 points)

You may want to interview local finalists, or better yet meet them at their office to discuss their responses. That way you can confirm the developers have the facilities and staff you'd expect and that the personal chemistry exists.

Reference Checks

Hiring a Web developer is no different from hiring a carpenter, a dentist, or an accountant. Check references! You might want to ask questions such as those in Figure 5.10. Check at least one reference at random that the bidders do not provide. Watch for several red flags in responses: difficulty communicating with clients, inability to deliver work in a timely manner; or constant turnover of staff.

Before signing with your choice of design and/or Web engineering firm, ask to see a sample contract. A contract may include as attachments the design description from your RFP, their proposal, a schedule of interim deliveries and review dates, and a schedule of payments. Make sure that you will retain ownership of the domain name, that you will be named the administrative contact on the domain name registration, and that you will have password control and access to the site to make changes yourself. Confirm that your company will own the copyright and that you will have physical ownership of commented programming code for the site (e.g., backup CDs quarterly). Having the code will make it easy to move your site, its development, or its maintenance to another provider, if necessary. This is particularly important if your designer is also your Web host.

The Design Process: What To Expect

The process of creating a Web site follows fairly predictable stages. While it may vary according to circumstances and complexity, the process generally incorporates the following:

For Developer Company Name_____

Reference Company Name _____

Name of Contact_____ Title_____ Date_____

Phone_____ Fax _____Email_____

URL _____

1. When did you start working with this developer: _____

2. Was your Web site new or a re-design? _____

3. Which of the following does the developer do for your company?

     _____Web Design   _____Programming   _____Multimedia

     _____Online Ads   _____Other (specify)

4. What are the developer's greatest strengths? Weaknesses?

5. How would you rate the overall quality of the work (1 to 5, with 5 best) _____

6. How would you rate the ease of working with the developer? (1 to 5) _____

7. How responsive is the developer to customer needs/budget? (1 to 5) _____

8. How accurate were developer's estimates of time and cost? (1 to 5) _____

9. Would you hire this developer again? (Y/N) _____

10. What, if anything, would you do differently in working with this developer?

11. What advice, if any, would you offer to another client of this developer?

Figure 5.10. Developer reference questionnaire. ©2002 Watermelon Mountain Web Marketing.

1. Initial design conference and schedule

2. Design "comps" for you to choose from

3. Navigation storyboards or flowcharts

4. Page templates for various levels of the site

5. Element production and content acquisition

6. Programming and integration

7. Testing and corrections

As described in the Timeline section above, the first five steps, along with your other preplanning, will absorb about half the time before launch. Steps 6 and 7 will each take roughly one quarter of the time.

Initial Design Conference and Schedule

Your RFP provides the designer with an excellent starting point for discussion at your initial design conference. Add to that your collection of site printouts and the URLs of sites you like and dislike. You may want to add a list of desired internal links (within the site) and external links (links to other Web sites) and where they belong. The more specific the information you provide to your developers, the easier it is for them to deliver what you want and the less expensive the design process will be.

Bring your calendar to schedule when deliveries from the design team can be expected and when you plan to launch the site. Indicate clearly at what points you want to see material and how long you will need for approval. Finally, review your budget with the developer to ensure that your expectations are still within the price quoted and that the level of effort will be adequate to meet your requirements.

Although it may seem counterintuitive, the earlier and more often you seek internal and external review, the less difficulty you will have with implementation and operation. Ensure that all appropriate members of your team (and others if necessary) have an opportunity to sign off on decisions before major funds are committed.

A review cycle is also an opportunity to confirm that content is ready and accurate. This is particularly true if others are providing technical information, bibliographical references, or up-to-date databases. Checking content from internal sources is just as important. You might discover that the Human Resources Department wants to update the Job Openings database daily, but the Web designer expected updates weekly.

Design Comps

As with print, a designer will generally provide several different graphic concepts (comps) for your Web site. The designer may use presentation software or PhotoShop to generate individual screen images that provide a "look-and-feel" sense of your site. Be aware that images may not transfer exactly from PhotoShop or other formats to HTML for the Web. The designer may include the layout for secondary and third-level pages, and/or a block diagram of screen elements (see Figure 5.11) for different types of pages. At this point, the designer uses "fake" text as a placeholder to show how a page will look.

After you select one approach and make suggestions, the designer will provide a final comp to confirm the look and feel of the site. Once you sign off on the final design, additional changes are likely to increase the cost. If the site is large, the lead designer or project manager should establish a standards book for the creative team to follow, especially if multiple contractors will be involved. A standards book establishes consistent icons, layout, typography, colors, graphics size, tone, style, and ad placement.

Navigation Storyboards or Flowcharts

Your Web designer might present the navigational elements of your site as a storyboard or a flowchart for your approval. A storyboard lets you

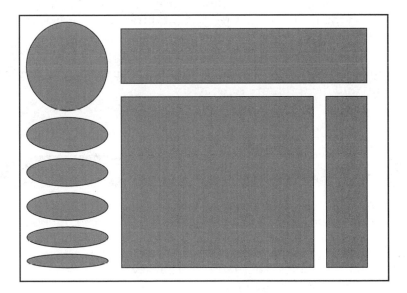

Figure 5.11.   Block diagram of sample screen layout.

answer the question "How well does this site work?" It looks like the cels from a cartoon and depicts activity using pictures of each page. You can easily rearrange these individual pages using sticky notes on a wall or index cards on a table to experiment with different ways of moving through a site. Many Web development packages supply a navigation flowchart that provides context, showing where users are, where they might have been, and where they are able to go.

Check the proposed structure against the navigation suggestions listed in the next chapter. Try to imagine how different visitors might experience it. Would navigation be obvious to someone who stumbled on the site by accident? Would an experienced, repeat visitor get frustrated at information buried too deeply? How many clicks does it take to get from one piece of information to another? Are there any gaps in your "story"?

Depending on the complexity of the site, your designer may build a prototype or shell before proceeding to actual programming. If the designer posts this prototype site on his or her own Web site, other members of your team can review it.

Strong visual cues help viewers find data and orient them in virtual space. Good structure is obvious and intuitive, such as in the site at *http://www.eskesbrewpub.com*, shown in Figure 5.12. Again, changes in structure after signing off on the prototype will probably incur additional charges.

Make sure the site organization is optimized for marketing, too. You may want the site divided so that different pages use different keywords, giving you better exposure in search engines. You might want splash pages designed with specific audiences in mind. If you want to reinforce messages with a click action, be sure the pages with the call to action and the result are separated.

TIPS FOR TIRED SITES

People don't want to play an adventure game, hunting high and low for information. If you're receiving complaints about navigation, bring in a focus group composed of naive users. Try to find people who match your expected audience profile closely and who have a range of computer or content knowledge. You can use focus groups online through a scheduled "conference chat" at any point in the re-design process, or you can interview a "live" group.

Figure 5.12. Good visual navigation cues, *http://www.eskesbrewpub.com/ food.html*. Courtesy Eske's Brew Pub and Brainwax.com.

You need to balance conflicting goals when it comes to outbound links. Every time you link outside your site, you risk losing your viewer. Not all users are familiar with the Back button or pull-down history features of their browsers. On the other hand, many outbound links will generate a reciprocal inbound link, which can help improve the visibility of your site. Generally, it's best to have your designer open a new window when a viewer clicks on an outbound link so your page remains on the user's screen.

Element Production and Content Acquisition

Some of the elements of the site—text, graphics, and photos—can be collected from company files; others will need to be created fresh. The less the designer has to create from scratch, the lower your cost. Perhaps someone in your company can write, edit, and proof the copy (see Chapter 6 for more on writing). Whoever handles the copywriting must optimize it for marketing purposes, with links and calls to action placed at strategic locations. On pages intended for search engine submission, the copywriter should consider the precepts discussed in Chapter 11 for improving rankings, particularly the ratio between keyword occurrence and the number of words on the page.

Since poorly written, ungrammatical text is a turnoff to readers and an embarrassment to your company, remember to proofread all content and check the spelling. Use focus groups to review the content for comprehensibility. If you are aiming a site toward children, you might want to assess readability level as well.

Do you have staff that could collect and digitize existing photographs, art, or database material, or review free sources for clip art, **sprites** (small GIFs used for animation), or digital photos? Do you need to arrange for other professionals to shoot photographs or create art? Will some content be contributed by other departments? Your designer should specify the format in which elements should be delivered. Generally, photos work best in JPEG format; graphics work best as GIFs.

The developer should have budgeted for the creation of any new multimedia material, such as animation or audio files, unless it was clear from the RFP that material would be provided independently. Depending on the project, either the Web producer or the lead developer will be responsible for making sure those pieces are created on time and in the required format. A good Web developer will bring to this project his or her knowledge of how to optimize the various pieces to get the best quality in the fastest download time. The developer usually is also responsible for establishing file-naming and version-numbering conventions and backing up all the various elements.

Programming and Integration

A Web developer decides how to code your site based on his or her familiarity with different development packages and languages, which packages will be supported by your selected Web host, and the server to be used. The programmer should also consider the Web skills and equipment capabilities of your target audience. It is sometimes tricky to put all the different elements together in a way that will be compatible with various versions of browsers, plug-ins, and computers.

Once a final design has been approved for the home page and for pages at different levels of your site outline, your developer will start coding these as master pages. Don't be surprised if your Web developer first programs your site with preexisting video clips or photos, instead of using your specific material. Often, it is easier to debug the programming portion of the site independent of actual images and content.

Finally, elements will be inserted into the program structure and you will be able to see your Web site. Generally, pages of a certain type or level come up at the same time. Then the developer will insert your content on additional pages of the same type. Be sure to check that text and images are on the correct pages! This stage of development is usually done on a local development server or a "hidden" section of Web site that is not available to the general public.

Testing and Corrections

Through internal testing and debugging, the designer should catch any obvious problems, such as images that don't fully download or pages that don't appear. Ask your designer to run a **syntax checker**, which confirms there are no errors in the code, and a link verifier to confirm that any links on your site are valid. (See Chapter 8 for more on testing and analysis tools.) Re-proof content that may have been edited to fit on the page or to flow around an image. Be sure to test any purchase or other process all the way through back office operations. Each round of corrections should be followed by a round of checking.

The designer's next task should include testing or emulating site performance on an assortment of equipment, with various plug-ins installed. Your Webmaster can simplify this by running a site checker like Web Site Garage (*http://websitegarage.netscape.com/O=wsg*). Make sure the site is tested with the minimal configuration your viewers might have: perhaps Windows 98, a Celeron processor, a 56K modem, 128 Mb of RAM, and a 15-inch monitor. Then move up to higher-level operating systems and more powerful hardware. Test on a Macintosh or when running on a local area network under Windows NT. Some of the tools described in Chapter 8 will allow you to emulate system performance under different load conditions.

Many sites that look beautiful on a large, expensive monitor can be cropped or distorted on a smaller display. Make sure the text font is large enough to be readable when viewed at high resolution. Test the appearance of the site under several versions of Netscape and Microsoft Internet Explorer browsers. Each browser operates slightly differently, so what looks great in Internet Explorer on a PC may not look right in Netscape on a Macintosh and vice versa. Check the appearance of your site whenever a new browser version is released. Your designer will optimize the site for appearance on multiple browsers; be prepared for some compromises. You may find support for browser compatibility testing at *http://www.AnyBrowser.com* or *http://www.cast.org/bobby*.

Even though many users now have high speed access, don't count on it. Dial-up users still decry slow download time as their chief complaint, and their patience is growing increasingly thin. If a page takes more than 15 seconds to download on a 56K modem, you may need to scale down, eliminate, or compress some images or multimedia. In the worst case, the designer may create a stripped-down version of the site as an option for those with less-capable equipment. One advantage of template-based sites is that much of this testing has already taken place. Minimum hardware configurations, plug-in versions, and software incompatibilities are well known; existing problems are usually documented. With a template, errors usually result from problems during the process of creating or integrating the elements, not from the program.

As a final test, make the site active, but don't publicize it yet for the world to view. Post a notice with a password or special extension asking for testing assistance and feedback from existing customers, members of newsgroups, mailing list subscribers, or a professional society. You might offer a small freebie or discount to those who fill out an online survey about the site and something larger if they catch a serious bug or make a suggestion you use. Ask testers to:

- Confirm that the directions, index, and structure are clear.

- Assess the value of the links and suggest others.

- Exercise any user-response or interactive mechanism, such as an e-mail registration form, contests, or games.

- See if there are problems with multimedia or plug-ins on any platforms.

- Check for errors in content, from spelling to facts.

This type of beta testing is done commonly in the software world, but has been used less frequently for Web sites. It should be best practice.

TIPS FOR TIRED SITES

To ensure that you're delivering excellent service and a positive Web experience, continue to re-test your site at least every three months. Test everything from placing an order to the length of time to receive a response to an e-mail request. Can you reach a "real" person easily? Can you find whatever information you're looking for? Does your search function work for someone not familiar with your products or services? Is customer information from previous visits accurately recorded and used? Once the initial excitement of a Web site has worn off, service may start to slide and errors may creep in. The price of excellence is constant attention.

Domain Name Registration

If you haven't done so already, you must select and register a domain name, sometimes called a **URL** (Uniform Resource Locator). Domain names are sorted into categories called **top-level domains** (TLD). You're most familiar with *.com*, which immediately signals that you are a commercial enterprise. The TLD *.net* designates a network, but some businesses register their name under *.net* as well. For most businesses, it doesn't make sense to buy a *.net* name unless you can get the *.com* version as well. The appellation *.org* designates a non-profit organization.

With more than 100 million registered names, the number of domain names started to run out in late 1999. To open up more URLs, **ICANN** (Internet Corporation for Assigned Names and Numbers) approved seven additional TLDs: *.biz*, *.info* (unrestricted), and *.name* (individuals) are already available, while *.coop* (cooperatives), *.museum*, *.pro* (doctors, lawyers, and accountants), and *.aero* (air transport industry) may become available shortly. While some companies are registering their domain names under these TLDs for defensive purposes, locking them up to prevent confusion or trademark infringement, many others are ignoring these "not-coms."

The shunning is for good reason. Both users and search engines will have trouble finding your site until these new TLDs are well-established and thoroughly publicized. It's not at all clear that users understand or will use them, given the difficulties they already have finding sites on the Web. Don't get taken by registrars peddling unsanctioned TLDs, such as *.shop*, *.arts*, *.school*, or *.church*, as a way to get the domain name you want. These won't necessarily be recognized by search engines or domain servers. You're far better off finding another domain name and keeping a *.com* identity.

Beware, too, of companies promoting other countries' domains. TLDs like *.ws* (Western Samoa), *.co* (Columbia) or *.cc* (Cocos Islands) are not easily recognized and may leave your site stranded in cyberspace, alone and visitor-less. (There are legitimate reasons to register in different countries you have targeted in your global marketing plan; registering with a specific country's TLD may make it easier to be found by search engines that serve that nation.) If you're serious about global marketing, consider multiple, multi-lingual domain name registration. Until 2000, Web addresses were available only in English, but now it is possible to register not only in languages like Spanish and Portuguese, but in non-Roman character languages—Chinese, Korean, and Japanese.

A Site by Any Other Name Might Not Smell as Sweet

How important are names? Very! Your Web identity and self-promotion start with your domain. Be as careful choosing your URL as you were selecting your business name; it's an absolutely critical Internet marketing decision. Look for a domain name that is:

- Easy to remember

- Easy to pronounce

- Easy to spell (try giving it out over the phone)

- Easy to type (short enough to type without errors)

Avoid special characters, including hyphens, abbreviations, and numbers, unless you already have brand recognition for a name that includes them. Domain names are not case sensitive, but many compound words are capitalized in print advertising to make the name easier to read.

Company names work well when you already have brand recognition (e.g., Sony.com) or a preexisting customer base. It's the first name most people will try online; many will never bother to use a search engine to find you. If the nouns in your business name are already taken, try adding "inc" or "company" or keywords describing what you sell, such as HealthyPlanetNaturalFoods.com, or HealthyPlanetInc.com.

If your business name isn't descriptive (e.g. Petunia's), perhaps your product description is: artsupplies.com. Descriptive or generic names like "quillpens.com" make for easy searching, increased traffic to your site, and can't be trademarked. They may be easier to use and say than your company name, and may be far more memorable.

You can also try for "clever." A name like *eat.com*, which Lipton, Inc., uses on its Ragu Sauces site, draws attention from the curious. Portals and businesses with an expansive online mission aim for short, flexible names that are easy to remember but won't limit them to specific products (e.g., Amazon.com, go.com, or snap.com.)

With the expansion of URLs from 22 characters to 63 (plus extensions), URLs created from compound words or phrases have become available. That's a good thing: 97 percent of the single words in Webster's dictionary have already been taken. Still stumped? Network Solutions (*http://www.networksolutions.com*) and many other registration sites offer a "Name Finder" feature that generates available multi-word domain name combinations from a list of keywords you enter.

Of the 140 million names currently registered, only about 25 percent are in active use. With the downturn in the economy, inactive name registrations are now expiring at the rate of 800,000 per month. With so many names available, you may yet find the one you want. You can back-order your first-choice name at *http://www.snapnames.com* for $69 per year per name, or you can monitor it there for free.

Registration Process

To reserve a name, registrants once had to use Network Solutions, Inc., at *networksolutions.com*, which had the original, exclusive contract with the U.S. government to manage domain name registration. Now 161 companies have been accredited by ICANN to register top-level domain names, of which 89 are active. They all use the expanded Shared Registry System, a central database currently stored at Network Solutions and at the Internet Network Information Center (InterNIC). For a list and more information on registration companies, go to *http://www.icann.org*. For more information on InterNIC policies, go to *http://www.internic.net*.

Initially, domain registration cost $70 for the first two years, with an annual $35 renewal fee thereafter. But competition has lowered prices. Shop around for registration bargains. Buydomains.com (*http://www.buydomains.com*) charges $16 per year; GoDaddy.com (*http://www.godaddy.com*) charges as little as $6.95 per year for a ten-year registration. Register.com (*http://www.register.com*) offers a free 3-page template Web site with domain registration for $35 per year. A number of sites, including Network Solutions and *http://www.bulkregister.com* offer discounts for bulk name registration. Watch out for special conditions, however. Some companies advertise reduced registration rates as a loss leader to entice clients into contracts for other services, such as hosting, design, or promotion, or they require a long-term registration contract.

You can register yourself at any of the ICANN sites, or let your Web host or ISP handle domain name registration for you. This service has become so competitive that you should not have to pay any charges beyond the regular registration fee. If you are hosting your own site, you will need to register your server first and then your name.

Standard registration procedures are easy. First, see if your desired name is available by searching the database at *http://www.internic.net* or on any of the registration sites. After you have selected a name, check for trademark conflicts through the U.S. Patent & Trademark database at *http://tess.uspto.gov*, or use one of the free trademark search links you find on a registration site, such as *http://www.nameprotect.com*. Then apply online through one of the registration services.

If you want to reserve several names until you make a final decision, you can "park" a name on someone's server temporarily. Some Web hosts will "park" names for free (e.g., *http://www.namesecure.com*) or for a modest fee (e.g., *http://www.domain.rshweb.com/parking.html*) until you are ready to go online. This is an enticement to use their service, but you can easily transfer the name elsewhere (sometimes with an administrative charge). If you've paid a "parking fee," the Web host will often apply the amount to your account if you select it as your host. A "parked" name is reserved until the payment period expires, 30 days after the date on the invoice you receive from InterNIC. Once you've paid for the name, of course, it's yours as long as you renew it.

Within the "name" marketplace, you can find other supplemental name services. For instance *http://www.mydomain.com* lets you direct visitors from a domain name to a free Web site (which usually doesn't have its own URL) or vice-versa, or forward e-mail from your Web site to another mailbox. For a $49 annual fee, RealNames at *http://www.realnames.com* will direct users from your business name or other keyword to your URL.

What's in a Name? Money and More

Names are important enough that some companies buy up any possible spellings (and misspellings) of their name, as well as any derogatory terms that could refer to them. Businesses may find themselves paying to reclaim their own brand names unless they have reserved them through trademark. This happened to Compaq, owner of search engine AltaVista, which paid $3.35 million to reclaim *altavista.com* in 1998. Court decisions and legislation have made **cybersquatting**—deliberately using someone else's trademarks within a domain name—illegal. Unfortunately, this doesn't help two companies that both have legitimate trademark interests within two different classifications of goods (Petunia's Pet Foods and Petunia's Café could both be trademarked). Then, it's first come, first served for each TLD. If your desired name is taken, you may be able to negotiate a purchase with the owner, whose name you will find in the WhoIs database. If a site is already active, the price may be higher.

Some companies and individuals went into the name game in the late '90s, buying up as many names as they could think of and then licensing or selling them. At one point, this was a lucrative enterprise. The name *WallStreet.com* was auctioned in April 1999 to a Venezuelan company for over $1 million. *Business.com* sold for $7.5 million in November 1999, and *America.com* was on the block for a cool $10 million. But with the decline in dot-coms and the expiration of many domain name registrations, the value of names has declined. Most names now sell for much less; even popular ones like *tv.com* or *internet.com* sold in the $15,000 to $150,000 range. More than 100 Web sites now broker names, either by auction or by soliciting private bids. For example, check out *http://www.domainnamebrokers.com*, *http://www.afternic.com*, or *http://www.greatdomains.com*.

Here Comes the Fun

In this chapter we reviewed preplanning requirements for staffing, budget, and development timeline, as well as how to select service providers, the design process and domain name registration. That's a lot to

TIPS FOR TIRED SITES

Could your domain name account for low traffic to your site? If your URL is hard to say or hard to spell, it's quite possible. Consider buying commonly misspelled versions of your name and redirecting those URLs to your main page. If you took an obscure version of your company name because someone else had already registered it, consider using the Real Names forwarding service described above. If you used your company name, but you lack brand recognition, you may want to obtain another URL that's more descriptive. For instance, RodriguezRailroadStore.com might not draw as much traffic as ToyRailroads.com. Buy that second URL and use it in your offline marketing instead. You might even create a separate "doorway" page that directs different segments of your audience to different parts of your Web site.

think about, and we haven't even talked about your actual Web site yet! In the next chapter, we'll finally consider the design piece of your Web marketing jigsaw puzzle. We'll focus on how to design a site for personality, clear content, easy-to-use navigation, appearance, and marketing effectiveness.

6

Step 5b: Design an Effective Web Site

Good Web design engages visitors; it keeps them on the site and brings them back as repeat viewers. Accomplishing this is not easy. As far as site visitors are concerned, competition from more than 36 million other active Web sites means that a better cyberworld is just a click away. You have only 3 to 10 seconds to grab viewers' attention and convince them they'll receive a benefit from remaining on your site. That's about as much time as it takes to roll a grocery cart down the cereal aisle!

In this chapter we look at design techniques for attracting visitors and making your site "**sticky**" so they stay longer, visit multiple pages, and return for more. Longer and more-frequent visits means viewers are more likely to read and remember a message, whether it is your own or from one of your advertisers. We'll explore ways that design enhances the marketing effectiveness of your site, delivers a clear marketing message, and reflects your commitment to your customers. You'll learn about:

- The goals of effective Web design

- Applying marketing communication principles to the Web

- Writing for the Web

- Using multimedia on your site

- Helpful hints for a successful site

- Free features and resources to enhance your site.

Goals of Effective Web Design

Besides the business goals your Web site must achieve, it must achieve three additional generic goals:

- Attract visitors' attention immediately.

- Keep visitors on the site as long as possible.

- Encourage them to visit again.

Designing a good Web site is like playing multidimensional chess! How can we use the analytical tools we've already discussed, our knowledge of human psychology, and the principles of marketing to make sense of this process? We can start by turning the five elements of site evaluation discussed in Chapter 1 into five elements of site prescription.

From Site Evaluation to Prescription

You may want to revisit the site evaluation rating sheet in Figure 1.21 as you read this chapter. Let's consider the five elements on that rating sheet in sequence: concept, content, navigation, decoration, and marketing effectiveness.

Concept
Concept is the most critical tool you have in attracting viewers' attention during those first critical one to three seconds after they arrive on your site. Concept is a visual metaphor, a graphic representation of an idea or feeling. It's a picture of your business's personality. (If you live in Santa Fe or Santa Cruz, call it your "business aura.")

Have you heard the axiom "form follows function?" In Chapter 3, you defined the purpose(s) your Web site will serve (its function) and what audience(s) you want to reach. The visual concept or "form" of your site—the instantaneous impression it creates—needs to be in sync with its function and audiences. The viewer needs an immediate visceral reaction that says, "This might be useful; it looks like quality; it's worth my time."

Start by making up a list of adjectives (use a thesaurus if necessary) like those in Figure 6.1. Describe the *feelings of* your audience before they arrive at your site and how you want them to *feel about* your site and your company. From this list try to select five to seven words to help your Web designer convey the personality, tone, and character of your business through colors, images, and sound. Your creative team

Adjectives on Site Arrival	Adjectives after Site Experience
angry	accomplished
annoyed	amused
anxious	calm
cautious	carefree
concerned	committed
curious	contented
depressed	delighted
discouraged	empowered
emotional	energized
fearful	entertained
happy	entranced
insecure	glad
laid-back	impressed
negative	lovable
neutral	mellow
outraged	open
pressured	positive
resistant	proud
rigid	reassured
sad	relaxed
serious	relieved
silly	satisfied
skeptical	secure
tense	self-confident
weary	triumphant

Figure 6.1. "Lizard brain" adjectives.

plays an essential role here, transforming your marketing message into a visual metaphor that carries through all the pages of your site. This metaphor immediately reaches our "lizard brain," the emotional, irrational core from which many decisions are made.

Content

A content-rich site makes visitors more likely to remain on your site or return for future visits. Web visitors have come to expect information, assistance, and value. A site unfolds for a viewer not just on the screen, but in time. Like a story, a site should have a beginning, a middle, and an end. The beginning (concept) grabs viewers' attention, the middle (content) is the value-added portion of the site, and the end is the payoff (when viewers' needs are satisfied—for example, by downloading a file) or the **call to action** (a specific suggestion of what step to take next—for example, register now). In sales lingo, the final call to action would be equivalent to a "**close.**"

At a minimum, you will need to tweak or "re-purpose" old content from brochures, spec sheets, or other sources for the Web. You'll want to shorten and reorganize the material, creating links or putting some information deeper in the site. Print graphics may not transfer well to a lower-resolution screen; photos may take too long to download.

Don't feel that you have to overwhelm visitors with every single bit of information ever created about your company. In fact, a site that stays tightly focused on your marketing mission will be more satisfactory to both the viewer and your bottom line. The tone of the writing should support the concept of the site. Consistency between image and text will energize your site.

Almost always, you or someone else inside your company will need to draft the initial content. An outside writer rarely knows a company's products or services well enough to start from scratch. Inside staff will probably also suggest external links and provide an initial hierarchy of information (the **site index**), structuring what should be on the surface and what belongs several clicks down. A gifted copywriter can take it from there, incorporating calls to action and following the principles of writing for the Web described below.

Navigation

Easy navigation is essential for hooking visitors in the third to tenth second after they arrive on the site. It's here that users decide whether a site is going to be easy to use. If they get that far, your content has a chance to carry them through multiple pages. Good navigation lets viewers know where they are, what options they have to go elsewhere, what they'll find when they get there, and how to get back where they came from. One recent study showed that 39 percent of online shoppers gave up just because they couldn't figure out what to do or how to locate the information they wanted!

Can you tell from using a site how it is organized? Most Web sites follow one of five basic structures seen in Figure 6.2.

- Sequential

- Grid

- Hub

- Tree

- Web

A *sequential arrangement*, best suited to a site with only a few pages, presents information linearly, organized by time, logic, or alphanumeri-

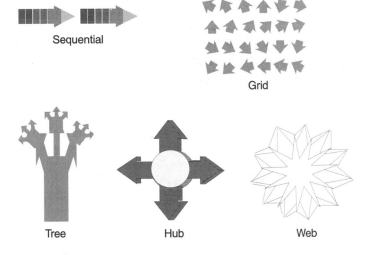

Figure 6.2.   Five basic site structures.

cally, with very few choices about where to go. A *grid or table structure* aligns topics and subtopics, taking advantage of internal links to help users search for related information within a category. Think of information arranged in a spreadsheet or database, tightly structured but with each cell of roughly equal importance. The *hub structure* also treats all information as equivalent in importance, with "spokes" to different pages radiating out from a center point and the user always returning to the hub (home page) to go to a different category of information.

By contrast, a *tree or hierarchical approach* divides content by degree of importance, with the most important (home page) as the root and all other pages branching off into progressively greater detail. Portal sites like Yahoo! often use this approach in their categorical directories, showing users how they have drilled down with a line of text: *business and economy > regional > healthcare > alternative medicine > massage therapy.*

A *web structure* allows access to all areas of your site at all times, without any predetermined hierarchy of information. It's often implemented with tabs or a row of secondary options along the header.

We know how to evaluate navigation: Is it simple? Intuitive? Consistent? Easy-to-use navigation makes customers happy and keeps them on a site. What gives navigation those characteristics? These techniques will help:

- Make sure the home page downloads quickly: a maximum of eight seconds, at your users' most common connection speed.

- Use **mouse-overs** to provide detail about subtopics available on following pages. Mouse-overs, which bring up a secondary menu when the cursor hovers over a selection, are not available with older versions of browsers. Pop-up and pull-down menus are generally effective for only the first three items in the list.

- Develop an identifiable menu structure that appears on all pages. Keep the menus on the top header and left margin so they are always visible, even if viewers use a low-resolution monitor that cuts off the right side of a page. Many developers will duplicate the menu in the footer in case viewers have scrolled down, but don't make that the only place the navigation resides.

- Change the color, shape, orientation, or type style of links on the menu and index so users can always tell where they have been and where they currently are. Whatever differentiation method you select, use it consistently across the site.

- Structure the site consistently, with similar elements always appearing in the same place on different pages.

- Limit the need to use the Back arrow on browsers; many people don't even know it's there, let alone know how to view the history of pages they've just visited.

- Take advantage of click actions to reinforce messages (i.e., ask viewers to request something specifically by clicking, thereby using their kinesthetic sense).

- If you use embedded internal links, make it clear where they go. Open external links in a new window, so your site remains on the screen.

- While used by only some viewers, a site index (sometimes called a map or directory) is useful for back-up navigation. The index affords an overview of the entire site in terms of both structure and content. Make the index available from every page and ensure that it contains active internal links to all pages.

- On a large site, include a site search engine so users can enter keywords to maneuver to their goal quickly. (See *http://www.tee finder.com*.) Select your search engine carefully; some, like the one in Microsoft's Front Page, provide inadequate results. You can use a free search engine algorithm (see *http://www.cgi-resources.com* or see the list in Figure 6.17 later in this chapter), or contract with a Web-based service to index your site for you. Some services are free if you allow advertising on your search results page.

- Assist users with on-screen help, especially for complex, information-dense sites.

Of course, like anything else creative, there are reasons to break all the rules. If the purpose is to entertain users and create an on-the-Web experience, a designer may choose to amuse, confuse, confound, and mystify the viewer, as the Haring Kids children's site does on its menu at *http://www.haringkids.com*, shown in Figure 6.3.

TIPS FOR TIRED SITES

If your site has been up for a while, you and your employees may be too familiar to provide objective feedback on navigation. Don't assume that other people use the Web or your site the same way you do. Ask customers, friends and family who are new to the Internet, or older users who aren't too familiar with the Web, to use the site. You may be surprised to find that people don't always recognize what is clickable and what is not. They may not realize they can type a URL in the address bar of the browser and hit Return to reach a site. (Many terms used on search engines are complete URLs!) Recruit half a dozen people who represent your target audience to come into the office. Watch them try to accomplish a specific task, whether it's researching a piece of information or making a purchase. Observe where they become stuck or get confused and how they try to solve the problem. Finally, look at two numbers in your statistics: how many people disappear after viewing only one page, and what pages people "exit" from. Review these findings with your developer and Web team as you restructure your site. Test the new navigation and refine as needed before you re-launch.

Figure 6.3. Unusual site menu, *http://www.haringkids.com*. Created by Daniel Wiener and Riverbed. ©Estate of Keith Haring.

Decoration: Backgrounds, Buttons, and Bars

A Web designer has almost infinite options for colors, buttons, backgrounds, textures, rules, typefaces, illustrations, photos, and multimedia to set the tone or style of your site in support of its visual concept. Should the buttons be three-dimensional, flat, or beveled? Should the imagery be realistic, abstract, or a combination of the two, like the surreal paintings of Magritte? Are cartoons or logotypes appropriate? It doesn't matter as long as the choices support the concept and remain consistent across the site. If too many variations are used, your site will have a split personality. Corporate colors, logo, and/or standard typefaces should be repeated somewhere on a site for the overall synergy of your marketing efforts.

Imagination is the only limit within the constraints of the Web. Your developer must select Web-friendly typefaces and a Web-safe palette, which optimizes colors for Web sites viewed on different platforms. (Users can override many of your choices in their browsers, but you'll just have to live with that.) Decorative elements should not replace commonly recognized symbols or imagery that viewers are familiar with. Viewers' ease of use is far more important than the small fizz of a developer's ego.

In the style book, the designer might want to specify more than just background colors and the grid layout. The style book might include specifications for:

- Icons and typography: style, size, line widths, colors, borders, button states

- Photography: cropping specs, special effects, color depth, resolution

- Windows: dimensions, textures, colors, placement

- Sounds: action effects, ambient sounds, volume, sampling rates, format

- File formats: file types, compression settings, naming conventions

Marketing Effectiveness

Everything you do on your business Web site is aimed at marketing effectiveness. From customer-centric design to calls to action, almost every decision on your Web site contributes to or detracts from its marketing effectiveness. If you can clearly state what action you want viewers to take *page-by-page*, you are halfway there.

As a matter of marketing preparedness, make sure your site is search engine–friendly, including relevant title tags and text links (you'll find much more on this in Chapter 11); that it has a page for exchanging related links; and that any e-commerce site follows the "two-clicks-to-order" rule.

After a brief detour into site organization, we'll devote an entire section to a discussion of how to apply marketing communication principles to a Web site design that subconsciously encourages viewers to take the action you want.

Refining Your Site Index

As part of the RFP, you created a site index to indicate how you thought the content should be arranged. That first draft may need revision as your site development progresses. Try writing the site index in outline form to reflect your navigation, as seen in Figure 6.4. You can use a standard outlining format to indicate how far down in the site different

I. **Home Page** (with flash animation to be supplied)

II. **Buy Socks Now** (links to catalog, shopping cart, secure checkstand)

III. **Sock It To Me**

    A. Kids Game 1 (sock design/coloring contest; code supplied)

    B. Kids Game 2 (follow the dots; code supplied)

    C. Kids Game 3 (mystery of the lost socks; code supplied)

IV. **About SillySox** (links to 4 other SuperSillyStuff, Inc. Web sites)

    A. About SuperSillyStuff, Inc.

        1. Company Directory

        2. Current Press Releases

          a. Archived releases

    B. Resources & Links

    C. Advertise With Us (traffic & demographics)

        1. Media Kit (rates)

V. **Register for SoxNews** (cgi form for newsletter)

VI. **Contact Us** (pop-up e-mail available from every page)

Figure 6.4. Sample site index outline.

pages will appear. The large Roman numeral pages would be the equivalent of the pages that appear as links from your main menu. Capital letters would be the pages with a direct link from one of those main pages, and so on. The index is not an exact map of the navigation, since you may let people reach specific pages deep in the site in a variety of ways. The index allows you to inventory your pages, which is essential for managing your site, as you'll see in Chapter 8. And for users, a site index yields security and a sense of control.

Consider using navigation to segment your viewers as WebTrends does on its home page (*http://www.webtrends.com*) in Figure 6.5. Quickly directing different audiences to the information they need is an effective marketing technique, and it reduces users' frustration.

You can gauge the "depth" and "width" of your site by viewing your outline as if it were a wedding cake, with the home page as the decoration on the top and each level down another tier, as seen in Figure 6.6. Unless you are doing an information-intensive site, you probably want to keep your site to no more than five tiers. You'll find that you are always juggling two parameters of site organization. On the

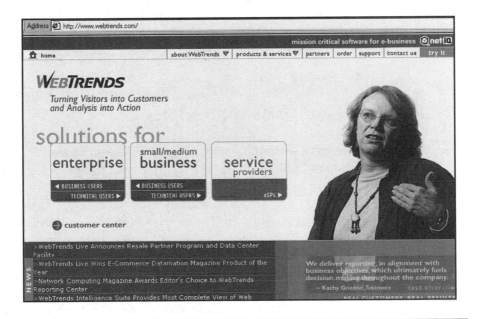

Figure 6.5. Audience segmentation through navigation, *http://www.web trends.com*. Reprinted by permission of New IQ Corporation. Copyright © 2002 New IQ Corporation. All rights reserved.

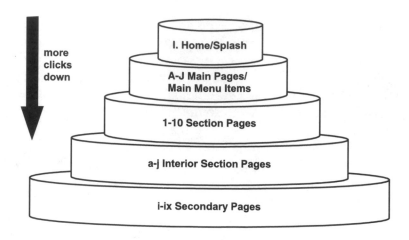

Figure 6.6. Site organization is like a wedding cake.

one hand, it's best not to have more than six to ten options available on a screen at a time. On the other hand, a user should be able to get to any point on a site with two to three clicks. It's nearly impossible to resolve both these demands simultaneously, but you can opt for judicious compromise. A broad and shallow Web site is easier to navigate than one that is narrow and deep.

Marketing Communications Principles

Just because we have invented new technologies doesn't mean we have new brains. Human beings still operate on the basis of age-old instinct, buried in the emotional part of our brains, the "lizard" brain. It's a truism in marketing that people make buying decisions based on feelings and then rationalize those decisions with facts. What kind of feelings? Fear, insecurity, loneliness, frustration, anxiety, anger, greed, pleasure, happiness, joy, love. (Do you hear echoes from Maslow's hierarchy of needs?) Marketing communications considers how the presentation of information affects these emotions and thus influences buying decisions. In terms of marketing communications, the goals online are no different from other selling methods, but applying those principles to the Web as a new medium can be tricky.

People buy when they feel comfortable with your company and your product; when they feel they can trust you to fulfill the promises you make online; and most of all, when they believe that buying will make *them* feel good. So what must your Web site do emotionally? It must convey that your company is reliable and trustworthy. It must inspire confidence. It must appear that you understand the viewers' emotional needs and material concerns; that you share their values; that your product or service will solve *their* problem (not yours!).

How can you do that on a Web site? Design, design, design! In our linear, word-soaked world, we tend to forget the emotional impact of layout, colors, fonts, photographs, and graphics. We tend to ignore the ability of good writing to convey an emotional jolt, as well as facts. And we tend to downplay the importance of customer testimonials, certification from the Better Business Bureau, or guarantees of satisfaction. A well-designed site draws viewers in; a poorly designed site pushes them away, without viewers' ever being able to articulate why they left. Perhaps you're beginning to see why those sites designed by the boss's teenage son leave so much to be desired!

Human Factors

Even if you resist the lure of the lizard brain (you're in denial!), perhaps you will at least acknowledge that the human brain has certain attributes in terms of memory, organization of information, and perception.

First, the brain is built for recognition, not recall. It's much, much easier to recognize information that's presented on the screen than to try to pull it out of mental storage. For instance, navigation buttons need text, not unidentified icons for menu choices—you don't want to force visitors to remember what each icon means. Second, the brain likes the number seven: it is the limit of the attention span (hence, the need not to overwhelm the user with too many choices on a page), as well as the limit for short-term memory. And it's the number of times a name or ad needs to be seen before it can be remembered.

Third, the human mind thrives on contrast. Without it, the mind begins to wander or becomes overwhelmed by massive information flowing in without differentiation. The interplay of visuals, text, and empty space must be handled carefully to energize viewers without confusing them. Designers, who call this dynamic tension, have many different ways to create contrast within an element, such as variations in type, color, illustration techniques, dimensionality, or positive versus negative (empty) space. Leave this to a pro!

Fourth, the brain likes to find patterns. It constantly searches for repetitive elements in the environment, looking to make sense of chaos, to create order from anarchy. That's why consistent design from one page to another and consistent operations from one task to another are so critical. The brain enjoys getting help—and the viewer will be grateful without knowing why. Try grouping objects with similar functions together, using proximity (e.g., all the shopping functions are along the right margin) and/or similarity (all the shopping functions are related by shape, size, or color). It's particularly important to keep menus and navigational cues consistent—same location, same style label, same color changes in different states, same associated sounds. An operation, such as "click here to start music," should be activated the same way on all pages.

As new pages are added and new people work on the site over time, it can be hard to keep the site from deteriorating and losing its hard-won consistency. To avoid this, maintain the layout grid and follow the precepts in the style book created by your designer. Enforce that style book as a matter of Web policy with other departments when they complain that you are behaving like "design police" and are handcuffing their creativity!

There is a kinesthesia of clicks. On a very basic level, every click users make binds them closer to your company and to your site. Taking a specific action actually creates a "body memory," so there may be reasons other than your own convenience to ask viewers to click to reach the next activity, or to enter a particular piece of information on a form.

Consider, too, human factors specific to your target audience. If you're concerned about the accessibility of your site to seniors, children, or people with disabilities, you need to assess many other factors, from readability levels to information-processing skills to sensory deficits. For information about how to address these issues and test your site's accessibility, go to *http://www.cast.org/bobby*.

Jakob Nielsen and many others have looked at how the operation of the brain should influence the human/computer interface, including the Web. (You can see his work at *http://www.useit.com/papers/heuristic/heuristic_list.html*.) Heeding his advice can improve the way people feel about your Web site. Among his principles, he recommends:

- Matching the Web with the real world, using viewers' language, not jargon

- Maintaining consistency and standards across the site, using well-recognized icons (e.g., shopping cart) and following Web conventions (e.g., underlined blue text for hyperlinks) whenever possible

- Keeping users informed of what's happening through feedback within a reasonable time; for instance, after submitting a form, let users know it has been received

- Making navigation, other actions, and alternatives visible, given that the brain prefers recognition to recall

- Keeping design and content simple, avoiding irrelevant or rarely needed information that competes for attention with what's important

- Ensuring that instructions and help are easy to access (both online and offline).

For more on usability, check out:

- CERN Usability Guidelines: *http://www.w3.org/WAI*

- Microsoft Usability Guidelines: *http://msdn.microsoft.com/workshop/management/planning/improvingsiteusa.asp*

- Philip Greenspun: *http://www.arsdigita.com/books/panda*

Color and Sound

Color is among the first sensory inputs processed by the brain. Color evokes a subconscious emotional response, influencing physiological reactions, moods, and buying behavior. "Warm" colors (red, orange, yellow) imply activity and excitement, while "cool" colors (green, blue, violet) are calming and relaxing. Can you predict which products would do best with "hot" colors (e.g., kids' toys) and which with "cool" (e.g., aromatherapy products)? As you surf the Web, see whether the colors used on a site match your expectations.

For your own site, your designer will pick two to four colors to predominate. Too many colors (on the wrong site) may distract or overstimu-

wers, with the unintended consequence of limiting sales. A good
designer will pay attention to color as a way to focus the viewer's
on on key messages or product features, while de-emphasizing
nformation. He or she may choose colors to organize material or
to convey the navigational structure through color-coding, using the
principle that warmer colors come to the front and cooler colors recede.

Alas, the Web imposes constraints on design that don't exist in print.
The designer must ensure that the colors are from the Web-safe palette;
text remains legible; the graphics don't increase download time to an
unacceptable level; the page remains readable when printed out in black-
and-white; and that the design will be compatible with different versions of browsers on different monitors using different operating systems.
Some things done in print, such as wrapping text around an irregular
object, simply won't work on the Web unless they are loaded as a complete graphic. That has a drawback in download time. If your designer
and programmer are separate individuals, be sure to have the programmer review the design for practicality before you approve it.

If you decide to include sound on your Web site (see the multimedia
section later in this chapter), remember that it is another mood modi-
fier. Slow-tempo music encourages leisurely shopping, while an up-tempo
beat increases activity. No matter what your personal taste, any music
used on your site should be compatible with your color choice to reinforce the mood you wish to create.

Layout and Images

As with any other design problem, there are an infinite number of ways
to lay out a Web page. The designer faces Web constraints: the layout
must not interfere with the navigation and it must avoid extraneous
design elements that users won't bother to learn. Even when a logo
appears on the page, most users ignore it, as they do mission statements, slogans, and anything else that isn't of immediate benefit to their
task at hand.

On the Web, as in a newspaper (in cultures with writing from left to
right), the eye starts in the upper right corner, moves to the upper left,
and then scans left to right. However, a clever designer can redirect the
visual path to the most important message on the page with a good
layout. A single dominant element—the largest or most colorful—will
draw the viewer's attention first; several smaller images will make the
large one even more important.

Don't be surprised if your designer avoids a symmetrical page; imbalance makes a page more dynamic. For a quick test, try dividing the visible portion of a Web page into thirds vertically and horizontally. The points of greatest interest—the points with inherent visual magnetism where important information should be placed—will be at the intersection of two of those lines, not in the center. You can see this principle applied in Figure 6.7.

To create a good page, a designer will take advantage of multiple elements of design: line, shape, value (lightness/darkness/shading), texture/pattern, and most of all white space. White space (also called **negativeZ** or **empty space**) is especially important on the Web, where users' eyes are fatigued from too much time in front of a computer screen. White space not only rests the eyes, it frames important information and demands that the design remain uncluttered. As tempting as it may be to fill every pixel of coveted screen real estate with information—avoid it. To isolate your layout from the impact of color, look at it on the screen in black and white. A good layout will hold up under the test.

Your choice of images depends significantly on your audience. If you're selling online, you absolutely, positively must show the product!

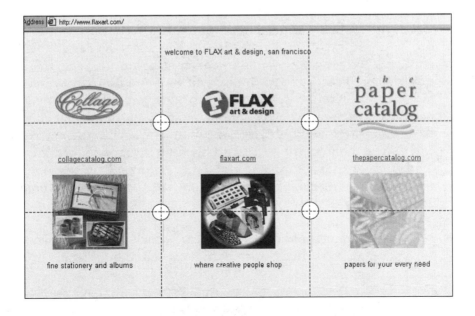

Figure 6.7. Points of visual magnetism at intersection of thirds, *http://www. flaxart.com.* ©Flax Art & Design.

Duh! On primary pages of a Web site, most consumers prefer dynamic photos that convey motion or realism, preferably with people in them. Static product shots are best relegated to your catalog pages. Engineers—but few others—love schematics, graphs, tables, flow charts, and cutaway views.

If you can afford it, shoot original photos. Otherwise scan in existing photos or consider using stock images. If you're scanning prints or using existing digital photos, remember to reformat them as low-resolution, Web-ready JPEGs. Other graphics and clip art should be saved as GIFs. Keep the size of each file in Kbytes as small as possible for speedy downloads.

Multiple Web sites sell stock; look for royalty-free images that you buy once and can use forever. Low-resolution (72 dpi) images, which will be the least expensive, are fine for Web-only use. If you plan to incorporate an image in print as well, buy the medium- to high-resolution version (depending on the size at which the image will be reproduced) for decent quality. Let your designer select the photos unless that's one of your fortes. As with everything else on the Web, your customers' needs and expectations come first.

Typographic Tips

Given the problems of reading a computer screen, how words "look" on the screen is as critical as the words themselves. Since designers can't control a Web page the way they can control a print page, this can be quite frustrating. Page appearance will vary on different browsers, different browser versions, different platforms, and different monitors. If users don't have the typeface you specify, their machines default to standard fonts preset only for large, medium, and small. You can treat the text as a graphic to avoid these problems, but that will increase download time. What's a writer to do? First, follow all the standard techniques for easy readability—e.g., avoiding all uppercase or all bold type. Second, consider these tips:

- Avoid italics and underlined text, which by Web convention is used only for links. Stick with normal and bold type.

- Use color contrast and unusual type position for emphasis (as long as the type is not vertical).

- Keep the most important information "above the fold," so users don't have to scroll to see it.

- Design for a 640×480-pixel screen for 14-inch monitors for an audience of predominantly home users; design for a 800×600-pixel, 15-inch screen for predominantly business users, who will have newer equipment.

- Keep text lines less than half a screen wide with hard returns.

- Use lots of white space around text to rest the eyes.

- Select a typeface that's been optimized for the Web, such as Verdana, Trebuchet, or Georgia.

- Reversed type, especially if the contrast is low, is hard to read on the screen. Don't make the mistake of using reversed type in two colors, or even colored text on a colored background, without testing to see how it will print in black and white. Two different colors at the same level of saturation may have almost no contrast in black and white.

- Keep headlines proportional to type size and relate them to both body type and images.

- Use a ragged-right margin.

- Use a double space between paragraphs rather than indents.

- Make it easy to download and/or print long articles for easy reading.

For more information on good Web design principles, see:

- Web Wonk: *http://www.dsiegel.com/tips/index.html*

- Page Resource: *http://www.pageresource.com/zine/index.html*

- Joe Gillespie's Web Page Design for Designers (great tips on typography): *http://www.wpdfd.com/wpdhome.htm*

- cNet: *http://builder.cnet.com*

- National Cancer Institute Web Design & Usability Guidelines: *http://usability.gov/guidelines*

- Yahoo!: *http://www.yahoo.com/Arts/Design_Arts/Graphic_Design/Web_Page_Design_and_Layout*

- Web Monkey: *http://hotwired.lycos.com/webmonkey*

- Georgia Institute of Technology: *http://www.lcc.gatech.edu/gallery/dzine*

Writing for the Web

Writing Web-style is an art in itself. Text on the Web needs to emphasize quick pickup of keywords. When viewers see something of interest, they stay on the page. Otherwise, it's "hasta la vista, baby." It's always hard for writers to throw out words, but they need to throw out even more of them for the Web. As we noted above, the low resolution and contrast of a computer screen present a physiological challenge for readers—text on a screen is hard to read and tires the eyes. It actually takes 25 percent longer to read the same passage on the screen than it does in print. To make things easier, surround text with plenty of white space and keep line lengths to less than half a screen width. That means only 8 to 12 words per line! Viewers might not know why, but they'll reward you for saving their eyes by staying longer on your site.

The Reader's View

Writing for the Web is thankless—you're writing for people who don't read. They scan text instead. Because they are in a hurry, viewers ignore the niceties of complete sentences and long explanations. Use plenty of indented, bulleted phrases, much as you would in a presentation.

Your task is complicated by the inherent nonlinearity of the Web experience. People may arrive at one of your pages from anywhere—from another page on your site, from a search engine, via a link from another site. Since they can enter your site on multiple pages and sequence text within any order within your site, you can't assume that people bring information with them from page to page. Consequently, you must establish context on each page, repeat critical information multiple times, and avoid using extended metaphors or pronouns without antecedents.

Inverted Pyramid

With viewers looking for information quickly, it makes sense to adopt the journalistic convention of the inverted pyramid, shown in Figure 6.8, on every page. Put the most important information at the top and the least important at the bottom. This approach ensures that key material appears before scrolling, the equivalent of "above the fold" in the newspaper world. Borrow another technique from journalism: Write a "**lead**" (the very first sentence) that grabs readers' attention. Use any technique that works to create a "hook": quotes, questions, comparison, contrast, conflict. To improve search engine ranking, consider the first paragraph as if it were an abstract of the entire page and load it with keywords.

Scrolling vs. Chunking

Structuring information within and between pages is another challenge. Even though it may cost more if your developer charges by the page, many short pages are better than one or two lengthy ones that require

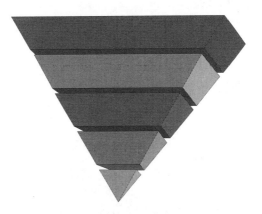

Figure 6.8.   Inverted pyramid style of journalism.

scrolling. **Chunk** text into paragraphs of fewer than 100 words and link them together. Each chunk should be understandable on its own, with a concise topic sentence and only one idea per paragraph. Two or more chunks with links are called a **stack**.

If you must have long scrolling pages, such as FAQs, put a linkable index at the top of the page, so users can jump immediately to their particular concern. Put a link back to the top at the end of each individual answer. Scrolled pages also work for archived articles that will be printed out.

The Written Word

Think short: short words, short sentences, short paragraphs of three sentences or less. You're writing a cross between journalism and ad copy, not a William Faulkner novel! A page of Web text is only 125 words—half a standard page of double-spaced type. Assume that your first draft of each chunk is probably twice the length it should be and cut, cut, cut.

Adopt yet another journalistic technique: stick with active voice (the subject does the acting). "The dog chased a car," not "A car was chased by the dog." Grammar checkers in most word processors can be set to highlight passive voice (not perfectly, but better than nothing). One clue that you may be using passive voice: forms of the verb "to be."

In spite of its inherent challenges, writing for the Web benefits from the same concepts that energize all good writing.

- Write for your audience and in their voice; teenagers expect completely different language than CEOs of Fortune 500 companies.

- Use vivid verbs and nuanced nouns. Avoid anemic adjectives; kill clichés; and junk the techno-jargon.

- Write clearly, using familiar words and simple sentence construction.

- Write concretely and avoid idioms, especially if you have an international audience.

- Write for an emotional jolt, humor, or entertainment on every page; the viewer wants a payoff for visiting your site.

- Above all, write correctly. Check for errors in spelling, grammar, and word usage. Either read your text out loud or ask someone else to proof your copy.

Keep your tone conversational, rather than authoritative. Some of the "no-no's" in standard written English are okay on the Web: contractions, colloquialisms, slang, sentence fragments. Writing in second person ("you"), which you would rarely do in formal English, is excellent on the Web because it forces you to focus on benefits to the reader. First person (I or we) is okay. Third person (he, she, it) can be deadly.

To get an idea of good writing, look at the product descriptions at *Gardeners.com* (*http://www.gardeners.com*) in Figure 6.9. They are brief but informative; with a benefits statement, up-selling, and calls to action. Check out the sites below for more information on writing for the Web, but don't forget the best book on writing—*The Elements of Style* by William Strunk and E. B. White.

- CERN Style Guide: *http://www.w3.org/Provider/Style/Introduction.html*

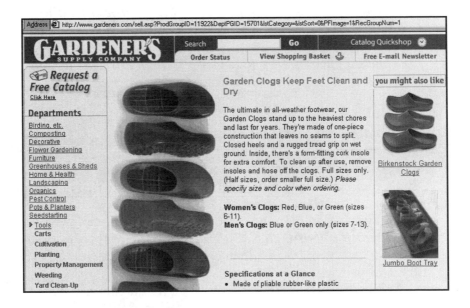

Figure 6.9. Well-written product descriptions with upselling, *http://www.gardeners.com*. Courtesy Gardener's Supply.

TIPS FOR TIRED SITES

Polish your prose! One of the easiest (and least expensive) things to fix on your site is the text. Try reading it aloud. Can you get through the first paragraph without snoring? Does it grab you by the mouse-hand and say, "Come here. Have I got a deal for you"? Is there even a whiff of a benefit for being on the site? No? Then fire up your keyboard or hire a copywriter to give a little flair to your text, at least on the home page. Hit the Delete key when you find passive voice, long sentences, or slithery jargon. Cut ruthlessly. If any page is longer than two scrolled screens (250 words), restructure the content into two or more pages. Finally, write a headline that aims directly at your target audience with a WIIFM (What's In It For Me) message.

- Yale Center for Advanced Instruction Media Web Style Guide: *http://info.med.yale.edu/caim/manual/*

- Web Writing Style Resources at Web Central: *http://cio.com/central/style.html*

- Jutta Degener's Writing Guide: *http://kbs.cs.tu-berlin.de/~jutta/ht/writing.html*

- Jakob Nielsen: *http://www.useit.com/papers/webwriting.*

The Promise and Peril of Rich Media

A sticky site retains visitors through multiple page views. To achieve "stickiness," more and more Web sites incorporate **rich media**, the Web term for **multimedia** incorporated on a site. "Rich media" refers to the presentation of animation, video, sound, real-time information feeds, 3-D, virtual reality simulations, games, interactive programs, and even aromas! Rich media is rich in another way: it's expensive to produce in time and money.

You may want rich media to create a unique Internet-based form of entertainment. Or perhaps your site is designed to promote your corporate identity as an innovative Web developer. Some reports show that rich media pages generate 20 to 60 percent more traffic than static pages and that rich media ads have 8 to 18 percent click-through rates, compared to 1 percent for regular banners. But many companies add rich media to their site simply because everyone else is doing it, or because they think it's "in."

As tantalizing as it may be to incorporate rich media, ask yourself whether it will enhance the communication goals for your site and whether it's appropriate for your target audience. Are there enough resources available in budget, personnel, and time categories to produce it? Will the user be able to download and play back the media easily? Just because something *can* be done doesn't mean it *should* be done.

Some rich media options—simple GIF animations, QuickTime movies, and some audio files—now run automatically on most browsers. While the newest browsers come with Java and Flash animation **plug-ins** (special pieces of playback software downloaded into a browser) already installed, many users on older browsers will need to download and install it.

Usually, it is straightforward to download and install plug-ins, but the time-consuming process may deter harried, casual, or inexperienced users. As new versions of browser and plug-in software are released, users may have to repeat this process. At the very least, users need RealPlayer from RealNetworks (*http://www.real.com*), an MP3 audio player, Acrobat Reader (*http://www.adobe.com*), Flash (*http://www.macromedia.com*), and Microsoft's Windows Media Player (*http://www.windowsmedia.com*) and/or Apple's QuickTime player (*http://www.quicktime.com*) to obtain good coverage of the various media formats on the Internet.

Most sites now include a quick test to see whether a plug-in is necessary ("If the pig is flying, you have Flash; if not, please click here to download."). Most plug-ins can be downloaded free from the developer's site. If possible, mirror the plug-ins so users can download them without leaving your site. Before you decide to implement rich media, go through the plug-in installation process yourself to decide whether your users are likely to do it.

Streaming media files, whether video (seen in Figure 6.10) or audio, play out as they are transmitted over the Internet to the user's computer. This is particularly valuable when files would be too big to fit into memory, when they would take an unacceptably long time to download, or when you want interactivity. However, to play streaming media or virtual reality files, users may need to reconfigure their machines and install additional plug-ins. You might want to offer viewers a choice of media as done in Figure 6.11.

In other cases, video and audio files are downloaded to a user's machine to be played later. Most new computers come with the built-in

Figure 6.10.   A site that uses streaming video, *http://www.atomfilms.com/ shockwave.com/af/home*. Courtesy AtomShockwave Corp. Copyright 2002 AtomShockwave Corp. and its licensors. "AtomFilms" and "PhotoJam" are trademarks and service marks of AtomShockwave Corp., its licensors, or other parties.

capability to play back downloaded video, audio, and 3-D graphics. By definition, however, users can't interact in real time with a downloaded file except to start, stop, fast-forward, or reverse it. Since it can take a while, viewers may be reluctant to download a long video clip they watch once and discard. Worse yet, they could end up resenting a business that requires this method to obtain information.

Several other factors may affect your rich media decision. Most streaming media require high-speed, wide-bandwidth connections to play well. Agonizingly slow delivery may result from low-speed modems, too many people online at any one time, bandwidth limitations, or the capacity of the server. Remember, only 17 percent of all Internet subscribers in the United States currently have high-speed connections, and the percentage is lower among home subscribers.

Compared to static pages, rich media sites also require that your users have more memory, faster processors, more recent system software and browsers, and better skills. Consider the importance of providing an alternative for users who lack adequate hardware and software

Figure 6.11.   Allowing multimedia options, *http://www.dreamtime.net.au/ creation*. ©2002 Australian Museum.

for rich media displays. Finally, make sure you can assemble the technical and financial resources to produce multimedia. Rich media compounds the complexity and expense of Web site development.

As an alternative, consider building an interactive application that is less resource-intensive. For an example of interactive rich media, check out Fireworks.com (*http://www.fireworks.com/interactive/fireworks_ show/default.asp*) in Figure 6.12. Users can select a variety of backgrounds, choose music, and select types of fireworks and colors in realtime. They are really selecting prepackaged, very short Flash animation files. Lots of fun, but only a fraction of the hassle of a long, prepackaged streaming video piece.

Helpful Hints for a Successful Site

What draws visitors to a site again and again? What enables you to build a relationship on the Web that turns a prospect into a customer? An existing customer into a repeat customer? According to a 2001 poll from Jupiter Media Metrix, U.S. surfers are more likely to revisit sites

Figure 6.12. Interactive rich media, *http://www.fireworks.com/interactive/ fireworks_show/default.asp*. Courtesy B. J. Alan Company.

that are "fast-loading, customizable, and more informative." Consumers ranked those three characteristics as far more important than expensive features like rich media or delivery to wireless handsets. Customizable elements included specifying a layout based on personal interest, polling, and chat capability. The need for information applies equally to retail sites; customers revisit sites that offer more product information and product suggestions.

You might want to check your Web developer's work against the list that follows. Keep a running list of ideas as you research other sites.

Splash Screens

A **splash screen** is often displayed as a distraction while a Web site loads. It sometimes lists the browser version for which the site is optimized or includes information about what plug-ins are needed to run special features. Links to plug-ins or suggestions about how to speed up the Web site if you have a slow computer may be included.

A splash screen might dissolve into the home page or ask the user to click for entry. Multiple splash screens can be customized according to their source, providing visitors with a submenu of choices appropriate to their interests. Splash "doorways" with different URLs make it easy to track the effectiveness of promotional activities by counting how many viewers arrive via each entry point.

Splash screens, like the one for the multimedia site Monster Interactive (*http://www.monsteri.com*), are an opportunity to make a first impression or establish a creative theme.

Home Page

You have only one chance to make a first impression, whether it is your lobby, window display, telephone receptionist, brochure cover, splash screen, or **home page**. Your home page is a welcome mat, main menu, and advertisement rolled into one. Whether your viewers consist of customers, suppliers, potential employees, or just casual visitors, your Web site makes a critical statement about your company.

The best home pages arrange pictures and text artistically to catch the eye of the viewer and lure him or her to explore further, like *http://www.scifi.com/set* in Figure 6.13. This streaming audio site uses visual images to "hook" listeners!

Requiring the viewer to scroll to see a complete image or description can be very distracting. If scrolling is unavoidable, try not to wrap text before and after an image. Instead, group text together so it will fit on one screen, with the picture on the next screen. In particular, try to avoid horizontal scrolling unless there is a valid aesthetic or display reason for doing so. The dinosaur home page at *National Geographic* (*http://nationalgeographic.com/dinorama*) is one of the few great examples of horizontal scrolling.

If it's too daunting to remember all this, use a Web host or developer that offers a gallery of templates you can customize, such as those from WyeNet at *http://www.wyenet.com*, shown in Figure 5.7 earlier. Additional template sources may be found in Figure 6.18 later in this chapter.

Avoid Causes for Complaint

According to a Cognitiative survey, Web buyers *avoid* sites for somewhat different reasons than they patronize them. The five most com-

Figure 6.13.   Enticing home page, *http://www.scifi.com/set*. Courtesy USA Networks.

mon reasons given to avoid sites are seen in Figure 6.14. Note that only *one* reason (bad customer service) deals with an off-site issue! One bad Web experience can turn a viewer off your site forever.

Reduce Download Time

As a rule of thumb, it takes one second to download 2 Kb of information with a 56K modem. Try to keep each page below 30 Kb. If it's more than that, decide whether the image or information is really necessary. If so, compress large files, even if it means sacrificing resolution for speed.

A high-contrast, print-quality photograph may take as long as two minutes to transfer across phone lines. Most photos can be converted to a much smaller, low-resolution JPEG file that downloads in less than 20 seconds. Tools like PhotoShop's WebVise further optimize JPEG and GIF files for the Web. Ask your developer about using size attributes to reduce perceived download time. Attributes allow the text to download without waiting for the browser to figure out picture size. If possible, reuse the same image more than once, since it won't need to be downloaded again.

Or consider using a series of thumbnail images, allowing viewers to click on the one or two pictures they would like to see expanded. Some-

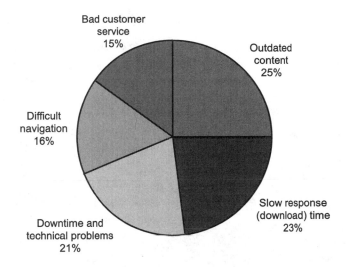

Figure 6.14.   Five most common reasons to avoid sites, *http://www.cognitiative. com*. Pulse of the Customer,^{SM} Cognitiative, Inc.

times it is more effective to display an image unfolding as it downloads, instead of waiting for it to finish and pop on. As alternatives, consider line drawings or illustrations: GIFs download much more quickly than JPEG files. Keep in mind that a plain white background will download faster than a colored or patterned one.

Other tips to speed download time include avoiding Java and selecting Web development packages carefully. Many common **WYSIWYG** (what you see is what you get) packages, like Microsoft's FrontPage, Adobe's Page Mill, or Claris's Homepage, slow down pages with irrelevant code.

Many users on dial-up modems still turn off Web graphics so that pages will download more quickly, clicking on an image only if it interests them. Be sure that your text and <alt> tags entice viewers to watch the image and that your layout and information flow works well without photos. You can check download time with commercial load-testing software such as Loadtesting.com (*http://www.loadtesting.com*), or by using some of the free online tools discussed in Chapter 8.

Since people can easily abort an image transfer and move to another site, try following Tetra's lead in Figure 6.15 (*http://www.tetra-fish.com/va/index.html*). Viewers build their own virtual aquarium on this site one fish at a time. By occupying viewers with decision making while an image downloads, Tetra makes the wait almost imperceptible.

Figure 6.15. Virtual aquarium, *http://www.tetra-fish.com/va/index.html.*
Courtesy Tetra.

Make Your Site Easy to Understand

Problems finding information and organizing what is found can be addressed in several ways. Return to the principles of good navigation described earlier. The complexity of your navigation scheme will suggest presentation needs for your pages. Secondary menus or mouse-overs may keep pages from getting too cluttered and offer more choices to those who need them.

Since viewers linking to your site may enter on pages other than your home page, maintain consistent access to a menu on every page, as Dancing Dear (*http://www.dancingdeer.com*) does in Figure 6.16.

Your page-naming conventions can help users organize information they collect. Use similar page names for similar information.

Consider a call to action that reminds users to bookmark your site.

Conduct Testing and Maintenance to Avoid Problems

A viewer perceives as a "crash" anything that keeps the site from operating as anticipated, including those infamous 404 errors generated by a broken link. Links (internal and external) are enormously powerful because they lead users through a chain of related information with the

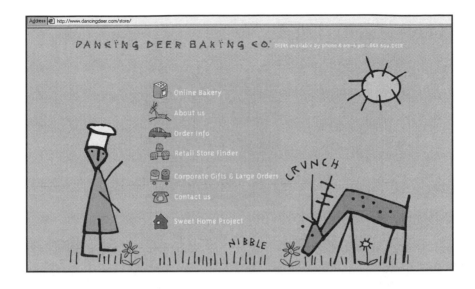

Figure 6.16. Consistent visual menu, *http://www.dancingdeer.com/store* Courtesy Dancing Deer Baking Co., Inc. Design by Slover [AND] Company.

simple click of a mouse button. This problem is easily avoided by running verification software at least monthly to monitor links for valid connections and obtain referrals to a new address. (See Chapter 8 for details.)

Don't forget that internal links (to other pages on your own site) can generate a similar problem if a page has been removed or renamed. This happens frequently on large sites with many stored documents. Development packages are supposed to handle page changes automatically, but they don't always do so. Be sure to search your own site for any links to an altered page whenever you update content.

Visitors might also become frustrated if they can't use your link to a popular URL, such as the Mars Pathfinder images at NASA, because the destination site is busy. Instead, obtain permission to **mirror** the information on your own site with appropriate credit. You can use mirroring creatively to draw visitors to your site and away from a jammed site. In fact, a mirrored site geographically closer to viewers' physical locations is often faster for them to access.

Don't shortchange yourself when reserving server space. Leave a cushion of 40 percent more space than you need. Of course, if the unthinkable happens and your site goes down completely, inform customers as soon as possible and offer refunds or coupons to make amends.

Want to make yourself feel better? Check out the mistakes that others have made at:

- *http://www.worstoftheweb.com*

- *http://www.webpagesthatsuck.com*

- *http://www.westegg.com/badpages*

To see how Web sites have evolved in terms of sophistication, try The Wayback Machine created by the Internet Archive at *http://www.archive.org/index.html*.

Forget-Me-Nots

Check your design against this compilation of pointers and reminders:

- Web or no Web, many people still prefer tangible sheets of paper in a manila folder stuck in a filing drawer. Offer users a print-and-save–friendly version of each page on your site. Many people don't realize that frame-based sites print (or save) only the frame that contains the cursor. Test that your pages will print out properly; for instance, yellow text on a black background may be nearly invisible in print. Offer the option of reverse printing (black text on white) if your site uses a dark background and be sure that multihued sites print legibly in black and white.

- Use many calls to action. In classic marketing terms, a call to action is the "close," the final step in a sale. You can ask viewers to demonstrate interest with smaller calls to action, moving them ever closer to a sale. On the Web, internal calls to action are almost always active intra-site links that ask users to take an action online, such as subscribing to a newsletter, signing a register, or bookmarking a page. They can also be used simply to move people through your site. External calls to action ask people to take an action off the site.

  Calls to action often use an active verb in the imperative: Save money, Get a free ..., Learn about ..., Check out our new ..., Try ..., Test drive, Register now, For more information contact .... Be specific, but gentle, if you want users to take action. Don't bury a call to action three levels down. Make different opportunities visible at the highest level and on every page. Whatever the call to action, it should be tied to marketing goals and objectives and should eventually lead visitors to the close. We talk more in Chapter 9 about using internal calls to action as a method of promotion.

- Include an e-mail address and point of human contact on your site, preferably on every page. If there are multiple points of contact, try to put the specific, relevant e-mail address on the page instead of using a generic info@yourcompany.com. It will shorten the time for response, making it more likely that you can stay within a 24-hour window to reply. It's a mistake to show an e-mail address only for your Webmaster (often your developer), who may not know enough about your business and staff to forward mail appropriately or promptly. If the Webmaster's e-mail address is on every page as well, specify that it's for technical assistance or problems with the site.

- Create a footer on each page that includes your street address, telephone number, and fax number. If you are selling goods or services, include your toll-free number as well. You can put an active "Contact Us" e-mail pop-up in the footer.

- Update the site frequently. For your own benefit, to improve search engine rankings, and to indicate that your site is current, show the date last modified and the name of the person who did it somewhere on the site. If your site isn't being updated regularly, remove the date of last modification. An old date is a turn-off.

- A What's New section directs repeat visitors immediately to new content on your site. Note the fish icon on the Fishing Online site (*http://www.pvisuals.com/fishing/whats_new/whats_new.html*), for example.

- Watch This Space. If you must remove some content and can't delete references to a page, post a construction icon. This may frustrate viewers, but it's better than an error message. Avoid posting frequent messages about coming pages that may never get built. To generate user interest in a return visit, announce an opening day for the page and include a call to action to bookmark the site for a return visit, perhaps with a chance to win something.

Freebies and Features

As you've learned, developing a good site is a detailed and time-consuming process. The more you can acquire elsewhere, the shorter and less expensive your development cycle will be. Features that required custom programming several years ago are now easy to add to your site as links, services, or downloadable code. You'll find sources for site improvements such as maps and search engines in Figure 6.17. Figure 6.18 offers sources for free Web and Internet services, and Figure 6.19 provides places to obtain decorative items like backgrounds, buttons, and bars. Sites for free tools may be found in Chapter 8; sites for free promotional options may be found in Chapters 9 through 12.

Features and Site Amenities

Use the added features and site amenities shown in Figure 6.17 when appropriate as a way to encourage visitors to linger on your site. For instance, contractors or architects might include a map and direction service linked to photos of their buildings so potential clients can drive by their projects. A children's site might encourage youngsters to create and send free greeting cards. A company that offers hundreds of products or documents would benefit from a site-based search engine. A

TIPS FOR TIRED SITES

Is traffic falling off? Are you losing repeat visitors? Perhaps it's time to spruce up your site with an amenity or two. Go through the list of amenities in Figure 6.17 to see what would most appeal to your audience. It could be anything from a "cartoon of the day" to a valuable, industry-specific news feed. Want to build a community of interest? Look for a chat room, scheduled conferences with guests, or a message board to make your site inviting. An on-site contest, a game, or a drawing with multiple opportunities to win entices repeat visitors. Personalized event and calendar services or free e-mail will bring people back to your site on a regular basis.

Type of Resource	URL	Free ✔
Affiliate program	*http://www.amazon.com/ exec/obidos/subst/associates/ join/associates.html*	Up to 15% to referring site
Calendar	*http://www.calendars.net*	✔
Shopping cart	*http://insitewebdesign.com/ shopcart.html*	<30 items
E-mail (offer on your site)	*http://www.zzn.com/informail/ signup.asp*	✔
Greeting cards	*http://www.regards.com*	✔
Guestbook, polls, and screensavers	*http://www.miatrade.com*	✔
Hub for affiliate programs	*http://www.refer-it.com*	✔
Hub for affiliate programs	*http://www.associate programs.com*	✔
Hub for other free resources	*http://www.totallyfreestuff.com*	✔
Map & direction service	*http://home.vicinity.com/ us/web.htm*	✔
Multiple: cartoons, classifieds, counters, forum, greeting cards, guestbook, mailing list, search engines, Web announcement	*http://www.bravenet.com*	✔
Multiple: chat room, e-mail list, guestbook, message boards, quiz-let, search box, site submission	*http://www.beseen.com*	✔
Multiple: perl cgi scripts, graphics, tools	*http://www.bignosebird.com*	✔
Multiple: animation, javascripts, tell-a-friend, quotes	*http://www.tripod.lycos.com/ build/welcome/accessories.html*	For members only
Multiple: games, greeting cards, screensavers, Web e-mail	*http://www.maxpatch.com*	✔
Polls	*http://www.infopoll.net*	✔
Polls, counters, guestbook	*http://www.pollit.com*	✔
Search engine	*http://www.freefind.com*	✔

Figure 6.17.   Free features and site amenities.

tourist-oriented company in San Diego or Puerto Rico might want to tout local weather, while one that sponsors conferences might create online forums for past participants. Too many features may detract from your marketing message and dilute the impact of your site.

Type of Resource	URL	Free ✔
Brand naming guide	*http://www.namestormers.com*	✔
E-mail forwarding and Web site re-direction	*http://www.mydomain.com*	✔
E-mail (Web-based)	*http://www.beseen.com*	✔
	http://www.email.com	✔
	http://www.hotmail.com	✔
Free and almost free hosting services	*http://www.clickherefree.com*	✔
	http://www.freehostingnavigator. f2s.com/hostlist.htm	✔
Hub for free Internet access sites	*http://www.lights.com/freenet*	✔
Internet access	*http://www.netzero.com*	for 10 hrs/mo
	http://www.juno.com	with ads
Template design (site builder)	*http://freesitetemplates.com*	✔
	http://desktoppublishing.com/ template/web/sitekits.html	for non-commercial only
Web site tune up and GIF optimizer	*http://websitegarage.netscape.com*	✔

Figure 6.18. Free Web and Internet services.

Affiliate programs offer a relatively easy way to generate some revenue from your site. They offer a commission on viewer click-throughs (prospects), qualified leads, or sales referred from your site. Bookstore programs from sites like barnesandnoble.com and Amazon.com probably are the best known—Amazon.com has hundreds of thousands of participating associates—but a myriad of affiliate programs are now available. Since affiliate programs link viewers away from your site to make a purchase, be sure they open in a new window and provide an on-site Back button to increase the likelihood that viewers will return. Most affiliates provide code to "cut and paste" onto your page and allow you to select certain items to highlight or sell.

Commissions usually run 5 percent, but a few go as high as 20 percent. Some offer only a flat fee per click-through or lead. Usually, you'll receive a monthly statement with payment made when commissions reach a certain level. Unless you spend a lot of time and effort driving

Type of Resource	URL	Free (✔)
Animated GIFs, e.g. bars, buttons, bullets	*http://www.beseen.com/beseen/free*	✔
Buttons and Backgrounds	*http://www.freegraphics.com*	✔
Clip art	*http://clip-art.com*	✔
Clip art, sounds	*http://www.maxpatch.com*	✔
Fonts	*http://www.fontsnthings.com*	✔
	http://www.1001freefonts.com	✔
Graphics (non-professional)	*http://members.tripod.com/ ~GIFPRO/index.html*	✔
Graphics, clip art, Web sets, toon-a-day, and more	*http://desktoppublishing.com/free.html*	✔
Graphics, design sets, fonts, design tips	*http://www.geocities.com/siliconvalley/ heights/1288/index.html*	✔
Graphics generator for logos, buttons, and bullets	*http://www.cooltext.com*	✔
Sound effects	*http://soundamerica.com*	✔

Figure 6.19.   Free decorative doo-dahs.

traffic to your site, don't expect to make a fortune. However, the right affiliation can be a convenient, value-added service for your visitors. Again, be selective. Choose no more than one or two affiliate programs, unless you want to be a virtual flea market! You can find a list of thousands of affiliate programs at *http://www.AssociatePrograms.com*.

There are conflicting opinions on the value of affiliate programs, with some forecasters arguing that up to 25 percent of retail sales on the Internet will originate on affiliate sites by the end of 2002, while other forecasters insist that affiliate programs are on the way out because too many content sites lose their own viewers to retailers. Experiment on your site and see!

Free Web and Internet Services

If you're really strapped for cash, the resources in Figure 6.18 may be a reasonable alternative. They are certainly better than putting up a free site without your own domain name on a portal like *http://geocities.yahoo.com/home.* These portals also make some free domain-named space available as long as you allow their advertisers to appear on your pages. As an alternative, many ISPs now include 3 to 5 MB of Web space in their monthly fee. Check to see if they will allow you to use your own domain name, or if they permit only an extension (yourcompany.ISPname.net or ISPname.net/yourcompany). Although search engines no longer index sites with such names, these small freebie sites may be useful as doorway pages to your main site, or you can use the redirection service at *http://www.mydomain.com* to send traffic to your free site.

Free Decorative Doo-Dahs

You'll have to decide whether the time it takes to search through the decorative resources in Figure 6.19 is worth it. You'll find many additional resources for free clip art and digital photos on commercial online services or by using a search engine.

In this chapter, we've conducted an overview of all aspects of design for a nonselling Web site, from marketing communication and graphics to writing, navigation, and multimedia. In the next chapter we cover specific issues related to the design, merchandising, and support of effective e-commerce sites. As you'll see, an online storefront adds layers of challenge and opportunity to the process.

7

Step 5c: Build an Effective Storefront

In the unpredictable world of the Internet, one trend is predictable: More and more transactions will be handled online. In 2001 only about 3 percent of $1.1 trillion in U.S. retail spending took place online, but that's not chump change: it amounted to $34 billion (excluding travel, prescriptions, and autos). Jupiter Media Metrix, Inc. projects online retail revenues will increase to $130 billion by 2006, as seen in Figure 7.1. It's not just that the same users are buying more online; more users are buying. Some 52 percent of those with Internet access are expected to buy online in 2002, up from 40 percent in 2000. As the global online population grows and as existing users become more comfortable buying online, the value of online sales will increase.

To capture some of that business, you need an effective storefront. E-commerce sites can be an order of magnitude more expensive to develop than an ordinary Web site. A recent survey by NetMarketing (*http://www.net2b.com*) priced development of a 7,500-item catalog site at anywhere from $30,000 to $1.2 million, with a median price of $479,000! Not to panic: There are less-expensive options—from free to $600 per year at the low end. The adage that "it pays to shop around" holds as much for building Web sites as for buying from them.

An online store requires three components. **Catalog** software displays your products. A **shopping cart** lets customers click on products they'd like to buy as they review the catalog. To pay, a customer goes to

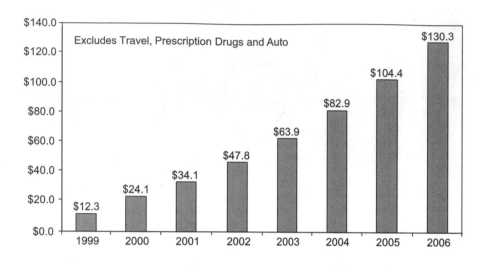

Figure 7.1. Online retail revenues, *http://www.jmm.com/xp/press/industry projections.xml*. Source: Jupiter Media Metrix, Inc.

a virtual **checkstand**, which totals the order, adds taxes and shipping charges, accepts shipping and billing information, and transfers the user seamlessly to a secure server for some form of payment. This suite of functions is sometimes called a **store-building** program.

Once you have your technology ducks in a row, you'll have to deal with merchandising, customer support, transaction methods, security, and ways to monitor what's happening with online sales. We'll look at these concerns in this chapter, as you learn about:

- Criteria for an effective storefront

- Different options for building a cyberstore

- On-site preparation for e-tailing through merchandising and on-line support

- Accepting payments online, including credit cards and their alternatives

- Credit card security for your customers and for you

- Using statistical sales reports to monitor your storefront.

Criteria for an Effective Online Store

To provide a positive shopping experience for customers, you must pay attention to the online shopping experience itself. A Forrester Research study confirmed that at least two-thirds of all buyers abandon purchases at checkout. Why? Figure 7.2 illustrates the top 10 reasons shoppers abandon their carts. To encourage purchasing, you need to:

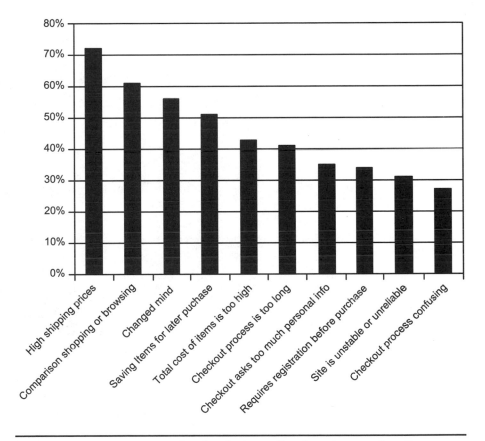

Figure 7.2. Top 10 reasons for abandoning online shopping cart, *http://www. vividence.com/public/news+and+events/press+releases/2001-11-05+shopping+cart+ abandonment.htm.* Courtesy Vividence Corporation® *(www.vividence.com).*

- Follow the "2 Clicks to Order" rule: It should never take more than two clicks from any page in your site for the customer to make a purchase. An "order now" link or "shopping cart" button on every page is an easy solution.

- Make it easy for buyers to keep shopping once they've put an item in their cart.

- Allow buyers to view and change their cart at any time; in particular, let them remove an item without emptying their entire cart.

- Allow buyers to see the running total of their purchases as they shop and to print out their order.

- Make the payment process secure and easy to access.

- Notify customers, preferably as they shop, when items are out of stock or on back-order. Better yet, remove items from your online inventory when they aren't available.

- Guarantee privacy.

- State privacy and return policies, warranties, and guarantees clearly and visibly.

- Inform buyers of shipping alternatives and costs early on.

- Incorporate step-by-step ordering directions.

- Develop an ordering process that includes order and shipping confirmations via e-mail, online order tracking, an order history, and courier tracking (see Chapter 3).

- Prominently display your toll-free number, as well as e-mail, regular phone, fax, and street address, so customers can reach you easily.

From an operational perspective, certain features are critical to online success. The first two features listed below—search capabilities and product information—not only affect shoppers' choice of online sites to use, but also help convert browsers to buyers by making online shopping more closely parallel the offline experience.

- Search capability, cited by 43 percent of shoppers as the most important feature of an online storefront, is essential if you stock more items than will fit on one double-screen page. The search function should be available from every page of your site and should allow users to find products quickly by category or name. With a large number of stocked items, include a more-advanced search function to sort by multiple criteria, such as price, size, and color.

- Detailed product information, including product reviews and in-stock status, is ranked by 40 percent of online shoppers as the most important feature.

- Offer close-up and enlarged product views, which can be done with a link to another page or with a smaller "pop-up" window; while showing your product is important, you also need to minimize download time.

- Offer e-mail registration capability to receive notification of sales, new products, special offers or other information; some 85 percent of buyers say they are more likely to return to a retail site after receiving e-mail.

- Customers should have opportunities to register and to provide useful information about their interests, such as registration for an e-mail newsletter or print catalog, or to store personal information on a site (e.g., shipping addresses, birthdays and anniversaries, gift "wish lists").

- Other niceties include a special "sale" area, live on-site customer service, real-time inventory confirmation, gift certificates for use online or offline, an FAQ section, gift registries, or personalization services, such as the cosmetic consultation found on the Clinique site (*http://www.clinique.com/templates/whatsright/index.tmpl*).

Many storebuilder packages offer sales reporting tools and customer support features, such as recommending related products. Such **intelligent agents** act like knowledgeable store clerks who **upsell**, encouraging additional purchases or suggesting that buyers upgrade to a more expensive model.

Some store sites place **cookies**, small data files with unique identification numbers, on users' machines and/or require a log-in with user name and password. Either method allows a site to personalize users' experience on follow-up visits. In theory, personalization makes for a more emotional connection with the viewer. It can be as simple as welcoming visitors by name or as complex as maintaining a database that presents products or information prearranged to be relevant to the viewer based on his or her past browsing or buying behaviors.

Cookies are a mixed blessing. Password entry can be a nuisance and people sometimes resent cookies as an intrusion on privacy. (Although users can turn off cookies in the Preferences section of their browsers, many do not know how.) Other viewers prefer the convenience of prerecorded shipping and charging information, an address book, a datebook of upcoming birthdays or events, or a list of past purchases. Most developers know how to do cookies, or you can purchase packages like Coravue that integrate customer information with your Web site (*http://www.Coravue.com*). In any case, if you collect personal information, post and follow a privacy policy to reassure your users. (See Chapter 14.) For more information on personalization, check out *http://www.personalization.com*.

For an inexpensive way to personalize your site, segment your audience and drive them closer to their likely purchase by asking them to select their interest from a simple, linkable list of options.

Remember, as customers click, they develop a relationship with your site. Personalization helps them feel better about their purchases, while providing you with data for analysis. Lands' End (*http://www.Lands End.com*), seen in Figure 7.3, includes both customized designs and personal recommendations on its site. For other shopping sites to learn from, look at Amazon.com (*http://www.amazon.com*); REI (*http://www.rei.com*); or The Sharper Image (*http://www.SharperImage.com*). To see how a portal design can suggest "great buys," check out the cNet Computer Shopper site (*http://shopper.cnet.com/?csredir=true*).

Storefront Options

There are hundreds of options for building a cyberstore that meet the criteria above. Like so much else on the Web, selecting the best one is harder than it looks. You need to know three things before you start: (1) your Web development budget, (2) how many products you plan to

Figure 7.3.   Good major catalog site, *http://www.LandsEnd.com/cd/frontdoor.* Permission granted by Lands' End, Inc.

sell, and (3) how you want to accept payment (discussed below). With that information, decide which approach best fits your general needs: a "browse'n'buy" prepackaged store; standalone programs to integrate with your site; or an integrated e-commerce solution. (These approaches are detailed below in order of cost and complexity. Figure 7.4 summarizes them.) Then decide which providers within the approach offer the features and flexibility you need at a price you can afford. You can always move up in capabilities as your store brings in revenues. Since it can be a hassle to constantly change storefronts, try to select an option that can grow with your business.

One note: In the olden days of the Web six to eight years ago, few sites took credit cards; most posted an online order form to fill out and return by e-mail, fax, or snail mail. Now, some 90 percent of online transactions are handled by credit card, and online card services let even the tiniest micro-businesses accept credit cards for purchase. Think about it.

Option	Components	Best For	Benefits/Drawbacks
Browse'n' Buy Store-builders	Integrated intro pages, catalog, check-stand, shopping cart, e-mail, reports, link to credit card services. Seller may include hosting & transaction services.	Pre-packaged templates for small start-up sites with tight budgets.	Easy to create and main-tain; may be hard to cust-omize; may include advertising. Canned software has constraints; problem if supplier goes out of business.
Standalone Packages to Integrate	Individual software for catalog, shopping cart, checkstand, and credit card processing. Usually have add-on modules for shipping, reporting, graphics, and special features.	Industry-specific applications, medium-size catalogs and stores. Good choice for growing company.	Usually maintained with-out tech support, but requires programming assistance to set-up. Must match host/server or use reseller. Custom look & feel.
Integrated e-Commerce Solutions	Fully integrated solutions for dedicated servers. Completely customizable, extensive reporting, customer service, and support capabilities.	Large companies expecting high sales volume, large catalogs.	Integrates with back-end software, such as CRM, accounting and inventory. Expensive; requires significant tech support.

Figure 7.4. Storefront options. ©2002 Watermelon Mountain Web Marketing.

Browse'n'Buy Storebuilders

Browser-based storebuilders let you quickly create and maintain a small, template-based store without programming help. All set-up entries and changes are completed by going online from your own computer, of-ten through simple "wizard"-style interfaces that walk you through the process. These turnkey solutions usually include a home page, an "About Us" page, a catalog, shopping cart, customer e-mail, tracking reports, and a link to credit card acceptance services. They are the most cost-effective option for a small e-commerce Web site. They are an obvious choice if you don't have a site already, but you can easily link between your existing site and storebuilder pages. Most storebuilders are offered in combination with Web hosting either from their creators or from re-sellers. Most, but not all, let you have your own domain name.

The cookie-cutter appearance of "browse'n'buy" storebuilders may turn off companies with a preexisting site, but some allow you to customize colors and appearance for better design integration. (Ask a graphic designer to help you select colors and customize the design.) Some hosts will accept credit cards on your behalf for a fee plus a percentage of your sales. Generally, these browser-based storebuilders start at $25 per month or less, and can run up to $250 per month for large catalogs. The really inexpensive ones make money by selling advertising space and assessing transaction fees on credit card purchases; they may require that you post their own or others' ads on your site. Following, you'll find a few of the many vendors that offer combination hosting and "browse'n'buy" storebuilders:

- Freemerchant (*http://www.freemerchant.com*) offers a small, basic storefront for $14.95 per month with credit card processing and a $25 set-up fee.

- Bigstep (*http://www.bigstep.com*) has a basic store for $44.90 per month for 25 items, which includes a catalog manager, merchant account, and credit card processing interface or PayPal compatibility.

- HyperMart (*http://www.hypermart.net*) has a basic store for $39.95 per month for up to 10,000 items, including modules for shipping and credit card processing.

- Bizland (*http://www.bizland.com*, seen in Figure 7.5) offers a suite of ShopSite storebuilders for different-size stores. ShopSite Lite, which is included with a $10.95/month Bizland membership, is for a five-page, 12-product store that doesn't plan to use credit cards or that already has a point-of-sale terminal for credit cards. ShopSite Manager, at $25/month with a $25 set-up fee, adds instant credit card processing, meta tag editing for search engines, an On Sale module, and unlimited pages and products. ShopSite Pro, at $50/month and a $50 set-up fee, contains all the ShopSite Manager features plus a searchable database and other merchandising

Figure 7.5. A template-based storebuilder, *http://www.bizland.com*. Courtesy BizLand, Inc.

tools. For instant credit card processing, you have to register separately for a Merchant Account and Payment Gateway.

- Advanced Internet Technologies, Inc. (*http://www.aitcom.net*) is an e-commerce Web hosting service that offers a card verification service, as well as store-building and statistical tools. Set-up costs range from free for a 20 MB starter site to $95, with monthly rates ranging from $7.95 to $199.95.

- Webhosting.com (*http://www.webhosting.com*) offers a fairly typical e-commerce turnkey selection starting at $34.95; prices increase by catalog size and feature selection.

- A similar package from NetNation Communications (*http://www.netnation.com*) runs $22.50/month for hosting and an unlimited catalog, plus $38.95/month for a shopping cart and secure server. There is a $99.95 set-up fee.

- The Yahoo! Store (*http://store.yahoo.com*) offers electronic commerce Web hosting. Prices start at $49.95/month for hosting, plus 10¢/month per product in your catalog, plus a 0.5 percent transaction fee and 3.5 percent revenue share per sale. Yahoo! offers fast point-and-click store building, lots of statistical and tracking tools, and great promotional tips. You have several payment choices: no credit cards; your own merchant account; or a contract with their Paymentech service, which processes cards for Yahoo! stores without their own merchant accounts. Paymentech, which accepts Visa, MasterCard, American Express, and Discover cards, charges a monthly service fee of $22.95 plus a 20¢ fee per transaction (six-month contract). Yahoo! stores are listed automatically in Yahoo's online mall (Yahoo! Shopping), its shopping search engine, its directories, and its main search engine. AOL.com offers similar store-building services.

- Amazon.com's Marketplace works like eBay, with postings that expire after a certain time, but you can set a fixed price up to a limit of $2,500 per transaction. There is no charge to post an item. When an item sells, Amazon.com collects from the buyer, deducts its commission of 99¢ per item plus 15 percent of the sales price, and deposits the rest in your account. You can sign up to accept credit cards with Amazon Payment. Transaction fees are included in the commission above. Amazon.com also has an auction site and zShops for those who sell frequently from a large catalog of posted items, with a complex scale of charges for posting and commission.

Many Web hosts re-sell specific storebuilder packages, such as Interland's ezAisle, Miva Merchant, Mercantec's SoftCart, eCongo's Powered Commerce, or OpenMarket's ShopSite. Select your Web host based on the storebuilder they offer, rather than trying to fit your store into their mold. Because "browse'n'buy" packages differ so widely in capabilities, flexibility, and ease of use, it's imperative to do some research before you make a decision:

1. Create a spreadsheet of the features you want, including the potential to grow into a larger store. Compare different packages to your list, using online demos and asking lots of questions. The checklist in Figure 7.6 offers some features you might want to look for.

Feature	Desired	Offered	Supplier
Technical Capabilities & Design			
Integrates with existing Web site			
Can be updated w/o tech support			
Tech support available 24 hours/day			
Notifies storeowner of orders			
Supports photos and thumbnails			
Templates for policies (shipping, return, privacy)			
Sales and traffic statistics			
Merchandising & Selling			
Ease of use for customer			
Built-in auction capabilities			
Customizable design			
Templates to choose from			
Preview capability before posting to store			
Allows sales & promotions, e.g., coupons, codes			
Searchable catalog			
Size catalog that can be supported			
Back-end & application integration			
Database import/export/support			
Inventory management			
Mailing list support for newsletters			
Packing slips and invoices created			
Multiple payment methods supported			
Transaction processing w/o merchant account			
Real-time credit card gateway			
Order numbers assigned to purchase			
Shipping module with customer tracking			
Multiple shipping options (e.g. UPS, FedEx, PO)			
Customer Service			
Cookies for tracking customers			
Customer registration			
E-mail confirmations sent to buyer			
International orders, language currency			
Buyer tracking of orders			
Personalization and upselling			
Ordering alternatives supported			
Costs			
Pricing structure			
Costs for transaction processing			

Figure 7.6. Storefront checklist. ©2002 Watermelon Mountain Web Marketing.

2. Take advantage of free trials, paying particular attention to how easy it is to create and update the catalog.

3. Visit other stores that use the same package. E-mail their owners to see how satisfied they are, particularly in terms of ease-of-use and tech support.

Stand-alone Packages to Integrate

Stand-alone packages for catalog display, shopping carts, checkstands, and credit card processing can be integrated into your current site. These generally require substantial programming and design skills, and are more expensive than browser-based storebuilders. These packages should still allow a nontechnical user to change the contents, image, copy, and prices of catalog items without assistance. Preferably, this would be done through a Web browser, but some packages require you to run a separate program on your computer and upload changes to your site.

Stand-alone store packages are usually sold as software for you to install on your own server. Your best bet, however, is to select a Web host and/or developer who resells and specializes in the particular software package you want. If you use stand-alone packages, you must be sure they are compatible with your existing site, with the server used by your Web host, and with each other. Stand-alone packages are often sold in modules, with costs ranging from $100 to $300 per module

---

TIPS FOR TIRED SITES

Take a look at your payment process. Are you still using a form that people need to print out, handwrite their order, and mail in with a check? Or perhaps they can complete the form online, but have to bounce back and forth between the catalog and the form to enter the items they want. In either case, you are probably losing an inordinately high percentage of potential buyers. Get a shopping cart and checkstand to automate order placement, price and tax computation, and shipping alternatives. Remember the "two clicks to buy" rule. Be sure there's a "Buy Now" or "Add to Cart" button on every item and every page! If you aren't accepting credit cards, it's time to rethink that decision, too. Look at iBill.com or Paypal.com for a method of accepting credit cards without a merchant account. It's very hard to get money out of people's wallets. The more difficult you make it for customers to spend, the less of their money you will see.

---

depending on the features. A total storebuilder suite might run $300 to $800, plus labor costs for development.

Specialized applications are available by industry, so it's worth exploring more than generic alternatives. For a guide to catalog, shopping cart, and hosted solutions, go to OnlineOrders.net (*http://www.onlineorders.net*) or Webcrafts.com (*http://www.webcrafts.com/ShopCartF.htm#shop*). To research your purchase, add specific compatibility and industry issues to the checklist in Figure 7.6 above and follow the steps described under the "browse'n'buy" option.

Catalog Software

You must stock your virtual shelves, setting up your products to be viewed in an organized fashion. Many Web hosting services now offer packages to create an online catalog. You enter the specifications and price of each product on a form that is included in a single table (called a **flat-file database**) and add thumbnail digital art if appropriate.

Expensive packages for larger stores use **relational databases,** which have related tables for different types of information. This approach allows sophisticated searches on multiple fields to present customized results on the fly. Databases are easy to update (e.g., if you change the supplier on all the coffee mugs you sell, you enter the new information just once).

Depending on the software you select, you may be able to:

- Choose one of several prepackaged styles

- Modify colors, fonts, background, and layout

- Have your Web designer completely customize your catalog

- Search the database of products by name, type, or other variables

- Import product data, and sometimes imagery, from a preexisting print catalog or inventory in electronic form.

Catalog software ranges in price from free with Web hosting deals, to several hundred or several hundred thousand dollars. The variables are catalog size, capabilities, searchability, flexibility, and operating system. As you would expect, the most complex and expensive software searches in real time through an ever-changing inventory for products like concert tickets or airline flights. Figure 7.7 shows the catalog software from Cus-

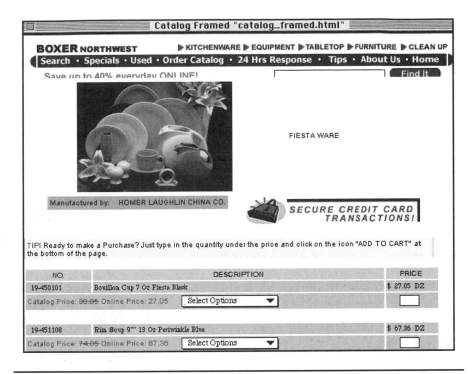

Figure 7.7. Catalog software from Custom Catalogs Online, Inc., *http://boxer nw.com/boxernw/images-f/b19-450.jpg.* Courtesy Boxer-Northwest Co.

tom Catalog OnLine, Inc. (*http://www.customcatalogs.com*) in use by Boxer-Northwest, a wholesale restaurant supply company, to manage more than 5,000 items, at *http://boxernw.com.*

If you already have an extensive print catalog, you might want to search for software that allows you to import your print catalog in Quark or PDF (Adobe Acrobat) format directly into your Web site. Such software usually preserves existing layout, photos, and graphics, while adding a zoom-in capability, thus speeding the development of large online catalogs.

If you have a modest-sized catalog (10 to 1,000 items), you can usually find a Web host that includes catalog software as part of its hosting package for $25 to $125/month. Preexisting software from a host may reduce design flexibility, but it dramatically simplifies and speeds the development process. The larger your catalog, the more expensive your solution will be.

Sources for catalog software include Catalog.com (*http://www.catalog.com*), which includes catalog and shopping cart software as part of its Web hosting service. Catalogs and shopping carts can be purchased from Miva Merchant (*http://www.miva.com/products/merchant*) and many other sources as add-on products for a freestanding site, with the price depending on the number of items and features selected. For example, NetCatalog (*http://www.grafix-net.com/netcatalog*), which automatically resizes scanned or downloaded photos into thumbnails and full-size images, starts at $99.95.

Shopping Carts and Checkstands

Shopping cart programs generally incorporate checkstands. Like catalog software, cart programs have a tremendous range in price and capability, and may be incorporated with a Web hosting package. Elaborate shopping cart software may allow you to create a registration database of shipping and billing information so repeat customers need not reenter their data.

Depending on the nature of your product (fruit? flowers? medicine?), shipping volume, and customers' needs, you may want to automate shipping options from UPS Ground or Federal Express, as described in Chapter 3, and/or generate shipping labels as part of the process. Free shipping and handling is becoming a competitive pricing feature on many merchandise sites. Since these costs must then be integrated into the overall price, adjust your prices so you don't lose money. If you plan to sell internationally, you need checkstand software that supports international currency exchange and shipping requirements.

If your Web host offers a shopping cart, check out the cart supplier's Web site to confirm that the product will meet your needs. For sample cart programs, take a look at:

- Hassan Shopping Cart (*http://www.irata.com/products.html*) is shown in use at A. L. Van Houtte Fine Coffee (*http://www.finecoffee.com*) in Figure 7.8. The Hassan Cart is a UNIX-based solution that supports UPS shipping. Costs range from $200 for a single license to $1,400 for a site license, plus charges of $200 each for a secure transaction or other modules.

- Hosting service Precision Web (*http://precisionweb.net/shop.html*) offers its free Ultrashop shopping cart software, otherwise priced at $200, with every site. Its shopping cart software is database-driven, secure-server-enabled, and customizable.

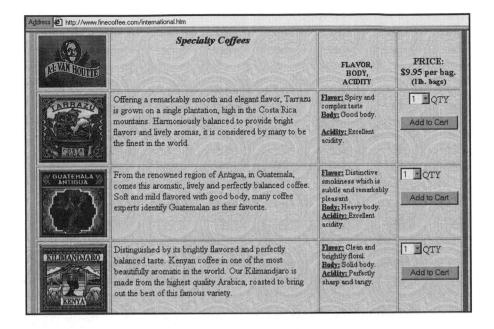

Figure 7.8. Shopping cart from Hassan seen at *http://www.finecoffee.com/ international.htm.* Courtesy Fruba Inc. DBA College Hill Coffee Shop.

- EZshopper, the basic cart product from Hamilton Associates (*http://www.hamassoc.com*), runs $600 for the server software. It has optional modules for real-time integration at $195 and database administration/statistics for $250. Their Minicart option for $250 is useful for companies with only a few items. After calculating the sales total, shipping costs, and tax, their products send both company and customer a sales confirmation receipt with the individual order number.

- GTA NetOrderForm (*http://www.gta-tech.com*) is a simple-to-use, turnkey shopping cart system that comes complete with online administration features, online credit card verification, customer feedback forms, and secure server capability.

- EasyCart (*http://www.easycart.com*) offers packages that run from $399 to $1,999 plus an annual maintenance fee. EasyCart is one of the few vendors that offers both PC and Mac options.

- QuikStore (*http://www.quikstore.com*), one of the least expensive but more flexible packages, offers a basic module for $199, with a choice of credit card gateways for an additional $49.95, and optional plug-ins for shipping, catalog-building, and customer transaction databases priced from $79.95 to $99.95 each.

- Web Genie Shopping Cart (*http://www.webgenie.com/Software/Shopcart*) licenses its cart, including an online catalog, tech support, and options for $495. Customized CGI to suit specific requirements is available for a fee.

Integrated E-Commerce Solutions

Integrated e-commerce solutions are the way to go for large companies with an extensive product line. These are sometimes offered by hosting companies, complete with technical support, but more often are purchased for use on a dedicated server or on a self-hosted site. Integrated packages include not only customizable modules for catalogs, shopping carts, and checkstands, but also expanded administrative modules that integrate the store with back-office applications such **Customer Relationship Management (CRM)**, accounting, inventory, mailing list, and supplier chain programs. These are total packages, complete with statistical analysis and personalization.

For these sophisticated solutions, you need both dollars and in-house technical staff. Costs range from $1,000 into the hundreds of thousands. Since you are likely to live with your choice for a long time to come, evaluate your options carefully, using the checklist shown previously in Figure 7.6 as a starting point, adding specific criteria for your situation, and following the research steps described under the "browse'n'buy" approach. For examples of modest to midrange product offerings, see:

- AbleCommerce (*http://www.ablecommerce.com*) development options start at $2,995 and offer sophisticated options for small to medium-sized businesses.

- E-cats (*http://www.e-cats.com*) sells a turnkey online store for $10,000.

- The ubiquitous Microsoft offers an integrated electronic commerce solution called BizTalk (*http://www.microsoft.com/catalog/display.asp?subid=22&site=10424&x=49&y=9*) that runs $9,749 for the server and $4,999 for the software license. BizTalk not only sells products online, it tracks supply and demand and communicates with vendors. It has been tested by such huge sites as 1-800 Flowers, barnesandnoble.com, Best Buy, Dell Computer, and Eddie Bauer.

Auction Options

By 2003, online shoppers will spend more than $19 billion per year on online auctions. Rather than maintain their own Web sites, many small businesses have decided to tap into that revenue stream, using eBay and other auction sites as a cost-effective way to sell. Typically, eBay collects a listing fee of 30 cents to $3.30 based on your opening bid and a commission of 1.25 percent to 5.25 percent based on the sales price of each completed transaction. eBay also offers a fixed-price option and runs its own store program starting at $9.95/month.

Some companies use auction services to set price points or test the viability of a new product, or even to direct shoppers to their own sites for additional items. Many sellers have discovered that shoppers caught up in the "game frenzy" of an auction will pay more for an item in an online auction than they would in either a regular "brick" or "click" store. For a look at the funny items people post (and buy) on auction sites, take a gander at *http://www.whowouldbuythat.com.*

If you're not in the consumer market, consider B2B auction sites like Wholesale Ramp at *http://www.wholesaleramp.com;* BidCom at *http://www.bid.com*; or Software and Stuff at *http://www.softwareandstuff.com,* which offers discounted or surplus computer and office equipment. Traditional surplus auctioneers, and the Defense Department's surplus disposal site at *http://www.drms.dla.mil,* also post auction opportunities online.

Industry-specific marketplace auction sites now abound, such as *http://www.metalsite.net* for the metal industry, *http://www.squaretown.com* for electronic components, or *http://www.farms.com* for livestock (seen in Figure 7.9). As a supplier, be cautious about these

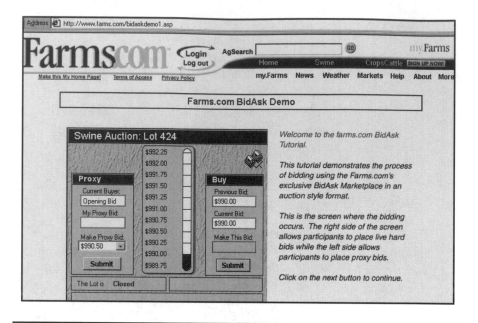

Figure 7.9. Sample industry auction site, *http://www.farms.com/bidask demo1.asp*. Courtesy Farms.com.

competitive, open-bidding sites run by industry giants, such as General Electric's Global eXchange, one of the world's largest B2B e-commerce networks. Such sites put tremendous price pressure on suppliers, often cutting out the small-business vendor.

More innovative companies, like Hemmings Motor News (*http://auctions.hemmings.com/index.cfm*), find that having an auction on their own site helps build traffic and increases return visits. Hemmings runs auctions for classic car parts, paraphernalia, books, and tools. Pre-packaged software lets you run auctions on your own site fairly simply. Vendors include Microsoft (*http://www.microsoft.com*), which has an auction extension to Site Server 3.0, and Beyond Solutions (*http://www.beyondsolutions.com/products.html*).

The Mall Alternative

Malls are virtual shopping areas on a server or online service that host or link related commercial sites. They generally charge for set-up, monthly listings and/or transactions. Some Web hosts define their own mall as a package of services that includes hosting, design, storebuilding, transaction services, and promotion.

A Web mall like Jewelry.com (*http://www.jewelrymall.com*) is really just a specialized advertising directory. Its service consists of home page links with promotional and merchandising opportunities by price, gemstone, birthstone, and types of jewelry. Simple links are free, but the mall sells retailers enhanced links with priority positioning and longer descriptions for $499 per year, as well as a variety of banner ads at a range of monthly rates.

Like every other Web service, rates vary widely depending on the mall and the benefits it provides. For example, the Cowboy Mall (*http://www.cowboymall.com*, seen in Figure 7.10) links sites and sells banner ads like the Jewelry Mall, but it also hosts sites for $95 per month and develops others for as little as $400 to $800.

Before you decide to open your cyberstore on someone else's mall, find one with similar industries or one where you'll easily be found. Malls that group together unrelated products do not perform well in search

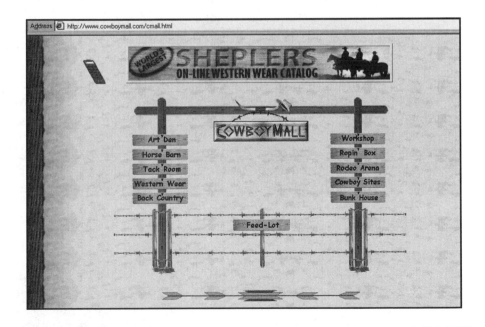

Figure 7.10. A mall alternative, *http://www.cowboymall.com/cmall.html*. Courtesy Cowboy Mall.

engines and are probably not a good business investment. If you decide to use a mall, make sure you'll have your own domain name. Check the traffic and other site statistics, see what promotional efforts the mall owner makes, and talk to existing businesses in the mall before you sign up.

If one store is not enough for you, perhaps you would like to build your own cybermall. BiznizWeb (*http://www.biznizweb.com/products/cditem.cfm?NID=2437*) lets you create an eMall on a portal-style site, giving shoppers the convenience of shopping from many merchants but paying only once. It comes with a shopping cart, payment transaction processing, and a common checkstand. Participating merchants can easily self-publish their own catalogs and stores without administrator involvement.

On-Site Preparation for E-tailing

Web development may seem simple, compared to the issues related to stocking your store and providing customer support. In Chapter 3 we discussed back office planning for shopping sites, considering issues like shipping and warehousing. But there are many other ways to fall short of customer expectations during their on-site experience. You may be displaying product you don't have in stock, the product information or price could be incorrect, or customers may not be able to get answers to their questions. Alas, all these shortcomings have significant consequences. About 57 percent of online shoppers polled by Jupiter Media Metrix in November 2001 said poor response time to customer inquiries would affect their decision to shop at that Web site again. Some 53 percent of buyers went further, saying they would be less likely to buy again at a merchant's *offline* storefront if they have a bad experience online. Can you really afford any of the problems described in Figure 7.11? Let's look at some ways to create happy customers.

Merchandising Your Online Store

Good product selection and attractive presentation are both essential. Products that sell well in a store don't always sell well online, and vice versa. You may decide not to offer inventory that is identical to your

Problem	% of Internet Buyers
Gift wanted to purchase was out of stock	64%
Product was not delivered on time	40%
Paid too much for delivery	38%
Connection or download trouble	36%
Didn't receive confirmation or status report on purchase	28%
Selections were limited	27%
Web site difficult to navigate	26%
Web site didn't provide information needed to make purchase	25%
Prices not competitive	22%
Site didn't offer enough gift ideas	16%

Figure 7.11. Top 10 problems experienced by Internet shoppers, *http:// cyberatlas.internet.com/markets/retailing/article/0,1323,6061_278991,00.html.* ©2002 INT Media Group. Inc. All rights reserved.

real-world storefront, or you may choose to alter your online pricing. Are product descriptions easy to read? Are close-ups available? Can thumbnail images, presented for quick downloading, expand with a click to permit a better look? You can choose to feature different items prominently on your home page or secondary pages, just as you would rearrange the display in your store window or place items for shoppers to see when they first walk through your door. Consider some of these merchandising tips:

- If you carry recognizable brand names, post this prominently on your site to build customer trust.

- Put seasonal and special event items on your home page, whether for Mother's Day or Halloween.

- If appropriate, use virtual reality or animation to display an item in 3-D.

- Be sure to include sizing information, such as how to measure.

- Include impulse-buy items at the checkstand, just as you would at the cash register in a brick-and-mortar store.

- Cross-sell to increase sales; where possible, feature complementary products that would appeal to the same buyers. This can be as simple as a link to other products under a reminder to "Also Look At ..." or "Coordinating Products." Gardeners.com, shown earlier in Figure 6.9, does this under the message "You might also like" in Figure 6.9.

As you know, every item in a good print catalog is placed carefully to maximize the eye appeal of high-profit items, to encourage additional purchases or up-selling, or to attract a viewer who is looking for a particular product. You can do no less with your online catalog. Think of each catalog page as a window display. Remember, many viewers will never scroll "below the fold," so your most attractive, popular, or profitable items should be at the top. Remember that the eye goes first to the upper right corner, so you might want to place your featured "item of the month" there. Set a size limit on the number of images per page to reduce download time.

If you have a large product line, avoid static catalog pages. A more expensive, database-driven solution will pay off quickly in ease of use and additional orders. A database generates new display pages "on-the-fly" on the basis of the keywords or search terms entered by the user. Just be sure you have entered a full complement of parameters for users to search on, and include ones that might be related. For instance, in response to a search on "green rainboots," viewers might be prompted to view green raincoats and umbrellas because the keywords were cross-referenced.

Product Photos

Try to include a picture of the product in use by people; it adds interest and allows viewers to assess scale. Make sure your product shots (thumbnails, expanded images, and close-ups) are good quality. (Big no-no! You cannot "borrow" someone else's product shots—they are copyrighted!) The most common errors of amateur photographers are poor lighting, blurry images, too much glare, not cropping out parts of the picture that distract from the product, shots combining multiple products, and omitting product close-ups. See how Skystone Trading solved these problems in Figure 7.12. Here are some hints for improving your product shots:

- For the best results, use natural (outdoor) lighting. A cloudy day is perfect to avoid shadows. Or light a product with two 40-watt incandescent bulbs, one from either side, aimed from above the product. Don't overexpose your images!

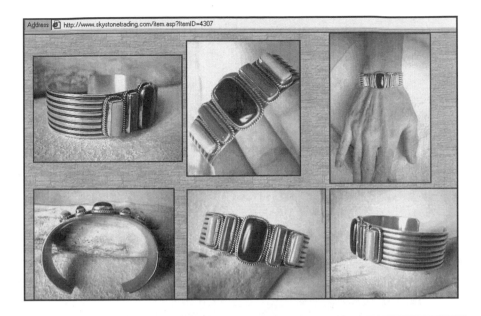

Figure 7.12. Close-up product photos, *http://www.skystonetrading.com/ item.asp?ItemID=4307.* Courtesy Skystonetrading.com.

- To avoid the glare of a flash, shoot from an angle (left, right, above, below).

- Use a tripod to avoid jitter-generated blurry images.

- Use a plain background in neutral or complementary colors to make your product stand out.

- If you use digital photo-processing software, don't overdo it. Spend your time cropping out any distractions, rather than trying fancy photo enhancements.

Check the Four Ps of Merchandising
Before you launch, review your site once more for the Ps of merchandising:

- Product mix

- Positioning

- Pricing

- Presentation

These four elements are just as applicable online. Do you have the right product mix for online shoppers, compared to what people buy offline? How are your products positioned compared to the niches filled by your online competition? Did you study pricing to see whether you are still cost-competitive, even if you have adjusted prices to incorporate shipping costs? Does your online catalog presentation work the way you intended? If possible, ask a focus group of potential customers to look at your site objectively.

Customer Support

Study after study has shown that customers expect the same, if not better, service online than they receive offline. They still expect orders filled on time, complaints resolved, and questions answered promptly. The basic issues should go without saying: Make sure orders are delivered, that charges are processed only on shipment, that return policies are clearly stated, and that returns are credited promptly. We already dis-

TIPS FOR TIRED SITES

Are sales drooping at your cybershop? You'd be amazed how neglectful online merchants can be! Are you still showing Christmas items in July? Have you simply pasted "out-of-stock" labels on products you no longer carry, instead of removing them from your site? Did you remember to drop poor sellers from your online catalog, or at least move them to a "sale" section of the site? How long has it been since you added products? Maybe it's time to freshen your stock. If that's out of the question, consider shifting items around to create interesting product juxtapositions. Real-world retailers call this product rotation, which can pay off without the expense of new inventory. For instance, match items that aren't selling well from two departments in your store, such as a navy-blue baseball hat and a lime-green T-shirt. Display them next to each other on the catalog page, or offer a deal if customers buy both. Letting your store display go stale is a sure way to lose customers, who will think you've "gone fishing" and no longer care about your products or about them. Don't let products gather cyber-dust on your virtual shelves—clean house!

cussed the importance of responding promptly to telephone calls and e-mail messages. Many sites are now going one better and are offering customers the opportunity to interact with a real human being in real time by chat, instant messaging, or voice without leaving the site.

For real-time chat features, check out the free trial at HumanClick (*http://www.humanclick.com*). HumanClick is owned by LivePerson (*http://www.liveperson.com/products/pro.asp*), whose small-business service runs $89.50 per month. Similar free trials are also available from ClickiChat (*http://www.clickichat.com/makeastore/features.htm*) or Parachat (*http://www.parachat.com*). FaceTime (*http://www.facetime.com*) offers instant messaging for customer relations. Other customer support services, like CorporateAsk.com from Jeeves, at *http://corporate.ask.com*, offer natural language-based automated customer support.

LiveHelper.com, one of many real-time customer support options available from Hotscripts (*http://www.hotscripts.com/Remotely_Hosted/Customer_Support*), offers the choice of either live text or voice chat to respond to customers' questions as does Instant Service *(http://www.instantservice.com)*. Hipbone *(http://www.hipbone.com)* adds co-browsing, allowing the user and customer rep to view the same screen simultaneously. Product costs range from free to $195 depending on the degree of sophistication and options. Many of these companies transition visitors to expensive call-center support when other options don't work, or will manage a call center for you on an outsourced basis.

Whatever the method, the purpose of customer support is to increase the number of shoppers who actually close a sale online. Even with automated or real-time support, be prepared to hire more staff in customer service; if your site is working well, you will have more customers calling, not fewer!

Accepting Payment Online

Before you "go live" with your Web site, you must integrate and test your methods of accepting payment. If you host your own site, you may find that you need to purchase software to support specialized functions; if you host elsewhere, your selection of a developer and host may well depend on their ability to provide such services as:

- Automated payment processing

- A secure server

- A gateway to a real-time credit card verification service

- Automated e-mail for order verification and tracking

- Feeding transaction data to your inventory and accounting software.

Depending on the size of your operation, payment processing may range from credit card processing on a secure server to full integration with inventory, warehousing, shipping, accounting, and other management information systems. The more sophisticated your financial processing, the greater the cost will be. Web hosts that specialize in online stores are best able to assist with handling transactions, especially for medium-to-large sites.

Just how sophisticated should you get when it comes to accepting payment? WebCom, formerly a host for Verio's e-commerce packages, recommended assessing your needs as shown in Figure 7.13. Keep this model in mind as you read through the software options that follow.

For the smallest businesses in the first column, hand-processing transactions is a cost-effective option. **Electronic funds transfer** (EFT), shown as a payment method, is the preauthorized transfer of funds from one bank account to another. (We discuss EFT more fully later in this chapter.)

	1- 2 Products < 50 transactions per week	2-10 Products < 50 transactions per week	> 10 Products < 50 transactions per week	> 10 Products > 50 transactions per week
Order Method	Phone, fax, e-mail	Electronic order form	Shopping cart with checkstand	Shopping cart with checkstand
Payment Method	EFT or credit card by phone, fax, e-mail, check money order	EFT or credit card by phone, fax, e-mail, check, money order	EFT or credit card by phone, fax e-mail, check, money order	CyberCash (real-time credit card processing)

Figure 7.13. Transaction needs by volume, *http://www.webcom.com*. Courtesy WebCom—worldwide host to small business. A member of the Verio Group.

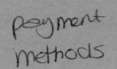

Almost any Web so   ate an **electronic order form**, seen in the second   payment information; just be sure your Web h   ipts. If you accept purchase orders or maintain   or your customers, such a form can become a l   credit cards. The completed form can be e-m   cure server, set up for automatic fax-back, or r   with a check or money order.

Real-time credit card processing follows the checkstand process with credit card authorization, the equivalent of running a card through an electronic swiper at a storefront. The customer is not charged until the product is shipped, while the merchant is assured that the card number is valid and the account holder has credit available to cover the transaction.

Let's look at these options in greater detail. In most cases, payment is made by credit card, but taking that number and processing the payment may be handled several different ways. Credit card data may be delivered offline, faxed, or e-mailed after completing a form on the Web, or processed directly by a bank.

In spite of the perceived risk, credit cards are actually one of the best ways for individuals to make payment online. A cardholder's liability for unauthorized online use is now effectively zero, and most cards act as a guarantee of satisfaction. That is, a consumer can easily cancel a credit card purchase and return unacceptable goods. Your risk as a merchant is far greater than your customers' risk, as you'll see later in this chapter.

Phone, Fax, and Snail Mail

Old-fashioned ways are both safe and inexpensive, allowing customers to mail a check, call in their order, or fax a printed form with a credit card number. Preferably, offer customers a toll-free number to place an order by phone or fax. The rates for setting up and running inbound toll-free numbers vary by vendor and location. It's worth a few calls to get the best price.

For a monthly and/or per-transaction fee, some Web hosts will establish an automated fax-back system. This allows consumers to fill out their form online (without bothering to print it out), but the information is faxed rather than sent over the Internet. This method also works for individual customers with established accounts who receive monthly bills. You can accept an online purchase order from business customers without requesting sensitive credit card information.

Even if you accept credit cards, always offer at least one alternative for customers who don't trust electronic methods. Given that 82 percent of small businesses themselves worry about credit card security, it's not a surprise that 43 percent of their customers do. Put your toll-free number for order-taking or questions on the checkstand page, as well as on all other pages of your site.

Credit Cards

By the end of 2002, an estimated 120 million people will have purchased online, and 90 percent of those purchases will have been by credit card. The median for B2C online transactions was $244, as seen in Figure 7.14. In contrast, the median B2B online order was $800.

After customers place an online order using their credit cards, the card issuer transfers their payments (minus a transaction fee) to your **merchant account**. Most card issuers provide free software to handle this transfer.

Although over a billion credit cards are in circulation, not all your potential customers will use one online, especially if they are buying internationally. (Europeans, for instance, prefer to use debit cards, checks, or COD.) In the case of unauthorized transactions, such as children using parents' cards without permission, the cardholder may refuse to pay and/or you may end up with the expense of processing returns. In spite of these caveats, you could miss many sales if you don't take credit

Size	Sample	B2C	B2B
$1 - 50	20%	22%	5%
$51 - 100	13%	15%	5%
$101 - 500	27%	26%	36%
$501 - 1,000	9%	10%	5%
$1,000 - 10,000	23%	20%	41%
+ $10,000	8%	8%	8%
Average	$4,622	$4,450	$5,580
Median	$300	$244	$800

Figure 7.14. Transaction size at commerce-enabled Web sites. *http://www. ActivMediaResearch.com*. Source: ActivMedia Research, LLC. © 2001. All rights reserved.

cards. Even the federal government now pays for most purchases under $2,500 (in some cases up to $25,000) using its own credit card equivalent, the IMPAC purchase card.

Setting Up a Merchant Account

Credit cards can be costly to merchants. If you are not already set up to accept credit cards, research costs thoroughly. A card issuer may ask you to estimate the percentage of credit transactions to be handled electronically, by phone, or in person; your anticipated annual dollar volume on credit cards; and the average charge amount. While there are only four major providers (American Express, Visa, MasterCard, and Discover), card accounts are offered by many sources.

Most, but not all, commercial banks offer merchant card accounts. You will have to provide basic business financial data and possibly personal financial information, especially if you are a sole proprietor or have recently established your business. You may also be required to create a second checking account into which all revenues from credit card sales will be deposited and against which all charges will be debited. Some banks are reluctant to establish merchant accounts for new, mail-order, or Web-only companies. If your local banks don't come up with a reasonable rate, try one of the national commercial banks or a company like Merchant Accounts Express that specializes in setting up Web-based merchant accounts (*http://www.merchantexpress.com*).

Most card issuers charge some combination of a one-time setup fee, a monthly fee for electronic swiping devices of around $35, a percentage of credit card sales ranging from 1.6 percent to 4 percent, and/or a fee per transaction of 25 to 30¢. Generally speaking, the lower the value of receipts and the lower the volume of transactions, the higher the percentage rate you will be charged for each transaction. Given the highly variable fee combinations and percentage rates, it is definitely worth shopping around for the bank or service company that offers you the best rates for the type and amount of business you expect to do. For instance, American Express now has a flat fee of $5 per month for small businesses, as long as their annual charge volume is less than $5,000.

Now that you have a merchant account, you need to arrange to handle credit card transactions online. You can choose between manual and real-time processing. The manual approach, in which information is collected on a secure server for later processing by hand, may suffice for small volume vendors. Large-volume e-tailers, or those that distribute their product online, will probably need a real-time solution. These packages validate the card number, verify the credit limit, and provide immediate confirmation to the user. VeriSign's Payflow at *http:// www.verisign.com/products/payment.html* is one of several server-side software solutions to manage electronic transactions securely in real time. Their add-on module, which is available from many Web hosting services, automates all credit card processing. Real-time card processing software generally carries fees for set-up, monthly or annual use, a percentage of transaction value, and/or a per transaction fee.

Merchant Account Alternatives

If merchant card rates are too high or if your transaction volume is too low to qualify for an account, consider using the services of CCnow (*http://www.ccnow.com*). For a $9.95 monthly fee and 9 percent of total sales over $100, CCnow acts as a reseller to process credit charges. When they reach the checkstand, customers transfer invisibly to the CCnow secure site.

A similar, though more visible, service is offered by PayPal at rates competitive with merchant accounts (*http://www.paypal.com*). If you use PayPal for payments, you must first register as a PayPal premium merchant, designating a bank account for deposit and entering a credit card number as a guarantee. When they are ready to check out from your site, buyers will be transferred to a secure PayPal page, where they are prompted to become members of PayPal (if they aren't already) and are asked to provide the credit card number to be charged. The charge will be processed and deposited to your designated bank account, less transaction fees. PayPal, which processes credit card transactions for eBay, offers store-builder templates on its own site, as well as event registration templates through *http://www.mollyguard.com*. Similar services are offered by Paybutton at *http://www.paybutton.com* or iBill at *http://www.ibillcom*.

All these services allow the tiniest of merchants with the smallest of inventories to offer shoppers the convenience of credit card payment. That alone helps build the credibility of your store and reduces the number of lost sales. Another hidden advantage: These companies, not yours, bear the burden of card certification and security.

Credit Card Security

Credit card numbers are at risk at three points: First, your online storefront and Web host have to be secure; second, card numbers should be encrypted during transmission over the Internet; third, numbers need to be secure when stored on your end of the transaction. The third link—your computer system—is often the weakest. We'll look at ways to conduct online transactions securely, as well as building customer confidence in your site.

Secure Storefronts and Hosts

Don't be afraid to ask prospective hosts or storefront software vendors about their security procedures and history. Check that any customer information, including card numbers, is stored on computers isolated from the Internet and that they are stored in an **encrypted** (scrambled) form behind a **firewall**, a combination of hardware and software that isolates a computer network from the Internet.

Credit card companies are starting to require online merchants and their Web hosts to comply with some common sense security procedures. Noncooperating companies may face fines, a cap in service volume, or termination of credit card service. Their requirements become a basic checklist for your host. In addition to the two statements above, make sure your host is up-to-date on security patches; encrypts data before transmission; uses updated antivirus software; restricts access to customer data to those who need to know it; doesn't use vendor-supplied default passwords; and regularly tests security systems.

A second risk comes from hackers who release viruses, modify Web pages surreptitiously, or temporarily shut down sites with coordinated **denial of service** attacks, which flood their targets with so many fake requests for information that sites can't respond. If you run a large, attractive site, your best bet is to install protective software and to maintain an alert system that quickly identifies and bans requests issued from specific computers causing any of these problems.

Secure Socket Layers for Transmission

Most browsers exchange secure transmissions across the Internet using **Secure Socket Layer (SSL)**, a technology developed by Netscape to enable authenticated, encrypted communications. Users can tell when SSL is used by looking for an icon on the page: Netscape 4.0 and higher shows a locked padlock; earlier versions showed an unbroken key; Internet Explorer shows a lock on the status bar. In addition, the URL on the secure page will generally change to one beginning with *https://,* with the "s" identifying a secure server.

Both the merchant's Web server and the customer's Web browser must use the same security system to exchange information. Because SSL can be used by all URLs that start with *http,* in most cases this is not a problem. SSL is included free on all commonly used browsers. Users can set most browsers to provide notification when they connect between secure and nonsecure servers. If you intend to process transactions or secure data online, confirm that your Web hosting service offers SSL. One-time setup charges to use a secure server differ by host, ranging from free to $90. Some charge a version (authentication) site license for $349.

Firewalls for Internal Security

A firewall should be used on your end to provide the third link of security. It can prevent unauthorized access to credit card numbers and other customer data stored on *your* computer systems. Your company may already have firewalls on its internal computer network to make it difficult for people who access one part of shared information, such as a product database, to reach another, such as financial records. Be sure your computer is protected from the Web as well. Good firewalls, combined with regular checking for viruses, can help ensure that your computer (and your business) stays up and running, while protecting vulnerable information from prying eyes.

The Biggest Risk Is to the Merchant

Standard credit card approval doesn't do much to protect merchants from fraud. It confirms only that a number is valid; that the charge doesn't exceed the cardholder's limit; and that the card has not been reported stolen. Consequently, merchants are far more likely than individual consumers to be victims of credit card fraud online than individual consumers. That risk is 12 times greater for merchants online than offline. While estimates vary, some analysts suggest that online fraud may range from 1.2 percent to 5 percent of all online transactions, or anywhere from $400 million to $1.7 billion of annual U.S. sales online. A CyberSource survey of online merchants found that they expect to lose about 4 percent of their total revenues annually. The exposure for a merchant includes:

- The chargeback from the bank for fraudulent transactions, a cost usually covered by credit card companies when traditional retailers have a signed receipt

- The costs of dispute resolution

- The low probability of winning against a challenge from a card owner, because there is no physical signature

- The risk of a fine or loss of service from a credit card company if there are too many chargebacks

- Increased rates for online businesses—up to 66 percent more than card issuers charge brick-and-mortar stores for the same service

The biggest risk is not from individuals, but from organized rings of hackers and thieves, particularly from Eastern Europe and Southeast Asia. They often target new sites, which are assumed to be more vulnerable. To combat these risks, store owners need to don self-protective armor. You can:

- Require complete information, including both work and home phone number

- Use address-verification services to confirm that the billing address given matches the address on file

- Follow up with an e-mail asking for additional information or more credit card data (three-digit verification number on the back, issuing bank, etc.)

- Follow up with a phone call for *any* potentially risky transaction; don't ship without confirmation

- Use a credit card aggregator like iBill or PayPal to absorb the burden and risk of security

- Avoid shipping to post office boxes

- Check that both addresses are legitimate when the shipping address differs from the billing address

- Buy third-party security programs or services that request additional verification, such as mother's maiden name or last four digits of a social security number, and confirm that against other online databases

- Set up a computer program to flag risky transactions and a "fraud file" with a historical record

Flag these specific risk factors for additional investigation:

- Unusual orders, such as unlikely items ordered together, or big orders for high-ticket or brand-name items

- Orders for multiple units (e.g., 20 Sony Play Stations)

- Orders for adult entertainment services and digital products like downloadable music

- Orders from untraceable, free e-mail services (e.g., Juno, Yahoo!, usa.net, or hotmail) or from an e-mail address whose source is a country other than the shipping location

- Express shipping, especially during a non-holiday period, on a high-volume or high-dollar order, and/or to a shipping address that differs from the billing address

- Shipping addresses in Romania, Macedonia, Belarus, Pakistan, Russia, Lithuania, Egypt, Nigeria, Colombia, Malaysia, or Indonesia

- Suspicious addresses like 12345 Big Street (You can check them easily with an online map service.)

- Expensive orders that say "leave at door." (This may mean someone is using an unwitting neighbor as a drop point; require a signature.)

More information on protecting your business can be found at:

- Internet Fraud Watch at *http://www.fraud.org/scams againstbusinesses/bizscams.htm*

- Scambusters.org at *http://www.scambusters.org*

- World-wide E-Commerce Fraud Prevention Network (you can become a free member) at *http://www.merchantfraudsquad.com*

Build Credibility

In addition to providing actual security, you want to reassure buyers who remain cautious about using their credit cards online. Join an organization that vouches for privacy and reliability, such as Trust-e (*http://www.truste.com*), BetterWeb from PriceWaterhouseCoopers (*http://www.betterweb.com*), or the Better Business Bureau Online (*http://www.BBBOnLine.org*), and post its logo on your home page. In the "About Us" section of your site, include background information about your company, such as how long you've been in business, number of employees, and business organizations you belong to. Other techniques to raise credibility include: supply testimonials from satisfied customers; provide a street address and phone number(s) on all pages; and post an online privacy policy. (For more on this, see Chapter 14.) You can choose to participate in a merchant rating program like Bizrate's free Customer Certification Program (*http://www.bizrate.com*), in which customers rate companies on their shopping experience. ePublicEye (*http://www.epubliceye.com*) offers a paid variation, with a "safer shopping" certification and a suite of promotional, fraud protection, and other business support services.

Payment Alternatives

In many cases, transactions are too small or infrequent to justify credit card transaction fees. Some banks have created an instant payment service, such as Bank One's eMoneyMail (*http://www.emoneymail.com*). The service is available to people who already have a Bank One ATM, credit card, or checking account, or to others who enroll with a credit card. eMoneyMail lets account holders transfer money to someone else or receive it from them, needing only both e-mail addresses to get started. Like PayPal, it is often used on auction sites; the seller doesn't need a merchant account and buyers don't need their credit card numbers.

Small Transaction Amounts

Credit cards aren't an appropriate vehicle for small transactions if the processing fee would exceed the value of the purchase. Depending on your product, you might consider following the example of Northern Light (*http://standard.northernlight.com/cgi-bin/new_account.pl?cb=0*, shown in Figure 7.15). Customers set up an account guaranteed by credit card. Northern Light charges the account monthly for any documents

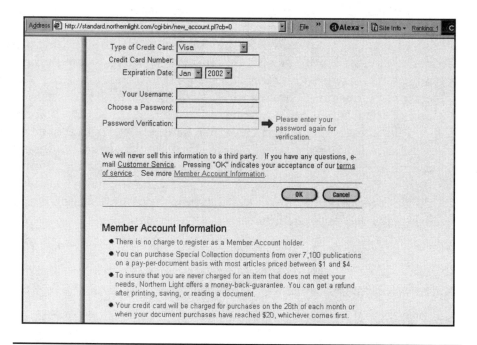

Figure 7.15. Sample small transaction account set-up, *http://standard. northernlight.com/cgi-bin/new_account.pl?cb=0*. Courtesy Divine, Inc.

downloaded from its collection at prices ranging from $1 to $4/ article. Other sites, particularly some of the music download sites like RealOne (*http://www.real.com/realone/services/music.html*) or eMusic (*http://www.emusic.com*), charge a monthly fee for a certain number of downloads to avoid the hassle of small unit charges.

EFT on the Internet

Electronic Funds Transfer (EFT) refers to electronic payments transferred between two checking accounts. It covers both an automated deposit to and a withdrawal from an account. Many people are familiar with EFT without knowing the term. Applications include the automated deposit of Social Security or payroll checks and automated withdrawals for such payments as dental insurance, gasoline credit cards, utility bills, or donations to a local public broadcasting station. Perhaps you have received a letter asking whether you want such a service instead of paying by check. By the end of 2002, almost all businesses and over 18 million households are expected to do some form of EFT. The federal government already makes all of its benefits payments via EFT.

EFT is extremely effective for the billing company because it guarantees payment (as long as there is money in the account). It saves the individual customer the time and effort of writing and mailing a check, while saving the merchant the cost of bill processing, mail and deposit delays, and bad checks.

This works particularly well with customers who buy from your Web site on a regular basis, and it is cost-effective for one-time purchases over several hundred dollars each from a number of different customers. With cost and labor for processing a standard check now running at least $4, it's worth seeing if you can save several dollars (or more) per transaction. If your company receives hundreds of checks on a regular basis (e.g., fitness centers, Internet service providers, online newsletters, cable companies), this may be an excellent option on or off the Web.

To explore this alternative, first survey your primary customers to see if they would be interested. Then talk to your bank. Most commercial banks are capable of handling EFT through the Automated Clearing House (ACH), which facilitates the transfer of funds between member banks. Some banks charge a monthly fee and/or a per-file transfer fee instead of, or in addition to, setup and transaction fees. Besides the bank's fees, there will be a charge for the software for your Web site, generally starting around $900. You'll find general information about EFT at *http://www.anypay.com/site/ml/eng/htm/business/eft_what.htm* or *http://www.ebseft.com/eft.html*.

Often called electronic bill presentation and payment (**EBPP**) software, some EFT products can be integrated into shopping cart/checkstand software. This option is available as a turnkey solution for your Web site and/or as a service from:

- *http://itransact.com/index.html*

- *http://webcs.com/checks/merchant1.html#carts*

- *http://www.electronicfunds.com/index.html*

- *http://www.checkfree*

- *http://www.simplehost.net/merchant_services.htm*.

It is possible to handle EFT without the automated software. If your transaction volume is low, consider an online form that users either fax or mail back. Since customers must provide a bank account number, a voided check or deposit slip, and a signature, they will need to print out the initial agreement form.

Online Purchase Orders

For many B2B sites it makes sense to establish online purchase order accounts. You can post the application online, do a credit check, and then reply to the customer with an account number and password. You can then bill offline, just as you would other customers. For an example see *http://btobshop.barnesandnoble.com/poaccounts*.

Selecting a Payment Option

As part of your online business plan, you need to weigh payment methods and their associated costs to decide which are best for you. If need be, make up sample spreadsheets estimating costs for transactions at various volume levels and average amounts. If it doesn't complicate your life or bookkeeping too much, you may want to hedge your bets by offering several payment options.

Make it clear on your site that you use secure transaction methods. Advertise on your Web page which payment methods you accept, just as merchants on Main Street place Visa, MasterCard, American Express, and Discover logos in their windows. The goal is to make it as easy as possible for consumers to buy on your site with confidence. Try to allow customers to select a payment method based on their level of comfort and what their browser will accept.

Sales Statistics and How to Use Them

Like any statistics, sales statistics are more than numbers. Obviously, you'll want to monitor sales and profits from your online store. If you're a "bricks-and-mortar" business, you should also assess the value of your Web site to your real-world storefront. Such "nontransactional" benefits as improved productivity and sales in your real-world store may dramatically increase the ROI of your site. Remember, about 45 percent of consumers use a merchant's online site for research before going to that same company's store to buy the product!

You're looking for the same kind of sales information from your Web site that you would want to know from a real-world storefront. For instance:

- Top-selling products sorted by number of sales

- Top-selling products sorted by dollars

- Average dollar value per order

- Number of orders per day

- Sales sorted by day (so you can tie sales to special promotions)

- Sales sorted by customer name (so you can personalize future communication).

You can see a simple statistical report in Figure 7.16 from Miva Merchant (*http://www.miva.com/products/merchant/features.html*). Unfortunately, some "browse'n'buy" storebuilders don't include statistics at all. In that case, you'll need to buy or lease a statistical package, such as WebTrends eBusiness Edition *(http://www.webtrendslive.com/ wtl_marcom/business_default.htm*) shown in Figure 7.17. You can also select a Web host that offers statistics for an additional fee.

Use your sales statistics in tandem with site traffic statistics (more on these in Chapter 8) to estimate the number of browsers who convert to buyers. Since the conversion rate is affected by product category, factor that into your calculations. Obviously, some purchases, like automobiles, are more likely to be researched in cyberspace than bought there.

Nothing is ever simple, is it? Don't worry. The planning you do really will pay off in reduced costs and increased sales. In the next chapter we'll see how to maintain and monitor the Web site you've planted and nurtured to ensure that it continues to bear fruit.

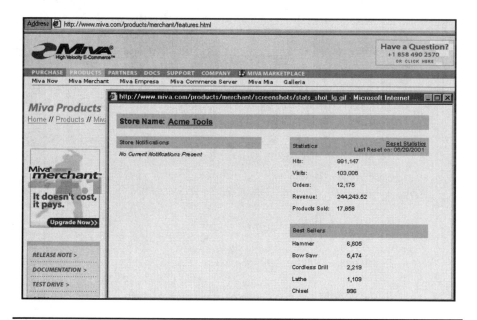

Figure 7.16. Sample sales report from Miva Merchant, *http://www.miva.com/ products/merchant/features.html*. Courtesy Miva Corp.

This report page displays a summary of all e-commerce transactions during the selected time period for the site being tracked.

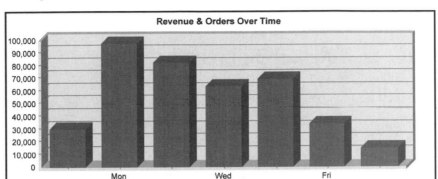

General Statistics	
Total Revenue	$394,710.73
% Revenue from First Time Buyers	83.46%
% Revenue from Repeat Buyers	16.54%

Top Revenue Producers		
Top Product	50 inch Toshiba Projection Television	$54,366.00
Top Category	Video	$169,457.00
Top Referrer	http://www.webtrends.net	$13,079.91
Top Entry Page	http://www.webtrends.net/tools/Whois/whois.asp	$0.00
Top First Visit Referrer	http://www.webtrends.net	$13,617.88
Top Ad Campaign	NBC News Ad	$85,909.04
Top Organization	rr.com	$18,993.71
Top Transaction Type	Business to Business	$226,121.78

Top Geographical Areas		
Top Country	United States	$197,644.85
Top Area of the World	North America	$206,105.03
Top Time Zone	GMT-0400	$139,338.09

Figure 7.17.   Transaction summary from WebTrends Live, *http://www. webtrendslive.com/wtl_marcom/business_default.htm.* Reprinted by permission of NetIQ Corportation. Copyright ©2002 NetIQ Corporation. All rights reserved.

8

Step 6: Maintain and Monitor Your Web Site

Your Web site is not finished when it goes "live." A site is an ever-changing marketing tool. Art goes "stale"; relevant links appear and disappear; unexpected errors crop up when developers release new versions of plug-ins or browsers; your product line grows. As your business and cyberspace change, your Web site must change with them.

In this chapter, we'll explore Step 6 for Internet success: maintain and monitor your Web site. You'll want to determine how well your site fulfills the objectives you set for it. Is it attracting as many visitors as projected? Are they clicking away as soon as they arrive on your home page, or do they continue to view additional pages? Does your newest call to action draw more or less response than the prior one? Instincts and anecdotal evidence, although critical, can be deceptive. Let statistical data cushion your decision making.

Consequently, planning for a Web site must take into account the budget and personnel needed for ongoing maintenance, updates, and monitoring. If you are working with an outside Web developer and/or Web host, include questions in your selection survey about update costs and available tools for analysis. In this chapter you'll learn about:

- A site maintenance schedule to keep your Web site at its peak

- Content management and updating tools

- Site and server statistics

- Analyzing statistical reports

- Available statistical tools

- Using statistical results.

Maintaining Your Site

Include a regular maintenance schedule in the Site Maintenance section of your Web notebook. Identify the people both in-house and outside who will be responsible for each maintenance activity. Designate the frequency with which each activity will occur, and coordinate these activities with your Webmaster and/or Web host. Your schedule should cover at least three types of checking:

1. Operational errors

2. Links

3. Content

Maintenance Schedule

Schedules for maintenance depend on the type of site you run. A complex multimedia site that relies on plug-ins for accessibility needs to be checked more often than a simple, static site. One with dozens of links, particularly to sites that themselves are new, will need more monitoring than a site with a few links to well-established databases at educational institutions. A site that updates price lists or inventory should be verified independently every time a change is uploaded to confirm that the right data appear.

As obvious as it sounds, check that your site is up and running every day. You might keep a list of priority features or pages to add, based on customer requests or internal marketing needs. Run a wish list of less important but attractive options as well. Then develop a schedule to add one item every week, month, or quarter, or as time and budget permit. At a minimum, plan on monthly additions or changes to your page.

Some of your most useful feedback will come from users who e-mail messages and queries to the Webmaster. Be sure you receive copies of all those messages, good and bad; you can always include a "copy to" option on the e-mail form so both you and the Webmaster receive complaints and praise. Keep these e-mails in the Site Feedback section of your notebook.

Check Syntax

Confirm that your Web developer uses a syntax-checking program to catch the inevitable typos and errors in his or her code. Your developer should have one, such as Dr. Watson (*http://watson.addy.com*). Most popular HTML editors like *Dreamweaver*, *GoLive*, or *Frontpag*e write code for you automatically, so there shouldn't be syntax errors. Other syntax checkers include:

- Weblint: *http://www.unipress.com/cgi-bin/WWWeblint*

- Site Inspector: *http://siteowner.bcentral.com*

- Imagiware: *http://www2.imagiware.com/RxHTML*

- Web Site Garage: *http://www.WebsiteGarage.com*

- Net Mechanic: *http://netmechanic.com*

Since some of these free services check programs online, the site must be up and running before it can be tested. If your developer uses one of those, consider publishing your site with limited password access or with a hidden URL until it has been validated, or have it checked on a private server before publication. Different checkers offer different features, so compare them carefully. For instance, Site Inspector checks spelling and links and builds meta tags, while Dr. Watson generates word counts.

Verify Links

Web surfers complain frequently about dead links that yield the frustrating message "404 Not Found" or "URL unknown." Once you have more than a few links, verifying becomes a painstaking and tedious task. Let a computer do it! Software is available to check all links automatically on a regular basis. Generally you will need to ask your Webmaster or developer:

- Whether he or she has link verification tools

- How often they are run (monthly at a minimum!)

- If there's a charge.

If the developer doesn't have these capabilities, see if your Web host will run a link verifier for you. You (or the host) might try Linklint 2.1 at *http://www.linklint.org* for free automatic link-checking software.

It's helpful to receive notification about links whose content has changed so that you can be sure the link remains relevant to your site. A **spider** is a program that automatically searches the Web for sites that link to yours, either inbound or outbound. MOMspider not only finds broken links, it also finds ones that have moved, changed, or expired. It is free at *http://www.ics.uci.edu/pub/websoft/MOMspider*.

Make Corrections and Fixes

Most programmers make and test changes offline and publish a finished page. A structured release of fixed, updated, or new pages allows your team to plan its work, while providing a clear way to assess whether your developer is meeting contractual terms. Be sure to discuss how much maintenance and upgrading time will be included when you negotiate your Web development contract. Some developers include one to two hours per month in their basic maintenance agreement and then charge an hourly fee for additional work.

In response to feedback from users or your own review process, you may have a collection of fixes that have been programmed and tested. Except for critical errors that must be repaired immediately, collect a small batch of changes for scheduled maintenance activity, perhaps weekly or biweekly. Every time you go into your site, you risk introducing an error. On the other hand, making too many changes at once may complicate identifying the source of a problem that occurs. Waiting too long to make changes suggested by the statistical findings doesn't make good marketing sense.

Be especially careful when more than one person makes changes. It is common in the software world to develop and test new modules independently and then integrate them into the existing structure. (A module can be a page, a database, or a function such as sound playback.) Your Web developer or editor should enforce some form of version management so that all developers and authors work from the same base. A systematic approach tests each new module with all the other revised modules in place to avoid negative interactions, particularly when the navigational structure changes.

Finally, each time significant changes are made or new features are added, retest site performance with different browsers, platforms, and monitor configurations. Emulation sites for download speed and appearance include:

- *http://www.cast.org/bobby*

- *http://www.AnyBrowser.com*

- *http://siteowner.bcentral.com*

Compatibility for the Disabled

If you are developing a site for a federal department or agency, your site must comply with U.S. Section 508 requirements *(http://www.usdoj.gov/crt/508/508home.html)* to make electronic information accessible to people with motor, auditory, and visual disabilities. The Center for Applied Special Technology (CAST) has detailed information on its site *(http://www.cast.org/bobby)* regarding these requirements and how to meet them, and a free option to test your site for compliance. At a minimum, it's a good idea to test any site drawing the general public or an educational audience for concurrence with Web Content Accessibility Guidelines 1.0. The CAST site also offers multiple resources and free assistance to enhance Internet access for the disabled.

Moving Your Site or Pages

The URL for a page or your domain name may change if:

- You change Web hosts and didn't have your own domain name.

- Information is moved from one part of a server to another.

- Your company or Web host sets up a new server.

You may also decide to move information from one page to another. As a result, links to your former address or bookmarks in user files will be incorrect. Be sure your Web developer and/or host sets up redirection information in such circumstances.

Take a few other steps as well:

- Notify everyone with whom you have established a reciprocal or outbound link.

- Notify everyone who has an inbound link to your site; you can find them by running an inbound link program such as *http://linkstoyou.com/CheckLinks.htm* or *http://www.linkpopularity.com*. Since inbound link finders are search engine–specific, make sure to review reports from several of the engines most often used by your site visitors.

- Notify visitors who have registered on your site via e-mail.

Content Management Tools

Do you know who is responsible for the content of each page, when it was last updated, and when it should be reviewed or removed? Companies with many people responsible for different pages on a large site may find it useful to create a content database that automatically (or manually) records such information as who is responsible for page changes, when a page was changed, and where archived versions are stored. Some owners of large sites create their own database-tracking system to monitor the status of each page and to ensure that the proper staff receive feedback on page performance. Figure 8.1 shows one such database developed by in-house MIS staff to support a Web redesign effort.

Often, page record-keeping and management features are tied into software packages that allow multiple authors to write, edit, and publish revised content without technical support. The ability to modify pages on your own is extremely valuable: You can add time-critical information to your site without waiting for your developer to be available, and it reduces costs. Commercial packages of this type are often expensive, since they are designed for large corporations with huge Web sites and Intranets. In some cases, Web developers or hosting companies buy one of these packages for use by their clients at an additional fee. Search under Content Management Software (**CMS**) in any search engine, or look at some of the products below.

Userland offers Manila (*http://manila.userland.com*), a server application that allows writers and graphic designers to manage and modify

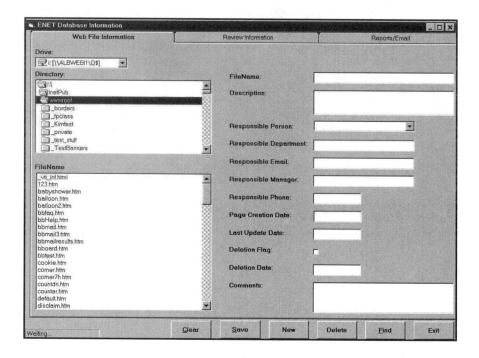

Figure 8.1. Example of database management system for a large Web site, *http://www.pnm.com.* Courtesy Public Service Company of New Mexico.

many different sites through a browser interface; it's part of Userland's $899 Frontier content-management system for Windows and Macintosh.

Global Internet Management (*http://www.gim.net/default.asp*) offers Web content management software that combines customized template design, content changes by multiple parties, record keeping, access control, and management of time-sensitive pages.

Ektron's eMPower 3.6, (*http://www.ektron.com/empower.cfm*), with licenses starting at $2,999 for 10 users, is a Web authoring package that lets companies manage and update Web sites running under Cold Fusion.

Content Updates

Updating content maintains interest and draws repeat users. It keeps your site alive and provides a reason for past viewers to return to your site. Your update strategy will depend on the goals for your site. An online archival database needs less-frequent updating than one pushing audio for a recording company's new releases. A sales site may constantly need to offer new promotions, quizzes, or contests.

You may be able to automate some content changes by referencing or uploading a file that is regularly updated by others or is dynamically modified (e.g., an inventory of auto parts). Real-time or daily information feeds are an obvious form of content updates. Use one of the free sources listed in Chapter 6 to provide weather, news headlines, daily quotes, or a cartoon-a-day. Adding a feed like this is a simple way to ensure that your site always has something fresh and convinces search engines that you maintain your site.

Many Web developers enable clients to modify site content on their own through a browser-based "administrative form" or template, or by uploading replacement text files to a particular location on the server. Although this approach lacks the record-keeping capabilities discussed previously, you may want to make "self-service" administrative capability part of your RFP, as discussed in Chapter 5. For a modest monthly fee per page, services like Suite Source (*http://www.suitesource.com*, seen in Figure 8.2) enable customers to modify text on their pages without knowing anything about programming.

Some event-driven updates, such as product announcements from a supplier, can't be prescheduled. Even if content updating doesn't apply to your site, schedule at least a monthly review to confirm that the information on your site is still accurate. At that time, you can also decide

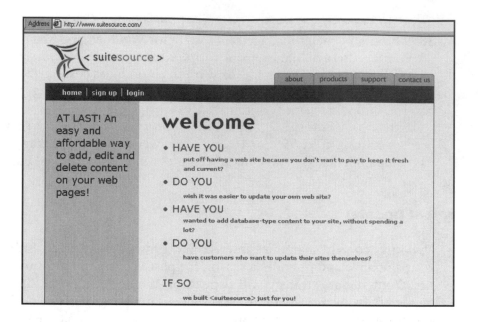

Figure 8.2. Site updating service, *http://www.suitesource.com*. ©2002 Bare Feet Studios *(www.barefeetstudios.com)*.

whether you want to incorporate any new links. Whatever method the updates take, be sure to **archive** (save offline) the old pages for record-keeping purposes.

Monitoring Results

In Chapter 3, we talked about writing quantifiable objectives. To see if those objectives are met, you must specify ways to measure progress and must decide how often data will be collected. In your selection survey for Web hosts, be sure to find out what statistical analysis tools they have and the types and frequency of reports you can expect. They should be able to provide you with reports showing both site statistics and server statistics. If you host a site on your own server, consider buying statistical software for your own use.

TIPS FOR TIRED SITES

As your site becomes more extensive or when you decide to redesign and relaunch it, you may discover that internal company policies need review. Has the site become incoherent? Cumbersome? Are there central policies regarding privacy? Design standards? Compliance with legal or regulatory requirements? You may find that you need to establish rules about:

- Who is allowed to post a page and who must approve the content

- How often pages must be updated or when they must be removed

- Style requirements for consistency and ease of navigation

- What external links are permissible

- Submitting pages for copy editing, search engine optimization, and content review.

Don't be surprised if you encounter opposition from people who used to post whatever page they wanted, or would intimidate someone in the IT department to post it for them.

Most hosting services offer at least a limited set of statistical reports for free; a few charge for more-extensive analysis or special reports. You usually access reports either on a hidden page of your site or by retrieving the reports with FTP. Before you select a Web-hosting service, be sure to check out their sample reports! If your host does not provide statistical reports, look for another host.

As more site owners become aware of the value of statistics, providing this information has become a competitive issue that differentiates hosts. Be sure to ask whether graphical presentations are available (these are much easier to understand!), how long data are kept, and the timeline for graphical comparisons. Find out whether you (or the host) can customize reports to meet your specific needs. Depending on the package used by the host, statistics may be available by minute, hour, day, week, or month. Don't be shy about asking your host to change reporting parameters to make the report more useful. The worst he or she can say is no.

What you are trying to accomplish with your site will determine what you need to measure and how you measure it. Various counts are valuable for determining the percentage of visits that convert to sales, and assessing whether your strategy for launch publicity met expectations. (In Chapter 12 we'll look at tools to measure the advertising value of your Web site and ad campaign effectiveness.) A high hit count does not always mean success. For instance, if your goal is to sell clear plastic lunchboxes, the number of hits on your site is not the ultimate measurement—sales volume and profit margin are. Web site statistics alone can't give you those answers, especially if you drive people from your site to a brick-and-mortar store.

Hit Rate: Fact and Myth

Not all hits are created equal. The number of **raw hits** or visits to your site may be quite misleading. Raw hit counts dramatically overstate the number of visitors because each separate text, sound, image, or CGI file on a page is counted as a separate hit. A page with four images, some text, and a menu bar generates six hits—one for the link to the page, one for the menu bar, and four for the pictures. Often, those selling ad space on their sites will quote raw hits because it's the highest number available.

The number of unique visitors is far more useful for marketing purposes than the number of hits. If you can't get this figure from your statistical reports, estimate it by (a) looking at the number of requests for the home page; (b) dividing the total hit count for a page by the number of files it contains; or (c) totaling the number of referrals by either URL or ISP. As a last resort, divide gross hit count by 6 or 8.

On the other hand, actual usage may be undercounted if a page is downloaded to a user's computer or LAN and is then viewed multiple times by the same person or others. To measure the frequency with which pages are **cached** (saved on a local computer or regional server), survey a representative sample of site users to see how often this occurs; then adjust your numbers upward accordingly.

Remember that the number of hits on a counter or in a log doesn't indicate how many of those hits came from the same person logging in at different times. Did you give your mother your new Web address? Even the number of unique visitors who accessed your site really tells you only which computers called your server, not which people. Was it the 10-year-old surfing after school or the parent with purchasing authority?

To obtain more specific information, some Web sites place a **cookie** on the computers of users who register (and occasionally on any computer that visits the site). This short identifier file assigns a unique number to the machine, which is recognized each time the registered user logs in. Some cookies have much more information: user name and address, purchasing history, shipping information, credit card numbers, reminder notes, e-mail address books, gift logs, or site preferences. Users don't have to reenter duplicate information each time they make a purchase, and the site owner can personalize greetings or upsell by suggesting new items based on past browsing and buying patterns. The convenience of cookies, however, comes at a price in user privacy, which is discussed further in Chapter 14.

On-Site Page Counters

Some small companies install simple counters on one or more pages to track the number of hits. You can obtain free counters from many sources, generally in exchange for putting the supplier's icon on your site. If you use one, be sure to note the date you started counting, at least internally! Better, try a free service like eXTReMe Tracking, where the counter is invisible; you log onto eXTReMe at *http://www.extreme-dm.com/tracking/?npt* to see your statistics privately.

Before you implement an on-screen counter, consider its implications from a marketing perspective. First, it should not be used in lieu of statistical analysis—a page counter is a raw hit count. Second, think how it will look to your viewers. Low numbers may reduce the confidence of potential customers. Do you really want to advertise a lack of success? On the other hand, if you're selling advertising online and your numbers are high, an on-screen page counter may be a psychological selling point for an advertiser who wants a quick way to monitor impressions, however inaccurate.

Analyzing Statistical Reports

Site Statistics

A good statistical package can provide a wealth of data about your site and its visitors:

- **Agent log:** Which browsers, spiders, or link verifiers have been used by someone to check out your site.

- **Browser:** Estimated number of computers that visited your site by name and version. Operating system platform usage is also available.

- **E-mail:** Feedback from users sorted into categories.

- **Entry page:** Which page of your site did visitors see first?

- **File:** Number of times a particular file is accessed.

- **History:** Analysis (preferably graphical) of various features over time; in some cases, such as a magazine site, a year-long history can be enormously important.

- **Impressions:** Number of times a logo or sponsorship was viewed.

- **Number and demographics:** User registration compiled automatically into a database.

- **Page count or pageviews:** How often whole pages were requested.

- **Path:** Frequent page sequences followed by viewers in aggregate.

- **Repeat visitors:** Number of repeat visits from the same address.

- **Referrer log:** Which URLs and/or domains generated a request to your site.

- **Sales:** By frequency, volume, revenue item, buyer, or category.

- **Sessions:** Count of all the times the site is accessed by one user.

- **Time:** Time users spend on site and/or on a page.

- **Unique home page hits:** Counts only one hit to home page per session.

- **User survey:** Data compiled automatically into a database and/or report.

- **Visitors:** Number of unique addresses from which calls were made.

- **Which pages and files** are most heavily used.

Even these numbers may be somewhat inaccurate. Browser numbers don't tell you whether several people share a computer, whether multiple people have arrived from a shared address (such as an ISP), or whether the same person has called several times from an online service like AOL that generates multiple source addresses. Some statistical reports eliminate AOL access from the totals because they can't be broken down to individual IP addresses.

Although you can determine how much time expired between page requests, you can't guarantee that users were actually looking at the previous page. They may have been chatting with a co-worker, talking on the phone, or taking a break to play Solitaire. They may have walked away or fallen asleep, leaving your site up for hours. However, you can get a sense of relative use.

By following users' paths through your site, perhaps you'll detect patterns that show which pages or links within your site are least or most effective. Compare usage before and after a page is updated. Instead of just raw numbers over a month, look at access rates by specific date to correlate what happens after you have reworded a call to action, changed a headline, or substituted a new photo. Did any of these make a difference in number of visits, length of time spent, or how often visitors proceeded to an order page?

To determine an internal conversion rate, compare the number of times people click on a banner (e.g., for a free offer) on one page, or arrive at a registration page, with the number of automatically generated "thank-you" pages issued after completion. Careful analysis can help you decide which parts of your site to delete, modify, or expand.

It is especially important to check how your visitors reach your site. A **referrer log** shows which URLs generated a click-through to your site. From an online marketing perspective, it's also extremely valuable to know which search engines were used to find your site and what keywords resulted in successful queries.

You also want to see whether other promotional activities successfully drove traffic to your site. If you don't usually obtain hourly, daily, or weekly statistics, ask your Web host to provide them following such events as new links, keyword changes, or the appearance of your site in a newspaper review. After their TV ads air on the Super Bowl, some advertisers actually monitor site access by the minute!

Server Statistics

Some of the most meaningful and accurate statistics about the server are very useful for your Web host, developer, or IT department (e.g., bandwidth, page download time, peak usage requirements, requests for secure pages). Besides showing activity on your site, this operational information monitors the performance of your Web host or internal server. Has it been down? Is it able to handle the volume of hits? Are visitors being turned away?

Server data also include such things as overall server usage by hour, day, and week; any network or communication problems; where errors were encountered; and comparative historical data. They can help you judge whether a site is so popular that access has become a problem, or whether some part of your site is generating many errors.

Amateur Statistics

In a pinch, you can download raw data files from the server as text, use the Find command in your word processor to search through it, and create your own reports. If the data seem incomprehensible, watch for a few key items in a long string of characters:

- A phrase that starts with "GET/..." This indicates the name of the first file requested by the browser.

- The referral source in the usual *http://* format. If this is a search engine name, it might be followed by the keywords used to locate your site.

- The browser information, preferably including version number so you can see if most of your viewers are using current or out-of-date technology.

- The acronym **cgi** (**common gateway interface**) often indicates a search engine address, since it means something was typed in by the user. Use the Find command in your word processor to search for that term, for the names of search engines, or for keywords or browser names.

Comparing Sample Reports

Let's compare extracts of reports provided by two different Web hosts, seen in Figures 8.3 and 8.4. The extract of the server report for the host in Figure 8.3 shows server access by day, hour, and domain, but it provides only the inflated number of requests or hits. The statistical report using WebTrends in Figure 8.4 includes the more useful totals of page views and user sessions as well. The report shown in Figure 8.3 provides only tabular data for a fixed time period, while the report in Figure 8.4 summarizes data graphically over variable selected time frames. Although not shown in the figures, both companies provide accesses broken down by files requested and by referrer URLs (same as "reversed subdomain"), but only the report in Figure 8.4 shows search words entered by the user. Knowing what reports you need may help you select the appropriate hosting service.

Statistical Tools for a Fee

There are many statistical packages, both for a fee and free. The fee-based ones include:

- AccessWatch ($40 for individuals, $400 per server for service providers, discount program). This UNIX-based program, which will run on any machine with Perl version 5.0 or greater, generates statistics on server use by hour or day and computes access by page, domain, host, browser, platform, and referral source. For information, go to *http://www.accesswatch.com/sample.*

- Accrue Insight (*http://www.accrue.com*) provides detailed user-analysis software to assess purchase behavior and marketing effectiveness. The cost is based on network configuration and traffic levels. (See Figure 8.5.)

- I/PRO (*http://www.engage.com/ipro/products_services/netline.cfm*) offers two expensive, high-end solutions for large sites: I/PRO

Totals for Summary Period: Dec 1 1998 to Dec 31 1998

Files Transmitted During Summary Period	765
KBytes Transmitted During Summary Period	36977.7
Average Files Transmitted Daily	26
Average KBytes Transmitted Daily	1275.1

Daily Transmission Statistics   **Hourly Transmission Statistics**

%Reqs	%KB	KB Sent	Requests	Date	%Reqs	%KB	KB Sent	Requests	Time
24.58	56.84	21018.4	188	12/1/98	6.01	8.61	3182.4	46	10
5.75	0.35	131.0	44	12/2/98	4.31	8.62	3188.3	33	11
1.05	0.14	53.0	8	12/3/98	11.11	21.02	7773.4	85	12
5.36	8.66	3201.6	41	12/4/98					

Total Transfers by Client Domain

%Reqs	%KB	KB Sent	# Reqs	Domain	Domain Name
1.70	0.94	346.2	13	cz	Czech Republic
0.39	0.13	47.2	3	nl	Netherlands
0.13	0.00	0.2	1	uk	United Kingdom
0.78	0.20	73.6	6	us	United States
48.37	60.06	22209.4	370	com	US Commercial
31.24	28.25	10447.6	239	net	Network
3.79	8.60	3178.6	29	org	Non-Profit Organization
13.59	1.82	674.6	104	unresolved	

Total Transfers by Reversed Subdomain

%Reqs	%KB	KB Sent	# Reqs	Reversed Subdomain
19.08	24.75	9152.1	146	com.aol.proxy
13.59	1.82	674.6	104	Unresolved
9.28	16.77	6202.6	71	com.nabisco
5.62	6.46	2387.4	43	net.psi.pub-ip.md.laurel
3.53	4.30	1591.8	27	net.flash.abq1.dialup.utc2
2.88	8.45	3126.3	22	org.frb
2.88	8.44	3120.2	22	net.uu.da.bos1.tnt3
1.96	0.33	120.5	15	com.intel.rr
1.96	0.21	77.3	15	com.aol.ipt

Total Transfers from each Archive Section

%Reqs	%KB	KB Sent	# Reqs	Archive Section
12.16	1.18	434.5	93	/
6.41	0.04	13.0	49	/blue_swirl3343.gif
8.24	4.18	1545.6	63	/chinapat.jpg
2.88	0.27	101.2	22	/client.htm
2.75	0.42	154.1	21	/open.htm
1.44	0.24	86.9	11	/ourstory.htm
2.09	0.27	98.8	16	/partner.htm
1.96	0.11	39.0	15	/philos.htm
7.06	0.05	16.9	54	/red_swirl12350.gif
1.70	0.06	22.1	13	/service.htm
6.54	0.32	119.8	50	/speckled_gradient1e3.gif
2.09	0.03	10.3	16	Code 404 Not Found Requests

Figure 8.3. Extract server report host 1. Courtesy ProcessWorks.

General Statistics

The User Profile by Regions graph identifies the general location of the visitors to your Web site. The General Statistics table includes statistics on the total activity for this server during the designated time frame.

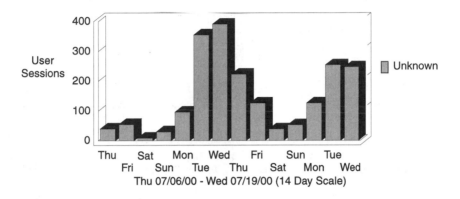

General Statistics	
Date & Time This Report was Generated	Wednesday July 19, 2000 - 14:51:09
Timeframe	07/06/00 00:00:00 - 07/19/00 23:59:59
Number of Hits for Home Page	N/A
Number of Successful Hits for Entire Site	75297
Number of Page Views (Impressions)	9386
Number of User Sessions	2044
User Sessions from United States	0%
International User Sessions	0%
User Sessions of Unknown Origin	100%
Average Number of Hits per Day	5378
Average Number of Page Views Per Day	670
Average Number of User Sessions per Day	146
Average User Session Length	00:09:15

Figure 8.4. Extract server report host 2. Courtesy American Hospital Association/Health Forum.™

Measures Original Ref Organization	Unique Visitors	Lifetime Value Total [$]	Lifetime Value Per Visitor [$]	Conversion To Buyer [%]	Orders Per Buyer
Yahoo	23,765	50,144.15	2.11	2.3	1.82
Google	11,954	75,668.82	6.33	7.0	1.97
Zdnet	10,922	59,350.15	5.43	6.0	1.45
Go	8,744	27,980.80	3.20	3.5	1.46
Altavista	8,011	16,903.21	2.11	2.3	1.62
CNET	7,950	56,524.50	7.11	7.8	1.51

Figure 8.5. Source for detailed user analysis software, *http://www.accrue.com/Products/Accrue_Insight/accrue_insight.html*. Coutesy Accrue Software, Inc.

Netline for site statistics and I/PRO Velocity, which monitors site speed and performance from different users' perspectives.

- Urchin at *http://www.urchin.com*, which is used by more than three million sites, offers great flexibility in setting time frames for analysis. Licenses for Urchin Pro start at $199 per domain name; more elaborate and expensive versions are available for hosting companies or large enterprises.

- WebTrends at *http://www.webtrends.com*, one of the most popular packages, ranges from $299 to $999 to purchase, or $59 to $199 per year to subscribe. An e-business version with sales statistics starts at $35 per month for up to 50,000 pageviews plus 65 cents per thousand pageviews thereafter. For higher-volume, sales-intensive sites, WebTrends has an Enterprise solution starting at $2,000 per month, which incorporates a comprehensive package of server tools.

Statistical Tools for Free

If you're doing your own site development or hosting, check whether your tools already include management and reporting software. Microsoft's Front Page and Adobe's Page Mill both include reporting capabilities, as do Microsoft's Site Server and Commerce Edition. If your Web host or developer can't provide the analysis you want and you can't afford to install one of these packages, request the access logs for your site. Then apply one of the following free statistical tools to analyze the data yourself:

- Analog, one of the most popular logfile analyzers, works on any platform and reports in 36 different languages. It is available free at *http://www.analog.cx*. Report Magic, a graphical add-on for Analog, is available at *http://www.reportmagic.org*.

- The Netstore, at *http://www.netstore.de/Supply/http-analyze,* has HTTP-ANALYZE 2.4, a log server analysis tool that generates images in PNG (portable network graphics) format. The program now incorporates 3D images of certain statistics.

- HitBox Central offers free statistical monitoring for small sites at *http://hitboxcentral.com/cgi-bin/hbcntrl.cgi?c=products/ details_hbf&ct=products_hitbox*, in exchange for putting its logo on the site. It reports results for 125,000 sites. HitBox Professional and Enterprise are paid versions without advertising that include additional features for more complex and e-commerce sites.

- Webalizer (*http://www.mrunix.net/webalizer*) offers detailed, configurable usage reports in HTML format, viewable in a standard browser.

- WebTracker (*http://www.fxweb.com/tracker*) provides limited statistics for free, including new visitors, return visitors, and browser and OS usage, as well as day-of-week and time-of-day records.

- WWWstat at *http://www-old.ics.uci.edu/pub/websoft/wwwstat* is a university freebie offering basic log analysis.

For an up-to-date list of various log analysis tools, check Yahoo's list at *http://www.yahoo.com/Computers_and_Internet/Software/Internet/World_Wide_Web/Servers/Log_Analysis_Tools*.

Lies, Damn Lies, and Statistics

Nothing is ever simple, including Web statistics. Because of their limitations, you must interpret them with some caution. First, remember that Web statistics count computers, not people! All you really know for sure is how many requests were made by some computer for some file on your Web site.

Second, not every statistical package counts things the same way. Different programs may have different definitions for such measurements as the length of a visit or what constitutes a new user or new visit. (Suppose someone leaves a site and then comes back 10 minutes later.) Gaps in visits (leaving a page and returning) may count as one visit in some packages but two in others.

Third, you may have a lot more visitors than you think! When people visit a site, the pages they view may be cached (stored) in their own browser or perhaps on a local or regional server. When those users revisit your site, they aren't seen because they view the site from their cache. When a page is stored regionally, such as on an ISP's server, completely new visitors may see that stored page without your Web statistics package ever counting it.

Fourth, there are a lot of things you can't know (including the meaning of life). Unless you ask for passwords, you don't know which individuals visit your site. Even with cookies or the most-expensive statistical packages, you can't always track an individual user's path through your site. Users may start with a home page from their cache and then go back and forth between new pages (so they appear to enter in the middle of your site) and other pages cached in their browsers (which you won't see).

As long as you don't try to read too much into your statistical tea leaves, you'll be fine. This isn't really different from offline marketing: you know for sure how many magazines you sell, not how many people read them! For more information on how statistics work, check out the explanations at Analog (*http://www.analog.cx/docs/webworks.html*), the National Library of Canada (*http://www.nlc-bnc.ca/publications/1/p1-256-e.html*), or Jim Novo's series on using statistics to improve ROI (*http://www.jimnovo.com/webtrends_tracking.htm*).

One other limitation: Statistical analysis packages can't track where someone saw or heard about your URL offline and decided to type it in. You can adapt a trick from direct-mail marketing to analyze this yourself. Create a new page for each of your advertising campaigns and run a slightly different URL extension, such as *www.maxpress.com/catalog/marketing.html* or *Marketing6.maxpress.com*, as an entry page that precedes your home page. This can be a visible new page or an invisible one that redirects to your home page. Then you can use a standard statistical package to monitor traffic on the entry pages. If you later take those pages down, remember to install an automatic forward; who knows when someone might pick up an old ad!

Alternately, you could use your main URL but include directions in each promotional campaign to link on different words. Then track the linked words used to reach the product page. By comparing the number of times each linked word was used, you can estimate the effectiveness of different promotional campaigns.

Using Results Effectively

So why bother with statistics? Think of statistics as relative performance measures, not absolute values. You can glean useful trends and insight from statistics as long as you don't use the data to calculate your trajectory to the moon.

From a marketing perspective, you can analyze data to help calculate your ROI or to assess visitors' online activities and preferences. You can use the results to segment visitors (how many visitors went to which pages within the site; which pages are never visited). You can postulate whether the navigation is driving visitors where you want them to go or whether it is so difficult that people abandon the site. Between the site statistics described in this chapter and the sales statistics discussed in the previous one, you can assess the relative success of marketing campaigns at driving potential buyers to the site.

To make the most of the data you accumulate, use information gathered from online registration to establish a demographic profile of visitors and compare that to buyers' profiles. Do younger viewers buy more online than in your brick-and-mortar storefront? Which viewers are most likely to buy? Be aware that registration information is not always accurate and that optional registration may inaccurately represent your audience. On-site data collection has been drawing increased concern about user privacy, which is discussed in Chapter 14. Freeware for registration is available at *http://free-guestbooks.com*, among others.

If you hope to derive income from your site, whether by selling product, leasing space in a mall, charging subscription fees, or carrying advertising, it's critical to define the visiting audience. Without a demographic analysis and a reasonable estimate of the number of impressions you or your advertisers can expect, it may be hard to attract advertisers or set reasonable rates.

By structuring pages on your site carefully, you can discriminate among types of buyers, such as those more interested in a possible purchase than in the information presented. For example, requiring an additional click to obtain price information or print out a coupon could distinguish between those interested in incidental products, such as an online game, and those interested in buying your real product.

Some things you can measure only offline. For instance, how much coverage did you get in other media when introducing your Web site? Does your sales staff find a difference in the e-mail it receives from the Web versus e-mail from other sources? (Use a unique e-mail address for "Contact Us" to distinguish e-mails generated from your site.) Compare daily online sales volume, average sale amount, and conversion rate to what occurs in your real-world storefront.

For assistance with tasks like these, companies offer **data-mining** tools to help identify trends and patterns in your data. For example, Personify analyzes user behavior at Web sites (*http://www.personify.com*), while iMarket (*http://www.imarketinc.com*) matches site registrants with Dunn & Bradstreet business data to prequalify sales leads.

As you've seen in this chapter, statistical analysis is a means, not an end. You must close the feedback loop by using the information to hone your online marketing efforts. Use the data you gather to improve your Web site: Increase the length of time on the site through a better visitor experience; build customer loyalty; or reduce time needed to check out. (Saving as little as 30 seconds can increase sales!) Take advantage of statistical information to revise marketing strategies so you draw ever-more-targeted audiences; to reconstitute your mix of products or services; and to improve customer service. You must use whatever resources you have, including statistics, to reduce costs and generate more revenues. That's the magic formula for higher profits and a greater ROI for your Web site.

For more information, check out the Online Advertising Discussion List at *http://www.o-a.com*. This moderated discussion group covers site statistical analysis, tracking, click rates, and many of the Web promotion topics addressed in the next four chapters.

9

Step 7a: Market Your Internet Presence On-Site

The Web can be a field of nightmares instead of a field of dreams. You can build a site, but visitors may not come. Or those who arrive may be "clicky-loos," visitors outside your target market who click onto your site and then click right off. The right visitors must know how and where to find you and why to look. Just as you reviewed long-term strategy before you began to design your Web site, you need to have a clear sense of where you're going before you start promoting it.

Be sure to bring the right people into this decision-making process. You wouldn't ask marketing people to write HTML; don't ask programmers to handle marketing. Some Web development houses staffed by specialists can do both, but most do only automated, one-size-fits-all submission programs. If you don't have the time or in-house staff to handle Web promotion tasks yourself, consider hiring outside help. There is simply no point spending thousands of dollars on a site that no one sees.

You can promote your Web site on the site itself, on or off the Web through a variety of techniques, through search engines, and through online advertising. This chapter covers the first of these four elements: promoting your site in the cheapest place of all—itself. In addition to reviewing the goals of site promotion, you'll learn:

- How to develop and write a Web promotion plan

- The value of internal calls to action

- Fanfare, freebie, and fun techniques

- How to build a loyal online community

Remember one of the basic laws of marketing: *When you find something that works, don't fix it!*

Goals for Site Promotion

Unless you have an advertising site (which means your audience is your product), your goal is more than the greatest number of viewers. The goals for site promotion are consistent with those for effective site design: First, you want to bring your target audience(s) to your site. Second, you want visitors to remain on your sticky site as long as possible. And third, you want them to return for multiple visits.

How People Find Sites

Viewers arrive at your site in three ways:

- Through search engine results

- By clicking on a link from another site, banner ad, or e-mail

- By typing in your URL, which they have learned from word-of-mouth, print advertising, or other offline promotions.

Your goals must maximize all three for success.

The Magic 3-Letter Word

Encouraging people to visit and explore your site requires that you put yourself in their shoes. The second-most-powerful word in marketing (we'll talk about the most-powerful word in just a bit) has only three letters: Y-O-U. As long as you focus on what your viewers and customers need and expect, you can't go far wrong. Write your copy in second person ("You'll receive; you'll enjoy; you'll earn …") as a reminder that your customer, not your business, is the focus of promotion.

A Web Promotion Plan

Site promotion is no different from other marketing activities. You'll follow the by-now-familiar drill for Internet success: research, plan, execute, evaluate. You'll need to add many items to the Site Promotion section of your Web notebook, as well as go back online for research.

Create a Promotion subfolder to bookmark sites that demonstrate the techniques discussed in this and the following chapters, as well as sites that might provide an inbound link, an announcement service, or an advertising opportunity. Save examples of good internal calls to action and banner ads. Collect promotional e-mail to see what others are doing. By all means, note any techniques your competitors use to attract an audience, from where they advertise to what promotional items they hand out.

Writing the Plan

Unless you have a photographic memory, it will be impossible to track all the details of your promotional plan without a written schedule and record. Among other things, a written plan helps you:

- Delegate responsibility for implementation and monitoring

- Avoid repeating what has already been tried

- Compare the results of different promotional methods

- Recognize when you have achieved your objectives.

Your Web promotion plan should include all the standard elements of other plans:

- Goals and objectives, including target audience

- Implementation methods

- Budgets for time and dollars

- Required personnel

- Schedule of activities from prelaunch to at least six months post-launch.

Goals and objectives for a promotion plan require a clear definition of the target audience(s) for your site and for each promotional activity. Your audience may include the press, stockholders, and potential employees, as well as customers and prospects. It may be as narrow as 100 current customers or as wide as the tens of thousands who might attend a rock concert.

Different pages with different purposes need to reach different audiences, so it's no surprise that they need different promotional techniques. Plan to repeat promotional activities on at least a monthly basis, and whenever you add a new page or function to your site.

The One-to-Two Rule

The promotion plan, especially the timeline and budget, should be in place long before you launch your site. You must absolutely plan to spend money (or at least substantial sweat equity!) to let people know how to find your Web site in the haystack of more than 36 million others.

RULE OF THUMB

Plan to spend $1 on site marketing and promotion for every $2 you spend on site development.

Help Available

When there is a need, someone on the Internet pops up to fill it. Your existing ad agency or PR firm may already provide Web promotional services. The Web has spawned an industry of promotional consultants, online agencies, and specialized Web marketing services.

Most marketing services aren't cheap. Rates range from $50 to $200 an hour depending on the nature of the service, the size of the agency, and the type of contract you have. In many cases, the trade-off is between your money and your time. Online guerrilla marketing can be inexpensive, but you will need to commit the time of someone in your organization to plan, execute, and track the results. At the inexpensive end of the scale, look at services like Microsoft's bCentral.com (*http:// www.bcentral.com*), which offers marketing packages starting as low as $24.95 per month. If you plan a site with a large advertising budget, you might need the services of a major ad agency.

For additional research on marketing and advertising services, try *http://www.ad-guide.com*, the discussion group at *http://www.iab.net,* or *http://www.adresource.com*.

Internal Calls to Action

We've talked about using calls to action to move site visitors toward the close, or toward your final objective. You can also use internal calls to action on an intermediate level to move visitors between pages, to encourage repeat visits, or to increase time on your site. Take a look at the clever calls to action on Ragu's home page, shown in Figure 9.1 at *http://www.eat.com*. This site is loaded! Four "click here" calls are found in the right column. Can you find at least four more internal calls to action on this page? If you click through this site, you'll find dozens of calls to action, from "Catch the Ragu Express" on the pop-up window to "Tell Everyone Your Favorite Places in Italy" on the "Talk to Mama" page. Keep a list of URLs or printouts in your Web notebook with great calls to action like these.

Consider including one or more of the marketing calls to action below:

Figure 9.1. Internal calls to action on Ragu's site, *http://www.eat.com.* Courtesy Lipton Investment, Inc. and Unilever USA, Inc.

- *Bookmark This Site/Page.* The simplest and easiest way for viewers to find your site again.

- *Make this site your browser home page.* The Discovery Channel does this at *http://dsc.discovery.com/utilities/about/makethismy.html*, as shown in Figure 9.2.

TIPS FOR TIRED SITES

If you have a problem with people leaving after visiting only one page of your site, take a look at your Calls to Action. If you don't suggest that viewers take an action, they may not think of it themselves. Is there a call to action on every page that encourages viewers to go deeper into the site? To go directly to purchase if applicable? Make a list of calls to action on your site page-by-page.

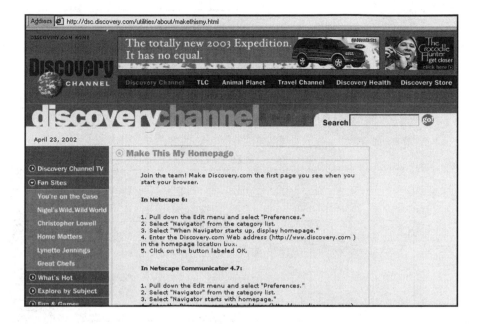

Figure 9.2. Make this site your browser home page, *http://dsc.discovery.com/ utilities/about/makethismy.html*. ©2002 Discovery Channel Online. Source: dsc.discovery.com.

- *Call us.* Users can now do this while online, even from a residence with only one phone line, using free software from Click2Talk (*http://www.net2phone.com/home.html*).

- *Complete a Survey.* Offer something for free in exchange for filling out a survey, as does NMrestaurants.com (*http://www. nmrestaurants.com*) in Figure 9.3. Make the form easy to complete with drop-down menus or check boxes, not typing. Surveys can be used to help you improve your site, better understand your customers' needs, or collect content information. Simple surveys are available from some of the sites listed in Figure 6.17. For a more complex survey, see Zoomerang's free survey templates (up to 20 questions; more with the paid version) at *http://www.zoomerang.com*.

  The two most common problems with surveys are asking too many questions and asking too many people. Keep your survey to 45 questions maximum. Unless you need statistically significant

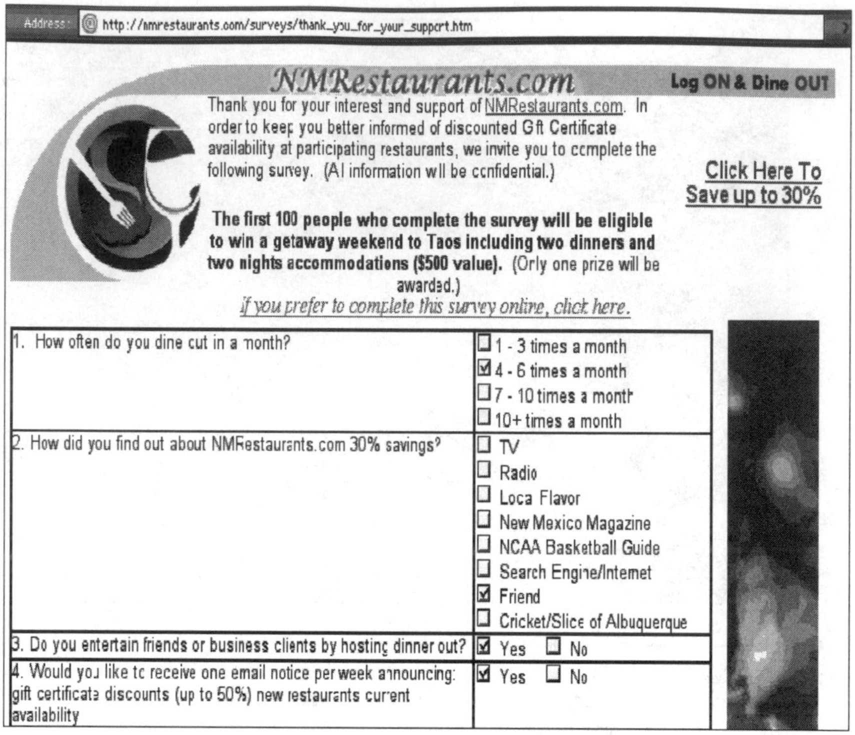

Figure 9.3. Sample survey with offer, *http://www.nmrestaurants.com/surveys/thank_you_for_your_support.htm*. Courtesy NMrestaurants.com.

data, you can probably stop after 100 responses to detect simple trends. Be sure to include screening questions so you know who your respondents are, and make sure each question has a purpose.

- *Take a poll.* "M&M's"® candy (seen in Figure 9.4 at *http://gcv.mms.com/us*) conducted a global poll in 2002 to choose the next color for M&M's. The site is replete with activities for children to influence other kids to vote, including newsletter sign-ups, and culminated in a live Webcast in June 2002 to announce the winner among purple, pink, and aqua. The site links to an affiliate program at *http://www.colorworks.com* to order a custom color mix for promotional purposes. A free polling tool is

Figure 9.4. Take a poll, *http://gcv.mms.com/us*. ©Mars, Incorporated 2002.

available at Hitbox Central's Tools page (*http://www.hit boxcentral.com/cgi-bin/hbcntrl.cgi?c=/tools/polls&ct=tools*).

- *Tell A Friend or Colleague.* Invite recipients to forward your marketing e-mail to a colleague or to send a friend the link to your site. The resource site HitBox Central does this at *http://www. hitboxcentral.com/cgi-bin/hbcntrl.cgi?c=/tools/ tellFriend&ct=tools*. This last call to action is a variant of viral marketing, one of the hottest trends in Web promotion, discussed below.

  For other "tell-a-friend" programs, see Let'Em Know (*http:// letemknow.com*), the Recommendation Script from BigNoseBird (*http://bignosebird.com/cgi-bin/birdcast.cgi*), or Recommend-It (*http://www.recommend-it.com/rec/homepage.jsp*). This last option is an affiliate-style program that enters viewers in a prize drawing for recommending your site, while paying you a fee if these viewers also subscribe to one of their e-zines. Your Web developer can add a tag to "tell-a-friend" links to track the source of the replies.

- *Tell Me When This Page Changes.* Many sites let viewers enter their e-mail address to receive notification when pages are updated (see Figure 9.5). This is particularly effective for event calendars, press releases, or What's New pages. The e-mail viewers receive usually includes a live link, encouraging an easy repeat visit.

Make the Most of On-Site Registration

Obtaining e-mail addresses through on-site registration is the most important internal call to action in terms of self-promotion. Use registration not just as a guestbook, but as a way to segment and prequalify

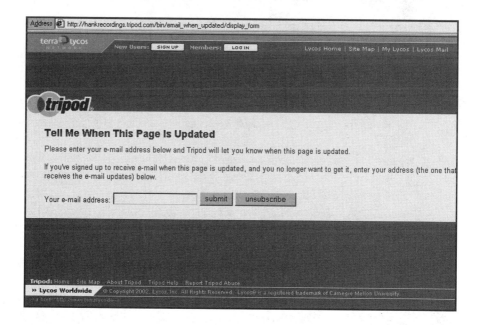

Figure 9.5. Page update notice, *http://hankrecordings.tripod.com/bin/ email_when_updated/display_form.* ©2002, Lycos, Inc. All rights reserved. Tripod® is a registered trademark of Lycos, Inc. Also courtesy Hank the Herald Angel Recordings.

prospects by collecting some basic information (see Figure 9.6). This is also an inexpensive way to establish circulation, which can be useful when negotiating reciprocal links, bartering an ad exchange, accepting paid advertising, or recruiting sponsors.

As we discussed in Chapter 4, on-site registration is one of the easiest ways to gain subscribers for your targeted e-mail newsletters. You can use this same list to notify viewers of changes to your Web site, thus encouraging a repeat visit.

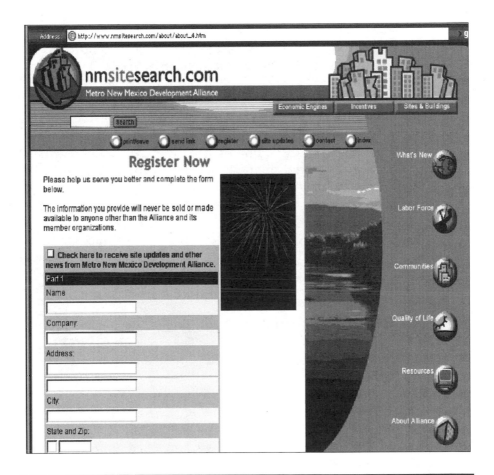

Figure 9.6. Sample registration with information request, *http://www. nmsitesearch.com/about/about_4.htm.* Courtesy Metro New Mexico Development Alliance.

Fanfare

Online promotional techniques frequently resemble comparable offline advertising methods. Awards pages, for instance, are a form of testimonial designed to reassure viewers that they've arrived at a quality site. Online fanfare encourages people to remain on your site for a longer period of time, thus reinforcing your company name and increasing perceived value.

What's New with You?

We've talked about the importance of changing content to draw return visitors to your site. A "What's New" icon or menu item is one of the most effective ways to make it easy for repeat viewers to find new information quickly. The icon should link to the new page or information, or to a submenu (maybe one that pops up or pulls down) of new material on a variety of pages.

By placing new information on a separate page, you may be able to generate another search engine submission with a new page extension and keywords. (For more on search engines, see Chapter 11.) Use any changes as an excuse to send a press release or to notify recipients on your e-mail list.

A few "What's New" announcement sites still accept changes in content or new site announcements, as do several press release pages, either for free (PRWeb at *http://www.prweb.com/urlwire.php*) or for a fee (Internet Wire at *http://www.iwire.com*). Also look at:

- Yahooligans, a section of Yahoo! for kids aged 7–12, at *http://add.yahoo.com/fast/add?+Kids*. The regular Yahoo "What's New" list posts only sites recently listed in the Yahoo directory (*http://dir.yahoo.com/new*)

- Click To New Sites at *http://www. click2newsites.com/press.asp*

- What's Nu at *http://www.whatsnu.com/cgi-bin/addlink.cgi*

Updating Service
Automatic notification of site updates is a service you can provide for a fee. (Of course, you can also do this for free with your e-mail list.) Pumatech

(*http://www.pumatech.com/mind-it_service/service.html*) offers "Mind-It for Webmasters" for $49.95 to $595 per year. It puts buttons on your site that let end users monitor changes to one or more pages.

Pat Yourself on the Back

Is your site on a list of Hot Sites or Cool Links? Did it win an award from one of the many organizations that recognize good Web sites? Shout it from your cybertop! Besides putting out a press release in traditional and Web media, incorporate a notice on your page. Award postings not only keep a record of your site, they act as a testimonial to your talent and will help draw new and repeat visitors. See all the awards won by Ragu at *http://www.eat.com/trophy-room.asp* in Figure 9.7. (This screen shows only a fraction of their awards.)

Think of awards as part of a press kit. A press kit would include a list of magazines, online and off, that have reviewed your site or mentioned your product or service. Preferably a kit would include copies

Figure 9.7. Award page, *http://www.eat.com/trophy-room.asp*. Courtesy Lipton Investment, Inc. and Unilever USA, Inc.

of the actual reviews. (Ask the original publishers for permission to reproduce their reviews on your site; reviews and articles are usually copyrighted.)

There are dozens of awards for Web prowess. They range from serious (the Golden Tag Award for excellence in HTML design or the IPPA Award for Design Excellence for commercial sites), to sarcastic (The Dancing Finger O'Sarcasm Award), to silly (The Cow Pie Awards). Some awards are designed for specific enterprises (Golden Tin Award for law-enforcement sites) or features (Red Eye Award for best use of plug-ins or Digital Media Awards for multimedia). Usually, sites must be nominated for awards, with the submission sometimes requiring a brief description as well as the URL. Review previous winners before nominating your site to ensure that your site will fit well with the nature of the award. The creators of the SpunkyMunky Awards probably have very different criteria than the people who compile Lycos' Top 5%.

Use one of the sites listed in Figure 9.8 or a search engine for a more-complete list of award URLs and links. Several sites (e.g., Award-It at *http://www.award-it.com* or Stealth Promotions at *http://stealthpromotions.com/awardlist.htm*) offer the opportunity to submit to multiple award sites, usually a few at a time. Spacing award submissions makes sense: Every new award or listing gives you a reason for a press release, an e-mail notification, an announcement on your What's New page, and an addition to your Trophy list. Maintain a spreadsheet or table in your notebook for award submissions, showing the name of the award, URL, date submitted, date of response, date notice appeared on the award site, and date you posted the award icon on your site.

> *http://www.award-it.com*
> *http://www.bizbotweekly.com/awards.html*
> *http://www.coolnetsites.com*
> *http://www.happymall.com/awards.htm*
> *http://www.ipages4u.com/Award%20Submission.htm*
> *http://members.aol.com/skycheetah/awardsites.html*
> *http://www.netprobe.net/body_submit.html*
> *http://picks.yahoo.com/picks*

Figure 9.8.   Some award submission sites.

The Webby, from the International Academy of Digital Arts and Sciences (IADAS), is one of the premier awards for Web designers and advertisers. Webbies, judged by professionals in the field, are given annually in 30 categories along with a People's Voice Award for a site chosen by the online community. Check out their home page at *http://www.webbyawards.com* to seek inspiration during your Web research forays. For more information on nomination criteria, go to *http://www.webbyawards.com/main/submit/rules.html.* Besides the 150 best sites of the year, the Webby site keeps archives of past winners. A great site to bookmark!

Freebies and Fun

Giveaways, coupons, and other offers are limited only by your imagination and your budget. Like similar offline promotions, they keep your name or brand in front of your audience and give viewers a reason to return. You can further entice repeat visits by highlighting future offers. Use your mailing list to tell people when a new game, drawing, or offer has been placed online and remind them to visit your Web site to see whether they have won.

A Four-Letter Word That Starts with "F"

The most powerful word in marketing is *free*! Offer something in exchange for registration, completing a survey, or even just trying your Web site. Jelly Belly combines the elements of a free sample with a survey and a game element, as seen at *http://jellybelly.jellybelly.com/ SurveyNew/survey_intro.asp* in Figure 9.9. Visitors receive jelly bean samples in exchange for filling out a survey, but only if they catch the random window each day during which the survey is accessible and if they are one of the first 500 entries.

Giveaways

Give away one of your products, a related item, or something with your name on it. Make it attractive enough that people will talk about your

Figure 9.9. FREE is a 4-letter word, *http://jellybelly.jellybelly.com/Survey New/survey_intro.asp*. ®Registered TMs of Jelly Belly Candy Company. Used with permission of Jelly Belly Candy Co.

promotion online and off. One site, Start Sampling (*http://www. startsampling.com*), does nothing but list sample offers. Since marketers are always looking for qualified users to complete surveys, the site gives away "Frequent Tryer Miles" for members who provide feedback, visit a manufacturer's site, or "Tell a Friend" about the site. These awards are used as gift certificates for other sites or to earn prizes. For other giveaways, consider these ideas:

- Baby Zone (*http://www.babyzone.com/Features/Offers/ FreeOffers.asp*) offers free items for new and expecting parents, ranging from coupons, gift cards, and discounts to magazine subscriptions and free samples.

- Offer a trial subscription to your fee-based e-mail newsletter or information service, or a free e-mailed report.

- Let users download free software, from demo software to an animated greeting or a screen saver, as Away.com does at *http://www.away.com/screensaver/index.adp*. You can purchase software to create your own screensaver, have your developer create one, or negotiate an arrangement with shareware developers who would like to attract customers for their products.

Distribute a Browser

For a unique way to drive traffic to your site, distribute a browser preset to have your home page appear when a user boots up. You could collaborate on this promotion with a local ISP or online service that offers a free trial period. An excellent Web site announcement, this CD-ROM–based promotion can be mailed out to current customers with an invitation to visit your new site or can be given away free at your physical location. You can distribute a customized Netscape browser for free, in exchange for filing a quarterly report on distribution, by going to *http://home.netscape.com/bisdev/distribution*.

Coupons

Discount coupons for use online or offline are surprisingly popular. An NPD Group survey found that nearly one-third of Web surfers utilize online coupons to save money. Many grocery store sites let users print a "ValuPage" (*http://www.valupage.com/Entry.pst*) of coupons with on-line specials to bring them into the store, with the additional temptation of getting additional Web dollars for future purchases. Ralphs of California (*http://ralphs.upons.com/upons/Start.do*) goes one better. It lets viewers pick the coupons they want and automatically adds the savings to their club card for use with their next in-store purchase. Coupons travel the opposite direction as well, with hard-copy coupons containing an offer code for online purchases. They may be distributed with in-store purchases or sent in direct mail.

Be cautious, though. Computer glitches with coupons may end up costing you dearly. Coupon message boards and posting sites, such as Fat Wallet.com (*http://www.fatwallet.com*) pass the word quickly to electronic coupon clippers by e-mail when an error allows multiple uses of an online coupon, or when there are typos in the price or quantity of merchandise offered. Even the biggies get hit: Amazon.com, Buy.com, Staples.com, AltaVista, and eZiba.com were all targeted by bargain-hunting consumers taking advantage of coupon programming errors. Be sure to test your coupon offer thoroughly on an offline server before posting it. Instead of, or in addition to, offering coupons on your own site, you can post them on such sites as Fat Wallet or MyClipper (*http://www.myclipper.com*) for a fee. Contact these sites for costs and process.

Contests, Raffles, and Games

Offer free entry in a sweepstakes, drawing, or contest with an online announcement of the winners. You may need to pitch your contest offline. For a sample sweepstakes offer, see *http://golfserv.nypost.com/ sweepstakes/default.asp?mainnav=games&subnav=games3*. Sweepstakes Advantage (*http://www.sweepsadvantage.com*) compiles a list of online sweepstakes, so post your sweepstakes there and on similar sites.

If a minimum number of entries is required before an award is given, provide a registration counter that shows the number of entries. Raffles, drawings, sweepstakes, and other contests must meet certain legal requirements, including a disclaimer with eligibility, dates of entry, dates of delivery, number of prizes, and more. Have your attorney check the text before you put it online. Gift certificates or online shopping sprees are good prizes because the winner stays on your site, and they encourage repeat business. Better yet, split the prize between the winner and a friend so you get two customers!

Games operate a little differently, since users may play against themselves, rather than against others, and may not win anything of tangible value. For example, Sony online offers multiple games *(http:// www2.station.sony.com/en)* as seen in Figure 9.10. Post your contest at *http://www.contestguide.com*.

Build a Loyal Online Community

Building an online community of interest is one of the newer approaches to retaining an audience for your site. The two-way communication of online groups encourages social and professional relationships between

Figure 9.10. Sample game site, *http://www2.station.sony.com/en.* "Jeopardy!" ©2002. Jeopardy Productions, Inc. All rights reserved. Jeopardy! is a registered trademark of Jeopardy Productions, Inc.

your company and your users, and among the users themselves. The process of users becoming "members" plays into the social and esteem levels of Maslow's Triangle, as discussed in Chapter 2. For an example of a site that built an effective community of interest for amateur auto tinkerers, take a look at Wrenchead (*http://www.wrenchead.com/ wh_mem/community/hangout.asp*).

Online communities pay off. One recent study showed that these online groups increase site traffic, average time on site, number of repeat visits, sales, and ROI. If you want to set up an interactive community on your site, consider all forms of people-to-people interaction organized around areas of interest: standard chat, real-time groups, instant messaging, e-mail, and message board discussions. You can install individual options or buy community-building software to incorporate these elements on your site. For instance, Build A Community from eCreations Software (*http://buildacommunity.com/ecardspro*) offers combinations of e-cards, games, forums, clubs, chat, and picture galleries at starting prices of $200–$600 per package.

Chat Rooms, Message Boards, and Events

In addition to basic ongoing chat rooms (including member-to-member help areas), consider scheduling a moderated live chat with a professional or a well-known personality, or offering opportunities for viewers to consult with business experts through a **message board** (nonsimultaneous chats in which messages are posted for others to read). Message boards are an ongoing feature available at any time, while celebrity chats are booked and promoted on the site (and sometimes off) well in advance. For example, Figure 9.11 shows how Third Age handles on-site promotion for its chats at *http://www.thirdage.com/chat/schedule.html*.

Free software for both chats and message boards is listed in Figure 6.17. In addition, Topica (*http://www.topica.com/create/index2.html*), Blogger (*http://www.blogger.com*) and Yahoo! (*http://groups.yahoo.com/start*) both offer free message boards you can link to. Or starting at $9.95 per month you can set up a chat room without banner advertising on your own site using software from Parachat (*http://www.*

TIPS FOR TIRED SITES

Looking for something special? Consider hosting a Webcast, an online event with live audio and/or video. Collaborate with some complementary businesses to share the cost, help with publicity, and bring in participants through their own sites. Each company's site promotion can be subtle—a logo link at the bottom of the Webcast page. For example, a company that makes monogrammed athletic uniforms could team with a manufacturer of soccer balls and the local soccer association for a real-time event that includes a coach or a player from a professional or local team. Use the event to discuss contemporary soccer issues, from its popularity as an intramural sport to good sportsmanship or the need for more sponsors for local teams. As always, promote the event offline, online, and on your own site. For example, see the billboard for a Webcast of the Gathering of Nations Pow Wow (*http://www.gatheringofnations.com*), shown in Figure 9.12. Post your event on Webcast announcement sites like *http://realguide.real.com/info/?page=submit*, *http://webcastlinks.com/live.html#Real*, and *http://add.yahoo.com/fast/add?+Events*.

Figure 9.11. On-site chat promotion, *http://www.thirdage.com/chat/schedule. html.* Courtesy Third Age, Inc.

Figure 9.12. Billboard promotion for online Webcast, *http://www.gatheringof nations.com.* Courtesy Gathering of Nations Web site.

parachat.com). Celebrity chats can be publicized both online and offline, including on television programs like "Entertainment Tonight."

Viral Marketing

Viral marketing is electronic word-of-mouth, the process by which viewers pass your message around the Internet. Viral marketing is inexpensive (even when tied to a reward), potent, and invaluable. As you know from your bricks-and-clicks business, a referral from a friend or colleague is one of the most common ways people learn about your company. Recent studies found that the average U.S. adult tells 12 others about his or her Internet shopping experience, almost twice those who recommend their favorite restaurant.

Their testimonials provide instant credibility for your business, cutting through the clutter of ads and their perceived lack of believability. Studies have shown that 81 percent of recipients will forward a message to at least one other person, and 49 percent will send it to two or more. (This doesn't sound unreasonable; just think of all those urban legends that circulate via e-mail forever.) In addition to e-mail, word-of-mouth may spread through chat rooms, newsgroups, message boards, listservs, ratings and comments on consumer sites like ePinions.com (*http://www.epinions.com*) or Planetfeedback.com (*http://www.planetfeedback.com*), on Web sites started by fans or critics of particular products, through negative annotations on manufacturer sites, or by information published on a user's own site.

A particular group of online opinion leaders, dubbed "e-fluentials" by advertising firm Burson-Marsteller, are particularly effective at influencing others through e-mail and other online venues. Representing about 10 percent of the online population, they pass along messages to 14 other people, well above the average rate.

ICQ (*http://www.ICQ.com*) instant-messaging software is famous for its use of viral marketing. If users of "I Seek You" want to set up instant messaging with friends who are not subscribers, they e-mail a link to download ICQ software to their friends. ICQ, which lets users scan their address books to send the download suggestion to everyone on their list simultaneously, claims to have signed up 115 million users using this method.

You've probably seen many other examples. Any message sent from HotMail, the free e-mail service, invites recipients to sign up for their own free account, leading to more than 12 million subscribers in less than 18 months. In a famous Valentine's Day promotion, Scope mouthwash invited consumers to e-mail a personalized, animated kiss to someone special, who in turn was invited to "pass it on." The success of the film "The Blair Witch Project" was built initially through online word-of-mouth, driving 75 million visitors to a $15,000 Web site. This approach to film marketing was so successful that many movie productions now copy it as a matter of course.

To succeed with pass-it-on viral marketing promotions, your product or service must be worth talking about! Keep your viral messages short and friendly, and see if you can identify influential groups of users, or at least one person who will be especially prolific with contacts. Be cautious, however: First, there's a fine line between sending a link request and spam. Second, as with all word-of-mouth advertising, negative experiences online are at least 50 percent more likely to be shared than endorsements.

Now that we've looked at promoting your site on itself through internal calls to action, fanfare, freebies, online communities, and viral marketing, let's go to the next chapter to see how other online and offline promotion techniques can drive an audience to your site.

10

Step 7b: Market Your Internet Presence Online and Offline

Almost every offline marketing technique has an online equivalent. There's no need to throw out everything you know about marketing; you just need to learn new methods. The techniques we discuss in this chapter use the Web for public relations, for garnering testimonials, for handing out the equivalent of flyers with your phone number, and for encouraging word-of-mouth communication among users. Most of these methods result in users either linking to your site from elsewhere on the Web or typing in your URL. In this chapter you'll learn about:

- Word of Web campaigns to publicize your site online

- Techniques for creating a "buzz" about your site

- Using inbound link campaigns to increase visibility and site popularity

- Promoting your site offline

- Coordinating a site launch

Word of Web Campaigns

"Word of Web" campaigns refer to all the various online techniques you can use to draw your target audience to your site. These include online PR, site reviews, newsgroups and mailing lists, chat rooms, and tie-ins to offline word-of-mouth. While there are no rules for site promotion, stealth won't drive traffic to your site! Let's consider these various techniques.

Online PR Campaign

Besides using your regular offline press mailing lists, utilize online press release/public relations services as a cost-effective way to let your Web light shine. PR in the broad sense includes any technique that builds your company's reputation without a direct marketing message. Stories and articles are viewed as more objective than ads. Good publicity establishes your company's expertise and credibility and encourages others to spread the word.

Since a mere Web site announcement is rarely newsworthy, try to tie your press releases to a new or unique element of your product or service, or something that will generate human interest. Information on how to write a good press release and other PR tips are available at:

- *http://marketing.tenagra.com/releases.html*

- *http://www.netpress.org/careandfeeding.html*

There are both listserves and Web sites for distributing releases online. Online News, which has a number of readers in the press and accepts *only* press releases, is a good listserve to try. To subscribe, e-mail *businesswire@topica.com.* In the body of your note, say *subscribe online-news <your e-mail address>.* Other press outlets on the Web (most charge a fee) include:

- *http://www.businesswire.com*

- *http://www.click2newsites.com/press.asp* (free)

- *http://www.internetwire.com*

- *http://www.newsbureau.com*

- *http://www.partylinepublishing.com*

- *http://www.pressaccess.com*

- *http://www.prnewswire.com*

- *http://www.prweb.com* (free; also offers free real-time news feeds to place on your site)

- *http://www.profnet.com*

- *http://www.solonews.com* (free B2B news portal)

For online media directories, try:

- *http://www.editorandpublisher.com*

- *http://www.mediafinder.com*

- *http://www.newsdirectory.com*

- *http://www.yahoo.com/News_and_Media/Newspapers*

Other ways of obtaining publicity abound. Write articles for e-zines, complementary Web sites, and offline publications with a link to your site. Produce an online and/or offline column and publicize it. Become a source for stories by journalists. Services like Media Map (*http://sourcenet.mediamap.com/sourcenet*) monitor requests for "recognized experts" on a topic. Take advantage of free publicity offered by organizations to which you belong. For instance, SouthWest Writers (*http://www.southwestwriters.org*) offers its published members free publicity for a period of time, including a link to the purchase location and a link to a Web site in exchange for carrying the SWW logo.

To monitor the success of your online press campaign, you might want to use an electronic clipping service to track the appearance of your site in various online venues. For an annotated list of clipping services, try E-releases (*http://www.erelease.com/clipping_services.html*) or look at:

TIPS FOR TIRED SITES

For relatively low-cost promotion, plan a regular and extensive program of press releases and media outreach. Create a press page on your site with the items below. You should also compile a hard-copy equivalent called a press kit, which will add brochures, product spec sheets, story reprints, and a business card to these items.

- Current press releases

- Recent stories about the company written by others (request permission)

- A corporate backgrounder

- A contact directory

- Brief biographies of key staff

- Digital photos of key managers, products, and processes

- An archive of past press releases and stories.

- eWatch from PRNewswire at *http://www.ewatch.com*

- News Index at *http://www.newsindex.com*

- Scoop at *http://www.intellisearchnow.com*

- Webclipping.com at *http://www.webclipping.com*

Hot Sites and Cool Links

Reviewed lists of Hot Sites or Cool Links are discretionary. The composers of these lists use their own intensely personal criteria to sift through sites, just as film critics and restaurant reviewers do. Cool Links lists range from a site-of-the-day maintained by an individual, to rankings from USA Today and Yahoo! A number of these sites are shown in Figure 10.1. For more sites with Hot Sites and Cool Links, check *http://www.bizbotweekly.com/awards.html*.

If criteria for a list are unpublished or too vague to determine if your site is qualified, evaluate the sites recommended on the list. Nominate your site only for lists that endorse sites similar to yours. As always, record your submissions and appearance so you can determine whether there is a correlation with traffic to your site. Sites like USA Today at *http://www.usatoday.com/life/cyber/cw.htm* review useful sites by category, much like an annotated bibliography. You'll need to search out such opportunities based on your business needs and target audiences.

Because appearing on one of these recommended lists can result in thousands of additional hits, competition for placement has become intense. An appearance on a Hot Sites or Cool Links list, which lasts between a day and a week, generates a brief but predictable flurry of hits. At the same time, the number of such sites has multiplied like bunny rabbits, saturating the Hot Sites/Cool Links field itself.

Create your own list with a unique, topical twist and accept nominations or allow viewers to vote. It's another way to generate repeat visits. Or exchange nominations with a complementary business that also maintains a Hot Sites list.

Some agencies and service providers specialize in getting your site listed as a Hot Site or Cool Link, just as some PR firms specialize in getting articles placed in the *Wall Street Journal* or local business magazines. The application process for most sites involves sending an e-mail with your URL and a short description (with style and verve) of your site, its features, and its value to the user. You must decide whether appearing on this list, or on any other award list, will draw the audience you are looking for.

> *http://coolsiteoftheday.com*
> *http://data.detnews.com/hotsites*
> *http://picks.yahoo.com/picks*
> *http://usatoday.com/life/cyber/ch.htm*
> *http://web.icq.com/cool-links*
> *http://www.100hotsites.com*
> *http://www.heritagenews.com/cool_links*
> *http://www.mediacom.it/siti2/hotsite.htm*
> *http://www.rosenet.net/hot*
> *http://www.yahooligans.com/docs/cool/index.html*

Figure 10.1. Some Hot Sites and Cool Links.

Newsgroups and Mailing Lists

In Chapter 4, we talked about using info-tools on the Internet to promote your business. These same tools promote recognition and repeat visits from a highly targeted audience to your Web site itself. Although newsgroup patronage is declining, it's still an exceedingly valuable means of reaching a prequalified audience. Some newsgroups and mailing lists now accept sponsors to defray the costs of maintenance and monitoring. To find such newsgroups, check out the FAQ files of well-trafficked topical groups such as:

- *comp.internet.net.happenings*

- *comp.infosys.www.announce*

- *misc.news.internet.announce*

Most moderated groups (e.g., misc.news.internet.announce) state that postings to the group are for new and revised Web site addresses only. Check the FAQ files if you are not sure. Many regional, event-oriented, or industry-, company-, and product-specific newsgroups may be appropriate, depending on your business. Search through the newsgroups on TopicA (*http://www.topica.com*) for names ending in *.announce*. Most of these sites allow you to post once for each unique URL.

Newsgroup announcements remain up for only a few days to a week. From a strategic point of view, spread out your announcements. Post to a different newsgroup each week to increase traffic without overloading your server. For this audience, your title, message, and form of announcement are all-important. If you post a press release on one of these groups, try to include a photo, sound file, or video, unless the site accepts only text.

Like newsgroups, some mailing lists now accept sponsors and Web announcements. Check FAQs and watch the types of mailings going out to determine whether a particular list is a good one to promote your site.

Chat Room Buzz

Find chat rooms on portals or complementary sites that address topics relevant to your business. Participate as an individual from your personal e-mail address, not as a company representative, to refer people to your site or talk it up as a great source of information.

Word of Mouth Buzz ... Buzz

Traditional online buzz is usually not enough to drive traffic to sites. Combined with advertising and offline word-of-mouth, however, buzz can be a very powerful reinforcement. You may combine an online buzz campaign with offline word-of-mouth techniques to spread the word faster: a direct-mail campaign targeted at industry leaders or conference attendees; getting product samples into the hands of consumers; or seeding distribution channels, power users, or "e-fluentials" with beta versions of software, book excerpts, or special pre-release samples.

Get people talking with online or offline marketing gimmicks, such as a stunt event, real-time video feeds, an online scavenger hunt, or an elaborate interactive game that links multiple sites. This approach was used successfully to promote the films *A.I.* and *Planet of the Apes*. Summon your marketing muse!

Inbound Link Campaigns

Inbound links from other sites do more than offer an opportunity for viewers to find you from other sites. Many search engines fully or partially establish your position in search engine results on the basis of your **link popularity**—that is, how many other "relevant" sites also on that search engine link to you. Here's the kicker: A search engine's definition of relevance is sites that share a keyword with your site! As you'll learn in the next chapter, each search engine has a unique, complex formula for ranking sites by importance. The number of domains and the number of pages that link to your site are part of this formula. Inbound link sites also rank higher if they have related content, have been reviewed by a human editor, or have many inbound links themselves. To get ideas for links, run a spider (see Chapter 8) to see who links to your competitors and to other sites that rank highly in results on coveted keywords.

Links from Other Sites

Links can be a reciprocal exchange with another site, one-way inbound, or one-way outbound. **Reciprocal** linking with other sites is one of the most-effective and least-expensive ways to attain greater visibility for your own. Be sure to visit the other sites to confirm that they attract the audience you want.

To establish an individual reciprocal link, e-mail a request to the other business, as seen in the sample request in Figure 10.2. Attach a digital logo in case the other site will let you have something more elaborate than straight text for your link. You can generate goodwill by creating a link to the other site's home page first. Try to find sites with more traffic than yours. Few sites link from their home page, but that doesn't matter for search engine popularity. You might want to direct the inbound link to a page other than your home page, bringing visitors directly to relevant information based on the referring source.

For a list of potential link sites, including industry-specific directories, and smaller search engines, check out *http://www.NetMegs.com/ linkage*. Beware of **Free-for-All** (FFA) link sites like Link-o-Matic (*http:// www.linkomatic.com*) or FFAnet (*http://www.ffanet.com/links/list.pl*). FFA sites rarely share keywords and may be ignored by search engines or rejected as spam for lack of relevance.

> Dear Webmaster:
>
> We have found your site so valuable to our viewers that we have established a link from our site, *www.oursite.com*. Our site, which [purpose of site, e.g. *is a resource guide for herbal remedies*], draws viewers who [describe viewers, e.g. *buy a variety of natural foods, clothing and NewAge music.*]. Since we share a similar audience, I would appreciate a reciprocal link to our site.
>
> I think you would find *www.oursite.com/bestpage* best suited to a link. For your convenience, I have also attached a GIF of our logo if you are able to use it. Please let us know when our link is posted. Thank you.
>
> Sincerely,

Figure 10.2. Sample request for a reciprocal link. ©2000 Watermelon Mountain Web Marketing.

Finding **inbound** links is a matter of good Web research. The trick is to identify places where your target audience is likely to be found online and encourage them to link to you from those sites. (The same process will work for banner ads.) Some sites are so open to inbound links, they post code for links and banner ads on their site for anyone to pick up.

Certain types of sites are more likely to support one-way outbound links to your site:

- Professional, business, and trade associations to which you, your company, or your target audience belong.

- Online sites for any magazine or other places where you advertise; often a link is included in advertising contracts for other media.

- Sites that offer directories of service providers or distributors.

- Shopping bot sites that help buyers locate products; you'll find a list of them at SmartBots (*http://www.smartbots.com*).

- Web sites with search engines that provide references for their viewers (your audience), such as *http://www.abcparenting.com*, shown in Figure 10.3.

- Home pages owned by satisfied clients or customers for whom you've provided service. (For example, Web designers often put a link from their clients' sites back to their own home page.)

- Newsgroup announcement sites.

An expanded listing in a directory is another variation on this theme. This is somewhat akin to a business card ad in a mini telephone directory of local businesses, but it draws focused traffic instead of a general audience. Netscape offers an excellent free card at *http://netbusiness.netscape.com/card*.

Some sites may charge a modest amount for a link, some may have a routine submission form, and some may need an individual e-mail contact. To track the status of link requests, you'll need another table in your Web notebook. Columns could include name of the site, URL where links appear, contact person, e-mail address, contact date, response date,

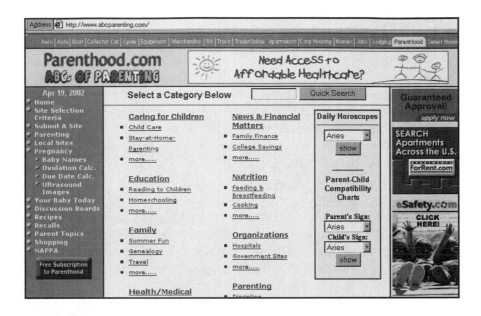

Figure 10.3. Links from a reference site, *http://www.abcparenting.com.* Courtesy Parenthood Web *(www.parenthoodweb.com).*

and nature of the link. Add columns to verify that the link has been established, and regularly confirm that the link (and the referral site) still exists.

Outbound links to complementary, informative sites add value for your user. Think of linking to your business customers, subsidiaries, suppliers, reps, or the manufacturers of products you carry. These links expand your virtual presence because the link title can be topical, using a keyword rather than the destination name. For instance, your veterinary hospital site might have a link reading "Hay and Oats," instead of "Burley's Feedstore." Ask your Web developer always to open outbound (external) links in a new window so that your site remains visible.

Think strategically about how many outbound links to include. You want to hold your visitors on your site as long as possible. If you provide too many links on opening pages, viewers may click away and never return. You may place external links in context throughout a site or collect them on a page fairly far down in the site structure.

Web Rings

Web rings (also called alliances) are multisite, reciprocal links connecting a group of sites, usually with similar content. Viewers click on a next, previous, random, or selected link to go to another site on the ring, eventually returning to their starting point.

To join a ring, you copy HTML code provided by the ring onto your site. A **ringmaster**, who maintains the ring database, may review each application for inclusion. Some rings have specific criteria; others may consist solely of personal pages or might include a number of competitors. Check out all the sites on a ring before you join.

You can obtain a list of rings on the Web by going to Ring Managers at *http://www.webring.org/#ringworld* or *http://www.daytaless.com/webring/webring.shtml*. If the Star Wars, fashion, personal coaching, or any of the hundreds of other rings don't meet your needs, you can always start a ring of your own.

Links from Meta-Indexes

Meta-indexes supplement the search engines and directories described in the following chapter. These lists of Internet resources consist of URLs organized by topic. The people who compile these indexes will often include your site for free, so it's worth requesting a link. Usually, a simple e-mail request is enough. Include the URL, a brief description, an explanation of why your site is appropriate for the index, and your contact information. Meta-indexes may also be potential sites for banner ads or for the purchase of a more prominent link with a logo. For a directory of meta-indexes, check:

- *http://allsearchengines.com*

- *http://cui.unige.ch/meta-index.html#5*

- *http://www.fys.ruu.nl/~kruis/h3.html*

- *http://www.indiana.edu/~librcsd/search*

- *http://www.zdnet.com/searchiq/directory/multi.html*

TIPS FOR TIRED SITES

Try affiliate programs to build traffic to your site. Instead of becoming an affiliate of another site, create your own affiliate program to encourage other sites to link to yours in return for a tangible award. These pay-for-performance arrangements mean that you pay for results, rather than for impressions as you do with advertising. You can run your own affiliates with software from My Affiliate Program *(http://www.myaffiliateprogram.com)*, or you can enroll in a network like Share-A-Sale *(http://www.shareasale.com)*, which matches affiliates with merchants. Be sure to list your affiliate program with directories like Associate Programs (http://www.associateprograms.com) so potential affiliates learn about your offer. For these links to be effective, you'll need to offer an attractive commission and to cultivate potential affiliates that already attract significant traffic.

Promoting Your Site Offline

Take advantage of all existing offline promotional methods to tell people about your Web site. Use the opportunity not only to provide your URL, but also to describe the benefits of visiting your site. You might tell customers to "see the flavor of the month" or "receive instant price quotes" or "place custom orders." As always, you'll want to track the results of offline advertising and promotional activities with a code that identifies the source of the contact. Create **doorway** pages with different URLs or extensions to act as special "ports of entry" depending on how visitors arrive at your site. Use your site statistics to correlate hits with ads spread over a period of time or across a geographical region. Like return address codes on direct mail flyers, doorway pages tell you which offline promotions are most successful. Dell created a URL called *http://www.dell.com/tv* to assess the payoff from its television commercials. The doorway URL redirects to a special page (seen in Figure 10.4) that reinforces advertised offers with the message "As seen on TV."

Literature, Stationery, and Packaging

Depending on your budget, you may want to update all your literature and stationery with your URL at once or replace the items as you run

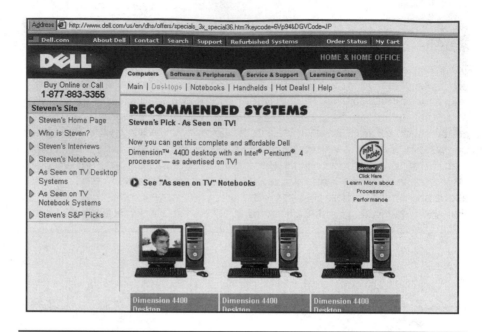

Figure 10.4. Good use of doorway page from TV ad, *http://www.dell.com/tv*. Courtesy Dell.

out. You may be able to add a designer-created label to existing brochures to draw attention to your Web site address. Don't forget to update your packaging. Labels on everything from Quaker Oats (*http://www. quakeroatmeal.com*) to Michelob Beer (*http://www.hopnotes.com*) now carry a URL as well as a toll-free number.

Promotional Items

Remember direct mail and other print promotion techniques. Avery inserts a paper with a call to action to visit their Web site into packages of labels, and eBay advertises on the back of ATM slips from Wells Fargo Bank! Web postcards to announce your site are now available for a reasonable price (500 for $99) from such sources as *http://www.wbcards.com*. Some sample print promotions appear in Figure 10.5.

When it comes to brand awareness, promotion is limited only by your imagination. In April 2001, Half.com (*http://www.half.com*) printed a discount coupon on the back of fortunes baked into fortune cookies

Figure 10.5. Sample print promotions. Clockwise from top: Coupon courtesy E-Stamp Corp. Shopping bag courtesy Reitman's Canada Ltd. Postcard courtesy *www.paintingsDIRECT.com*, painting by Marie-Louise McHugh. ATM slip courtesy eBay, Inc.

for restaurant distribution, and put ads on bags of roasted nuts sold by New York City street vendors. (The ads read: "Why pay full price when you can get it for peanuts at Half.com?") EarthLink, the well-known ISP and Web hosting company, dropped silver pouches with cookies into thousands of lunchbags delivered by dozens of carryout restaurants in six cities. (The bags read, "Do you know where your cookies come from? EarthLink.net.") Their program was created by SmartBags, a San Francisco company that also puts URLs on toothbrushes! Southwest Airlines applies window clings with its URL to airport windows, and Superfast Ferries in Athens, Greece, paints its URL on window awnings as seen in Figure 10.6.

Order your next batch of giveaway pens imprinted with your URL as well as your company name, or send customers a desk magnet or calendar imprinted with it. For reasonably priced options like these, check out Promo of the Month (*http://www.promoofthemonth.com*), which lets you select different promotional items (imprinted with your URL, of course) in small quantities each month. Companies like DotCom Gear (*http://www.dotcomgear.com*) specialize in labeling clothing and computer products with URLs. Figure 10.7 shows a range of promotional options, from T-shirts and coffee mugs to magnets, screen cleaners, and ice cream sticks!

Community Events

Community efforts require more time than money, but the investment can pay off in goodwill and credibility. It doesn't have to be as expensive as a postseason college football game like the Insight.com Bowl sponsored by the discount computer software/hardware house, or the racing events sponsored by Wrenchead shown in Figure 10.8 (*http://www.wrenchead.com/wh_mem/default.asp*). Instead, you can accept speaking engagements, attend conferences, or run seminars.

Doing good for others often does well for you. Sponsor several runners (or walkers) in a 5K charity race who agree to wear T-shirts with your company name and URL. The URL for your RV or powerboat Web site might work well on the back of shirts worn by a local bowling team. If you deal in computer-related products, enlist in a business-to-school partnership. Or see if any of your employees, wearing that ubiquitous T-shirt with your URL, will volunteer for litter or graffiti cleanup campaigns.

Figure 10.6. Sample large-scale promotions. Top, window clings courtesy Southwest Airlines. Bottom, window awning courtesy Superfast Ferries S.A.

Figure 10.7. Promotional items can drive traffic to your site. Clockwise from top: T-shirt courtesy Pablo's Mechanical. Screen cleaner courtesy IEI Marketing, Inc. Magnet courtesy American Hospital Association/Health Forum.™ Ice cream stick courtesy Blue Bunny. Mug courtesy Black Lab Advertising and Marketing.

Figure 10.8. Sample community and event sponsorship, *http://www.wrenchead. com/wh_mem/community/events_promo.asp*. Courtesy Wrenchead, Inc.

Launching Your Web Site

If you've invested a lot of money developing a Web site, treat its launch as you would the opening of a new storefront or introduction of a new product, coordinating both online and offline efforts. The launch need not correspond with the day the site first becomes available to the public. In fact, it's better that the site run solidly for several weeks before you launch promotions that will drive substantial traffic.

You may want to piggyback your site launch on another event, such as a trade show, a sales or stockholder meeting, a holiday promotion, or the introduction of a new product. Your goal for the launch is to create enough word-of-mouth and word-of-Web buzz to generate good baseline traffic. You need to build a sense of anticipation and excitement.

Coordinate Your Campaign

Advertise your new site in other media—print, radio, billboard, or TV— as well as online as your budget permits. (We discuss advertising in

Chapter 12.) Here are some launch ideas drawn from the promotional concepts described above:

- Coordinate press releases online and offline.

- Do several sequenced direct mailings and e-mails to an audience of customers, clients, suppliers, sales reps, and employees to announce your plans in advance of "opening" day.

- You can't control when your site will appear on a search engine, but you can time postings on appropriate newsgroups, mailing lists, and announcement sites.

- Create special tag lines in your signature block, and write anticipatory stories for newsletters and e-zines about the coming event.

- Copy the "sneak preview" and "teaser" aspects of movie sites like *http://www.spiderman.sonypictures.com*, which provided changing trailers, "behind-the-scenes" information, message boards, and more. The momentum increased as opening day approached.

- Announce special "opening day" or "inaugural week" site offers, whether these are deep discounts, free gifts for every order placed online that day, or special contest drawings. Announce these offers on the Web, through other Internet venues, and offline.

- Offer a premium above your normal registration payoff (e.g., a discount coupon redeemable for several months) for those who register on your site during the first month.

- Plan a live event for opening day, such as a celebrity chat (practice first); promote that event online and offline.

- If you have a storefront, put computers running your Web site on the show floor.

- Your formal inaugural week may be worth an advertising buy for a well-targeted audience; it might even be worth creating a special banner ad.

- If you are selling from the site, provide an incentive for both customers and sales reps who book orders online. (Be careful how you handle this; you don't want buyers holding orders while they wait for the big event.)

- Create an event. Try to think of something surprising or with a dramatic human focus that will draw attention. Host a special event with a school or perform some community service that draws local or trade press while you unveil your site.

- Partner with a not-for-profit to make a contribution for each site visitor, thus encouraging the not-for-profit to help with promotional activities.

- Partner with suppliers or manufacturers for the event, asking them to assist with online promotion from their own sites.

We've now looked at both online and offline methods to draw an audience to your site. In the next two chapters, we look specifically at two more primary techniques: search engines and advertising.

11

Step 7c: Market Your Internet Presence with Search Engines

Viewers find new sites in a variety of ways: Search engines, word of mouth, and random surfing (inbound links) are by far the most common, as seen in Figure 11.1, which ranks viewers' most often used strategies for finding new sites. Of course, many viewers use more than one strategy, and they may use different techniques, such as bookmarks and direct navigation, to find a site a second time. In any case, with an estimated 275 million searches per day and 80 percent of all Internet user sessions beginning at the search engines, it's time to address this form of online marketing. The benefits of search engine promotion are clear. In a recent study by the NPD Group, search listings outperformed online ads by every measure:

- Users were six times more likely to click on search listings than on banners.

- Users were four times more likely to remember a company in search listings than in banners.

- Fifty-five percent of purchases originated with search listings compared to 9 percent with banners.

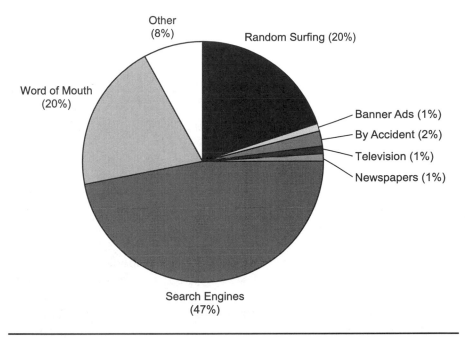

Figure 11.1. How users discover new Web sites, *http://www.metagroup.com.*
© 2002 META Group, Inc. All rights reserved. Used by permission.

Many Web site owners don't realize that their presence remains
unknown to search engines unless they submit their sites. In this chapter you'll learn how to tame the search engine gorilla to garner the maximum visibility for your site. We'll cover:

- How to submit your site to search engines and directories

- Optimizing your submission process

- Strategies to improve search engine ranking

- Optimizing pages

- Details about keyword selection

- Pay-for-position search engines

About Search Engines

The terms *search engine* and *directory* are often used interchangeably, but actually these sites are quite different. A **directory** like the Yellow Pages is a hierarchically organized database arranged by categories and subcategories. A directory generally indexes only a site's home page. **Search engines** like Alta Vista, on the other hand, use indexing agents called **spiders** (also known as robots, crawlers, or wanderers) that automatically explore the Web, visiting and revisiting URLs to collect links and pages of text that eventually are analyzed for **keywords**.

Assuming there are internal links to every page on a site, search engines will ultimately review an entire site. Once the pages and URLs have been collected, search engines apply various logic **algorithms** (computer formulas) to check the relevance of keywords. From these results and link popularity standings, engines rank sites in response to a search request. Most engines no longer index sites without a registered domain name.

The growth of the Web makes search engines' tasks nearly impossible. A December 2001 study compiled by Search Engine Report showed that the major search engines individually index no more than one-half of the estimated 4 billion "surface" Web pages. Google leads the pack (2 billion pages), followed by Fast (625 million), AltaVista (550 million), Inktomi (500 million), and Northern Light (390 million). If BrightPlanet, the purveyor of a database search engine, is correct, another 550 billion documents are stored in dynamic databases ignored by surface-skimming search engines. A list of the 103,000 database sites they've found is located on *http://www.completeplanet.com*. InvisibleWeb offers a similar directory.

To promote your site on search engines and directories, you need to accomplish two things:

1. Your site must be found.

2. It must be ranked in the top 10 or 20 sites resulting from a search of likely keywords, which is all most surfers bother to look at.

Theoretically, search engines eventually visit URLs whether or not a formal submission has been received, as long as enough links exist for the site to be identified. In reality, search engines have so many submissions that the likelihood of automatic recognition is extremely low.

Consequently, submitting your URL to search engines is an essential part of Web promotion.

There are about a dozen major search engines (some are shown in Figure 11.2) and directories (some are shown in Figure 11.3), and thousands of lesser-known ones. Don't dismiss the latter out of hand. If they are specific to your business area, smaller engines and directories may be the most likely to be searched by your target market. Combined, search engines and directories have literally millions of entries and receive tens of thousands of submissions a day. Among other sources, there are lists of search engines at *http://www.refdesk.com/newsrch.html* and *http://cui.unige.ch/meta-index.html*. There are even search engines for search engines at:

- *http://www.searchengineguide.com/searchengines.html*

- *http://www.searchability.com/atoz.htm*

- *http://www.allsearchengines.com*

Name	Submission URL	Time to Appearance	Cost
All the Web	*http://www.alltheweb.com/add_url.php*	After review	Free
AltaVista	*http://www.altavista.com/sites/search/addurl*	4-6 weeks	Free
AOL Search	*http://search.aol.com/add.adp*	After review	Free
Ask Jeeves	*http://static.wc.ask.com/docs/addjeeves/ Submit.html*	7 days	$30/yr
Google	*http://www.google.com/addurl.html*	After review	Free
Hotbot	*http://hotbot.lycos.com/addurl.asp*	30 days	Free
Inktomi	*http://www.inktomi.com/products/ web_search/submit.html*	48 Hours	$39/yr
Jayde	*http://www.jayde.com/submit.html*	seconds	Free
Looksmart (includes search.MSN. com)	*http://listings.looksmart.com/submit/? requestid=16180*	Faster posting for higher fee	$49 for basic submit plus PPC
Lycos	*http://searchservices.lycos.com/ searchservices*	6-8 weeks	Free

Figure 11.2.   Some major search engines.

Name	Submission URL	Time to Appearance	Cost
BizWeb	*http://www.bizweb.com/InfoForm*	A few days	Free
Open Directory Project	*http://dmoz.org/add.html*	After review	Free
SuperPages	*http://www.superpages.com/about/ new_chg_listing.html*	Immediate	Free
Where 2 Go	*http://www.where2go.com/binn/ su.w2g?function=form*	A few days	Free
Yahoo	*http://docs.yahoo.com/info/suggest*	7 days	$299/yr
Yellow Pages	*http://www.bestyellow.com/addurl.html*	48 Hours	Free

Figure 11.3. Some major directories.

- *http://www.invisibleweb.com*

- *http://www.beaucoup.com*

To see how well your initial keyword selection works, submit to Fast/All the Web (*http://www.alltheweb.com/add_url.php*), or Inktomi (*http://www.inktomi.com/products/web_search/submit.html*). When you're satisfied with the results, try to submit by hand at least to Google, AltaVista, and HotBot as well. Check the FAQs of each search engine if you have questions. For example, the FAQs for Alta Vista at *http:// help.altavista.com/search/faq_web* show that you can submit up to five URLs as part of their free basic submission process.

In spite of the one to eight weeks that search engines claim in Figure 11.2 that it takes to be published, a recent study found that it takes more than six months *on average* for a new listing to appear. If you don't find your listing within two weeks after the anticipated time, re-submit your site.

As tempting as it may be to submit your URL to search engines as soon as you decide to have a Web site, wait until at least the home page for your site is up and running. Many things can change or go wrong. You could easily turn off a future customer or directory researcher who reaches a page under construction or a page whose content has nothing to do with the keywords you anticipated using.

If you do the most critical search engine submissions by hand, you can use a free, one-stop submission service for additional ones. For freebie submission sites, check out:

- Eighteen free engines at AddMe: *http://www.addme.com/submission.htm*

- Twelve free submissions at Register-It: *http://register-it.netscape.com/O=wsg*

- A shareware program (varied submissions) at *http://selfpromotion.com/CF=per.koch@aviana.com*

These sites and many others offer additional submissions for a fee. For instance, Submit It! starts at $49 for one URL submitted to hundreds of engines. These services consider each announced page to be a separate URL. All sites are submitted to the same engines and directories, regardless of where your target audience might be. Be careful: Some engines have started to refuse these multiple, simultaneous submissions, considering them to be spam.

Most search engine submission services offer to resubmit your site every month or every other month to multiple search engines, whether you need it or not. SearchTrends (*http://www.searchtrends.com*), Submitter (*http://www.submitter.net/default.asp*), and others offer resubmissions and a number of other promotional services.

About Directories

Sites can't be found by directories unless you submit your URL, usually with proposed keywords and categories. Yahoo! and the Yellow Pages allow only a single URL per site, with a single description and title or keyword. Most other directories permit multiple pages from the same site, as long as each page has a different description, keyword list, and URL. (Change the page extension following your domain name, e.g., *http://www.yourdomain.com/extension.*)

Every directory has a slightly different registration form and process, so you may want to individualize submissions; look at online forms and existing listings to see what's appropriate. In most cases, you simply fill out the Web-based form with your site name, the URL, and a brief descriptive paragraph that will appear in a list of results. A few locations require that you e-mail your entry instead of submitting on the Web. You'll find a list of business directories at *http://www.bizynet.com/web-dirs.htm* or *http://www.laisha.com/business.html*.

Directory-wise, list in the AT&T White Pages and at least one Yellow Pages directory, such as WorldPages (*http://www.worldpages.com/TWP/twpwebsite/modform.html*). Other companies also maintain free Yellow Page listings. Try:

- *http://www.superpages.com/about/new_chg_listing.html*

- *http://www.comfind.com*

- *http://www.switchboard.com*

- *http://www.anywho.com/yp.html*

Don't forget business directories like AllBusiness (*http://www.allbusiness.com/directory/selectListing.jsp*), which has a free link option, or the Dunn & Bradstreet database (*http://www.dnb.com*). For the latter site, you need to get your free D&B number, which you can do onsite at *https://www.dnb.com/duns_update/duns_update_US*. Both are worth it depending on the size of your company, the purpose of your site, and the audience you are trying to attract.

Yahoo!

Yahoo! is unique among the search engines and directories because it shares the characteristics of both. Like a directory, it is hierarchically organized; you'll be asked to suggest placements within 14 categories and subcategories. Follow the directions at *http://docs.yahoo.com/info/suggest*. Yahoo! also has a robot that searches collection points on the Web, but human beings evaluate your site for keyword relevance and category accuracy. If those aren't correct, your site won't get posted.

TIPS FOR TIRED SITES

When submitting to directories, consider carefully the categories to which your site belongs. Directories may define the same category names differently and may divide up broad categories into subcategories on a unique basis, so this submission process can become quite cumbersome. Search each target directory until you find other companies like yours. If you can't find a subcategory that fits, suggest a new one. There is no point in going into a less-appropriate category—your audience won't find you. Resubmit to directories whenever your URL, category classification, or description changes.

Yahoo! recently announced an *annual* submission fee of $299 for all business listings, guaranteeing to review your site within seven days but not necessarily post it. To make sure your Yahoo! submission is successful—it may take several months to find out—note the following:

- Commercial sites for the directory or Yahoo! site matches must be placed in a Business and Economy subcategory.

- Locate up to two good subcategories by searching until you find businesses like yours, or use a likely keyword to see where responsive sites have been categorized.

- Since you can't suggest keywords for Yahoo!, the Title and Description fields are particularly important. The title can be a maximum of 60 characters; try to include keywords in that count. The page description, which appears in the Results list, has a maximum of 25 words. Try to create a complete sentence that includes keywords while describing your company's products or services. (Other search engines differ: Most clip the page title at seven to nine words and the page description at 256 characters.)

Optimizing Submissions

With the time it takes to do search engine and directory submissions, it makes sense to prioritize them. Select first those engines and directories where *your* target audience is most likely to be found, not just the ones with the most referrals (seen in Figure 11.4) or the ones on which users spend the most time (seen in Figure 11.5). Your site statistics will show which search engines your users favor. In general, business users gravitate toward Yahoo! and Google; academic users to Lycos and Alta Vista; and home users to AOL, MSN, and Looksmart.

Yahoo! is the grandma of all the directories, with more search engine referrals than any other site, but Google has been gobbling Yahoo!'s market share and may soon surpass Yahoo! as the leading referral engine. Since information is reviewed by real people for Yahoo! and the Open Directory (*http://www.dmoz.com*), their search results may be more accurate than other engines. The widest net is cast by meta-engines like MetaCrawler, ProFusion, and SavvySearch, which search other search engines. However, meta-engines don't accept direct submissions.

Inktomi, one of the best-known indexes based on relevance, licenses its technology to HotBot, Iwon, Snap, Looksmart, MSN Search, and other European and Asian search engines. In contrast, Google ranks

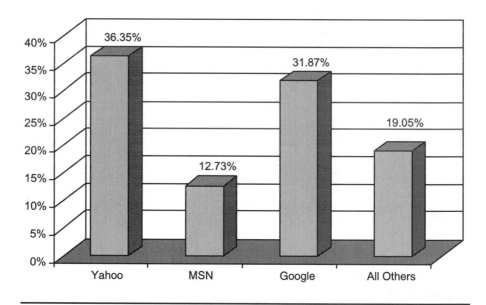

Figure 11.4. Top referring search engines, WebSideStory on *http://www.stat market.com/cgi-bin/sm.cgi?sm&feature&week_stat*. Source: WebSideStory.

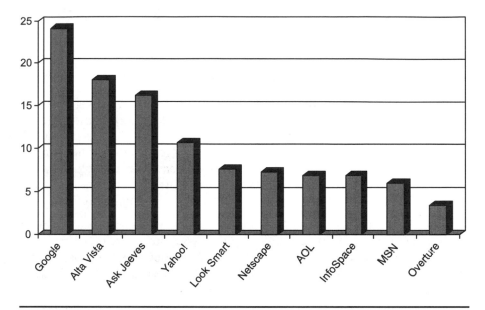

Figure 11.5.   Average minutes spent searching per visitor, February 2002, *http://www.searchengiatch.com/reports/mediametrix.html.* Source: Jupiter Media Metrix, Inc.

pages based on the number of inbound links, and Direct Hit ranks popularity based on user clicks on prior searches.

Resubmission Strategy

Search engines are not static. To increase the likelihood of getting your Web site ranked highly, submit multiple pages with different URLs whenever possible, optimizing them for different keywords. If you use multiple doorway pages, be sure to change the meta tags for each one. Besides your home page, submit major topic pages, unique content, or pages describing a special product or service.

Finally, submit new pages as they are created and resubmit pages if their content changes significantly. Although these changes should eventually be caught on a revisit by a spider, submission will speed up the process. Check your site's standing in search engines every month or

TIPS FOR TIRED SITES

Trouble getting found on the major engines? Many B2B sites include smaller, faster, less-likely-to-be-bogged-down specialized search engines in their submission strategy. These business sites, located through one of the search engine directories listed at the beginning of the chapter, may be excellent places to submit. The big search engines are also less than stellar when it comes to shopping, since they don't index product databases. If you're a B2C e-commerce site, seek out specialized search engines, such as Dealtime.com, PriceSearch, or Bottomdollar.com; well-known price comparison sites like Shopper.com or MySimon.com; and shopping search agents found at BotSpot.com and SmartBots.com. These sites generally require product descriptions and current prices; some demand a fee per listing, per referral, or per sale.

If your site includes searchable online databases, you might want to register at InvisibleWeb.com and CompletePlanet.com. If your site sports rich media, image databases, or streaming video, be sure to submit to specialized sections of search engines like *http://multimedia.alltheweb.com, http://www.google.com/imghp?hl=en,* and *http://www.altavista.com/sites/search/svideo.*

two to monitor for changing algorithms and random drop-offs from the search databases. Resubmit your site if your rankings drop. Keep track of all your submissions and rankings in your Web notebook.

Improving Search Engine Ranking

Thousands, if not hundreds of thousands, of matches may be found in response to a search on a particular topic. Most directories present results of a search in alphabetical order, which you can't change. Most search engines rank by relevance or popularity, which you *can* affect.

Given the delay in appearance on many engines, it can be frustrating to realize that you need to optimize your submission, resubmit, and wait again to see what happens. To avoid this, you can purchase software like WebPosition at *http://www.webposition.com* to test your keywords on the major search engines before submitting. Some vendors allow you to download trial positioning software from their sites.

Some Web marketing consultants use Web Position or other tools like 1st Position (*http://www.1stposition.net*) or Trackbot Pro (*http://www.position-it.com/trackbot*) to improve their clients' placement and/or provide an optimization service on a per-page basis. Before you go with a consultant, read the fine print in the contract regarding guaranteed results—which may be a myth—and ask for references from other customers. Some of these sites, such as Coastal Sites (*http://www.coastalsites.com*) say that you pay only for rankings achieved, but they require a minimum purchase.

Many sites offer search engine tips online, through e-mailed newsletters, or in newsgroups. Look at:

- *http://www.submit-it/subopt.htm*

- *http://www.webposition.com*

- *http://www.searchenginewatch.com*

- *http://www.searchsecrets.com*

These reports usually provide suggestions to improve ranking according to the approach used by each engine. The engines change their algorithms over time, partly to increase accuracy, partly to outwit people who are trying to outwit them, and partly to distribute visibility among indexed pages. If you want to get really fancy, you can optimize splash or **doorway** pages (special entry pages) based on different search engine techniques. In spite of differences, there are some general principles about the way most search engines determine ranking.

Site Popularity

Many engines judge your value to the world by the number of inbound links to your site. This increases the importance of reciprocal and inbound links (described in the previous chapter). Several sites list your inbound links. Use the free link checkers below or go directly to AltaVista, Google, or HotBot. At AltaVista you simply type "*link:url.com*" on the screen without *www.* to obtain the number and identity of sites that link to yours. At HotBot, enter the URL and select search for "Links to

This Site." It's worth running more than one of these spiders. They rarely produce identical lists!

- *http://www.linkpopularitycheck.com*

- *http://www.jimtools.com/link.html*

- *http://www.hb2k.com/check.html*

- *http://linkstoyou.com/CheckLinks.htm*

- *http://www.linkpopularity.com*

Optimizing Your Pages

By adjusting your Web pages to optimize each one for three to four of your keywords, you can increase the likelihood of a high ranking on a search engine for one or more of your pages. Here are some tips to share with your Web designer:

1. Use the page description **meta tag** in the source code header to specify keyword-rich text that will appear as the summary of your site in a results list, instead of a sentence fragment from your first paragraph of text. Meta tags are especially important when a site uses Netscape frames or Java script at the top of the page. Your Web designer will know the syntax and location for meta tags (see the example in Figure 11.6 from *http://www.lunarcow.com*), but you need to provide the content, preferably from a marketing perspective.

2. Keyword meta tags can encompass keywords that appear on other pages and incorporate singular, plural, and other forms of keywords (e.g., clothes, clothing; shop, shopping). Since not all search engines score on meta tags, be sure to utilize keywords within page content as well. Repeating the same word too many times in a meta tag can get a site bounced from an engine.

3. Include one or more descriptive keywords in the <title> tag of the document. This <title> tag is what a browser displays in the title

Figure 11.6 Good meta tags for a site, *http://www.lunarcow.com* © ™ 2000 Lunar Cow Design.

bar of a page. See Figure 11.7 from *http://www.finecoffee.com* for an excellent example of title bars with different keywords.

4. Provide keywords in a comment tag in the first few lines of HTML code, as well as in a header tag.

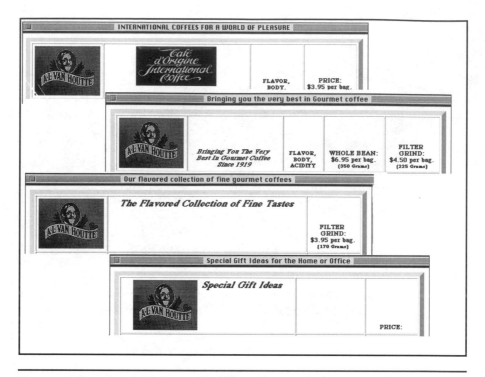

Figure 11.7. Good title bars with different keywords, *http://www.finecoffee.com.* Courtesy Fruba, Inc. dba College Hill Coffee Shop.

5. Since the top of a page is assigned greater relevance, the first two paragraphs of text are most important. A graphic near the top should have text immediately above or next to it.

6. If the site uses multiple photos or graphics, which search engines can't "see," use text within <alt> tags to give search engines a way to find keywords.

7. After indexing a home page, search engines return at a later time to index internal links. In a frame-based site, frames are treated as internal links, delaying a correct analysis of the home page. Since this may result in a poor ranking initially, include descriptive text between the <noframes> and </noframes> tags of the source code. This gives the search engine something to work with.

8. Use keywords in internal text links, on menu bars, or in headings set apart with a different font size, style, or color.

9. Substitute keywords in URL extensions for a page instead of a generic word like *index*.

Keyword Weighting

This is a ratio between the occurrence of a keyword and the total number of words on a page. Try to keep your total word count per page to 250 to 350 words. Look at what percentage of the total words on the page are keywords, counting all occurrences of all keywords on that page. Keywords should represent somewhere between 3 and 10 percent of total words. Instead of trying to get the maximum number of different keywords on a page, try to focus your pages so that different keywords pop out as the most relevant on different pages.

Keyword Emphasis

Make your headline and the first 25 words of your page keyword-rich. Most search algorithms expect keywords specific to a page to be located near the top, relatively close to each other (as in an abstract), and then scattered in various places around the page. Each search engine has a unique, proprietary set of criteria to determine keyword emphasis.

Keyword Density

Sophisticated algorithms not only count how often a keyword is used on a page, they watch where keywords appear with high frequency. Some engines will bounce sites that try to boost their ratings by repeating keywords over and over behind a graphic or hidden in one section of the background. Draw a delicate balance between good repetition of a keyword (six to ten times each per page) and overuse.

A Few More Words about Keywords

For search engines that operate by using keywords to rank relevance, an accurate and extensive list of keywords is crucial to improve your ranking. An online florist who stops with the obvious keywords *flowers*, *bouquets*, and *florist* will lose anyone who searches for "gifts," "weddings," "houseplants," "funerals," or "floral arrangements."

Think like the audience you are trying to reach. What words or phrases might they type in? People looking for a small, intimate hotel in San Antonio might type "bed-and-breakfast San Antonio." The more narrowly focused the phrase or keywords used, the smaller the list of search results and the higher in the rankings you are likely to be. For instance, instead of the word *gifts*, try "women birthday presents," "fresh flowers $30," or "office-warming plants." Try "electronic funds transfer software," not just "software program."

If you find a phrase that returns a reasonable number of results (say, less than a thousand instead of several hundred thousand), optimize your page for that phrase: You're more likely to end up near the top of the list. Of course, you can't choose words just because they return a good result—it's a meaningless victory to rank first if no one in your target audience would type that keyword or phrase.

The following list of tips may come in handy:

- Your company name should be one of your keywords, especially if it is not obvious in your domain name or if it could be spelled or abbreviated several ways. If your company name isn't obvious, you may want to arrange for it or your brand name(s), trademark, or slogan to map to your Web site. RealNames (*http://customer.realnames.com/Eng/Eng_Corporate_RealNamesHomepage.asp*) charges $49 annually per keyword.

TIPS FOR TIRED SITES

If you are already listed in search engines, type in your existing keywords and see where you rank. If you are not in the top 20 sites for at least one page in each engine, start revising your keywords. Create a spreadsheet or table with a proposed list of keywords and the list of search engines and directories you have already submitted to. Which competing sites result from a search on those words? Are the results similar in nature to your company? If so, you're on the right track. Optimize your pages for those words to improve your ranking. If you're not on the right track, work backward. Go to competing sites that consistently rank well in search engines. Look at their source code (right-click on the page or look under "View/Source" on the browser tool bar) to see their keyword list. Or ask potential viewers what keywords they would use to find your site. Everybody's brain works differently; you might be surprised. Rework your pages for some of those words.

- Use only keywords that apply to your site. In the end, any other choice of words will be self-defeating for a business presence.

- In general, use two- to three-word phrases instead of individual keywords.

- Make sure your keywords are spelled correctly.

- Include commonly misspelled words deliberately (e.g., Caribean for Caribbean).

- Don't use **stop words**, common words that search engines skip (e.g., a, an, the, and, but, or, of, that, Web). Try to avoid "the" as the first word in a title, since it might reduce the prominence of keywords in the title tag. If you must use a stop word, put it in quotes.

- If you have purchased banner ads (discussed in Chapter 12), co-ordinate keywords with words in the ad.

- Don't be afraid to include regional words or phrases to target your audience (e.g., Appalachian).

- Use long versions of words, such as *photographer* instead of *photo*. The short "root word" will usually be derived by the engine.

As described earlier, some sites try to increase keyword frequency by hiding the words behind graphics or in a text color that matches the background. This technique, called **keyword stuffing**, may temporarily increase the ranking if it is based on absolute numbers or on the ratio of keywords to text, but not for long. Most search engines now set a limit on the number of occurrences per word per page they will accept.

If you try to stuff the ballot box or "spam" an index by submitting too many pages or too many keywords (more than six to ten uses per word per page), or by using keywords unrelated to the content of the site, you may find your submission rejected. If you persist, many engines will permanently ban all your pages. "Web watchers" like *cNet* also review the Web for stuffing techniques and the use of keywords inappropriate to a site.

WordTracker

WordTracker at *http://www.wordtracker.com/trial* is a tool that simplifies the keyword selection process. Brainstorm about 100 words and run them through WordTracker, which ranks potential keywords for their likelihood to produce high rankings in search engine results based on the number of times surfers are likely to use a word, compared to the number of other sites that use the same word. (See Figure 11.8.) There's a free trial on the site, or you can license the commercial version of WordTracker by day, week, month, quarter, or year. Use WordTracker to narrow your list to 20–25 words. Since some engines restrict the number of keyword entries, you might not be able to use them all. However, spreading keywords around to different engines and assigning them to different pages will improve the likelihood of attaining a reasonable ranking somewhere. If you find WordTracker cumbersome, you might check out the keyword usage and suggestion tools at Overture (*http://inventory.overture.com/d/searchinventory/suggestion*) or

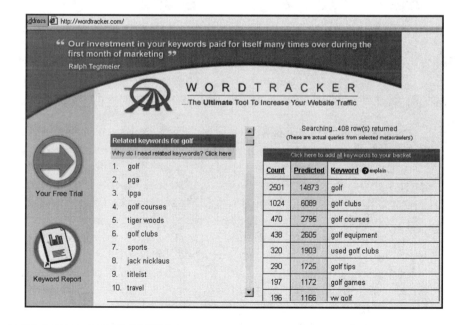

Figure 11.8. Sample WordTracker suggestions for related keywords, *http://www.wordtracker.com*. Courtesy Mike Mindel, Managing Director, Word Tracker.

see *http://www.keywordwizard.com/index.html* for a list of most commonly used keywords.

Paid Search Engines

The search engine world has become so competitive that several engines, including Yahoo! ($299), Inktomi ($39), and Looksmart ($149–$299 depending on time to index) now require payment for any business listing. Most engines accept paid advertising (sometimes called premium sponsorship, which we discuss in Chapter 12) for appearance at the top of a results list for a particular keyword. In the past several years, a new model arose. Overture and FindWhat are two of the most popular **pay-per-click (PPC)** sites, which require that you place a bid per keyword stating what you will pay for each viewer who clicks through to your site. The higher you bid, the higher your site appears in search engine results.

Of more than 250 pay-per-click engines, the single most valuable one is Overture, since its results are shared with AltaVista, Netscape, MSN, Yahoo, and Ask Jeeves. If you're in the top ten at Overture, your link will also appear when someone searches using the Dogpile meta-search engine. If you're in the top six, you'll also appear in Metacrawler searches. Overture has a minimum bid requirement of 5¢ per click-through, with a minimum payment of $20 per month. You can select the free bid for three keywords, or pay for assistance and the right to use more keywords. If you already have high rankings in search engine results, these PPC sites may not be worth the additional traffic you would receive. Figure 11.9 lists some of the most popular PPC engines.

For more information about pay-per-click search engines, see the articles at:

- *http://searchenginewatch.com/links/paid.html*

- *http://www.payperclicksearchengines.com*

- *http://spider-food.net/paying-to-play.html*

We've now reviewed search engine marketing, including keyword selection, page optimization, and submission optimization. In the next chapter we look in detail at the fourth and last method of Web promotion, online advertising.

7Search.com	http://www.7Search.com
About.com	http://About.com
Ah-ha.com	http://www.ah-ha.com/addurl
Alpha Omega Cyberspace Guide	http://www.alpha-omega.net
Bay 9	http://www.bay9.com
e-find	http://www.efind.com
e-pilot	http://www.epilot.com
Find What	http://www.findwhat.com
Overture	http://www.overture.com
HitsGalore	http://www.hitsgalore.com
iWon	http://iwon.com
Kanoodle	http://www.kanoodle.com
Rocketlinks	http://www.rocketlinks.com
Webcrawler	http://www.webcrawler.com/info/add_url

Figure 11.9.   Some popular pay-per-click search engines.

12

Step 7d: Market Your Internet Presence with Online Advertising

It's amazing how quickly the advertising industry has found ways to sell the Web audience as a product. Both space and time have been carved up in multiple ways, creating the online equivalent of every form of advertising and promotion that exists offline: display ads, event sponsorships, product placement, classifieds, and logos, logos everywhere. In this chapter we first look at online advertising in the context of all other forms of advertising and then explore the online world in greater detail. By the end of the chapter, you'll learn how:

- Online advertising compares in effectiveness and cost to other forms of advertising

- Online advertising dollars are spent

- To identify the types, sizes, and rates of different forms of banner ads

- To take advantage of online sponsorships, search engine advertising, and Web classifieds

- To sell advertising on your site

- To track the success of online ads

Trends in Web Advertising

Three significant trends have affected the nature of online advertising in the past several years. First, the economic slowdown in early 2001 (even before the trauma of September 11) and the failure of many dot-coms produced a downturn in overall advertising and a slowdown in online ad spending. As a result, the distribution of online and offline dollars for Web promotion shifted among categories. For instance, spending huge amounts of money on broadcast advertising for major events like the Super Bowl lost favor; only 6 dot-coms used the Super Bowl in 2002 compared to 17 in 2000. E-commerce companies have turned instead to infomercials, radio, billboards, and online advertising. They also increased their use of much less-expensive e-mail and direct-mail campaigns. In 1999, dot-coms spent $82 to acquire each customer, compared to only $12 spent by catalog and store retailers. The dot-com rate had dropped to $20 per customer a year later. Under the pressure from lower demand, the cost of online ads has declined.

Second, advertisers and content sites argue about the validity of applying the traditional payment-per-impression model to the Web. Consequently, several new advertising models have evolved. **Pay-per-click** (PPC), which was pioneered on search engines, charges advertisers for the number of click-throughs they receive, instead of the number of times an ad is served to a viewer. **Pay-per-action** (PPA) is more controversial, charging advertisers only when a viewer clicks through from an ad *and* proceeds to take a specified action, whether registering or making a purchase. Affiliate arrangements, in which the source site receives a commission on a sale, is one example of a PPA model.

At the same time, ad agencies have defended pay-per-impression models and stagnating **click-through rates** (CTRs) of 0.5 percent (until a sudden uptick in February 2002) with studies showing that online ads are effective for branding, even when users don't click through.

Third, the industry continues to devise new forms of online advertising, such as special banner sizes and ads enhanced with rich media. At least during their period of initial novelty, these new forms attract ad dollars and improve click-through rates.

How Ad Dollars Are Spent

No matter whose study you look at, Internet advertising declined in 2001 compared to projections. Still, roughly $7.3 billion was spent on Internet advertising in the United States for all of 2001, up 60 percent from the $4.6 billion spent in online advertising in 2000. Perhaps in a triumph of hope over experience, most analysts forecast gradually increasing online ad revenues in the future, as seen in Figure 12.1.

Look at the distribution of $46.5 billion in U.S. non-Web advertising expenditures for the first half of 2001 shown in Figure 12.2. The dollars spent online during that time frame ($3.76 billion) would have represented barely 7.5 percent of these selected expenditures. Surveys project that advertisers will continue to switch gradually to online ads from print, radio, and TV, with the share of online revenues growing slowly in coming years.

The corporate kahunas, many of them Internet-related themselves, spent millions in online ads in 2001: eBay, $45 million; General Motors, $43 million; Providian Financial, $29 million; Amazon.com, $27 million. A list of top online advertisers ranked by impressions can be

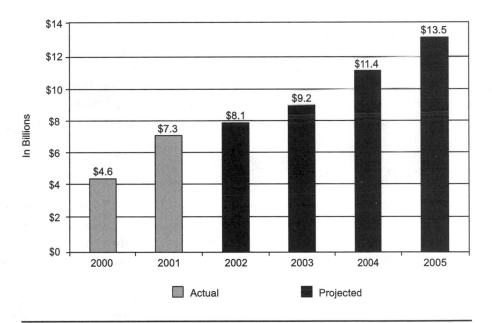

Figure 12.1. Estimated Web advertising revenue.

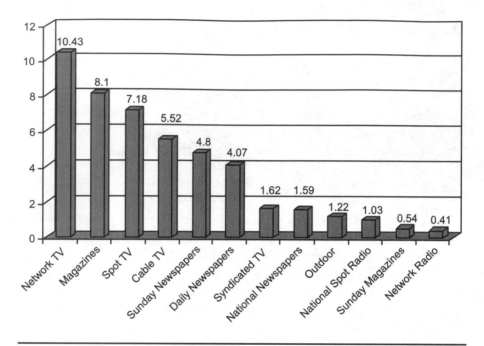

Figure 12.2. Advertising spending by media type for first half of 2001, *http://www.medialifemagazine.com/news2001/sep01/sep03/3_wed/news1wednesday.html.* ©2001 Media Life.

seen in Figure 12.3. For all their complaining, you know one thing: Major advertisers wouldn't pour billions of dollars annually into online ads if they didn't think they were getting something for their money.

How Online Ad Dollars Are Spent

Figure 12.4 suggests how various forms of online promotion compare in terms of cost per customer acquisition (not the same as cost per thousand viewers). As you can see, typical banner (online) advertising is the most-expensive option for acquiring customers, in the sense of a click-through leading to a purchase.

However, recent studies show that online ads are effective in building brand awareness (name recognition), brand image (marketing message), and purchasing intent, even if viewers don't click on them. These studies, which may be somewhat self-serving, contend that a focus on

Rank	Advertiser	Impressions (000s)
1	Amazon.com	12,316,972
2	eBay, Inc.	5,746,873
3	Providian Financial Corporation	5,559,735
4	Columbia House	5,438,788
5	Orbitz	5,040,898
6	ClassMates.com	4,909,343
7	Barnes & Noble, Inc.	4,902,329
8	Cassava Enterprises	4,042,223
9	Bertelsmann AG	3,814,016
10	AOL Time Warner	3,433,876

Figure 12.3.   Top online advertisers by impressions, Q3 2001, *http://www.jmm.com/xp/jmm/press/adIndicators.xml*. Source: Jupiter Media Metrix, Inc.

CTR underestimates the value of online campaigns, especially since the immediate recall level for an ad online is about the same as that for television and since the Web has roughly the same potential reach in audience size.

Online display ads, called **banners,** are basically hyperlinks dressed up with graphics. As you can see in Figure 12.5, banners have dropped to only 36 percent of total online ad revenue. This is down from 80 percent in 1997 and 50 percent in 2000. Sponsorships and classifieds are now responsible for a large percentage of ad formats. **Slotting fees** (premiums paid for preferential ad placement or exclusivity) and key-

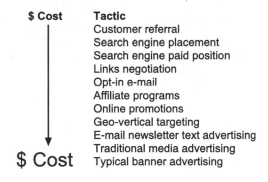

Figure 12.4.   Online promotional tools ranked by increasing cost of customer acquisition, *http://www.markneting.com/mservices.htm*. Courtesy MARKnETING, markneting.com

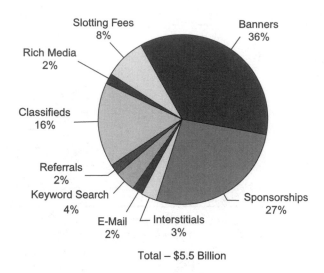

Slotting Fees
8%

Banners
36%

Rich Media
2%

Classifieds
16%

Referrals
2%

Keyword Search
4%

E-Mail
2%

Interstitials
3%

Sponsorships
27%

Total – $5.5 Billion

Figure 12.5. Popular online advertising formats by revenue, January-September 2001, *http://www.iab.net*. Source: IAB Internet Advertising Revenue Report, IAB/PricewaterhouseCoopers.

word searches have risen in popularity, while interstitials (separate screens, now called Pop-Ups and Pop-Unders) and other forms of online advertising have remained stable.

As their novelty wore off, banner ads lost their destination appeal, with click-through rates settling for a time below 0.5 percent, as seen in Figure 12.6. Recent DoubleClick research indicates that average CTR may be on the rebound, shooting up for the first time in two years to 0.83 percent in February 2002. DoubleClick hypothesizes that the increase is due to reduced clutter from fewer ads per page, and the use of larger and more intriguing ad formats. For comparison, a good response in direct mailing is 1.5 to 2 percent. For more information on advertising, check out the following sites:

- Ad Resource has an Ad Rate Guide at *http://adres.internet.com/adrates/article/0,1401,,00.html* and an advertising primer at *http://adres.internet.com/glossary/article/0,1401,,00.html*.

- BizReport provides advertising articles and a directory of service providers at *http://www.ad-guide.com*.

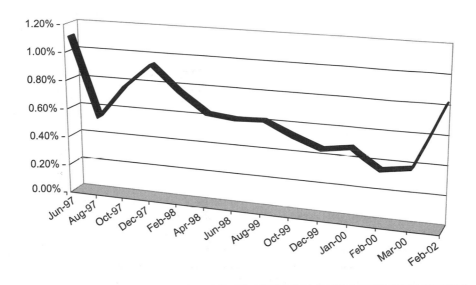

Figure 12.6.   Historical tracking of banner ad click-through rates.

- The Interactive Advertising Bureau provides news, research, events, and member information at *http://www.iab.net.*

- InternetNews carries stories from the Internet Advertising Report at *http://www.internetnews.com/IAR.*

- Yahoo! offers advertising statistics at *http://solutions.yahoo.com/ advertiser_center/research/index.htm.*

- The advertising section on Cyberatlas at *http://cyberatlas.internet. com/markets/advertising.html* offers multiple reports on ad rates and trends.

Web Site Ads

Banners generally take one of the forms shown in Figure 12.7. New standardized large-format ads like Skyscrapers, Large Rectangles, and Large Squares appear to yield better branding value than standard full-

Type	Description	Size in Pixels
Full Banner	Banner	468 × 60
Half Banner	Banner	234 × 60
Vertical Banner	Banner	120 × 240
Micro Bar	Banner	88 × 31
Button 1	Button	120 × 90
Button 2	Button	120 × 60
Square Button	Button	125 × 125
Square Pop Up	Pop Up	250 × 250
Rectangle	Rectangle	250 × 180
Medium Rectangle	Rectangle	300 × 250
Large Rectangle	Rectangle	336 × 280
Vertical Rectangle	Rectangle	240 × 400
Skyscraper	Skyscraper	120 × 600
Wide Skyscraper	Skyscraper	160 × 600

Figure 12.7.   Standard online ad sizes as seen on *http://www.iab.net/ iab_banner_standards/bannersource.html.* Courtesy Interactive Advertising Bureau (IAB).

and half-width banners. They have become quite popular, making up as much as 9 percent of all online ads, as seen in Figure 12.8.

Major advertising sites will have either a contact name and number or an online media kit, which usually includes online advertising rates, site demographics, ad dimensions, and graphics requirements. Most media kits spell out the submission process (ads can be placed on the site's server or called from yours), purchasing method, tracking reports, and special offers. Sizes for online ads have begun to standardize, but exact dimensions may still vary from site to site. Most ads must be supplied in GIF or JPEG format and must be below a certain size in Kb. Check required dimensions, file size, and format before submitting an ad.

Pop-Ups and Pop-Unders

Two recent forms of **interstitials** (full-page ads that appear between page clicks) are more likely than static banners to generate click-throughs, as much as consumers decry them. **Pop-ups** load into a browser's storage area and overlay the Web site. **Pop-unders** appear beneath the chosen site and may remain on display even after viewers have closed the origi-

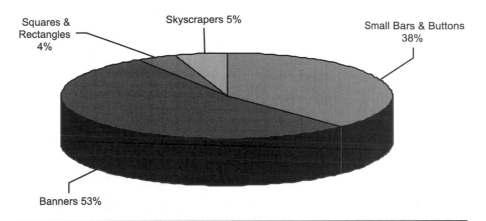

Figure 12.8. Popularity of online ad sizes by paid impressions, January 2002, *http://www.jmm.com/xp/jmm/press/2002/pr_030602.xml.* Source: Jupiter Media Metrix, Inc.

nal site. The advantage of interstitials is that viewers see your page without requiring a click-through.

Adsubtract (*http://www.adsubtract.com*) and Junkbusters Proxy (*http://www.junkbuster.com*) have the Web equivalent of cable zappers, allowing viewers to block your banners. Numerous utilities, like the freeware programs KillAd (*http://wwwin.wplus.net/pp/fsc*) or POW! (*http://www.analogx.com/contents/download/network/pow.htm*), block pop-ups. Although such tools have been around for several years, fortunately only about 1 percent of viewers appear to use them, either from lack of knowledge or because they are perceived as too much hassle for the benefit.

Rich Media Ads

Rich media—ads containing some type of animation, audio, video, or interactive programming—and **javamercials** (ads done with Java script) have up to a 340 percent higher CTR, as well as improved brand perception. At the high end of rich media, companies like Enliven (*http://www.enliven.com*) create **live banners**, which allow viewers to complete a survey, play a game, or print a coupon without clicking through to the advertiser's site.

Besides being more expensive to develop, rich media and live banner ads download slowly on low-speed modems, require broadband connections, clog heavily trafficked sites, or crash servers and browsers. Not all places accept such ads, including AOL. Check first. As long as rich media and live banners show high CTRs, major advertisers will spend the extra dollars on development to target high-end consumers with broadband connections.

Banner Exchanges

Banner exchanges, which work like link exchanges discussed previously, are available at many places: *http://www.exchange-it.com, http:// usa.bpath.com/Services_info/servservice.dbm?IncName=banner_ exchange.dbm,* or *http://www.ceramlinks.com/cerambanners/us.* You can specify categories of sites that would be a good fit for your business, but it's hard to control which ads you display (unless they're offensive). Usually, you must place exchange ads near the top of a page, and some services demand exclusivity.

Most banner exchange sites offer a 2:1 or 3:2 ad ratio. In the first instance, your ad would be placed once for every two ads from others that you display. (The other ad is sold to a paying customer.) Credit ratios have become more competitive, so keep searching. Banner Co-op (*http://www.bannerco-op.com*), for instance, has a 1:1 ratio. Some banner programs are fee-based: *bCentral* (*http://www.bcentral.com*) includes banner advertising with its Traffic Builder bundle for $249 per year.

Sign-up is simple. Register with the exchange, designate desired categories of sites, and provide your ad in the required format. Check each exchange site for details on ad size, credit ratio, placement control for your own ad, and other requirements. For a list of other banner exchanges, go to *http://adres.internet.com/feature/article/0,,8961_559081,00.html* or search Yahoo! for banner exchanges.

Web Site Advertising Rates

Web advertising on major portals, which can cost far more per month than Web design and hosting combined, is best used to reach a mass audience, promote well-known brands, or build name recognition. For a small business, targeted niche marketing may have a much more positive impact on your bottom line. You may be surprised to learn that you can advertise on niche sites without driving your company into bankruptcy.

As you may recall from Chapter 1, advertisers use **CPM** to compare the cost per thousand possible viewers or listeners. The table in Figure 1.13 compared CPMs for various media. Generally, the higher the CPM, the smaller but more targeted the audience. Many sites charge higher CPMs for premium page position (upper corners, **above the fold**—on the first half of the page so ads are visible before scrolling down) or offer different targeting options (e.g., appearance only when certain keywords are selected on a search engine). Others set a minimum on the number of impressions you must buy. Just to confuse things more, different ads may rotate in the same position on different content pages or rotate after a fixed time on a single page. Rates will vary by the number of ads sharing the rotation.

Although a CPM rate may seem reasonable, the absolute cost on a major site is boggling. Given the online ad rates seen in Figure 12.9, it's clear that sites such as portals, search engines, news organizations, and financial services are now a promotional playground primarily for deep-pocket corporations. A portal site with 60 million visitors a week could easily guarantee 2 million impressions per month, costing over $44,000! For more information, go to *http://adres.internet.com/adrates/article/0,1401,,00.html.*

TIPS FOR TIRED SITES

Ready to experiment with online ads to stimulate new traffic? If you decide to use paid advertising, set a dollar limit first, then decide how to distribute the funds. Keep your advertising expenses in line with the amount you spend on site development. Many advertisers report negotiating significant reductions from published rate cards. It's worth a try. Or look for a marketing support service that buys ad space in bulk on portals to resell at a rate affordable to small businesses. Always test a handful of ad locations to see which ones work best before you lock up your budget in long-term contracts. Ask for a 30-day trial. Look around for options or negotiate your own ad with a site you'd really like to be on. It may be cheaper to advertise on several smaller sites than on one premium site. Ten sites with 100,000 visitors each may cost less than a single site with one million visitors, yet can yield the same total exposure with an audience better targeted to your needs.

National Newspaper Site		E-Mail Newsletters*		Search Engine/Portal	
Impressions	Rate	Impressions	One Month	Run of Site	One Month
500,000	$40/CPM	1,000,000+	$14/CPM	1–249,000	$29/CPM
860,000	$35/CPM	750k–999k	$18/CPM	250–499k	$28/CPM
2,000,000	$30/CPM	500k–749k	$22/CPM	500–999k	$27/CPM
4,000,000	$25/CPM	250k–499k	$26/CPM	1.0–1.9 mil	$24/CPM
8,500,000	$20/CPM	249k or less	$30/CPM	2–2.9 mil	$22/CPM
				3–4.9 mil	$20/CPM
				5 mil+	$18/CPM

* Rates for ads across all newsletters

Ad Network		Portal-Financial Section		Technology Site	
Type of Buy	CPM	Type of Buy	CPM	Monthly Impressions	One Month
Single Site	$40+	Run of Property	$20.50-$31	100k–250k	$70/CPM
Content Channel	$20-$39	1-3 Demo Targets	$27-$48	250k–499k	$61/CPM
Run of Network	$10-$19	3 Month Frequency Discount	2%	500k–999k	$58/CPM
		6 Month Frequency Discount	5%	1 mil +	$56/CPM

Figure 12.9. Sample online advertising rates, *http://adres.internet.com/ adrates/article/0,1401,,00.html.* ©2002 INT Media Group. Inc. All rights reserved.

With the downturn in online advertising, the median online CPM dropped from $33.75 in 1999 to $25.00 in 2001. The decline is also partially due to an increased supply in ad space as more sites seek advertisers.

Even if your business exists only in cyberspace, don't spend all your advertising dollars on the Web. Although the Internet has reduced ad expenditures on other media, a July 2000 survey (seen in Figure 12.10) showed that time online still accounts for less than 20 percent of users' weekly media consumption.

Once you've determined which places work, stay there, whether online or offline. An advertising message repeated multiple times in one place is better than an ad that appears once in many places. You can change creative approach or content, but viewers get used to seeing your name in a particular location.

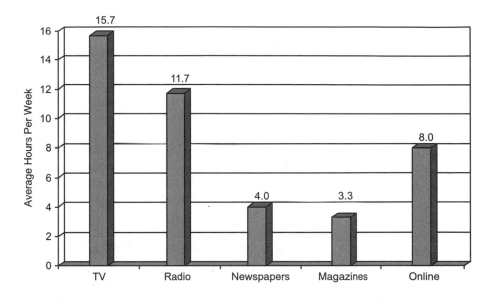

Figure 12.10. Media consumed by online users in hours per week. Source: Jupiter Consumer Suvey (7/00); n=2312. Jupiter Media Metrix, Inc.

When making ad placement decisions, consider audience size, demographics and CPM, as well as absolute cost. This is tough, because Web advertising can be priced by impressions (number of pageviews) or click-throughs (executed links to the advertiser's site). The following factors affect ad rates:

- Past history for the number of unique visitors to the site, page views for the page on which the ad appears, and/or number of click-throughs.

- Ad size, generally given in pixels.

- Placement on the screen.

- Frequency with which the ad runs. Most sites rotate ads in each screen location based on the relative number of impressions purchased. Ads are usually refreshed each time a page is requested, but some are now sold by fixed length of visible time. Confirm the length of time and the frequency with which your ad will appear.

- Specified time of appearance. You may want ads, such as those advertising a specific sitecast, to appear at a certain time or on a certain day. Late-night placement might be available at a discount.

- The number of impressions, exposures, or click-throughs purchased.

- How many other advertisers share the same space.

- Demographics—the more targeted the audience, the higher the CPM.

In the end, sites charge what the market will bear. The ultimate proof of market pricing is a pay-per-click advertising site like the Adwords Select program at Google (*http://adwords.google.com/select/overview.html*). For assistance with advertising for a major site, you may want to try a large online ad agency like Beyond Interactive (*http://www.gobeyond.com*) or DoubleClick *http://www.doubleclick.com*). These companies usually deal only with sites pulling 500,000 to 1 million viewers per month. Most ad agencies take a 10–15 percent commission on ad buys or sales. Alternately, try a site like *http://www.overture.com/d/advertisers/p/bjump/?o= U2895&b=15*), which charges only on click-throughs.

Improving Online Ad Effectiveness

Increasingly, major advertisers try to match ad presentation to behavioral patterns online, seeking to hawk products and services specific to

---

TIPS FOR TIRED SITES

There's one other way to cut your ad costs. If you carry brand items, see whether the manufacturers will let you apply co-op marketing dollars (ad costs shared between the manufacturer and retailer) to online advertising. Manufacturers may require that their logos appear in your ad. You might also get them to place a link from their site to yours and/or pay you to place a link from your site to theirs.

the interests of an individual Web surfer. To maximize the return on your investment in advertising, you should do the same. Research advertising rates, record the locations of your competitors' ads, and look at good ads to decode what works.

Create tempting banners that give viewers a reason to click through to your site. Provide an incentive in your ad: a call to action, a teaser, a free offer. Since banner ads also lose their punch after seven to ten views by the same user, you may need to create multiple banners that are swapped on a regular basis.

The five top banner ads for a one-week period, seen in Figure 12.11, represent a cross section of intriguing ads (some with animation) that encourage click-throughs or brand memory. Nielsen NetRatings shows the top 10 weekly banners at *http://pm.netratings.com/nnpm/owa/ NRpublicreports.topbannerweekly*. It also displays the top 10 banner ads for the prior month at *http://pm.netratings.com/nnpm/owa/NR publicreports.topbannermonthly*. Or look at the ad gallery on Yahoo! at *http://solutions.yahoo.com/adspecs/gallery.html* for examples of good campaigns. If you're still intimidated or need a less-expensive way to design a campaign, consider Admine (*http://www.admine.com*), an ad syndication site that lets you license ads in various media that were developed by ad agencies but either were never used or were used only briefly in a specific region. You view ads in an online showroom, license rights for your own market for a particular time period, and have Admine customize them.

Coordinating with an Offline Ad Campaign

Besides simply including your URL in an ad, you can create ads in any medium specifically to increase awareness of your Web address. Depending on the nature of your business, you may find the best response

RULE OF THUMB

The success of an ad is based 40 percent on the audience it reaches, 40 percent on the nature of the offer it makes, and 20 percent on the quality of the creative design and copy of the ad.

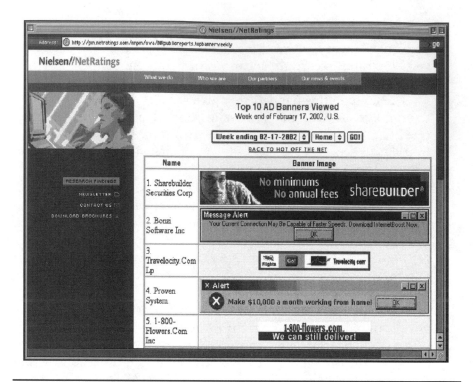

Figure 12.11. Top banner ads, *http://pm.netratings.com/nnpm/owa/ NRpublicreports.topbannerweekly*. Source: Nielsen//NetRatings. Reproduced with permission. © NetRatings, Inc. 2002. All rights reserved.

from TV, radio, billboards, or print. An ad created to drive traffic needs to be constructed to provide a specific benefit or provoke interest. Dell promotes a separate Web page (*http://www.dell.com/tv*), seen earlier in Figure 10.4, in its television ads.

Other companies like Gazoontite (*http://www.gazoontite.com*), which sells household products for allergy and asthma sufferers, have found that infomercials are an effective and relatively inexpensive tool for driving traffic. Sometimes called "long-form ads" or "direct-response TV," half-hour infomercials are lead generators; they cut the cost of acquiring new customers.

When you build an offline campaign, make sure that the design, tone, and content of ads in other media are consistent with online ads and with the design and tone of your Web site. This synergy promotes recognition, reinforces the benefits of repetition in different media, and reduces potential confusion in users' minds.

Online Sponsorships

Sponsorships take many forms. You can sponsor an e-zine, a newsletter, an on-line mailing, a discussion group, a content site, or a not-for-profit organization. Sponsorships of all types now account for about 27 percent of Web advertising purchases, as seen in Figure 12.5.

Newsletter, Discussion Group, and E-mail Sponsorships

Newsletters, discussions groups, and e-mail offer highly targeted audiences, self-qualified prospects, and higher click-through rates. Prices for sponsorship run from $25 or $50 per issue to thousands of dollars based on the size of the mailing list or number of participants in a discussion group. Find the right vehicle and then negotiate with the owner of the newsletter or e-mail list to place your ad as a sponsor. Most of these are 50-to-75-word, text-only ads with a link to your site, but some also involve a logo ad on the owner's Web site as well. Figure 12.12 shows sponsorship information for the O-A newsletter.

Publishers of HTML newsletters will be able to tell you the number of people who opened the newsletter and the number of click-throughs. Otherwise you will know only the number of recipients. If you use a separate link for each newsletter (each one can redirect to your home page), you'll be able to tell from your site statistics which sources are most productive.

Content Site Sponsorships

Content sponsorship is similar to advertising, but generally means a lower price tag, a smaller banner ad, and lower placement on a page. Softer by nature than a banner ad, sponsorships are more comparable to corporate ads on TV than to 30-second spots on soap operas. Be sure

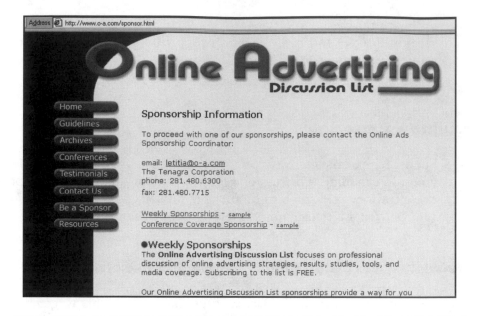

Figure 12.12. Sponsorship arrangement for the O-A newsletter, *http://www. o-a.com/sponsor.html.* Copyright 2001 The Tenagra Corporation, *http://www. tenagra.com.*

the content sites you sponsor relate to your field of business and that they draw your target audience. An exclusive version of sponsorship, sometimes called **co-branding,** is a partnership with a content site, with the link to your site provided as a source of additional data. Like ad rates, sponsorship rates are usually determined by a Web site's circulation and the number of impressions purchased.

TIPS FOR TIRED SITES

If you are creative with your selection of sites, you may find ways to locate your target market at a low cost or perhaps establish a barter arrangement. For instance, a CD store in a college town might sponsor student sites around campus to reach its target market. Students often put up highly creative sites, heavy in multimedia or pop culture. It's certainly easier to sponsor students' music sites or e-zines than to create your own. Popular student-created sites might trade a sponsor ad in exchange for space on your server. (Student pages with heavy hit rates are often removed from university servers because they slow down the system.)

Charity Sponsorships

To bolster your reputation as a good corporate citizen and your affinity with your customers, sponsor a not-for-profit site that's related to your business. For instance, a nursery specializing in native plants could sponsor some of the costs associated with a Web site for the local chapter of Tree People. A not-for-profit might agree to take a donation for every hit or registrant you receive from their site, instead of asking you to pay up front.

Figure 12.13 shows the "Shop & Give" program at GreaterGood.com (*http://www.greatergood.com*) that allows not-for-profits to benefit from dozens of shopping affiliate arrangements. GreaterGood splits the royalties it receives from merchants with its member not-for-profit organizations. You might affiliate with a specific charity or other sites similar to GreaterGood such as:

- *http://www.givingboard.com*

- *http://www.iGive.com*

Figure 12.13. An interesting way to sponsor not-for-profits, *http://www. greatergood.com/cgi-bin/WebObjects/GreaterGood*. Courtesy GreaterGood.com.

- *http://www.shopforchange.com*

- *http://www.thehungersite.com*

Search Engine Advertising

The latest twist in advertising is "text sponsorship," the Web equivalent of buying a vowel on "Wheel of Fortune." Instead of a vowel, however, you "sponsor" a keyword. Most major search engines, like Google and Yahoo!, now accept text-only ads "tuned" to keywords; they appear only when viewers enter a particular search term. Unlike pay-for-position arrangements, which affect the actual ranking of sites, AdWords (displayed in the right column) or premium sponsorships (displayed above the results) are independent of the listings.

AdWords

These ads provide extra visibility for your site when you want to reach a highly targeted audience. And they allow you to "jump over" competing sites when your search engine rankings would place you below the first page. If you are already within the first three listings on a particular keyword, these ads are only frosting on the cake. Your search engine ranking is more valuable, and you probably don't need the ad as well. Figure 12.14 shows an AdWord sponsored link in the right-hand column on *Google.com*.

AdWords, particularly on Google, are set up as a self-service, easy-to-use, low-cost alternative to display advertising. A small, boxed classified ad with a link, AdWords are pay-per-impression with a CPM of $8 to $15 based on position. This approach is excellent for sites aimed at small, tightly targeted niche markets. If your target audiences use Google or Yahoo! as their primary search engine, you should definitely consider these options.

Google lets you pre-test keywords to estimate your costs and allows you to modify all the terms of your campaign, from starting and ending dates to the dollar limit on spending. Google requires no minimum deposit and charges fees to your credit card. Google's new AdWords Se-

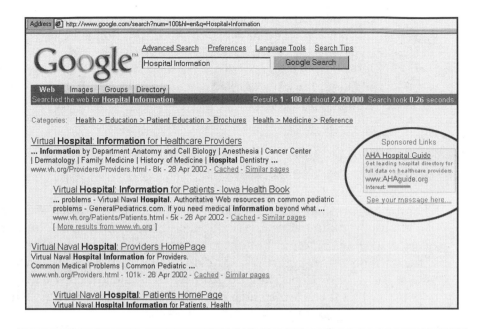

Figure 12.14. Sample Google AdWords advertisement, *http://www.google.com/ search?num=100&hl=en&q=Hospital+Information.* Courtesy Google, Inc. Courtesy Health Forum.

lect™ program combines the features of AdWords with pay-per-click pricing. Try their demo at *http://www.google.com/ads* to see how these work. Yahoo! offers something similar at competitive prices, but it's not as easy to use.

Premium Keyword Sponsorships

Premium sponsorships on Google or Yahoo! are also linkable, text-only ads. Like AdWords, premium sponsorships are text-based ads tuned to keywords, with a limit of two displayed per word. Unlike AdWords, premium sponsorships have a minimum price of several thousand dollars per month and a minimum contract length. The price is not tied to either impressions or clicks. Sponsorships are still less costly than a regular display ad on these portals because the number of viewers is limited.

It is also possible to purchase a text-based ad that appears on the search results page across a network of 50 destination sites and portals whenever a viewer enters a particular search term. Pioneered by askJeeves (*http://www.static.wc.ask.com/docs/advertise/advertising.html*), the Direct Hit and Direct Linx Networks are auction-based with bids opening at $5 per 1,000 impressions.

Classified Ads on the Web

Classified ads, which appear in a section organized by subject, are available on all the online services, on USEnet, and on many individual sites. As a growing percentage of online advertising, classifieds, like the AOL ClassifiedPlus ad in Figure 12.15, can be one of the best advertising buys in the world. Depending on your target audience, classifieds may be a better buy than display ads; classified viewers preselect by search-

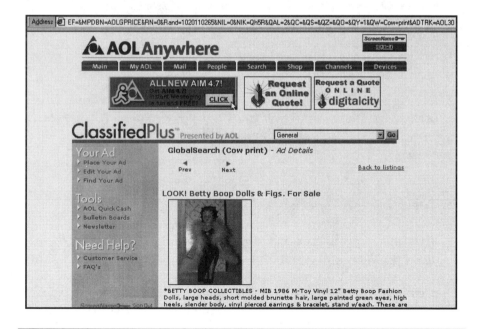

Figure 12.15. AOL classified ad, *http://classifiedplus.aol.com*. AOL screenshot ©2002 America Online, Inc. Used with permission.

ing specifically for the category that interests them. Most people who read classifieds are ready to buy: They are the ultimate in prequalified customers. Classifieds are relatively inexpensive—often free or just a few dollars per week to reach a potential audience of millions.

For example, AOL's classifieds reach 44 million viewers on five sites. AOL's charges, which are category-based, range from free for AOL and CompuServe members to $8 per month for a featured ad with photo and unlimited text. By comparison, print classifieds may run from $1 per day for a four-line ad in a paper with a circulation of under 100,000 to $244 per day for a similar ad in a paper with a circulation of several million, like the Monday-through-Thursday edition of *USA Today*. Many newspapers and magazines include a free online classified, or at least a free link, when you purchase a print classified or display ad. Others, like the *Los Angeles Times*, offer an online classified at a reduced rate when you buy a print run. The *LA Times* also offers online-only classifieds for $35 per week. Some 700 newspapers belong to a service called Abracat (*http://www.abracat.com/abracat/about/index.jsp*) which shares online classifieds, so you can obtain national coverage from one ad.

USEnet and Classified Sites

If your budget is really tight, consider USEnet classifieds, which are free to both buyer and seller. USEnet classifieds are found mainly in the *.forsale* newsgroup, but some others accept them. (Check, for example, *.wanted*, *.jobs*, or *.marketplace*.) Starting with the *.forsale* newsgroups, ask members for their help in locating others that accept classifieds.

TIPS FOR TIRED SITES

Are you getting traffic from your classifieds? Writing a good classified ad is an art. You'll need a good headline and concise body copy. Study the ads that appear online, check out the tips for writing an ad at AOL Classifieds, get a book from the library, or run a comparison ad in a paper. Remember to track your ads so you know which ones work best. Do this by coding e-mail response addresses, or even by creating a separate Web entry page for each ad. You'll know within several days if your classified ad is successful. Change the language if it doesn't draw.

You can localize your ads by going to regional newsgroups. For example, if you want to sell your old family car in Chicago, the *chi.forsale* newsgroup would be the best place for you. Join the group and type an article that becomes your ad. As always, post only items for sale that are relevant to the subject of a newsgroup. Use a newsgroup search program like the one at *http://www.topica.com/news* or *http://tile.net/news* to locate good "for sale" sites.

Web classified sites, such as Classifieds 2000 at *http://www. infospace.com/info.cls2k,* have more features than USEnet. Most have the capacity for photos and parameter searches. Classifieds 2000 is free at the moment. TraderOnline (*http://www.traderonline.com/ traderpaa.html*) offers a basic text ad for free, but more extensive classifieds range from $20 to $51 for four weeks, depending on the item you're selling and the features you want in the ad.

Selling Advertising on Your Site

What if you want to reverse the advertising process? You're not alone. Unfortunately, of approximately 3,300 sites in the United States that sell ads, the top 10 raked in 70 percent of all online ad revenue in the first half of 2001, according to the Interactive Advertising Bureau. (The top 25 earned 88 percent; the top 50 hauled in 96 percent.) A list of the top ten Web sites hosting ads can be seen in Figure 12.16. For most sites, however, advertising is only a modest source of revenue. If you're counting on major income, your site must generate a great deal of traffic or deliver content reliably to a highly prized, selected demographic.

In preparation for selling ads, designate locations and sizes for ads in such a way that you can meet advertisers' demands for space above the fold without disturbing the look of your site. Confirm the amount of traffic your site currently draws. Make sure you can obtain meaningful statistics from your host. If its statistical package doesn't count unique users and requests for a specific file, supplement your host's statistics with HitBox, WebTrends, or some of the other tools described in Chapter 8. Demographic information from user registration will help you recruit advertisers.

You will also need to provide feedback to your advertisers. For a quick solution, ask your Webmaster to add some server-side scripting

Rank	Site	Impressions (000s)
1	MSN	27,677,368
2	Yahoo!	26,467,701
3	iWon	11,776,485
4	Excite	8,182,850
5	AOL.com	7,302,325
6	Netscape	6,669,230
7	eBay	5,645,619
8	Juno	3,628,618
9	About.com	2,075,530
10	The New York Times	2,071,839

Figure 12.16. Top 10 Web sites hosting ads, Q3 2001, *http://www.jmm.com/xp/jmm/press/adIndicators.xml.* Source: Jupiter Media Metrix, Inc.

that redirects to the client's URL to track click-throughs from your site to the clients'. (A common Perl script for this, called *redir.pt,* can be downloaded free at many sites.) A free tracking program called Admentor 2.21 (*http://www.aspcode.net/aspcode/download.php*) also serves and rotates ads. For more program options, check *http://www.ad-tracking.com* or *http://dmoz.org/Business/Marketing/Internet_Marketing/Traffic_Measurement.* Iron out any technical details with your Webmaster and host before you start selling ads.

To become a major ad-supported site, you may need to install such third-party auditing software to confirm viewership for advertisers, or contract with an independent company like I/PRO (*http://www.engage.com/ipro*) to supply such statistics as session length, multimedia access, ad impressions, and click-throughs. Generally, only the most heavily trafficked sites on the Web can afford expensive services like these.

Estimating charges for advertising on a small site is a bit tricky. Advertising prices are based on a combination of impressions from the desired audience and the frequency with which ads run. Start with a guesstimated CPM of $10 per month and adjust within a $5–$70 range based on your traffic and the specificity of your demographics. If you're essentially a small local site, price yourself like one of the coupon advertisers, such as *http://www.valpak.com/index.jsp.*

You can research ad pricing information by e-mailing a request to similar, but noncompeting, sites that accept ads. Or survey potential advertisers to see what they pay to advertise on other sites and what they pay (CPM) for other media. Set up a trial rate card (media kit) with the types, sizes, and prices of ads you are willing to sell. Unless you expect to be a truly major advertising link, don't worry about ad rotation. (Major ad servers use special software to rotate ads, track impressions, and change creative content for each advertiser on a regular basis.)

Assume that you will need to discount rates for early advertisers and for those who sign up for longer terms. Once you have an experience base and an established viewer rate, selling online advertising will be more straightforward.

If the process of finding buyers for your ad space seems too daunting, list your site for free on WebConnect's W.I.S.E. database of sites that accept advertising (*http://www.webconnect.com,* and click on W.I.S.E.). WebConnect is one of the few "open network" agencies that will sell space on sites not owned by its clients. An online media strategy and placement firm, WebConnect will place ads on sites with relatively light traffic as long as the sites deliver their clients' target audience.

Other companies, like Burst Media (*http://www.burstmedia.com*), promise to sell your ad space on specialty content sites. Revenue Avenue (*http://www.bcentral.com/products/ra/default.asp*), one of bCentral's programs, matches sites with pay-for-performance advertisers through Commission Junction. To be sure these companies execute this well, check with other clients before signing a long-term exclusive agreement.

Tracking Advertising Success

Since advertising and promoting your site may be expensive in both time and money, you want to know whether your expenditures brought results. If you advertise on other Web sites, they should be able to give you CTRs. If they provide only the number of impressions, use the referrer URLs in your statistics (see Chapter 8) to determine which online ads have the greatest pull. If you divide the number of visitors you received from a specific ad by the number of impressions, you will get the CTR.

At the very least, ask for a copy of the site's statistics to tease out the visitor profile. Try to avoid sites that offer only ad or page hit rates, since that rate inflates the number of impressions. The number of unique visitors is apt to be lower than the number of impressions implies, since visitors may repeatedly visit the same site and often ask for more than one page of information. Remember to delete hits from spiders or robots trolling the Web: They don't have eyeballs!

If the site owner won't provide statistics, subscribe to a service such as ROIbot Ad Tracker (*http://www.roibot.com/features_at.htm*), which will track the effectiveness of your campaigns on multiple sites for only $17 per month. ROIbot also has tools to track from click-through to order form submission. A somewhat more sophisticated analysis program that tracks from click-through to sale is available from PromotionStat (*http://www.promotionstat.com/whati_sinfo.shtml*) for $50–$100 per month, plus an initial set-up fee.

With statistical information, you can quickly optimize your advertising schedule for preferred sites, placement, graphics, wording, and special offers. Track results to see whether traffic builds and then drops off, whether it increases steadily, or whether there is no difference. If you manage an extensive advertising campaign with multiple ads on multiple sites, you might want to purchase one of the very expensive software packages that tracks ad performance in real time. Accrue Software (*http://www.accrue.com*) and Straight Up! (*http://www.valueclick.com/promo/adin.htm*) track ads from impression to sale, so you can determine the cost of sale or cost of inquiry for each ad.

The variety of methods available for Web promotion may seem overwhelming, but don't be daunted. As with offline marketing, it's more important to do something consistently than to try to do everything. Once you find a marketing method that works for you, stay with it! Now that we've concluded the seven steps to Internet success, let's see in the next chapter how ten model sites have applied these principles.

13

Model Web Sites

Repeat this mantra: "Before adding a new feature or page to my site, I will see what other sites do." Each model site illustrates a different aspect of marketing on the Internet. View these sites online to see how their design matches their business concept. Flow through their Web pages as if you were a customer. Look at them from the standpoint of your own product or service. How could you adapt their ideas? Can you borrow their marketing wisdom? When you check these sites, the pages may have changed from the ones shown here. See if you can infer why changes were made.

Most business people are generous with advice and experience. If a noncompeting site uses a technique that interests you, e-mail the owner to ask how well it works. You'll be surprised at the useful information you'll receive and the mistakes you can avoid as a result. You might want to bring the sites in this chapter when you meet with your developer. For more examples of model sites, visit the annual Webby Awards (*http://www.webbyawards.com*) or the Inc. Magazine Web Awards (*http://www.inc.com/home*). Now let's look at sites that:

- Attract customers through content and service

- Exemplify good marketing techniques

- Maintain a strong customer focus

- Marry a traditional service business with cyberspace.

Tempting Customers Beyond the Home Page

This is basic. You can't sell something to a prospect who leaves your site within 20 seconds. As you've learned, you need to create a desirable destination, one that immediately offers potential customers access to the information, product, or service they want.

Virtual Voyages Makes the Most of the Web: All-Outdoors Whitewater Rafting at *http://www.aorafting.com*

All-Outdoors Rafting is a 40-year old company with $2 million in revenues. Located in Walnut Creek, California, it draws on a customer base in Silicon Valley and San Francisco that is wired for the Web. AO Rafting developed its site with specific goals in mind: to increase revenues, to reduce the complexity of its marketing program, and to improve customer service.

They've come out a winner on all three. Revenues from the site alone rose from $55,000 in 1997 to $760,000 in 2000. At this point, 84 percent of the company's business derives from the Web. In the mid-1990s, AO Rafting was spending $150,000 per year on marketing to generate $1 million in total revenue. The marketing program was complex and time-consuming to manage, with a print catalog, brochures, display ads, yellow pages, direct-mail campaigns, and group discounts. Although AO Rafting still spends $150,000 on marketing, they generate $2 million a year and 90 percent of their marketing expenses are Web-related. They still use print to support the Web effort, as well as search engines, strategic inbound links, and word-of-mouth.

The site offers photos glorious enough to feel the spray, clean design, easy navigation, and the virtual tours shown in Figure 13.1. It also provides terrific customer support, thus reducing the cost of a call center. Visitors can plan trips, book reservations on one of 12 California river tours, check river conditions, price gear, learn about discounts (offered to fill up spaces on rafting trips and run more trips), and collect

Figure 13.1. Virtual Voyages makes the most of the Web, *http://www.aorafting. com/ipix/ka-cyanotic.htm.* ©2001 All-Outdoors Whitewater Rafting. Courtesy Search Engine Marketing.com Consulting Services: Jamie@search enginemarketing.com.

Company: All-Outdoors Whitewater Rafting

Year Founded: Non-Profit 1965/For Profit 1972

Web Site First Established: 1996

Gross Annual Revenues: $1-2 Million

Annual Revenues from Web Site: $600,000-$900,000 for reservations generated from site traffic

Percentage of Revenues from Sales on Web: 60-70%

Site Start-Up Cost: $7,500; peaked at $80,000 in 1998.

Site Maintenance Cost (monthly): $1,000 for in-house site maintenance; online advertising, newsletter, and database maintenance extra.

Most Successful Feature of Site: Depth of content.

Lessons Learned: Users trust a favorite search engine and the opinions of friends.

Marketing Techniques Used: Search engines, word-of-mouth.

Advice about Marketing on the Web: First impressions are critical. Be the "best" compared to your competition.

Jamie Low, Consultant

free (there's that word again) stuff, from screensavers to e-mail post-cards. Are you ready for adventure?

Turning Offline Needs into Online Opportunity: The Connoisseur.cc Ltd. at *http://www.low-carb.com*

There's no community like the community of people trying to lose weight. Low-Carb.com (seen in Figure 13.2) was started in 1997 by two sisters. They opened their Web site in 1998, their first café in South Carolina in 1999, and another in 2001. Both the cafés and the Web site sell a line of low-carb products and offer support to dieters. Low-Carb.com has a clear mission: to provide the best shopping experience on the Internet.

The site sells more than 400 specialty items, from beverages to vitamins, cookbooks to beauty aids. Besides selling low-carb products, the site affiliated with Johns Hopkins Hospital to distribute special ketogenic foods for children with severe childhood epilepsy.

With two message boards (including the "Low-Carb Confessional") and an "Ask the Expert" page, the site offers dieters the proverbial online community, an excellent way to draw repeat visitors. In another incentive for repeat visits, some 4,700 mailing list subscribers receive a code for biweekly specials and coupons.

In a unique move, The Connoisseur opened a constellation of Yahoo! satellite shops—Southern Connoisseur, The Chocolate Box, The Low-Carb Bakery, 1st Women's Health—to market existing inventory to new customers with a slightly different spin. This move has proved financially rewarding: It spreads fixed expenses over new Web sites, turns over inventory faster, and increases overall company sales. All this, and the foods sound yummy!

Log On, Dine Out: NMRestaurants.com at *http://www.nmrestaurants.com*

Just when you think there's nothing new under the sun, up comes an entrepreneur with a new business model. On the surface, NMRestaurants.com, shown in Figure 13.3, looks like an online interactive restaurant guide with 1,700 searchable listings. But that's just the start. The company acts like a restaurant mall and co-op advertising venture, providing a Web presence to more than 40 restaurants. The restaurants pay in a combination of

Figure 13.2. Turning offline needs into online opportunity, *http://www.low-carb.com.* Courtesy The Connoisseur.cc, Ltd.

Company: The Connoisseur.cc Ltd.

Year Founded: 1997

Web Site First Established: 1998

Gross Annual Revenues: $731,000-$1.34 million

Annual Revenues from Web Site: $600,000-$1.1 million

Percentage of Revenues from Sales on Web: 82%

Site Start-Up Cost: $2,000

Site Maintenance Cost (monthly): $1,250

Most Successful Feature of Site: Extensive product line paired with customer education and support.

Lessons Learned: You need to anticipate market and economic trends to maintain optimum inventory levels and not be caught off-guard holding excessive, expiring, or unwanted merchandise.

Marketing Techniques Used: Targeted satellite Web sites; pay-per-performance keyword placement; sponsoring recipe exchange and support mailing lists, bulletin boards, newsletters, and Web sites; opt-in newsletter (most effective).

Advice about Marketing on the Web: Determine a niche market, a customer base whose needs are not being met. Exceed their expectations in your product offerings and customer service.

Elaine Payne, Owner

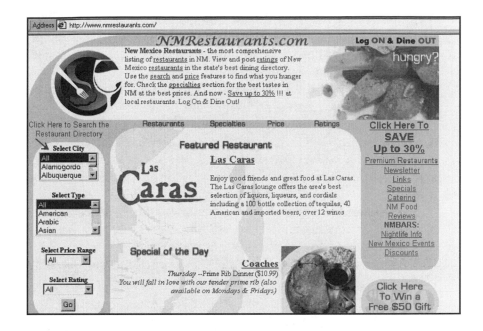

Figure 13.3. Log on, dine out, *http://www.nmrestaurants.com*. Courtesy NMrestaurants.com.

Company: NMRestaurants.com

Year Founded: 2000

Web Site First Established: 2000

Gross Annual Revenues: NA

Annual Revenues from Web Site: NA

Percentage of Revenues from Sales on Web: 35%

Site Start-Up Cost: NA

Site Maintenance Cost (monthly): NA

Most Successful Feature of Site: Selling gift certificates online at a 30% discount.

Lessons Learned: Internet must be used with other forms of traditional media to reach its full potential.

Marketing Techniques Used: Television and print advertising search engine referrals.

Advice about Marketing on the Web: Determine your audience and listen to their needs. Integrate your marketing efforts through online and traditional media. Study site statistics regularly to determine effectiveness of marketing tactics.

Brett Hills, President

cash and credits, which are then sold as discounted gift certificates (30 percent off) online. This not only provides a second income stream to the company, it also allows the restaurants to track the value in actual customers who present the gift certificate.

The site advertises heavily on TV, radio, and in print, sponsors local events, and conducts an active online marketing campaign through links and search engines. President Brett Hills is a fanatic about tracking statistical results to evaluate marketing tactics. A leader in its field, NMRestaurants advertises on wireless handheld devices with digital images of daily specials, to catch impulse diners, business visitors, and tourists.

Customers have an incentive to log on for daily specials and a chance to win a gift certificate. Special offers are presented by e-mail to subscribers. Hills followed the B-school approach: business plan, focus groups, market research, financial projections, measurable objectives. NMRestaurants is proof that approach works.

Marketing Magic

Marketing specialists have created Web equivalents for almost every form of promotion and customer interaction, not just advertising. These range from giveaways to product tie-ins, from catalog displays to product demos. Let's take a look at some companies that have applied these marketing techniques to increase their cybersales.

Free Is a Four-Letter Word: MagicTricks.com at *http://www.magictricks.com*

Many four-letter words are used in marketing, but by far the most common one is "free." For MagicTricks.com in Figure 13.4, "Free" is as effective as "Open Sesame!" With its free one-page Magic Club Web sites, free newsletter, free directory of magicians, free magic library, free supply directory, free classifieds, and an online magic museum, you could disappear forever on this site like a rabbit in a hat. This site is exceptional for value-added content that keeps visitors on the site, while continually tempting them with items to purchase.

Figure 13.4.   "Free" is a four-letter word, *http://www.magictricks.com*.
©2002 Magic Tricks, Inc.

Company: MagicTricks.com

Year Founded: 1971

Web Site First Established: 1996

Gross Annual Revenues: NA

Annual Revenues from Web Site: NA

Percentage of Revenues from Sales on Web: 100%

Site Start-Up Cost: $0; one of the owners does all site maintenance and promotion.

Site Maintenance Cost (monthly): $200 for hosting, licensing, and shopping cart maintenance; labor not included.

Most Successful Feature of Site: The Magic Directory.

Lessons Learned: Focus efforts on specific products for specific customers.

Marketing Techniques Used: Word-of-mouth, primarily, as well as links, constant site updates, a few pay-per-click programs. Also free search engine submissions, directory listings on other sites, and press releases.

Advice about Marketing on the Web: Personalize, communicate, and give great customer service.

Peter & Jackie Monticup, Owners

Now one of the largest magic suppliers in the world and the largest one online, MagicTricks.com began as a bricks-and-mortar store in 1971. After moving the physical location of the store several times, magician Peter Monticup started the Web site in 1996. By 2000, it became clear that cyberspace was a better deal than real space and offered an endless number of potential customers; the retail storefront closed. A mom-and-pop business—Jackie Monticup, a former marketing professor and self-taught programmer, does all the site maintenance and promotion—MagicTricks.com has been magic for its owners.

Site navigation is simple. In spite of making it easy to buy with one-click, the site is loaded with value. As Monticup points out, "If a Web site has interesting, relevant, and free content, the site will be bookmarked and considered as authoritative ... and therefore automatically rated as a better place to purchase."

A Passionate Business: The World of the Walking Stick at *http://www.walkingstickworld.com*

Good writers write what they know; good business owners sell what they know. In this case, Liela Nelson created a business from her walking stick collection, which she started in 1988 and which was the topic of her NYU Master's thesis in decorative arts in 1994. Displaying a collection of 150 to 200 one-of-a-kind, antique canes, WalkingStickWorld.com (seen in Figure 13.5) caters to an elite audience devoted to a hot collectible: custom-crafted walking sticks from around the world ranging in price from hundreds to thousands of dollars. The inventory changes constantly as pieces are added and sold.

While Nelson indulges her passion with travels to Europe and the Far East for research and product acquisition, her Web site has made her one of three major American dealers in walking sticks. Her decorative, ethnic, folk art, and system (or gadget) canes sell internationally on a straightforward site. Her site includes a well-commented catalog, but eschews online purchasing for 800-number and e-mail requests.

Like several of the other sites in this section, Nelson takes advantage of eBay to auction items and to draw new customers to her Web site. In addition, she uses the cachet of a "private" mailing list for early announcements of new items and also uses Microsoft's LinkExchange program through bCentral.

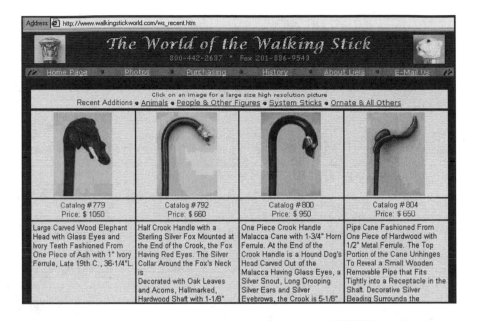

Figure 13.5.   A passionate business, *http://www.walkingstickworld.com/ ws recent.htm*. Courtesy KW Productions, Clifton, NJ.

Company: The World of the Walking Stick

Year Founded: 1991

Web Site First Established: 1998

Gross Annual Revenues: NA

Annual Revenues from Web Site: NA

Percentage of Revenues from Sales on Web: 50%

Site Start-Up Cost: NA

Site Maintenance Cost (monthly): NA

Most Successful Feature of Site: Visual catalog, which allows potential customers to view pictures of inventory, descriptions, and prices at any time.

Lessons Learned: Exposure helps.

Marketing Techniques Used: Search engines, print ads in antique magazines and antique fair newspapers, brochure, postcard mailing, links, eBay.

Advice about Marketing on the Web: Keep it correct, complete and easy to understand.

Liela Nelson, Owner

The Light Stuff: StreetGlow, Inc. at *http://www.streetglow.com*

A classic basement start-up, StreetGlow was founded in 1990 by Jack Panzarella when he accidentally damaged a neon bulb under a show vehicle. Initially focused on automotive neon accessories that were durable and affordable, the company now also manufactures neon for clocks, in-line skates, bicycles, motorcycles, and custom signs. A multi-million-dollar company, StreetGlow manufactures its products in New Jersey and China. It has been featured in many entrepreneurial and business publications and is one of the Inc. 500.

StreetGlow (see Figure 13.6) initially catered to a niche market of car enthusiasts, but it drew interest from a mainstream consumer market. For the niche community, the site maintains a message board, chat room, multimedia section, photo gallery of screaming-neon cars, and screensaver downloads. As a B2B company that sells through distributors and retailers, StreetGlow has had to manage channel relations. To avoid alienating the distribution channel, the site offers a dealer locator service and doesn't discount prices.

Visitors who request a free catalog online must complete a survey with useful marketing information such as types of car modifications they've made, where they buy accessories, and how much they spend annually on vehicle upgrades. The data are analyzed for market segmentation, with different groups (e.g., buyers versus prospects) receiving different mailings, product news, and incentives. In a creative offline marketing effort, StreetGlow created "Glow-Off®" competitions, in which neon-lit vehicles vie for prizes.

Putting Customers First

The next sites focus on their customers through a combination of personalized product and personal contact. They all illustrate the importance of service in spite of their difference in size and product.

Personal and Personalized: Victorian Fireplace Shop at *http://www.thevictorianfireplace.com*

The VictorianFireplace.com (seen in Figure 13.7) is a bricks-and-clicks operation for the Victorian Fireplace Shop in Richmond, Virginia. To-

Figure 13.6. The light stuff, *http://www.streetglow.com/site/auto3.htm.*
Courtesy StreetGlow: The Leaders in Auto-Neon® and Performance Lighting.

Company: StreetGlow, Inc.

Year Founded: 1990

Web Site First Established: 1999

Gross Annual Revenues: NA

Annual Revenues from Web Site: NA

Percentage of Revenues from Sales on Web: 3%

Site Start-Up Cost: $1,000

Site Maintenance Cost (monthly): $450; host own site

Most Successful Feature of Site: Message Board.

Lessons Learned: Listen to your visitors. Keep the Web site easy to navigate, and provide as much information as possible.

Marketing Techniques Used: Web site survey responses to customize communications, print catalog distribution, and segmented direct-mail database.

Advice about Marketing on the Web: Offer quality products and quality service to both B2C and B2B customers.

Adam Daley, Network Administrator/Webmaster

Figure 13.7. Personal and personalized, *http://www.thevictorianfireplace.com.* ©Karen Duke.

Company: Victorian Fireplace Shop

Year Founded: 1992

Web Site First Established: 2000

Gross Annual Revenues: under $1 million

Annual Revenues from Web Site: $300,000-$400,000

Percentage of Revenues from Sales on Web: NA

Site Start-Up Cost: Less than $100; done by owner

Site Maintenance Cost (monthly): Hosting $50, marketing $3,000-$5,000 depending on the season.

Most Successful Feature of Site: Personal, conversational tone combined with detailed product specs and educational articles.

Lessons Learned: Pick a product niche that is small enough to dominate, but large enough to sustain sales. If you become an expert in your niche, competitors will send business to you.

Marketing Techniques Used: Extensive link campaign to related sites, search engine optimization, pay-per-clicks, cross-marketing the site with newspaper ads, yellow pages, and business cards.

Advice about Marketing on the Web: Resist the temptation to discount price. Shoppers' primary concern is convenience, not cost. Marketing is the key to Internet sales success.

Karen Duke, Owner

gether with its sister site, DukeFire.com, this site sells fireplace products and installation services; DukeFire also offers a menu of chimney services. Another mom-and-pop operation, the two sites are owned by Karen Duke and her husband Michael, with Karen as Webmaster.

Duke is adamant about maintaining profit margins. "If you live by price, you die by price," she insists. Noting the pressure to discount from "big-box" building supply chains, she suggests differentiation by quality and customer service to capture a niche market at premium prices. DukeFire has experienced another form of pressure. Manufacturer Vermont Castings posted a policy discouraging consumers from buying its fireplaces and woodstoves over the Internet, fearing that online sales would draw traffic away from local dealers. Duke has posted a letter to her customers (*http://www.dukefire.com/page62.html*) explaining why the site will no longer sell Vermont Casting products outside Richmond and asking for public comment on whether manufacturers should be able to prevent Internet sales. What do you think?

The company is known for more than its backbone. As a unique "see-it-before-you-buy" service, they will take a photo of an old fireplace and digitally superimpose a new surround, mantel, hearth, or whatever accessories the customer wants. Duke claims close to a 100 percent closing rate with this method!

Book Lovers of the World, Unite: Abebooks at *http://www.abebooks.com*

Abebooks (see Figure 13.8) takes advantage of the Internet's unique features: real-time communication, interactivity, and the ability to match fluid pools of buyers and sellers. The site matches book seekers with a network of more than 9,000 independent dealers of secondhand, rare, and out-of-print books worldwide. Their combined inventory constitutes an Oracle database of more than 30 million books.

To meet global demand, Abebooks has German (*http://www.abebooks.de*) and French sites (*http://www.abebooks.fr*), and partners with reseller sites in Japan and Australia. A private Canadian company begun in 1996 by Keith and Cathy Waters, the site has been profitable from its inception. It is now the largest online community of independent booksellers and has over 100 employees.

Booksellers pay a monthly fee of $25 to $300 based on the number of books they list. In exchange, they receive free software for inventory management, and Abebooks' coordination of accounts, payments, and

Figure 13.8. Book Lovers of the world, unite, *http://www.abebooks.com.* Courtesy Abebooks.

Company: Abebooks

Year Founded: 1995

Web Site First Established: 1996

Gross Annual Revenues: NA

Annual Revenues from Web Site: NA

Percentage of Revenues from Sales on Web: 100%

Site Start-Up Cost: NA

Site Maintenance Cost (monthly): NA

Most Successful Feature of Site: Matching process that links book buyers to sellers to give buyers the option of purchasing directly from seller.

Lessons Learned: Upwards scalability is a must; database now houses an inventory of over 30 million books and we anticipate further growth.

Marketing Techniques Used: Reseller partner programs that permit bookseller members to market their books internationally through major online shopping outlets. Extensive customer support for sellers.

Advice about Marketing on the Web: Open-mindedness is essential. Don't necessarily follow the current trends for online marketing.

Sue Handel, Marketing

customer service. Now able to compete with large online chains, these small sellers receive a significant portion of their revenue from the site and through Abebooks' reseller partners, which include Barnes & Noble and Half.com.

Buyers may purchase directly from booksellers or use Abebooks' e-commerce option for a nominal fee. To further encourage booklovers, the site features "reading rooms," author interviews, and expert panels to help collectors. A supremely "sticky" site with many repeat visitors, Abebooks ranks among the 100 busiest sites on the Web.

Up Close and Close Up: Skystone Trading at *http://www.skystonetrading.com*

Turquoise is the "fallen skystone hidden in Mother Earth." On their site in Figure 13.9, Henry and Julia Theobald share their knowledge and love of turquoise and of Zuni fetishes. After 25 years selling Native American jewelry and crafts either wholesale or retail, they closed their retail storefront within three months of going online, confident their future was on the Web.

Like WalkingStickWorld, Skystone has found eBay an excellent source of customers, as well as auction revenue. Like TheVictorianFireplace, they adopt a folksy, personal tone to let visitors know that there are "real people" behind the Web site. They have added value to the site with detailed content about turquoise, heishe (shell beads), jewelry crafting, and Zuni fetishes, believing that education builds appreciation, which in turn leads to sales. And like the other model sites, they've learning to take addresses for an e-mail newsletter.

The site is particularly astute in providing multiple close-up images of their jewelry and fetishes—an important feature when you're selling products for hundreds of dollars. The Theobalds also made an intentional design effort to convey a sense of "a warm place ... that is both calming and soothing to the eyes and stimulating to the mind. We deal with things of spirit, so we wanted ... a friendly, yet professional feeling."

Service in Cyberspace

Any small business that adapts its service delivery to the electronic world deserves tremendous credit. Such is the case with our last model site.

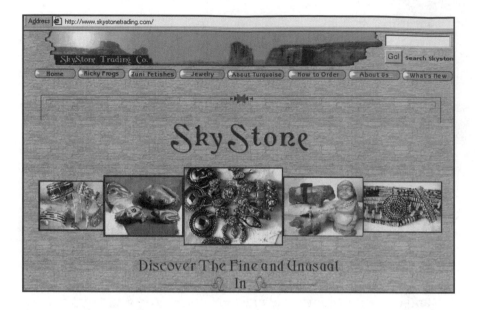

Figure 13.9. Up close and close up, *http://www.skystonetrading.com*. Courtesy *www.skystonetrading.com*.

Company: Skystone Trading

Year Founded: 1996

Web Site First Established: 1998

Gross Annual Revenues: less than $500,000

Annual Revenues from Web Site: NA

Percentage of Revenues from Sales on Web: 100%

Site Start-Up Cost: approx. $5,000

Site Maintenance Cost (monthly): $499 for a dedicated server.

Most Successful Feature of Site: Easy for customers to navigate and find what they're looking for. Use education to build appreciation and add value.

Lessons Learned: Visit many Web sites to learn what you like and don't like. Keep your site clean, crisp, and to the point; you have 60 seconds or less to get people's attention.

Marketing Techniques Used: Posting on eBay to attract new customers most effective, use Goto.com (pay-per-click) for search engine placement, and rely on repeat customers.

Advice about Marketing on the Web: Do your homework. Clarity of purpose and direction will keep you focused. Don't throw money at areas where you are weak. Use education to build appreciation and add value.

Henry & Julia Theobald, Owners

Repairing the Virtual World: Quality Transmission Service, Inc. at *http://www.quality-trans.com*

If you don't think a Web site makes sense for an automobile transmission repair company, think again. Quality Transmission (seen in Figure 13.10) has taken one of the most mundane (and maligned) businesses— auto repair—and used the Web to clean up its image. The site also lets visitors book appointments, print out Web-only discount coupons, and learn about transmission systems.

From the multiple awards and Better Business Bureau credibility labels posted at the top of the home page to its customer testimonials, nationwide warranty, employee certifications, and codes of ethics, the site works hard to increase the credibility not only of Quality Transmission Service, but of the industry as a whole. The company itself has been family-owned and operated in Tempe, Arizona, since 1977.

Quality-trans.com uses e-mail forms to schedule appointments, to "Ask Bob" questions or request free assistance with transmission problems, to complete a customer survey, or to provide suggestions about improving the site. "Ask Bob" has proved particularly popular, generating e-mails from countries as far away as Russia and the Philippines. FAQs, a collection of newsletters, and a transmission quiz round out the value-added content sections of the site. Like several of our intrepid, go-it-alone entrepreneurs, Bob Jones does all the site maintenance himself. There probably aren't many places better than Tempe to have your transmission break down!

Nearing the Finish Line

We've now looked at a variety of sites that utilize Web marketing techniques to achieve their business objectives. Most of these businesses achieved their Web success with tiny budgets and huge passions. If they can do it, why can't you? These sites have several things in common: They make the Web experience a pleasant one for their customers, add value with content, follow through with support, offer quality products, and provide good service.

In the concluding chapter, we look at global marketing and long-term business trends in Internet marketing, as well as review the integration of Web activities with the rest of your business.

Figure 13.10. Repairing the virtual world, *http://www.quality-trans.com*. Bob Jones is the sole creator and maintainer of this Web site.

Company: Quality Transmission Service, Inc.

Year Founded: 1976

Web Site First Established: 1998

Gross Annual Revenues: $400,000

Annual Revenues from Web Site: $50,000 (indirect)

Percentage of Revenues from Sales on Web: 12.5% comes indirectly through the site; nothing actually sold online.

Site Start-Up Cost: $800

Site Maintenance Cost (monthly): $0, owner does all maintenance.

Most Successful Feature of Site: "Ask Bob," a free service to educate consumers on auto repair, helps the industry's reputation and builds company credibility. FAQs and transmission quiz are also very popular.

Lessons Learned: Don't try to predict what Web site visitors will want. Include everything and provide a feedback feature. Just when you think you have provided everything, someone will make a suggestion or ask a question that you didn't think of. Review as many sites as possible before creating your site and keep notes of features you like.

Marketing Techniques Used: NA

Advice about Marketing on the Web: No other medium allows you the capacity to present more information than the Web. With good navigation, viewers can choose what interests them.

Bob Jones, Owner

14

The Future Is Yours

Clearly, the Internet is redrawing the map of the business world. With business life online running at "Internet speed," there is as much change in one year as there used to be in seven. The horizon for strategic planning has shrunk from three years to 18 months. And it's often impossible to foresee new technologies and applications beyond six months. Take comfort in the knowledge that the more things change, the more they stay the same. As long as you remember the basics of business, you'll be fine.

The Web is not disappearing. If anything, its global use is growing. If your online activities reflect a desire to build a long-term relationship with customers—the most basic of business rules—the rest is window dressing. In this chapter, we look at:

- The global aspects of Internet marketing

- Online legal issues that affect Web operations

- Trends in technology, legislation, regulation, and taxation

- Trends in B2C and B2B commerce and the fallout from the dot-com implosion

- The importance of integrating online marketing with other business activities.

The Web Is Global

As we saw in Figure 3.4, global commerce opportunities abound. To reach an international market effectively, it will pay to adopt some specific techniques. If you're not certain where to start, try the United Kingdom and Germany; they both have a high number of Internet users and are easy to work with.

If your product or service has international appeal, consider **localizing** your site and info-tools for different countries. Localization addresses cultural issues, offers local contacts, and includes items of country-specific relevance, such as a local singing star on a site that sells CD-ROMs. It also recognizes that different countries may require different marketing, pricing, and payment strategies (e.g., should your product be positioned differently since your competition and user needs differ?).

Localization may mean maintaining a virtual overseas office with a local voice-mail/fax contact point or registering your URL with your target country's top-level domain name. If your product will have different names in different countries, you may need a second trademark registration. Encryption standards, consumer protection, and privacy policies also differ from country to country. Dozens of organizations are trying to deal with international distinctions on everything from the length of time for buyers to change their minds about online purchases to publicizing an unconditional refund policy, to the use of comparative advertising, and to the enforceability of digitally signed contracts.

Multilingual Sites

Major computer dealers, such as Apple, Dell, and Cisco, have taken the lead in international marketing. Dell Computer, for instance, has unique Web sites for 82 countries in 21 different languages, and 40 currencies. Major multinationals are not the only ones. Look at how Spy Zone (*http://www.spyzone.com*) lets viewers know it has a global presence in Figure 14.1a. The screen shots in Figures 14.1b and 14.1c show a Spy Zone splash screen translated into two other languages.

Figure 14.1. (a-c).   Spy Zone splash screen in English, Arabic, and Korean, *http://www.spyzone.com* and *http://www.spyzone.com/foreign/index.html*. All three images courtesy C.C.S. International, Ltd. and the Counterspy Shops of Mayfair, London.

A number of companies offer site translation and localization services. Expect to pay $50 to $80 per Web page for a professional translation from a linguist, with discounts for multiple pages or languages. For example, see *http://www.wetranslate.com* or *http://www.berlitzglobalnet.com/english/services/translation.html*.

You can try to use automatic translation software, including free packages, at *http://translator.dictionary.com/urlhtml* and *http://www.tranexp.com:2000/InterTran*, or machine translation products from sites like *http://www.translation.net/tsfaq.html*, but beware. Such solutions, while inexpensive, can lead to some hilarious errors—and to some offensive ones. (For a funny example, check out *http://babelfish.altavista.com.*) You might be better off with an e-mail translation service at $2 a pop!

Payment and Shipping

Consider how you will handle payment and delivery. Can you consolidate pricing to a single price per item and then add shipping, tariffs, and local taxes by country? That will make it easier to handle pricing through an electronic checkstand. What about currency exchange instead of requiring dollars? For amounts over $10, the simplest solution is to accept credit cards. However, not all countries are credit card–oriented. Europeans, especially Scandinavians and Germans, prefer COD, being billed for check payment, or debit cards like the Eurocard. Debit and prepaid cards are popular in Latin America. Explore other options in international currency exchange, such as the Virtual Trading Desk and other payment options offered by Thomas Cook (*http://www.fx4business.com*). Delivering goods in a timely manner at a reasonable price can be difficult overseas. Your options will vary by shipping location, size, weight, and type of product.

International Promotion and Advertising

Start with major search engines like Yahoo!, which offers at least 18 country- or continent-specific engines. Some of the many other international search engines are shown in Figure 14.2. More can be found at *http://www.searchenginecolossus.com*. You may want to seek help from companies capable of promoting your site in other languages and countries. They will submit your Web page to international indexes and search

Region/Language	Name	URL
Asia/English, Chinese	Globe Page	*http://www.globepage.com*
Canada/English	Alta Vista Canada	*http://ca.altavista.com*
Europe	Euroseek	*http://www.euroseek.net*
France/French	Alta Vista France	*http://www.i3d.qc.ca*
France/French	Lokace	*http://www.lokace.com*
Germany/German	Alta Vista Germany	*http://altavista.de*
Greece	WebIndex	*http://www.webindex.gr*
Hong Kong	Hong Kong Search Engine	*http://www.chkg.com*
India/English	Search India	*http://easyway4u.com/index.asp*
Ireland	In2 Ireland	*http://www.searchingireland.com*
Japan/Japanese, English	MOSHIx2	*http://www.moshix2.net*
Netherlands	Search NL	*http://www.Search.NL*
New Zealand	Search NZ	*http://www.searchnz.co.nz*
Scandinavia, Iceland	Nordic Web Index	*http://nwi.dtv.dk/index_e.html*
Singapore	TechnoFind	*http://www.technofind.com.sg/index.html*
South Africa	Ananzi	*http://www.ananzi.co.za*
South Africa	Zebra	*http://beta.zebra.co.za/zebra-cgi/webdriver*
Spain/Spanish	El Faro (The Lighthouse)	*http://www.apali.com*
Switzerland/English, German	Swiss Search	*http://www.search.ch*
Ukraine	Sesna	*http://www.uazone.net/sesna*

Figure 14.2. Some international search engines, *http://global-reach.biz/gbc/indexes.php3*. Courtesy Global Reach.

engines in your target language. To be listed on many of those sites, you must translate at least a localized page, a home page, or a one-page summary of your site, along with keywords, categories, and page descriptions.

Most offer Web promotion services besides index listings: registering local domain names, monitoring search engine rankings, optimizing pages in the target language to improve placement, strategic linking, and banner advertising. These services will also handle a variety of Internet marketing tasks off the Web, such as posting to newsgroups, preparing autoresponders, handling mailing list submissions, participating in chat rooms, and answering your e-mail. For international support, try:

- *http://www.global-reach.biz*

- *http://www.asia-links.com*

- *http://www.clickexperts.com*

- *http://www.blueskyinc.com*

International Resources

You must be able to answer some essential questions before you can do business internationally. Are you set up for export? Do you know how to find distributors in other countries? Handle letters of credit? Process items for customs and international shipping?

Take advantage of free or low-cost government programs. For information, check out the Office of International Trade at the Small Business Administration (*http://www.sba.gov/oit*). Try a local international trade council, visit the International Trade Administration Web site (*http://www.ita.doc.gov*), attend a Department of Commerce export training session, or check out some of the other sites listed in Figure 14.3. Most of these sites offer extensive information, including publications, links to export counseling services, trade statistics, financing options, and educational programs. The Department of Commerce offers a low-cost "virtual booth" at its cybermall—E-Expo USA—for as little as $100 per year. For more information, go to *http://e-expousa.doc.gov/ExpoWeb2.nsf/pages/Registration*.

Business Sense: Things to Watch For

You can trip over many legal and regulatory requirements as you develop and promote your Web site. Watch out for the following.

The Privacy Zone

For good reason, Web visitors are concerned about protecting their personal information, financial data, and credit card numbers. Sites have tried to sell information they've collected about users' whereabouts and

Name	URL
Dept. of Commerce (DOC) homepage	*http://www.doc.gov*
DOC, Bureau of Export Administration	*http://www.bxa.doc.gov*
DOC, E-Expo (electronic trade show)	*http://e-expousa.doc.gov/Start.html*
DOC, International Trade Administration	*http://www1.usatrade.gov/website/website.nsf*
DOC, Trade Compliance Center	*http://www.mac.doc.gov*
DOC, Trade Information Center	*http://www.ita.doc.gov/td/tic*
Export-Import Bank	*http://www.exim.gov*
National Trade Data Bank	*http://tradeport.org*
Small Business Administration, Office of International Trade	*http://www.sba.gov/oit*
Stat-USA/Internet	*http://www.stat-usa.gov*
U.S. Census Bureau, Foreign Trade Statistics	*http://www.census.gov/foreign-trade/www*
U.S. Customs Service, Automated Export System	*http://www.customs.ustreas.gov*

Figure 14.3. Government trade resources.

personal information, often without the users' explicit knowledge. Things are improving. Of the 100 most popular sites, the number that collect personal information fell from 96 percent in 2000 to 84 percent in 2002; 93 percent now offer consumers a choice before sharing their information with third parties.

Develop and maintain a privacy policy like Microsoft's in Figure 14.4. Inform site visitors of your policy on any registration or order screen with a simple statement such as, "We sincerely honor your online privacy. We will not sell or share your e-mail address or other personal information with any third party." Your policy should apply not just to e-mail, street addresses, and credit card numbers, but also to demographic information and purchases.

Kids Are Special

Because of concerns about collecting data from young children, Congress passed the Children's Online Privacy Protection Act in April 2000. It prohibits Web sites from collecting personal information—including names, e-mail addresses, and zip codes—from children under 13 without verifiable parental permission. Companies in violation are subject to thousands of dollars in fines. A scan by the FTC in July 2000 found

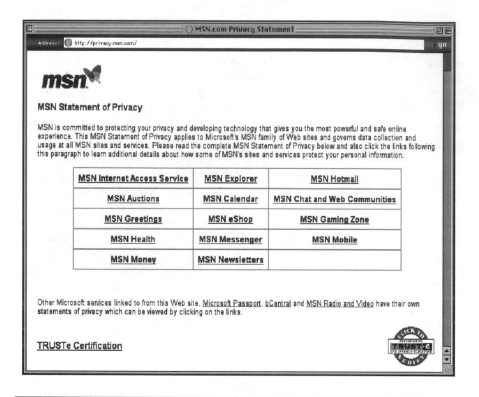

Figure 14.4. Sample privacy policy, *http://privacy.msn.com.* ©2002 Microsoft Corporation. All rights reserved.

that of the 75 percent of children's sites that collect data, about half still had a substantial compliance problem.

Privacy Options
The World Wide Web Consortium Platform for Privacy Preferences established P3P, a standard for computer-readable privacy policies. Once consumers select their desired level of privacy, their browser automatically scans only for sites that meet or exceed that level. For resources on privacy, check out these Web sites:

- World Wide Web Consortium Platform for Privacy Preferences (*http://www.w3.org/p3p*)

- Federal Trade Commission (*http://www.ftc.gov/privacy/index.html*)

- Electronic Privacy Information Center (*http://www.epic.org*)

- OECD Privacy Statement Generator (*http://CS3-HQ.oecd.org/scripts/pwv3/pwhome.htm*)

- Internet Privacy Working Group (*http://www.cdt.org*)

- Privacy.org (*http://www.privacy.org*)

Added Security

We discussed encryption and firewalls as part of basic security in Chapter 7. If you are actually concluding business or signing contracts online, consider adding **authentication**, which guarantees that the person who receives the message is the person for whom it was intended and that the sender is the person who was supposed to send it. This is done through a **digital signature,** which can now be used legally to verify personal identity and age, to sign a contract or e-mail, or confirm credit card charges.

The next line of defense is **public key cryptography.** The key holder encodes his or her message with a private key; its matching public key is used to decode it and vice versa. A **digital certificate** ties a digital signature and public key together. A new standard, called strong encryption, uses a 128-bit key, making it almost impossible to unscramble the message. The Digital Millennium Copyright Act of 1998 made it illegal to create or distribute devices that circumvent encryption. Expect this law to be tightly enforced after the terrorist attacks of September 11, 2001, and anticipate pressure to give the government access to private keys.

Legalese

In its early days the Internet was an electronic Wild West. People grew fairly cavalier about **intellectual property** (any idea protected by copyright, trademark, or patent). Now that the Web has become a popular commercial trading route, instances of intellectual property infringement have skyrocketed. Large corporations increasingly use intellectual property rights to shut down sites that infringe on copyrights or trademarks, including unofficial movie fan sites and sites that critique a company's operations.

TIPS FOR TIRED SITES

Have you protected yourself? You need to protect your own online material as well as ensure that you do not misuse the property of others. Be sure that any agreement with Web contractors specifies that you own all intellectual property rights in their work, which should be designated as "work for hire." If your site is designed in-house, your employment contracts should include a notice that your company owns the intellectual property of all work performed by employees. Make outside Web contractors responsible for clearing rights to use whatever elements (e.g., photographs) they obtain from another source; if your in-house staff acquires elements, the responsibility is yours.

Copyright

Copyright applies to the design (look and feel) and content of audiovisual and print media. Copyright covers text, data, icons, graphics, audio, video, music, and software programs. Although copying MP3 music files and online game software receives the greatest publicity, copyright infringement is also a potential issue with databases and other compiled information that appears on sites.

Republishing copyrighted material on a commercial site without permission is a giant no-no. When a copyright notice appears on others' material, you cannot use it on your Web site without permission, period. Government material is not copyrighted. If you wish to republish or mirror the contents of a site, obtain permission first. Start by sending a letter with a permission form, such as the one in Figure 14.5. If you are unable to negotiate permission, consider linking to the owner's clearly identified site.

It's easy to provide common law copyright protection for your own site. A simple notice consisting of the symbol © or the word "Copyright" or "Copr.," followed by the year of publication and the name of the copyright owner (usually your company name), confers common law copyright protection. At a minimum, this notice should appear on your site; you can supplement it with a statement of rights and permissible uses as ThirdAge (*http://www.thirdage.com/copyright.html*) does in Figure 14.6.

For a nominal fee of $30, you can obtain more complete copyright protection by registering your copyright with the Library of Congress (*http://lcweb.loc.gov/copyright*). Registration gives you greater rights

The undersigned authorizes Maximum Press, 605 Silverthorn Road, Gulf Breeze, FL 32561 to print electronically, publish on its Web site at *http://www.maxpress.com*, and otherwise distribute throughout the world in all languages and versions, the following (information) (article) (screenshot) (art).

Material covered by this permission: (attached)

Please specify the credit line you would like to have appear:

Please sign this permission and enter your desired credit line. You may return it in the enclosed SASE or fax it back to:
Thank you.

Signature: Date:
Printed Name: Title:
Company
Address:
City: State: Zip:
T: F: E:

Figure 14.5. Sample copyright permission letter.

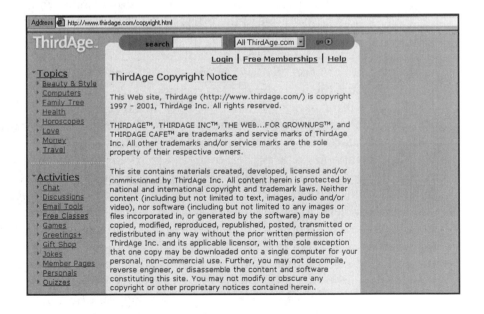

Figure 14.6. Sample trademark and copyright notice, *http://www.thirdage.com/copyright.html*. Courtesy Third Age, Inc.

in court and allows you to collect additional damages and legal expenses if someone infringes. Carefully read the information on the Library of Congress Web site to determine which form(s) of copyright (Visual Arts, TX for nondramatic works, or other forms for multimedia) you need. Mail the completed forms with printouts of your pages and a check to the Library of Congress. Within several months, you will receive official notice that your copyright has been registered.

Trademarks

A trademark or service mark confers the right to use a particular name or logotype within a specific class of commercial activity. Recent court decisions have held that trademark rights apply to domain names. Federal legislation signed in 1999 made **cybersquatting** (i.e., registering someone else's trademark or a celebrity's personal name as a domain name with the intent to resell it at a profit) illegal. This applies internationally as well: The UN World Intellectual Property Organization recently finalized its rules against cybersquatting. You might infringe a trademark if you use someone else's marks in your list of keywords, depending on the circumstances. A dealer carrying a trademarked product would have a legitimate use, whereas a competitor or unrelated business would not.

A name may be available in the InterNIC database but still be trademarked. To determine trademark status and ownership, go to the free online search engine for the U.S. Office of Patents and Trademarks (PTO) at *http://tess.uspto.gov*. To trademark your own company or product name, you must file with the PTO at a cost of $325 per name per class of use. More information on what qualifies as a trademark and how to file is available from the PTO home page. Some states also maintain a trademark database for registration only within that state.

Many companies refer to their own trademarked names or the trademarks of other companies within their pages. Put the ® symbol after a registered trademark the first time it appears, and provide a notice of trademark ownership somewhere on your site. (The symbol ™ is used when a trademark application is pending.) Use a statement such as "Quaker is a registered trademark of the Quaker Oats Company." For multiple trademarks, use a blanket statement such as "All trademarks are the property of their respective owners" as ThirdAge does at *http://www.thirdage.com/copyright.html* (see Figure 14.6 above). Or have fun with the legalisms as Ragu does at *http://www.eat.com/site-credits.asp* (see Figure 14.7).

Figure 14.7. Fun trademark and copyright notice, *http://www.eat.com/site-credits.asp*. Courtesy Lipton Investments, Inc. and Unilever USA, Inc.

Patents
A patent covers an underlying concept or idea that has been "reduced to practice." The Patent Office is under fire for its generous granting of "business method" patents. Some businesses contend that the USPTO has awarded rights to broad claims that are "obvious" to practitioners in the field. For instance, the PTO granted patents to Priceline.com for the concept of "reverse auctions" online and to Amazon.com for its "one-click" checkout process and its affiliate program software. Be careful about using technology you haven't licensed or that isn't marked "freeware." Obtaining patents is a complex and expensive process; if you think you have a patentable invention, consult an intellectual property attorney.

Hyperlinks
Federal judges have ruled that linking without permission is acceptable as long as consumers understand whose page they are on, even if the link goes deep within a rival's site. Although it is not required, notifying

another site when you link to them is good business practice since you may be able to obtain a reciprocal link. Be careful that you don't eliminate someone else's identifying information, implying that you have created their work. Also, avoid manipulating a link to make it seem that others have endorsed your site or company, unless, of course, they have.

Nasty Beasties: Liability, Disclaimers, and Fraud

Activities that are illegal off the Internet are illegal on it. For instance, you can't operate a pyramid scheme or other scams. Any liability you have off the Web for unsafe products, false advertising, or financial fraud you also have on it. Many Web sites post an online disclaimer and/or consumer license, similar to the one that appears on their packaging. ThirdAge uses its own general disclaimer, seen in Figure 14.8.

Content and the First Amendment

The content of the Internet is covered by the First Amendment. However, in some recent cases, courts have ruled that online and Web hosting companies have the same responsibility as publishers for what appears on pages they host. You can't sell alcohol, gambling chances, or pornographic material to minors online, but so far these laws have proved difficult to enforce. The Supreme Court has upheld a federal law aimed at limiting obscene material in e-mail as well as on Web sites. Many interest groups now demand that Web sites carry warnings if they contain material that might be objectionable, although not legally obscene, if seen by children. Some organizations provide their own lists of "inde-

---

TIPS FOR TIRED SITES

Are potential customers worried about doing e-business with you? According to the Internet Fraud Watch, a system maintained by the National Consumers League (*http://www.fraud.org*), online auctions account for 63 percent of all Internet-related complaints (see Figure 14.9). If your Internet business is a likely target of complaints, boost consumer confidence with the credibility measures discussed in Chapter 7. Or offer to use a third-party online escrow service, such as *http://www.safebuyer.com* or *http://www.escrow.com*. Unhappy customers can submit their gripes to the National Fraud Information Center at *http://www.fraud.org/info/contactnfic.htm* or post negative ratings on one of many consumer review sites like *http://www.eopinions.com*.

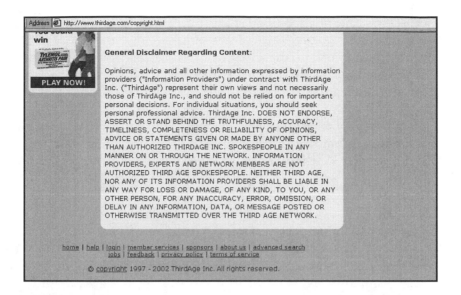

Figure 14.8. Sample disclaimer notice, *http://www.thirdage.com/copyright.html*. Courtesy Third Age, Inc.

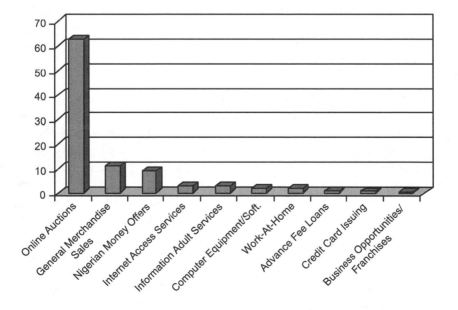

Figure 14.9. Top 10 Internet related fraud reports in 2001, *http://www.fraud.org/ internet/intset.htm*. Courtesy The National Consumers League's Internet Fraud Watch.

cent," violent, or hate-filled sites; others recommend the use of blocking and filtering software.

Litigation about these issues continues. If you're not sure what you want to do is legal, consult an attorney. Background information on computer law is available at The Computer Law Association (*http://www.cla.org*) or the American Bar Association Committee on the Law of Cyberspace at *http://www.abanet.org/buslaw/cyber/home.html*. Or contact the Electronic Frontier Foundation (*http://www.eff.org*), which seeks to protect the open exchange of ideas and expression on the Internet.

Insurance

One way to reduce your exposure to all these issues is to obtain insurance for your Web operations. Insurance companies have started to offer policies that address the various legal risks of doing business online. They may cover expenses or lost business due to hacker attacks, product liability claims for an item sold on your site, or your liability for infringing on another firm's trademark. Check your current business owner policy for coverage—most do not cover intellectual property issues, which generally appear only in professional liability policies.

Trends to Watch

The fastest-growing communications technology in history, the Internet reached 50 million people in less than five years. It took radio 38 years, television 13 years, and cable 10 years to reach the same audience. With that kind of impact, it's no surprise that the Internet has drawn vastly different interest groups into action. Communications conglomerates jockey over who will own broadband channels; state governments worry about losing sales tax revenue; not-for-profit organizations battle over censorship (pro and con); citizens complain to Congress about junk e-mail; and investors sue over profits lost when online stock brokerages are shut down by heavy traffic. If you market your business online, you need to keep your antennae up for trends that will affect your ability to survive and thrive on the Internet. Here are a few things to watch in the next several years.

Technology

High-end computing capabilities teamed with high-speed Web access will create a tantalizing Internet feast for more and more viewers. Changes are coming in two main areas:

- Faster access to information from the Internet

- Increased use of hand-held, wireless devices

Remember that the overall system can run only as fast as the slowest piece in it. We spoke in Chapter 1 about the increased use of cable and DSL for high-speed, broadband access. Even faster options are on the way.

Pipe Dreams: Faster Broadband Access

Frustrated by the increasing commercialization of the Web, the explosion of sites and users, and subsequent slow transmission speeds, the military long ago created MILNET, a network independent of the Internet. In addition, some 60 corporations and academic institutions turned on the Abilene Project in February 1999 to develop extremely fast Web access. Other groups are working to change the naming convention for IP addresses, so more devices can connect to the Internet. Internet Protocol Version 6 (IPv6) will solve a problem familiar to phone companies—the original 4.3 billion IP addresses just aren't enough. For more about the future, check out:

- The Abilene Project at *http://www.time.com/time/index.html*

- The Internet2 Initiative at *http://www.internet2.edu*

- The Next Generation Internet Initiative (NGI) at *http://smithsonian. yahoo.com/nextgeneration.html*

High-speed, broadband connections increase expectations. From a marketing perspective, the changes in technology translate into:

- The potential to attract new customers with sophisticated, value-added sites replete with video, animation, and sound

- New forms of product and service delivery with value-added features such as voice and video teleconferencing and live performances

- New products and markets in the form of pay-per-use software applications, such as word processing and spreadsheets

- More satisfied online customers, which implies more online sales.

Hand-Held, Wireless Devices

One of the most rapid changes in Internet access is narrowband transmission for hand-held devices. These devices contain a mini-browser that sees only sites written in **HDML** (handheld device mark-up language) or **WML** (wireless markup language). Wireless connections display minimal, but essential, text information on the small screens of cell phones, two-way pagers, or wireless messaging devices like the RIM Blackberry. According to a study by IDC, wireless users could grow from 5 million in 2000 to more than 84 million by 2005.

Internet providers are busy reformatting content and sites so wireless users can change plane reservations, book theater tickets, or send an order to buy stock. Major Web sites seeking to position themselves at the top of the wireless click-list include Ticketmaster.com, Travelocity.com, and E-Trade. Amazon Anywhere and Barnes & Noble's On the Go services aim at impulse shoppers, while Starbucks gratifies customers' cravings for a mocha cappuccino by pointing them to the closest outlet with a "store-locator" service. Such sites are expected to generate additional revenue streams for wireless providers from advertising and transaction fees.

WebTV Appliances

Inexpensive, easy-to-use WebTV appliances are on their last legs, in spite of Microsoft's offer of free Internet access for its WebTV owners. A WebTV appliance connects to a regular TV, with an optional wireless keyboard and/or printer. Set-top terminals run $99 to $149, with $30 to $50 additional for the keyboard. Subscriptions to one of the Internet TV access services run $12 to $25 a month. In spite of the low cost, which opened the possibility of reaching a broader, more economically diverse market, forecasts for Internet TV were far too rosy. For up-to-date news about what's happening with Web appliances, see *http://ruel.net/top/box.news.htm.*

Legislation and Regulation

When it comes to the Internet, many people are saying, "There oughta be a law." Pretty soon there will be many of them! More legislation has been proposed at the federal and state levels to deal with data privacy, encryption, online fraud, spamming, access by minors to salacious information, and online gambling. With the exception of the last, some form of regulation or legislation has already been enacted for all of these.

Spamming

Spam mail costs ISPs an estimated $1 billion annually. The costs for larger servers and greater telecommunication capacity are underwritten by legitimate users, while the burden of a clogged Internet affects everyone. A dozen states and the U.S. Congress have considered laws similar to the state of Washington's, which requires e-mailers to use real return e-mail addresses and makes it a crime to put false or misleading information in e-mail solicitations. Legislation passed the House in March 2001 that would give the Federal Trade Commission, ISPs, and consumers the ability to sue spammers. A similar bill is pending in the Senate.

Access to Sites

So far, the U.S. Supreme Court has found that attempts to restrict access to the Internet in public settings like libraries run afoul of the First Amendment. Various courts have ruled against federal legislation requiring Web hosts and online services to restrict access to certain sites for those under 17, against mandating the use of software filters, and against attempts by libraries to install software filters on publicly accessed computers. The Children's Internet Protection Act, which requires libraries and schools to use filters, remains under court challenge.

Regulation

Some issues are more likely to be addressed through regulation than legislation. For instance, the Federal Trade Commission (FTC) is attacking online fraud and is fining companies that don't notify consumers of shipping delays. Consumer affairs departments in several states are actively pursuing complaints about online auction houses. Other laws crop up where least expected. For example, 30 states restrict the ability of wineries and breweries to ship some products into their states. To monitor the status of federal legislation on these and other Internet-

---

TIPS FOR TIRED SITES

If your site includes "hot-button" words, software filters may cost you viewers. Filters and site rating systems are often used by parents at home and are offered as an option on most online services. Filtering software may deny access to information on topics such as breast cancer or AIDS in an attempt to limit access to sexually explicit sites. Other filters prohibit access to information on subjects like homosexuality or Wiccan religions. If your Web site contains such content, monitor commercial filtering software, object to the manufacturers, and use publicity to counteract the filter if their search algorithms block your legitimate site.

---

related topics, go to one of the sites that track the progress of bills through Congress, such as *http://thomas.loc.gov*.

Taxation

It's obvious that projections of $100.3 billion in B2C online revenues by 2003 would attract the attention of state and local governments wondering how to collect taxes. State governments worry about the eventual loss of sales tax revenue, as well as the loss of Main Street businesses. Most governors are searching for ways to tax Internet commerce, citing a recent study by the University of Tennessee that by 2011 states will have lost an estimated $54 billion in sales taxes on Internet commerce.

Without sales taxes, states and municipalities argue there will be a shortfall in services. Alternately, other taxes will need to be raised to make up for the loss, or low-income consumers purchasing on Main Street will end up bearing the brunt of local taxation. To some, the Internet should always remain a tax-free zone, but brick-and-mortar businesses on Main Street argue that not taxing the Internet gives their online competitors an advantage. For others, the patchwork of multiple state and local taxes provides even greater impetus for a national sales or value-added tax. The challenge is to figure out an equitable way to deal with the complexity and cost of collecting and distributing taxes across more than 7,800 taxing jurisdictions around the country. This will be a national issue; the Supreme Court previously ruled that Congress must authorize the imposition of state taxes on interstate mail order sales. Currently, a business must collect taxes only in states where it has a physical presence.

In 1998, Congress, heeding cries that taxation would impede the growth of online commerce and stifle small businesses, passed the Internet Tax Freedom Act. The Act initiated a three-year moratorium on state and local Internet taxes, which has since been extended until 2006. Stay tuned to events in the tax arena. They could affect your bottom line or, at the very least, the checkstand software you use. You can review current information at *http://www.vertexinc.com* or *http://thomas.loc.gov*.

B2B and B2C

We've already learned that U.S. B2B online revenues will exceed B2C by a factor of 8.5:1 by 2005. Now that the lumbering giants of industry have finally boarded the cyber-train, they are using it to restructure how they manage their own supply chain.

The B2B Explosion
Online marketplaces now affect purchasing practices in every major business from hotels, electronics, computers, shipping, office supplies, and energy to automobiles, aerospace, and agriculture. Such purchasing alliances reduce procurement costs and erode national borders as global companies cut costs by pressuring suppliers around the world. Watch for the impact on small suppliers, whose own ability to respond quickly while maintaining a profit will come under attack. In 2000, the number of marketplaces peaked at roughly 1,700 and has now started to consolidate. For the best of these marketplaces, go to *http://www.btobonline.com/netMarketing200/index.html#top*. The highest-rated B2B sites in 2001 are seen in Figure 14.10. Figure 14.11 provides a breakdown of the B2B sector by industry and size. More information on what to expect in the B2B sector is available at the Business 2.0 site, *http://www.business2.com* or at *http://www.cba.hawaii.edu/aspy/aspyimkt.htm*.

A B2C Implosion?
The Internet is the fastest-growing segment of retailing. Today's hot areas in small-ticket e-tailing are apparel, toys and video games, books, and music. In the big-ticket arena, airline tickets, computer hardware,

Rank	Company Name	Industry
1	American Express Co.	Financial Services and Insurance
2	FleetBoston Financial Corp.	Financial Services and Insurance
3	Merrill Lynch & Co. Inc.	Financial Services and Insurance
4	National City Corp.	Financial Services and Insurance
5	3Com Corp.	Manufacturing: High-Tech
6	Dell Computer Corp.	Manufacturing: High-Tech
7	IBM Corp.	Manufacturing: High-Tech
8	CDW Computer Centers Inc.	Wholesale/Retail/Distributor
9	PNC Financial Services Group Inc.	Financial Services and Insurance
10	Cisco Systems Inc.	Manufacturing: High-Tech
11	Compaq Computer Corp.	Manufacturing: High-Tech
12	Gateway Inc.	Manufacturing: High-Tech
13	Microsoft Corp.	Software

Figure 14.10. Highest-rated B2B Web sites 2001, *http://www.btobonline.com/netMarketing200/index.html#top*. Courtesy *BtoB Magazine*.

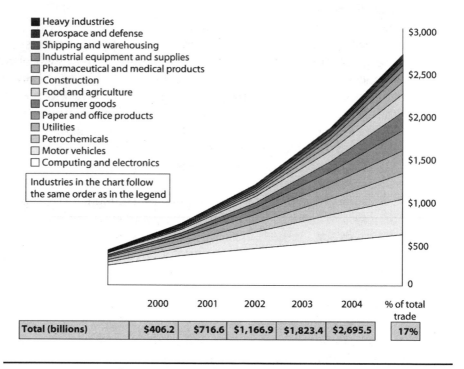

Figure 14.11. Online B2B growth by industry. Source: February 2000 "eMarket Places Boost B2B Trade," Forrester Research, Inc.

consumer electronics, and hotel reservations predominate. The "cold" areas are garden supplies, furniture, and appliances. While the catalog companies took to the Internet early like hummingbirds to nectar, it's only in the past several years that major retailers decided they have an online future. Even as traditional retailers built Web sites, online merchants started mailing print catalogs, blurring the distinctions between stores, mail order companies, and e-tailers.

Large "clicks-and-mortar" retailers like Wal-Mart and K-Mart have a formidable edge: brand name, customer base, supplier relationships, warehousing and distribution capacity, inventory control, and the ability to supplement online shopping with in-store returns and service. Recognizing their weaknesses, however, companies like Target.com and Toys R Us have contracted with Amazon.com to fill orders and provide customer service!

As early as 1999, Forrester Research warned that the Web could reduce local commerce in favor of national-brand stores. In 1999, the top ten online B2C companies already accounted for 32 percent of e-commerce revenue, up from 27 percent the year before. In the Forrester forecast, the share of online sales by local retailers would decline from 9 percent in 1999 to only 6 percent in 2003. This compares to the 50 percent share of retail dollars small and medium-sized business garner *offline*. As you saw from some of the stories in the previous chapter, nimble, creative businesses can still thrive. In particular, local service providers are well off in the new environment, the Forrester study notes (*http://www.forrester.com/ER/Press/ForrFind/0,1768,0,FF.html*). More information on B2C changes by product category is available at the Business 2.0 site, *http://www.business2.com*.

The Dot-Com Jitterbug and the Wall Street Waffle

No longer does www translate into World Wide Windfall for investors. The dot-com world was a frenetic dance, with IPO (initial public offering) valuations soaring higher than Baryshnikov and then crashing to the floor. More than 500 Internet companies bit the dust in 2001 alone. (You can find a list of dead-coms, from Boo.com to Pets.com, at *http://www.hoovers.com/news/detail/0,2417,20_2694,00.html*. For more information on the dot-com dance, see *http://www.webmergers.com/editorial/article.php?id=49*.) The only bright spots are the perennially profitable eBay and the news that Amazon.com's original book, music, and video division finally turned a profit.

This is not a good time to seek equity financing for your online enterprise from venture capitalists or **angel investors** (smaller investors

TIPS FOR TIRED SITES

The lessons to be learned from the dot-com fiasco sound like Business 101. Just throwing money at marketing doesn't work; you have to build brand. Tying staff loyalty solely to stock valuation is a disaster. Back office infrastructure for order fulfillment (inventory, warehousing, distribution, order tracking, return policies) is essential. Customer service and support are critical. You can't spend more to acquire your customers than they purchase. The numbers have to work. You must have a plan to improve margins and increase profitability. Duh?

seeking smaller returns). Venture money for Internet startups will continue to be tight in 2002. If you insist, have a credible plan that realistically offsets expenses with revenue, and that shows when and how profitability will be reached. Be sure you will have enough cash to last until then. The same holds true if you're seeking debt financing (a microloan, a bank loan, a small-business loan) or financing your business from your own savings.

Many states now run programs for local angels and microlenders. For a venture capital directory, try *http://www.nextwavestocks.com/ vcindex.html*. Angel investors can be found at *http://www.vfinance.com/ angelsearch/as_searchtest.asp*, *http://ace-net.sr.unh.edu/pub*, or *http:// www.biz-angels.com*. Find your local Small Business Development Center at *http://www.sba.gov/regions/states.html*. The SBA site also has a list of microlenders at *http://www.sba.gov/financing/lender.html* and a list of certified participants in the Small Business Loan program at *http:// www.sba.gov/gopher/Local-Information/Certified-Preferred-Lenders*.

The Corporate Pas de Deux

The 15 top U.S. Web sites, seen in Figure 14.12, are all large corporations, most of which control multiple sites. According to Jupiter Media Metrix, by March 2001 a mere 14 companies controlled 60 percent of users' time online, down from 110 companies two years before. Watch for the increased importance of these corporate portals.

Portals are seen as adding not only advertising value, but informational worth. They are expected to make the Web a more-organized place to exchange both data and dollars. What they organize, however, is corporate depth, not Web breadth. Portals are now the entry point to

Rank	Properties	Unique Visitors (000) [home & work use combined]
1	AOL Time Warner Network - Proprietary & WWW	91,899
2	MSN-Microsoft Sites	83,010
3	Yahoo! Sites	78,647
4	Terra Lycos	40,954
5	About/Primedia	36,016
6	Google Sites	33,000
7	Gator Network	32,154
8	eBay	29,334
9	Amazon Sites	29,259
10	CNET Networks	26,232
11	InfoSpace Network	24,991
12	Walt Disney Internet Group (WDIG)	23,588
13	Viacom Online	21,266
14	Vivendi-Universal Sites	20,766
15	Real.com Network	20,479

Figure 14.12.   Top 15 U.S. Web properties, March 2002, *http://www.jmm.com/xp/jmm/press/mediaMetrixTop50.xml.* Source: Jupiter Media Metrix, Inc.

the network of multiple sites owned by a single corporate entity, which can influence, if not control, what viewers read and even say online. Consider how Microsoft bought up many small online marketing sites and combined them into *bCentral.com.*

As the Web segments into monster sites, increasingly linked to one another to reinforce marketing messages, it retains buyers within a cyber-conglomerate for purchasing. Portals are like broadcast networks. To make the numbers work for their investors, these sites have to deliver one thing: eyeballs. They sell an audience to advertisers, particularly to huge corporations concerned with brand-name imaging. Several strategies exist if you are trying to reach the consuming public: You can affiliate with one of the mega-monsters, participate in a segment at a lower tier (equivalent to cable television), or stick it out as an independent. The answer, as always, depends on your business goals. As for your eyeballs, keep one eye on trends influencing activity on the Internet, but keep the other on your bottom line.

The Web Is the Tail; the Business Is the Dog

Let's reconsider the basic issues of doing business. First, put yourself in your customer's place. Is the message clear? Will the customer know how to take the next step toward a purchase? Does the message impart a sense of trust? Customers, clients, future employees, even suppliers like to be stroked and made to feel important. Successful online marketing makes it easy for customers to do business with you. They can find you easily; they can communicate with you easily; they can navigate through your Web site easily. When you offer useful information or entertainment, you offer value that tells customers they are worth the effort. In the end, the most meaningful measures of success are the return of existing customers and the arrival of new ones.

Second, a solid Internet marketing effort starts with something of value—a product, a service, technical support, or additional information. Customers who hear of others' bad experiences often shy away from purchasing online. They worry about guarantees, quality, service, and misuse of credit cards. Although you are not responsible for online problems created by others, you must overcome misgivings about using the Internet.

Third, apply your off-line marketing know-how to the Internet. The more you know about the results of your marketing activities, the better off you will be. Closely monitor the rate of response to various forms of Web promotion online and offline. Then repeat the successful ideas and drop the losers. Online marketing takes work, but it is not rocket science. Don't be afraid to talk to your online customers to see what they like or don't like about your site, your service, or your products. Your customers know you best.

Fourth, even if you sell only in the virtual world, the rest of your business functions in the real world. From marketing to finance, order processing to supplier relations, banking to warehousing, a business deals with human beings in physical space and real time. Ignoring these elements of your business can lead to a downfall, no matter how brilliantly you execute your online marketing strategy. Think before you act electronically. For most companies, online activities are only a portion of their overall marketing and promotion efforts, only one sector of their sales, and only one element in their customer service or employee recruitment tool kit. Staff buy-in and involvement will help you integrate online business techniques successfully.

Have Fun

Extrapolating from its growth, the Web—with its sizzle, graphics, entertainment, and information—will eventually draw in almost everyone with serious business intentions. Try to approach the Web in a spirit of discovery and delight. You're going to spend a lot of time online researching, monitoring your site, and looking at what others are doing. If you experience sheer horror at dealing with computers, delegate Internet marketing tasks to someone who enjoys it. Like anything else worthwhile in business, marketing online takes time. But you can make it fun for your employees, your customers, and yourself with realistic goals and the right attitude. Log on and good luck!

Index

Reader Feedback Sheet

Your comments and suggestions are very important in shaping future publications. Please e-mail us at *moreinfo@maxpress.com* or photocopy this page, jot down your thoughts, and fax it to (850) 934-9981 or mail it to:

Maximum Press
Attn: Jim Hoskins
605 Silverthorn Road
Gulf Breeze, FL 32561

_____

_____

_____

_____

_____

_____

_____

_____

_____

_____

_____

_____

_____

_____

_____

_____

_____

_____

*101 Ways to Promote
Your Web Site,
Third Edition*
by Susan Sweeney, C.A.
488 pages
$29.95
ISBN: 1-885068-57-3

*Marketing
With E-Mail,
Third Edition*
by Shannon Kinnard
352 pages
$29.95
ISBN: 1-885068-68-9

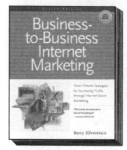

*Business-to-Business
Internet Marketing,
Fourth Edition*
by Barry Silverstein
432 pages
$34.95
ISBN: 1-885068-72-7

*Marketing on
the Internet,
Sixth Edition*
by Jan Zimmerman
488 pages
$34.95
ISBN: 1-885068-80-8

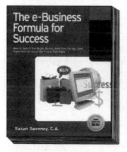

*e-Business Formula
for Success*
by Susan Sweeney, C.A.
360 pages
$34.95
ISBN: 1-885068-60-3

*The Business Guide to
Selling Through
Internet Auctions*
by Nancy Hix
608 pages
$29.95
ISBN: 1-885068-73-5

*101 Internet Businesses
You Can Start
From Home*
by Susan Sweeney, C.A.
520 pages
$29.95
ISBN: 1-885068-59-X

*Internet Marketing for
Less Than $500/Year,
Second Edition*
by Marcia Yudkin
352 pages
$29.95
ISBN: 1-885068-69-7

To purchase a Maximum Press book, visit your local bookstore
or call 1-800-989-6733 (US/Canada) or 1-850-934-4583 (International)
online ordering available at *www.maxpress.com*

Exploring IBM @server pSeries, Eleventh Edition
by Jim Hoskins
and Robert Bluethman
344 pages
$54.95
ISBN: 1-885068-81-6

Exploring IBM @server iSeries and AS/400 Computers, Tenth Edition
by Jim Hoskins and
Roger Dimmick
560 pages
$39.95
ISBN: 1-885068-43-3

Exploring IBM @server zSeries and S/390 Servers, Seventh Edition
by Jim Hoskins
and Bob Frank
432 pages
$59.95
ISBN: 1-885068-70-0

Exploring IBM e-Business Software
by Casey Young
308 pages
$49.95
ISBN: 1-885068-58-1

Exploring IBM @server xSeries and PCs, Twelfth Edition
by Jim Hoskins, Bill
Wilson, and Ray Winkel
432 pages
$49.95
ISBN: 1-885068-83-2

Exploring IBM Technology, Products & Services, Fifth Edition
edited by Jim Hoskins
272 pages
$54.95
ISBN: 1-885068-82-4

Building Intranets with Lotus Notes & Domino 5.0, Third Edition
by Steve Krantz
320 pages
$39.95
ISBN: 1-885068-41-7

Internet Marketing for Information Technology Companies, Second Edition
by Barry Silverstein
464 pages
$29.95
ISBN: 1-885068-67-0

To purchase a Maximum Press book, visit your local bookstore
or call 1-800-989-6733 (US/Canada) or 1-850-934-4583 (International)
online ordering available at *www.maxpress.com*